CALIFORNIA STUDIES IN THE HISTORY OF ART

Walter Horn, *General Editor*

GEORGE CALEB BINGHAM

Self-Portrait of the Artist, 1834/1835
(A11), oil (28 x 22½), City Art Museum,
St. Louis, Missouri.

GEORGE CALEB BINGHAM

THE EVOLUTION OF AN ARTIST

by E. MAURICE BLOCH

University of California Press
BERKELEY AND LOS ANGELES
1967

UNIVERSITY OF CALIFORNIA PRESS
BERKELEY AND LOS ANGELES, CALIFORNIA

CAMBRIDGE UNIVERSITY PRESS
LONDON, ENGLAND

© 1967 BY THE REGENTS OF THE UNIVERSITY OF CALIFORNIA

Library of Congress Catalog Card Number: 65-10714

DESIGNED BY WARD RITCHIE

PRINTED IN THE UNITED STATES OF AMERICA

TO MY PARENTS

PREFACE

George Caleb Bingham's name was long missing from the annals of American art, and it is only in relatively recent years that he has come to be recognized as one of the country's foremost genre painters. No serious investigation of his life work was actually attempted until almost forty years after his death. Apart from newspaper and magazine articles that appeared during his lifetime and from time to time afterward, mainly in Missouri, the artist was generally neglected or forgotten. Among historians of art only Henry Theodore Tuckerman gave him recognition, and that in five lines in his Book of the Artists (see Bibliography), published in 1867.

In a small, compact monograph which appeared in a limited edition in 1917 Miss Fern Helen Rusk (later Mrs. John Shapley) first recognized Bingham's true importance and attempted to organize all the available information concerning his life (see Bibliography). She also considered his work on the basis of style and appended a checklist of pictures. Unfortunately, the record was then incomplete. Much documentation, such as the invaluable series of letters written by Bingham to his friend Major James Sidney Rollins, covering more than four decades, and still to be located. And the larger part of Bingham's significant genre paintings was missing too, so that any final estimate of his achievement could not approach a definitive form at that time.

Albert Christ-Janer's monograph on Bingham, published in 1940 (see Bibliography), made extensive use of the then recently discovered Bingham–Rollins correspondence, as well as of the figure compositions located since the appearance of the Rusk volume. By that time the belated recognition of Bingham's contribution to American painting had become more firmly established, chiefly as the result of the great interest aroused in his work by the important exhibitions held in St. Louis in 1934 and in New York during the following year. Christ-Janer's book, an answer to a popular demand, introduced color plates of the paintings, as well as good black-and-white reproductions, the most valuable of which were the fifty-six drawings from the St. Louis Mercantile Library collection. However, the paintings considered were limited in number, and no catalogue or checklist was included.

A publication by Lee Larkin which appeared in 1955 (see Bibliography) treats Bingham's life from a journalistic viewpoint and avoids any critical consideration of his work. Although certain family letters are introduced for the first time, Larkin's book is actually a fictionalized approach to history. No catalogue of pictures is attempted.

The latest monograph, by John Francis McDermott, published in 1959 (see Bibliography), is a more ambitious work in which the author attempts to bring together the vast amount of factual materials that bear upon the artist's activities during his lifetime. Through diligent effort McDermott has uncovered details that help to fill out the picture, but there is no attempt to utilize those valuable materials in terms of an evolution of the artist's pictorial style. A checklist is included. By far the most important contribution of this work is the publication, for the first time, of the entire series (109) of Mercantile Library drawings (The John How Collection). (I had planned to reproduce ten of these drawings here, chiefly as demonstrations of the artist's procedure. Although the owners of the drawings, The St. Louis Mercantile Library Association, were evidently willing to coöperate, they were restricted by an agreement made in connection with McDermott's book of 1959. Regrettably, the publisher of the book, the University of Oklahoma Press, has steadfastly refused to give permission.)

In the present work I have endeavored to evaluate the accomplishment of the artist through an intimate analysis of his style and derivations, clearing away all traditional implications and establishing a more concrete biographical fabric based on documentation and pictorial evidence, as well as on actual conditions of the time. My study was undertaken in an effort to define the style of a major figure in American painting, but in a larger way it is perhaps even more a consideration of those artistic influences—the working tools, as it were—that helped to shape developing talents and artistic tendencies from the third decade of the nineteenth century. In a further effort at a systematic concentration on style, facts relating to the nonartistic experience of the painter have been deliberately held to the minimum necessary for depicting the relevant background. Similarly, much of the detail concerning individual paintings has been transferred to the comprehensive catalogue of Bingham's works which is being published in conjunction with this text (George Caleb Bingham: A Catalogue Raisonné [Berkeley and Los Angeles: University of California Press, 1967]).

From the Bingham–Rollins correspondence, and also from family and other documents, it has been possible to glean a substantial amount of information about the artist's work. Unfortunately, however, the painter rarely affords us a glimpse of his thoughts about his art or about art of his time.

Even his lecture on "Art, the Ideal of Art, and the Utility of Art" (see Bibliography), prepared for delivery in his role of professor of art at the University of Missouri near the close of his life, fails to give us any clue to the sources of his own artistic style and development, nor is it of much aid in clarifying our ideas in that direction. Bingham's intention was to appeal to an intellectual audience, and he therefore employed notions of an art or aesthetic philosophy which were obviously derived from the writings of others. Although this reveals the artist as an avid reader and even as a thinker along such lines, any extended consideration of the published lecture has been eliminated from this study, chiefly because it offers no evidence in support of the purely stylistic discussion that is the main concern of the present book.

For those who seek the "complete man" in this estimate of Bingham, there may be some feeling of disappointment, for my concentration on the art historical aspect rendered a total study of this many-sided personality unfeasible. The man actually reveals himself only occasionally in his pictures, although the definition of his character comes through clearly and brightly in connection with his active political career, revealing him as a vital figure participating in the vigorous and stimulating events of his age. It still remains for the scholar of American history to make use of the rich materials about Bingham and his time now readily available.

This work represents the major part of a manuscript that was completed in 1956, but the present text has been revised to incorporate materials discovered since that time, as well as to include those ideas which have finally been brought to maturity after many years of research and contemplation. The basis of the present study actually relies on the organization and analysis of materials assembled over a period of eighteen years. The work was begun in Columbia, Missouri, while I was a member of the faculty of the art department of the University of Missouri, and later carried forward in St. Louis and Kansas City, as well as in New York, Philadelphia, and Washington—all areas with which Bingham had active contact. Correspondence during the progress of the work covered most of the states of the nation. In this connection, a letter received in 1947 from another prominent Missourian, former President Harry S. Truman, then resident in the White House, gave valuable suggestions for additional information on the artist during his residence in Independence. The letter revealed an intimate knowledge of Bingham's work.

During the many years occupied in research, I became indebted to a large number of individuals who have come forward generously, but they are too numerous to list separately here. Nevertheless, I recall with particular affection the late Mrs. Mayme Wallace Walter and the late C. Lester Hall, Jr., who from the first gave unselfishly of their time and afforded me every assistance. My special thanks go to the artist's granddaughter Mrs. Clara King Bowdry, who sent me copies of family letters and other documents which have been of the greatest importance in filling gaps in our knowledge of Bingham's early artistic career. Her own unpublished material about Bingham family history was also made available without restriction (see appendixes A and B). To Charles van Ravenswaay are due grateful thanks for the use of his excellent file of references to the artist, as well as to Mrs. Nadine Neff Roberts for placing at my disposal early photographs of Bingham's works. I am indebted also to Alfred Frankenstein for his courtesy in communicating with me in connection with the discovery of a long-lost painting by Bingham.

To the late Professor Walter W. S. Cook of the Institute of Fine Arts, New York University, whose guidance and encouragement will always be remembered with deep affection; to Professors Harry Bober, Walter Friedlaender, Robert J. Goldwater, and Dimitris S. Tselos for lending so generously of their skills and wisdom on many occasions; and to Lloyd Goodrich, Director of the Whitney Museum of American Art, for an always willing assistance during the long progress of this work, and for actively supporting its publication —my grateful appreciation.

For the able assistance afforded me by the staffs of the State Historical Society of Missouri, the Missouri Historical Society, the Frick Art Reference Library, the Pennsylvania Academy of the Fine Arts, the New-York Historical Society, and the New York Public Library, I tender my thanks.

E. M. B.

University of California
Los Angeles

PHOTOGRAPHIC SOURCES AND ACKNOWLEDGMENTS

The majority of the illustrations are from photographs generously made available by museums, libraries, university archives, dealers, and the owners of pictures. Many photographs were made specifically for the present work.

The following photographs are reproduced by courtesy of the institutions named:

Art Commission of the City of New York: Pl. 124.

Boatmen's National Bank of St. Louis, St. Louis, Missouri (*Color plates:* Neil Sauer): Pls. 95, 103, 104.

Brigham Young University, Provo, Utah: Pl. 76.

Brooklyn Museum, New York: Pl. 86.

City Art Museum, St. Louis, Missouri (*Photographs:* Piaget): *Frontis.*; Pls. 7, 17, 61, 62, 66, 94, 110, 133, 160, 194.

Detroit Institute of Arts, Detroit, Michigan: Pls. 35, 48, 83.

Fogg Art Museum, Harvard University, Cambridge, Massachusetts: Pl. 82.

Frick Art Reference Library, New York: Pls. 25, 26, 189.

Institute of Fine Arts, New York University, New York: Pls. 57, 58, 88, 89, 165, 166, 167, 168.

Isaac Delgado Museum of Art, New Orleans, Louisiana: Pls. 10, 11.

Kennedy Galleries, New York: Pl. 51.

Los Angeles County Museum of Art, Los Angeles, California: Pl. 117.

Metropolitan Museum of Art, New York: Pl. 50 (Morris K. Jessup Fund, 1933).

Missouri Historical Society, St. Louis, Missouri (*Photographs:* Piaget): Pls. 3, 24, 43, 112, 113, 123, 134, 145.

Museum of Fine Arts, Boston, Massachusetts: Pls. 47, 74.

National Gallery of Art, Washington, D.C.: Pl. 32.

Peabody Museum, Harvard University, Cambridge, Massachusetts: Pl. 75.

State Historical Society of Missouri, Columbia, Missouri: Pls. 67, 135, 148, 149, 150, 151, 164, 170, 176, 187.

Wadsworth Atheneum, Hartford, Connecticut: Pl. 118.

Washington University, St. Louis, Missouri: Pl. 87.

William Rockhill Nelson Gallery of Art, Kansas City, Missouri: Pls. 1, 2, 9, 23, 56, 69, 91, 101, 102, 106, 116, 120, 121, 136, 137, 140, 142, 154, 155, 156, 157, 158, 159, 172, 181, 183, 184, 190, 196.

CONTENTS

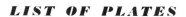

LIST OF PLATES

LIST OF PLATES

(plates follow p. 341)

FRONTISPIECE. *Self-Portrait of the Artist,* 1834/1835, City Art Museum, St. Louis Missouri.

1. *Dr. John Sappington,* 1834, Missouri State Park Board, Jefferson City, Missouri.
2. *Mrs. John Sappington,* 1834, Missouri State Park Board, Jefferson City, Missouri.
3. *Meredith Miles Marmaduke,* 1834, Missouri Historical Society, St. Louis, Missouri.
4. *Mrs. Meredith Miles Marmaduke,* 1834, collection Mrs. Grover F. Stephens. Marshall, Missouri.
5. *Dr. Anthony Wayne Rollins,* 1834, collection Mrs. James S. Lackey and Mrs. Jessie B. Terrill, Richmond, Kentucky.
6. *Mrs. Anthony Wayne Rollins,* 1834, collection Mrs. Ellsworth A. MacLeod, Columbia, Missouri.
7. *Major James Sidney Rollins,* 1834, estate of Curtis Burnam Rollins, Columbia, Missouri.
8. *Josiah Woodson Wilson,* 1834, collection Mr. J. Dozier Stone, Columbia, Missouri.
9. *Colonel John Thornton,* 1835, collection Mr. and Mrs. Charles P. Hough, Jr., Kansas City, Missouri.
10. *Portrait of a Man,* 1835, Isaac Delgado Museum of Art, New Orleans, Louisiana.
11. Reverse, *Portrait of a Man,* 1835, Isaac Delgado Museum of Art, New Orleans, Louisiana.
12. *General Richard Gentry,* 1837, collection Mr. William Richard Gentry, Jr., St. Louis, Missouri.
13. *Judge Warren Woodson,* 1837, collection Mrs. William Ashley Gray, Clayton. Missouri.
14. *Thomas Miller,* 1837, State Historical Society of Missouri, Columbia, Missouri.
15. *Priestly Haggin McBride,* 1837, collection Mrs. Howard Hammond, Fayette. Missouri.
16. *Mrs. William Johnston,* ca. 1837, collection Mr. John Lawrence Johnston, New York.
17. *Mrs. Anthony Wayne Rollins,* 1837, estate of Curtis Burnam Rollins, Columbia, Missouri.

18. *Mrs. James Sidney Rollins*, 1837, collection Mrs. Curtis Field Burnam, Baltimore, Maryland.

19. Thomas Sully, *Frances Anne (Fanny) Kemble as "Beatrice"* (1833), engraving, John Cheney after painting. Ill.: *The Gift ... for 1836*, frontis.

20. *Mrs. David Steele Lamme and Son*, 1837, estate of Curtis Burnam Rollins, Columbia, Missouri.

21. Sir Thomas Lawrence, *Lady Georgiana Dover and Son* (1830), engraving, James Henry Watt after painting.

22. *Miss Sarah Helen Rollins*, 1837, collection Mr. Rollins Field Burnam, Shreveport, Louisiana.

23. *Mrs. Thomas Shackelford*, 1838/1839, collection Mrs. Harold E. Edwards, Santa Fe, New Mexico and Miss Margaret Shackelford, Brandywine, Maryland.

24. *Mrs. John Fletcher Darby*, ca. 1839, Missouri Historical Society, St. Louis, Missouri.

25. *Judge Henry Lewis*, 1839, collection Mrs. Richard Hawes, St. Louis, Missouri.

26. *Mrs. Henry Lewis*, 1839, collection Mrs. Richard Hawes, St. Louis, Missouri.

27. *Jacob Fortney Wyan*, ca. 1838/1839, collection Mrs. Curtis Pigott, Merrick, New York.

28. *Thomas Erskine Birch*, 1839, collection Mr. George Harrison Whitney, Upland, California.

29. *Mrs. Lewis Bumgardner*, 1839, collection Mr. Rudolph Bumgardner, Jr., Staunton, Virginia.

30. *Leonidas Wetmore*, 1839/1840, Market, St. Louis, Missouri.

31. Robert Walter Weir, *Sa-go-ye-wat-ha (Red Jacket)* (1828), engraving, Moseley Isaac Danforth after painting.

32. *Richard Henry Robinson*, ca. 1838/1839, collection Mrs. William Patterson, Lexington, Kentucky.

33. *Miss Sallie Ann Camden*, 1839, private collection.

34. *John Quincy Adams*, 1844, collection Mr. James Sidney Rollins II, Columbia, Missouri.

35. *John Quincy Adams*, ca. 1850, Detroit Institute of Arts, Detroit, Michigan.

36. *John Quincy Adams*, ca. 1850, collection Mrs. W. D. A. Westfall, Columbia, Missouri.

37. *Daniel Webster*, 1844, Thomas Gilcrease Institute of American History and Art, Tulsa, Oklahoma.

38. *Mrs. George Caleb Bingham and Son Newton*, 1840/1841, collection Mrs. W. P. Bowdry, Dallas, Texas.

39. *The Sleeping Child: Horace Bingham*, 1843/1844, collection Mrs. George Bingham King, Stephenville, Texas.

40. *Mrs. George Caleb Bingham*, 1842, collection Mrs. W. P. Bowdry, Dallas, Texas. (Reproduced from a daguerreotype.)

41. William Fisher, *Portrait*, engraving, W. Osborn after painting (?).

42. *Mrs. Hartwell Peebles Heath*, 1841, collection Mrs. Randolph Crump Miller, New Haven, Connecticut.

43. *The Dull Story*, 1843/1844, collection Mr. Charles van Ravenswaay, Boonville, Missouri.

44. *Miss Anna Rives Heath*, 1841, collection Mrs. Ernest P. Buxton, Jr., Richmond, Virginia.

130. *Dr. John Sappington*, ca. 1844/1845, collection Mrs. C. Lester Hall, Jr., Kansas City, Missouri.
131. *Mrs. John Sappington*, ca. 1844/1845, collection Mrs. C. Lester Hall, Jr., Kansas City, Missouri.
132. *Mrs. Jacob Fortney Wyan*, ca. 1845, collection Mrs. Curtis Pigott, Merrick, New York.
133. *Dr. Oscar F. Potter*, 1848, City Art Museum, St. Louis, Missouri.
134. *Colonel William Franklin Switzler*, 1849, Missouri Historical Society, St. Louis, Missouri.
135. *Mrs. William Franklin Switzler*, 1849, State Historical Society of Missouri, Columbia, Missouri.
136. *Mrs. George Caleb Bingham*, 1849/1850, estate of Mrs. Arthur Palmer, Independence, Missouri.
137. *Mrs. James H. McGee*, 1849/1850, collection Mrs. Webster W. Townley, Kansas City, Missouri.
138. *Self-Portrait of the Artist*, 1849/1850, collection Dr. Eleanor Cook, Lake Charles, Louisiana.
139. *Miss Mary Elizabeth Rollins*, 1849, collection Mrs. Sidney Rollins Overall, St. Louis, Missouri.
140. *Mrs. Sallie (Thomas) Moore or More*, 1849/1850, collection Mrs. Thomas B. Hall, Kansas City, Missouri.
141. *Mrs. James H. Bennett*, 1849, collection Mrs. Stephen McCready, Ocala, Florida.
142. *Miss Vestine Porter*, ca. 1849/1850, William Rockhill Nelson Gallery of Art, Kansas City, Missouri.
143. *Mrs. Anthony Wayne Rollins*, after 1850, collection Mrs. James S. Lackey and Mrs. Jessie B. Terrill, Richmond, Kentucky.
144. *Washington McLean*, after 1850, Market, New York.
145. *Thomas Hart Benton*, after 1850, Missouri Historical Society, St. Louis, Missouri.
146. *Elijah S. Stephens*, 1855, collection Mr. E. Sydney Stephens, Jr., Columbia, Missouri.
147. *Mrs. David McClanahan Hickman*, ca. 1855/1856, collection Mr. Arch Y. Guitar, New Orleans, Louisiana.
148. *Thomas Jefferson*, 1857/1858, destroyed by fire, Capitol, Jefferson City, Missouri, 1911.
149. *Thomas Jefferson* (copy after Gilbert Stuart), 1856, State Historical Society of Missouri, Columbia, Missouri.
150. *Henry Clay*, 1860, destroyed by fire, Capitol, Jefferson City, Missouri, 1911.
151. *Baron Friedrich Heinrich Alexander von Humboldt*, 1860 (present state), State Historical Society of Missouri, Columbia, Missouri.
152. *Mrs. Robert Levi Todd and Daughter, Matilda Tete*, ca. 1860, collection Mrs. James P. Bennett, Berkeley, California.
153. *Mrs. Almerin Hotchkiss*, ca. 1860, collection Mrs. Frank Hotchkiss Jordan, Des Moines, Iowa.
154. *Miss Sally Cochran McGraw*, ca. 1860, collection Mrs. Frederic James, Kansas City, Missouri.

155. *Judge James Turner Vance Thompson*, ca. 1859/1860, William Rockhill Nelson Gallery of Art, Kansas City, Missouri.
156. *Mrs. James Turner Vance Thompson*, ca. 1859/1860, William Rockhill Nelson Gallery of Art, Kansas City, Missouri.
157. *Dr. Benoist Troost*, 1859, William Rockhill Nelson Gallery of Art, Kansas City, Missouri.
158. *Mrs. Benoist Troost*, 1859, William Rockhill Nelson Gallery of Art, Kansas City, Missouri.
159. *Mrs. James M. Piper*, ca. 1860/1862, estate of Mrs. Arthur Palmer, Independence, Missouri.
160. *General Nathaniel Lyon and General Francis Preston Blair, Jr., Starting from the Arsenal Gate in St. Louis to Capture Camp Jackson*, ca. 1862/1865, collection Mrs. Frank Rollins, Columbia, Missouri.
161. Charles Wimar, *Colonel Franz Sigel, General John Charles Frémont, and Captain Constantin Blandowski*, 1861, collection Mrs. Edwin H. Conrades, St. Louis, Missouri.
162. *Thread of Life*, ca. 1862, collection Mr. A. J. Stephens, Kansas City, Missouri.
163. Peter Frederick Rothermel, *The Angel of the Opal*, engraving, John Sartain after drawing (?) Ill.: *The Opal* . . . (1849), frontis.
164. *Martial Law* or *Order No. 11* (2), ca. 1869/1870, State Historical Society of Missouri, Columbia, Missouri.
165. *Apollo Belvedere*, Vatican, Rome.
166. Masaccio, *Expulsion*, ca. 1427, Brancacci Chapel, Sta. Maria del Carmine, Florence.
167. Jean-Baptiste Greuze, *The Father's Curse*, Louvre, Paris.
168. Fra Bartolommeo, *Pietà*, Pitti, Florence.
169. *General Nathaniel Lyon*, 1867, destroyed by fire, Capitol, Jefferson City, Missouri, 1911.
170. *Major Dean in Jail*, 1866, William Jewell College, Liberty, Missouri.
171. Edward Matthew Ward, *Napoleon in the Prison at Nice*, engraving, J. Outrim after painting.
172. *James Rollins Bingham*, ca. 1870, collection Mrs. John B. Hutchison, Independence, Missouri.
173. *Hugh Campbell Ward*, ca. 1869/1870, collection Mr. Hugh C. Ward, Cohasset, Massachusetts.
174. *General Francis Preston Blair, Jr.*, 1871, Market, New York.
175. *Major James Sidney Rollins*, 1871, collection Mr. David Westfall, Columbia, Missouri.
176. *Major James Sidney Rollins*, 1871, State Historical Society of Missouri, Columbia, Missouri.
177. *Thomas Hoyle Mastin*, ca. 1871, collection Mr. Hoyle M. Lovejoy, River Forest, Illinois.
178. *John Jerome Mastin, Jr.*, ca. 1871, collection Mr. G. Edgar Lovejoy, Jr., Port Lavaca, Texas.
179. *Mrs. James Sidney Rollins*, 1871/1872, estate of Curtis Burnam Rollins, Columbia, Missouri.

THE EVOLUTION OF AN ARTIST

ABBREVIATIONS

AAU	American Art-Union, New York
AFS	Artists Fund Society, Philadelphia
B.	George Caleb Bingham
M. B.	Mary (Amend) Bingham
MHR	Missouri Historical Review
MHS	Missouri Historical Society, St. Louis
NAD	National Academy of Design, New York
NYHS	New-York Historical Society, New York
PAFA	The Pennsylvania Academy of the Fine Arts, Philadelphia
PAU	Philadelphia Art Union
R.	James Sidney Rollins
S. E. H., S. E. B.	Sarah Elizabeth (Hutchison) Bingham
SHSMo	State Historical Society of Missouri, Columbia
WAU	Western Art Union, Cincinnati

(Full bibliographical details of works cited briefly in the notes are given in the Bibliography.)

I

AMERICAN PAINTING IN THE 1830's

We can perhaps more readily appreciate the problem that faced an aspiring young artist like George Caleb Bingham once we have a clear picture of the general conditions prevailing at the time he began to consider following the profession of a painter.

It is undoubtedly true that in the United States the period about 1830 was scarcely encouraging to the young hopeful in the art, particularly in the field of painting; yet it is surprising to note how many Americans were then concentrating their energies and devoting their lives to it, despite the obvious practical hazards.

All through the eighteenth and continuing into the first quarter of the nineteenth century, portraiture had been almost the only means of a livelihood available to the American painter. Although Benjamin West had earned an enviable reputation as a painter of historical and religious subjects and, following his example, John Trumbull had attempted to establish himself as a history painter in this country, the majority of painters at work in America still received little encouragement beyond portraiture. In those days before Daguerre, painters who could most faithfully record a good likeness would at least find a ready market for their work, regardless of the artistic merit of the production. Gilbert Stuart (who was dead by 1830) had been a notable exception, and younger painters idealized him. The brighter lights among his successors included John Wesley Jarvis, Thomas Sully, Matthew Harris Jouett, and Chester Harding, some of whom were undoubtedly inspired by his example.

The primary problem for the young artist was the inadequacy of art instruction. Art training on any formal scale was concentrated in eastern cities such as New York and Philadelphia, but even in those centers the opportunities offered to the student were frequently hopelessly limited, and they were hardly conducive to the development of any real talent. The National Academy of Design in New York had been founded in 1826, but four years later it afforded instruction in no more than drawing from the antique, along with lectures on anatomy. Henry Inman, addressing the students as an officer of the Academy in that year, could promise that "during the next season, in addition to the Antique School, *the living model*, and, that besides the usual course, practical lectures on portrait painting, architecture and engraving, will be delivered by able professors of these several departments."[1] But it was not until the fall of 1834 that a life school was "ordered to be opened, if a sufficient number of persons subscribed to pay the actual cost of models."[2] The Pennsylvania Academy of the Fine Arts, in Philadelphia, was older; and there, drawing from casts was available to students as early as 1807. Sometimes a young artist might obtain the special privilege of working under an established painter, or could at least submit his work for criticism and advice. Less frequently, he might secure an opportunity to study abroad (in 1830, the artist's dream was usually to go to Rome).

Inland from the eastern seaboard, opportunities for art training were fewer and much less positive. An artist was usually self-taught, and frequently he gained his first contact with the medium through sign painting. If he was lucky, he might meet with some itinerant portrait painter who at least afforded him a flesh-and-blood contact with the rudiments of the craft and whose works, poor as they often were, served to inspire a talented youth to higher efforts. He often knew no pictures other than the daubs of the itinerants, together with the few engraved reproductions that might come his way. Some periodicals and the already popular literary annuals and gift books of the time included engraved illustrations after the works of contemporary artists or the old masters. In the large centers there were the annual exhibitions of the works of living painters at the academies, and sometimes special shows of collections of old masters. In the period under discussion, for instance, the collections of Richard Abrahams and Richard W. Meade[3] attracted considerable attention in the press when they were placed on view in New York; the Abrahams pictures were described as "one of the finest collections of old

1. T. S. Cummings, *Historic Annals of the National Academy of Design . . .* (Philadelphia: G. W. Childs, 1865), p. 117. From an address delivered March 22, 1830.
2. *Ibid.*, p. 134.
3. Exhibited at the National Gallery, Clinton Hall, in the fall of 1831. The collection was said to have been formed in Spain and included "specimens from the Italian, Spanish, and Flemish schools, all by masters of distinguished reputation, and several by those of the very first class." Examples cited were attributed to Titian, Jordano [Giordano], Veronese, Bassano, Rubens, Rosa, Domenichino, Murillo. From review, *New-York Mirror,* IX (Sept. 17, 1831), 86-87.

paintings ever brought to the city."[4] Artists such as Thomas Sully eagerly took advantage of such opportunities to see "original" pictures.[5]

The rather restricted instruction in the schools in the East and the almost total lack of training available in other regions compelled many young painters to seek other means of gaining a formal knowledge of their profession. Certainly the art instruction books (published mainly in England), which will be discussed below, played a vital part in the training of a young artist, and at times these works served to inspire his future direction in the field. Thomas Cole, as a youth in Steubenville, Ohio, in 1820, became acquainted with an itinerant portrait painter who lent him one such volume, a book that "treated of design, composition, and colour."[6] As he later related to Dunlap: "This book was my companion day and night, nothing could separate us—my usual avocations were neglected—painting was all in all to me."[7]

Except for the patronage of those people of all classes who provided a steady demand for family likenesses, and thus a means of livelihood for the painter, there were comparatively few other outlets for an artist's work along other lines. There were some exceptions, to be sure—collectors such as Luman Reed, Philip Hone, Robert Gilmor, Jonathan Sturges, and Henry C. Carey, who apparently did more than their share in encouraging the painters, not only by buying their pictures but also by assisting many of them to continue their studies abroad. The vast majority of American artists, however, still had to struggle to survive, and it was some years before any concentrated effort was made to "promote" the arts through the creation of a larger, more centralized market. In time, that was what the American Art-Union was to provide.

Yet the prospect was not a completely depressing one. Signs of a change were clearly in the air, with the rise of the Jacksonian democracy of the 1830's, bringing with it a greater awareness of a certain pride in country and culture, and a feeling by the people that "the nation belonged to them at last."[8] A strong bourgeois class was arising now, and its interest in art, however limited, began to broaden, turning in directions other than that of mere self-perpetuation through portraiture. A pride in the nation that was

---

4. Cummings, *op. cit.*, p. 118. The collection was on exhibition at the gallery of the American Academy of the Fine Arts by March, 1830. "It contained a beautiful 'Hobbiman' [Hobbema], a 'Claude' of great excellence, a 'Murillo' superb—indeed, the whole good" (*ibid.*).
5. W. Dunlap, *History of the Rise and Progress of the Arts of Design in the United States...* (New York: G. P. Scott, 1834), II, 280. Sully saw the Abrahams collection in May, 1830, and made color notes of the pictures.
6. *Ibid.*, II, 352.   7. *Ibid.*
8. Van Wyck Brooks, *The World of Washington Irving...* (New York: Dutton, 1944), p. 314.

5

cutting its last ties with the mother country brought with it as well a growing demand for delineations of the homeland in terms of the country's vast landscape, as well as for portrayals of American life, customs, and history. Thus an artist at the turn of the third decade might have discerned signs that promised well for him and his calling.

Writers on art, too, were beginning to give more and more space to reviews of the annual art exhibitions, such as those of the National Academy, with each picture discussed individually. At the same time, the public was being energetically prodded to support and encourage the efforts of both the Academy and the artist:

It is very certain that we shall never have arts or sciences or literature, unless we know and reward those who devote themselves to their promotion. There is no excuse for apathy among us. Our country is flourishing, our people are free, peaceful, and happy. The earthquakes, both moral and physical, which shake the eastern continent to the centre, are not felt on these shores. We have neither tyrants, nor revolutions, nor want; our public coffers are overflowing. When shall we reach a more proper period for cherishing those elegant establishments of civilization, among which the art of painting holds such prominent rank? A good painter here in *want*, unless from his own idleness or extravagance, is a rebuke to the taste and liberality of the whole city; and, we may add, an exhibition like the present, comprising the works of so many talented men, and not noticed by the editors, visited by the community, and honored with ample encouragement, is a proof that we are progressing much more slowly towards the real refinements of cultivated life than we are willing to allow.[9]

Although the large exhibitions of works by living painters were still made up predominantly of portraits, the public and the art critics were obviously tired of rooms mostly filled with paintings of faces, and they yearned for something new. Typical of the attitude is the criticism of a contemporary critic, aimed at the National Academy show of 1830:

The great fault of the exhibition, or rather defect, for it is not the fault of any one connected with it, but that of the egotistical particles which make up the public, is the great number of portraits. Portraits of ladies and gentlemen meet the eye in every direction; and not even the splendid talents of Inman and Ingham, principally exercised in this branch of the arts, can reconcile us to the undue preponderance of "the human face divine" in the exhibition.[10]

The most admired works in the show included a landscape by Cole, which was deemed "among the most attractive to our eyes"[11]; others, by Doughty and Wall, were called "delightful."[12] The literary subjects of paintings by Weir inspired the suggestion that it was "a great pity that this species of

9. *New-York Mirror*, IX (June 9, 1832), 391.
11. *Ibid.*

10. *Ibid.*, VII (May 15, 1830), 359.
12. *Ibid.*

composition is not more encouraged."[13] The Academy's exhibition of the following year called forth much the same sort of criticism over the excessive display of portrait paintings, but there was a refreshingly favorable note about a genre subject by William Sidney Mount.[14]

Such significant signs of change, of course, were as yet infrequent in the inland cities and towns, where the demand was still heavily concentrated on portraits. Nevertheless, a painter such as Bingham visiting Philadelphia and New York in the last years of the decade would find enough indications of a change of taste favoring greater variety in the pictorial expressions of his colleagues to encourage him to extend his own first efforts beyond the familiar "pot-boiling" face paintings.

13. *Ibid.*
14. *Ibid.*, VIII (May 7, 1831), 350.

7

II

BINGHAM'S FAMILY BACKGROUND

George Caleb Bingham was known during his lifetime as "The Missouri Artist," and he will always be actively identified with the history of that state; yet he was born in Augusta County, Virginia, a descendant of at least two generations of Virginians. And in after years, although from his childhood on he recognized Missouri as his home, the artist still proudly recalled his native state. Late in life, disgruntled over the terms of a commission granted him by the state of Missouri, he declared, "if my life and health shall be spared so as to enable me to execute the picture, it will more likely become the property of my native State of Virginia than of my adopted State of Missouri."[1]

Bingham apparently knew very little about his family origins before the generation to which his parents belonged, but it is now believed[2] that the Binghams of Virginia came from England during the latter half of the seventeenth century. Where they first settled in this country is still a matter of some conjecture, but the artist himself asserted that his grandfather, the Reverend George Bingham, came "from some one of the New England States" at about the end of the Revolution. Another source indicates that the grandfather actually came from Pennsylvania. Old records point to the first settlement of the family in New London, Connecticut; this was during the latter part of the seventeenth century, when two brothers, the sons of one Thomas Bingham, a Master Cutler from Sheffield, Yorkshire, came to the American colonies. One of the brothers died in New London, and there is good reason

1. Bingham to Rollins, letter, Jefferson City, Mo., April 18, 1877, coll. State Historical Society of Mo., Columbia (*Missouri Historical Review*, XXXIII [1939], 380).
2. All details in the following pages which refer to the paternal and maternal ancestry of the artist are based on research made by Mrs. Clara King Bowdry. Mrs. Bowdry kindly made her manuscript available to me. See Appendixes B and C.

to believe that a son of this Bingham was James (1668-1714), who had considerable property in New Jersey. James Bingham, by 1705, resided in Philadelphia. It was his son, also named James, who purchased land in who accumulated additional land in Virginia at an even earlier date. Three Orange County, Virginia, in 1735, and it may have been this second James Binghams—Christopher, George, and John—possibly the sons of the second James, were in Augusta County, Virginia, in 1745. Another son, William, was married in Philadelphia in that same year, to a Mary Stamper, and it is usually assumed that George, the grandfather that the painter George Caleb Bingham recalled, was born of that Philadelphia marriage. The grandfather, George, was living in Hanover County, Virginia, in 1782, about the time he married Louisa Vest of that county, and of this union the oldest son, Henry Vest Bingham, born in 1783, became the father of the painter.

Bingham's material grandfather, Matthias Amend, was the grandson of Johann George Amend, who came to America (probably from Germany) in 1732 and settled in York County, Pennsylvania. This settler's son was George Elias, who apparently married twice and spent his entire life in the same region. Matthias, born in 1753 of the union of George Elias and his second wife, moved to Virginia in 1781 after seeing service in the Revolution. He married Elizabeth Bushong, of French Huguenot descent, and these two became the parents of Mary, who married Henry Vest Bingham.

Later in his life, George Caleb Bingham started to set down what he may have intended to develop into an autobiography, but he never carried it beyond an account of his memories and impressions of his Virginia forebears. This account, in the artist's own words, reads:

I have no knowledge of my ancestry beyond my maternal and paternal grandfathers. The former was born of German parentage near the city of Little York in the state of Pennsylvania. His name was Matthias Amend. He was by trade a millwright and a most excellent workman in his line. Before the close of the last century he migrated to the valley of Virginia and settled at the place on which is the celebrated cavern known as Wier's Cave. Through his grounds flowed the beautiful little South River which forms one of the three branches of the Shenandoah that intersect each other near the village of Port Republic. Upon this never-failing stream he erected a sawmill and gristmill which furnished lumber and breadstuff to the community for miles around. Its revolving wheels were the earliest wonder upon which my eyes opened, and as an evidence of the skill with which they were constructed, they are yet in motion after a lapse of more than three score years. But two children were born to my Grandfather Amend, a son and a daughter. The former died in early childhood. The death of the mother soon followed, and the daughter, Mary, was the only remaining solace to the bereaved mill-wright. Upon her were very naturally centered all his hopes and affections. Having been the child of poverty himself and, consequently, favored with none of the advantages of education, his experience of the evils of such a deprivation impelled him to obtain

9

for his daughter such means of instruction as the country then afforded. The nearest school was six miles from his residence. This Mary attended from the house of a kinsman nearby, to which she went every Monday morning, never failing to return to her father on the succeeding Saturday, in the evening of which and the Sunday following she would impart to him the lessons she had received during the week.

Thus father and child were educated together, the child obtaining a good English education, and the father learning to read and write and to cast up accounts.

My grandfather, George Bingham, was born and raised in some of the New England states, from which at about the close of the Revolution he migrated to Virginia and settled on the east side of the Blue Ridge, about eighteen miles west of Charlottesville, the home of Jefferson and the seat of the Virginia University.

He was what is termed a local Methodist preacher and as such ministered to a congregation in a meeting-house erected for their accommodation upon his plantation. He cultivated tobacco and grain by the aid of a number of slaves, to whom he was exceedingly kind and indulgent, never using the lash or allowing it to be used upon his place.

I remember him well as a tall and white-headed old gentleman, overflowing with the milk of human kindness. He had three sons and four daughters who reached the age of maturity. My father, Henry V. Bingham, was the oldest son and the oldest child. He was blessed with a good constitution, and leading from early boyhood an active life, he presented in his person at the time of my remembrance a fine specimen of vigorous manhood, measuring six feet in height and weighing over a hundred and eighty pounds. His education was only such as could be acquired in the common field schools of the time, but he was a constant reader, and his mind became stored with a good amount of historical and political information.

After reaching his twenty-first year he had the charge of his father's plantation and conducted its affairs with energy and industry, laboring in the fields with the slaves and taking the annual crop of tobacco to market in Richmond.

The present era of railroads and rapid transportation furnishes a striking contrast to the roads and locomotive powers which then furnished the Virginians with the only means of reaching a market with the staple upon which he predicated his hope of future wealth. Not even the common wagon was used. Each hogshead of tobacco was strongly hooped from end to end, the heads were made of thick and substantial material, and in the center of each was inserted a strong hickory pin to which a pair of shafts were attached, and by which a single horse could roll a hogshead of tobacco from the shed in which it was prepared from fifty to a hundred miles, as the distance might be, to the market which furnished a purchaser.

This was generally done at a season of the year when the roads were dry, and when the labor both of horses and men could be best spared from the fields. As such times the roads to Richmond would be filled for miles at a stretch with "tobacco rollers" who enlivened the hours with singing songs and cracking their jokes. Some of the latter were occasionally of a practical nature and calculated to test the temper of their unfortunate subjects.

Taking his provisions and blankets with him, each roller would encamp, and frequently alone, wherever he might be at the approach at night, and in the event of a cloudy morning it not infrequently happened that a roller, after attaching his horse and travelling several miles, would be astonished by meeting a roller travelling exactly

10

the opposite of the course which appeared to him to be the way to Richmond. Questions and answers would be immediately exchanged which would make it clear to his mind that the shafts of his hogshead, which were toward Richmond when he laid down, had been reversed by some wicked rival while he was asleep, and that deceived thereby he was wending his way homeward instead of lessening his distance to Richmond. Should he meet in Richmond the wag who thus tricked him, a fight might ensue, or a jolly laugh and a drink all around, as the humor of the parties might happen to be.

In consequence of the entire failure of the mill streams on the east side of the Blue Ridge during a period of drouth, it became necessary for my father to take a load of grain "over the mountain" to my Grandfather Amend's mill on the South River. While there he became acquainted, as a matter of course, with my mother, Mary Amend, fell in love with her, and in due time offered himself in marriage and was accepted.

As my mother, Mary, was the only treasure which my Grandfather Amend valued, in giving her away, he also surrendered to my father his entire earthly possessions, stipulating only that he should have a home with his daughter during the period of his natural life.

As soon, therefore, as the wedding was consummated, my father became the proprietor of the lands including the mill and Wier's Cave, so called in honor of its discoverer, a little Dutchman named Barnett Wier, who was in the habit of roaming among the hills and forests with his dog and gun.[3]

The marriage between Henry Vest Bingham and Mary Amend probably took place on September 8, 1808, and thereafter the couple resided at the Amend mill. It was there also that six of their eight children were born. George Caleb, the couple's second child and their second son, was born on March 20, 1811.

In 1819,[4] probably as a result of a financial loss, the Augusta County holdings were sold. Soon afterward, Henry Bingham, his wife and children, and his father-in-law set out for Missouri, in the hope of regaining their fortune. They settled in Franklin, the county seat of Howard County and already a town of considerable importance and prosperity. In July, 1819, the year of the Bingham family arrival, it was described as a town of "about one hundred and twenty log houses of one story, several framed dwellings of two stories, and two of brick, thirteen shops for sale of merchandise, four taverns, two smiths' shops, two large team-mills, a post office, and a printing press issuing a weekly paper."[5] The newspaper was the *Missouri Intelligencer,* which informed its readers during the latter part of the same year:

3. MS. in coll. SHSMo.
4. A year earlier Henry V. Bingham, Sr., made an exploratory trip west, then returned to Virginia for his family. The record of that trip is contained in his diary, now in coll. SHSMo and published in M. G. Windell ed., "The Road West in 1818, the Diary of Henry Vest Bingham," *MHR.* XL (1945), 21-45, 174-204.
5. "Account of an Expedition from Pittsburgh to the Rocky Mountains Performed in the Years 1819, 1820... Under the Command of Maj. S. H. Long," in R. G. Thwaites, ed., *Early Western Travels, 1748-1846* (Cleveland, O.: A. H. Clarke, 1905), XIV, 148.

Emigration to this Territory, and particularly to this County during the present season, almost exceeds belief. Those who have arrived in this quarter are principally from Kentucky, Tennessee, &c. Immense numbers of waggons, carriages, carts, &c., with families have for some time past, been daily arriving. During the month of October it is stated no less than 271 waggons and four wheeled carriages, and 55 two wheeled carriages and carts, passed near St. Charles bound principally for Boone's Lick. It is calculated that the number of persons accompanying these waggons, &c., could not be less than 3,000. It is stated in the St. Louis Enquirer of the 10th inst. that about twenty waggons, &c., per week passed through St. Charles for the last nine or ten weeks with wealthy, respectable emigrants from various states whose united numbers are supposed to amount to 12,000. The county of Howard, already respectable in numbers, will soon possess a vast population; and no section of our country presents a fairer prospect to the emigrant.[6]

Intellectually, the town had advanced to the point of having a library company by 1819,[7] superseded by a public library in 1822,[8] and an academy, which was incorporated in 1820.[9] What was called "the first real school" was opened there in 1821,[10] and two years later provision was made for the education of both sexes, "in which the primary branches and, for an extra fee, geography and history were taught."[11]

In 1820 Henry Vest Bingham operated a tavern at Franklin "at the sign of the Square and Compass,"[12] and during the next two years he also took a partnership with one William Lamme in a tobacco manufactory producing chewing tobacco and cigars.[13] He became a prominent citizen of the town, was appointed a judge of the county court for Howard County in January, 1821,[14] and a circuit court judge from 1822 to 1823.[15] His property during this period included a 160-acre farm at Arrow Rock in Saline County; presumably he grew tobacco there. Matthias Amend evidently lived on the farm, but he is said to have met his death by accidental drowning in the Missouri River near Arrow Rock. Henry Vest Bingham, George Caleb's father, died at Franklin on December 26, 1823,[16] leaving his widow with their several chil-

6. *Missouri Intelligencer*, Nov. 19, 1819, 3-1.
7. J. Viles, "Old Franklin: a Frontier Town of the Twenties," *Mississippi Valley Historical Review*, IX (March, 1923), 281. The Franklin Library Company was closed in 1822.
8. *Ibid*. References to books indicate that the library's collection included Volney's *Ruins*, Burns's *Poems*, the works of Shakespeare, Junius' *Letters*, Gregory's *Economy*, *Heathen Mythology*, and *Peregrine Pickle*.
9. *Ibid*.
10. *Ibid*. There were itinerant teachers in the town in 1820 and 1821. The "first real school" was apparently the one opened by one Jonathan S. Findlay.
11. *Ibid*.
12. *Missouri Intelligencer*, May 6, 1820, 2-4.
13. *Ibid*., Nov. 13, 1821.
14. *Ibid*., Jan. 1, 1821, 3-1.
15. *Ibid*., July 9, 1822. His activities while in office were noted in later issues of the same paper: July 16, 1822; Aug. 20, 1822; May 27, 1823; Aug. 12, 1823.
16. *Ibid*., Dec. 27, 1823.

dren to support. The family encountered immediate financial difficulties, with claims against the estate evidently using up the available resources.[17] The interest in the tobacco factory was also lost, and eventually only the Arrow Rock farm property was salvaged. It was to this refuge that the widow and her children finally moved, four years later.

17. *Ibid.*, Jan. 15, 1824, 3-2; notice of list of property to be sold to settle claims against the estate. A week later the same paper (Jan. 22, 1824, 4-2) contained an announcement of the public sale of "household and kitchen furniture," Jan. 24, at the "dwelling-house" of H. V. Bingham in Franklin.

III

THE EARLY YEARS: FIRST PAINTINGS (1834-1837)

The question of George Caleb Bingham's first artistic efforts has already been seriously considered by Rusk.[1] It seems credible enough that the future painter could have displayed artistic tendencies at an early age, and the first published account of his life, one to which Bingham in all probability contributed the salient details, advises us that "his first propensity for Art manifested itself when he was about four years old, in an attempt to copy a foreshortened figure which had been rudely but vigorously drawn by his father upon a slate."[2] This insistence on the artist's early talent for drawing is repeated in another essay prepared by his friend Rollins at a later date during Bingham's lifetime.[3]

It thus appears highly probable that Bingham already displayed some artistic talent during his Virginia childhood and that the interest in drawing continued after the family moved to Missouri in 1819. As his first biographer further relates: "Much delighted with this first effort he continued a similar practice with the lead pencil upon paper, until he reached his twelfth year— at which time he had so far advanced as to be able to copy, with considerable facility, such engravings as chance or friends threw his way."[4] (The importance of this statement in connection with the influence of engraved reproductions on the artist will be discussed fully in a later chapter.) The specific mention of his contact with engravings at an early age, and his copying of them, suggests a means of self-instruction that was entirely acceptable and even recommended to the young artist.

In any event, Bingham continued to draw with diligent effort until his

1. Fern Helen Rusk, *George Caleb Bingham* ... (Jefferson City, Mo.: Hugh Stephens, 1917), pp. 13-14.
2. *Bulletin of the American Art-Union.* II (Aug., 1849), 10: "We have lately obtained from a reliable source, some particulars of the biography of this artist."
3. W. B. Davis and D. S. Durrie, *An Illustrated History of Missouri* ... (St. Louis, Mo.: A. J. Hall; Cincinnati, O.: R. Clarke, 1876), p. 469.
4. *Bull. AAU.* II (Aug., 1849), 11.

14

twelfth year, when the death of his father made it necessary for him to contribute to his family's support by helping on the Arrow Rock farm. We are further informed that young Bingham was only rarely in a position to pursue his artistic inclinations during the following ten years.[5] At this point the narrative skips over the events of those ten years—a period that actually was to prove of decisive importance to the artist, marking his choice of painting as a career. The later biographical sketch fills in some of the missing details by indicating that Bingham's health was impaired by the rigors of farm life and that, at the age of sixteen, he left for Boonville, where he was apprenticed to a cabinetmaker (probably the Reverend Justinian Williams). The account also reveals: "It was the intention of young Bingham to embark in the legal profession, and as soon as his apprenticeship expired, he commenced the preparatory studies thereof. A portrait painter, however, casually visiting Booneville [sic] at that time, turned his mind in another direction. ... A sight of the productions of this painter fired his ambition to become distinguished, as an artist."[6]

The Boonville sojourn, and the accidental meeting with the itinerant artist, would therefore seem to mark a turning point in Bingham's life, for he apparently devoted himself completely to painting from that time on. One might thus assume that Bingham now had the opportunity of observing the itinerant artist working directly from the model, as well as experiencing first-hand the technique of the use of the palette and brushes in the application of oil colors to canvas. However, a reporter in 1835 revealed, presumably in speaking of this earlier period of the artist's career: "Except those of his own execution, he never saw a portrait painted in his life."[7] Supposedly the latter information was supplied by the painter himself, and, of course, it dramatically underlines the idea that he was a self-made artist. Moreover, it was often said that itinerants were at times reluctant to permit others to watch their technical procedure, and this can be substantiated by Chester Harding's testimony about his own experience with the Pittsburgh painter Nelson.[8] Thus it is not improbable that Bingham, like Harding, was per-

5. *Ibid.*
6. Davis and Durrie, *op. cit.*, p. 469. Another source indicates that Bingham worked near Arrow Rock with Jesse Green, a cabinetmaker, and "here sketched his first pictures with chalk, before he went to Boonville" (*History of Saline County, Missouri* ... [St. Louis, Mo.: Missouri Historical Co., 1881], p. 201).
7. *Missouri Intelligencer*, March 14, 1835, 3-1.
8. W. Dunlap, *History of the ... Arts of Design in the United States* (New-York: Scott, 1834), II, 290: "Mr. Nelson was one of that class of painters who have secret modes of painting faces, and would sell a 'receipt,' but saw no advantage that could possibly grow out of his *giving* his experience to another; so that I never saw my own portrait in an unfinished state, nor would he let me be present at the painting of my wife's portrait." (Harding had commissioned Nelson to paint the portraits in the hope of being able to watch him at work.)

15

mitted to view the finished product only and had to base his first studies on it.[9]

Of course, Bingham may have used color earlier, although it could have been merely a kind of sign pigment. An old friend of his, Washington Adams, who knew him when he first came to Boonville, noted Bingham's artistic efforts before the meeting with the itinerant painter: "He commenced drawing on the ground with his fingers and would make horses, cows, chickens and other birds without any trouble—soon began to use pencil and paper, and afterwards colors. He painted old Danl Boone in a buck Skin dress with his gun at his side for a sign for Judge Dades Hottel [sic]. The likeness [sic] was very good. It was one of George's first attempts. . . ."[10] This would suggest that Bingham, like many another American painter before him,[11] had his earliest patronage as a sign painter; yet, on the basis of the limited evidence available, it is reasonable to assume that the young artist indulged only rarely in that timeworn activity.

Undoubtedly the itinerant painter at Boonville must have made an important impression, and his production, whether seen in the completed state or in process, may indeed have stimulated Bingham with a desire to emulate what he had seen. We can assume that idea with even greater probability, for we are told that upon his return to Arrow Rock "four young men of his

9. *Ibid.* Harding, continuing his autobiographical sketch, still referring to Nelson's portraits of himself and his wife, noted that the finished work served as a basis for his study of portrait painting: "These pictures, although as bad as could well be produced in any new country, were, nevertheless, models for my study and objects of my admiration. Soon after I took these pictures home, I began to analyze them; and it was not long before I set a palette, and then seating myself before my wife, made my first attempt. In this I was eminently successful."

10. W. Adams, to J. S. Rollins, letter, Boonville, Mo., March 20, 1882, coll. SHSMo (*MHR*, XXXIII [1939], 207, note 8). Not so readily acceptable is the suggestion that the artist painted earlier, using "axle grease, vegetable dyes, brick dust mixed with oil, and even his own blood, obtained by clipping the ends of his fingers" (quoted by Rusk, *op. cit.*, pp. 13-14, from an unpublished biographical sketch of the artist prepared by his niece Mrs. Louisa J. Bingham Neff). And scarcely more acceptable is the supposition that because ochre was to be found on the Virginia farm of the Binghams, a boy of seven could have learned about its color properties and made use of it (Rusk, *op. cit.*, p. 14).

The reference to the Bingham signboard may perhaps be further strengthened by a notice that appeared in a St. Louis newspaper during the artist's lifetime: "At New Franklin, Howard Co., in Alsop's Store, there is an old painting hanging upon the wall upon which is the following: DANIEL BOONE / Liberty. Some claim that it was painted by a young artist at the old fort at Boonsboro, from Boone himself, and afterwards to Mr. Alex Alsop who died a few years ago in Franklin. Others say it was painted by Gen. Geo. Bingham, while a boy, and presented to Mr. Alsop" *(Missouri Republican*, Feb. 13, 1879, p. 7). The "painting" was probably a tavern signboard. Despite the apparent flimsiness of both references, there would seem to be good reason to assume that they either refer to the same sign, or to a form of activity to which Bingham may have given some attention on more than one occasion during his early years. An engraving of Daniel Boone could well have served as Bingham's source in this instance—very probably (as McDermott suggests) the stipple engraving (1820) by James Otto Lewis (1799-1858) after Chester Harding's portrait, which seems closely related to the old description of the signboard.

11. Chester Harding ran a sign-painter's shop in Pittsburgh before he turned to portrait painting, and William Sidney Mount was a sign-painter's apprentice in New York as a youth (Dunlap, *op. cit.*, II, 290, 451).

acquaintance," admiring his work, commissioned him to paint their portraits, and he accepted the opportunity, "and with such colors as a house-painter's shop could supply, and a half dozen stumps of brushes left by a transient artist in a neighboring town, he commenced his career as a portrait painter."[12]

The "transient artist in a neighboring town" could only have been the painter Bingham met in Boonville. The identity of that painter is never revealed and it is more than possible that Bingham himself could not recall his name. He was probably one of the many itinerants who made his living by traveling from town to town. There were many such painters and not all of their names have come down to us. Certainly, relatively few were artists of any marked ability.

It has been repeatedly stated that Bingham met Chester Harding while serving his apprenticeship and that "upon Harding's advice he gave up all else and turned to painting as his life work" and received from him his first instruction in painting.[13] This would appear to be an attempt to identify our unknown transient painter with Harding. It is inconceivable that this could have been so and that Bingham would have neglected to mention, or indeed have forgotten, the identity of his first instructor, especially had he been the well-known Chester Harding. Bingham knew Harding's name and work, for later in life he recognized him as a representative American portrait painter.[14] At no time, however, did he record any personal connection with Harding, although tradition has always tended to establish such a contact. This may, of course, stem from the fact that Harding was active in Missouri and his name was almost as much a household word in the state as that of Bingham.

The further suggestion that the nine-year-old Bingham may have seen Harding painting his portrait of Daniel Boone or that he, "must have seen some of Harding's work; for he himself has told of becoming interested in and receiving his first impression of portrait painting from Chester Harding when the latter was temporarily residing in Franklin in 1820 . . ."[15] seems mere heresay. The documentary "proof" for the statement is contained in a letter written by James Harding, a son of Chester Harding, in 1902.[16] And the basis for the meeting in Boonville with Harding at the later date is

12. *Bull. AAU*, II (Aug., 1849), 11.
13. Rusk, *op. cit.*, p. 17.
14. B. to R., letter, Natchez, Miss., May 6, 1837, coll. SHSMo (*MHR*, XXXII [1937], 7): "I am aware of the difficulties in my way, and am cheered by the thought that they are no greater than those which impeded the course of Harding and Sully and many others." (It seems evident that Bingham based his knowledge on the biographies of the artists included in Dunlap's *History of the Arts of Design*, published in 1834.)
15. Rusk, *op. cit.*, p. 14. Albert Christ-Janer, *George Caleb Bingham of Missouri; The Story of an Artist* (New York: Dodd, Mead, 1940), p. 13, notes the "improbability" that Bingham could have witnessed Chester Harding painting Daniel Boone's portrait in 1820, and "discounts the idea that Harding was the single potent inspiration of the boy."
16. Rusk, *op. cit.*, p. 14, note 5.

included in a letter also written in 1902 by James Rollins Bingham, the painter's son.[17] Such indirect documentation is too frequently inaccurate to be relied upon.

As if to add still more to the confusion surrounding the early artistic training of Bingham, and demonstrating with even greater emphasis the unreliability of secondhand documentation, in 1905 James Rollins Bingham came up with yet another theory regarding his father's early background. At that time he prepared a long paper about his family, which included a detailed account of his father's life and work. At one point he stated:

...he left the home farm some time about 1830 and went to Boonville, some twenty miles, where he learned the cabinet maker's trade. While there Gilbert Stuart, the painter, came also to Boonville to paint portraits of some wealthy residents there and discovered that my father had undeveloped talents as an artist. Stuart advised a course of study and that my father adopt that profession.[18]

What caused Rollins Bingham to substitute Stuart for Harding is not known, but it is obviously an even less digestible supposition.

We can accept the idea that Bingham decided to become a painter during his Boonville period. Cabinetmaking was soon set aside and his law studies were to be of important use to him only in his later political activities and official connections with the State. About 1833 he returned to Arrow Rock,[19] fully determined to embark on the career of a painter. As his first commission, he painted the portraits of four young men, "taking upon themselves the risk of his success."[20] We are further informed that

by becoming to some extent an itinerant, and painting upon moderate terms, he found himself full of business, and though in total darkness in regard to color, his drawing generally gave so strong a likeness that many of his unsophisticated patrons looked upon his productions as the perfection of the "divine art." He astonished them, too, by his facility of execution, frequently commencing and finishing a portrait in the same day.[21]

Unfortunately, it has not yet been possible to locate any of the 1833 portraits of the "four young men."[22] The earliest portraits extant can be dated 1834, painted at Arrow Rock, and it must be assumed that these reveal the style that was also characteristic of the first portraits. They show an approach to technique and composition which prevailed in all of Bingham's work in portraiture for at least the succeeding three years.

17. *Ibid.*, p. 17, note 3.
18. MS. coll. SHSMo. See Appendix A.
19. *Bull. AAU*, II (Aug., 1849), 11.
20. *Ibid.*
21. *Ibid.*
22. Washington Adams (1814-1883) claimed that his portrait, painted in Boonville, was one of Bingham's first attempts at portraiture, thus antedating the 1833 group (subject to Rollins, letter, Boonville, Mo., March 20, 1882, *MHR*, XXXII [1937], 7).

The earliest Bingham portraits now known are those of Dr. John Sappington (A3; plate 1) and his wife (A4; plate 2), and his son-in-law, Meredith Miles Marmaduke (A5; plate 3), and his wife (A6; plate 4). The four portraits were unquestionably executed at about the same time, and bear similar dates and inscriptions, although apparently added by another hand. Bingham himself rarely signed or dated a portrait, and judging from the large number of his known portraits, probably did not do so at all before his late years.[23] The Sappington and Marmaduke portraits all reveal characteristics that Bingham repeated with little variation in all of his early paintings. The pictures are bust-length, the heads turned toward the left looking out toward the observer in three-quarter view against neutral brown backgrounds. This formula was never changed during these early years, yet there is considerable variety in the portraits, gained largely through the artist's ability to catch the distinguishing traits of his sitters and to set them down firmly on canvas. His subjects turn toward the spectator with a certain forcefulness and sense of stark reality which make it easy to understand why his work was soon in demand.

The type of portrait composition he adopted was a standard one used by many of his contemporaries, and one which, because of its simplicity, was particularly popular among itinerant portraitists. Accessories such as hands were not admitted, and the backgrounds were always the same. Costume varied but slightly. It would be impossible to attempt to discover any immediate source for our artist's use of this formula, but in all probability it was the one used by his Boonville mentor. Also, of course, the inspiration gained from engravings then available after portraits by Stuart and others must be taken into consideration. Indeed, the sharp, decisive handling of paint by Bingham would seem to presuppose a strong leaning toward engravings in his work, most likely those reproduced after portraits by Stuart and his circle.

The hardness of the delineation is accompanied by a somewhat brittle sense of modeling. The use of ruddy, high-keyed flesh tones set against the dark brown neutral backgrounds serves to give Bingham's portraits a remarkable vitality and compelling presence. There is a lack of subtlety in the color handling and a general unsophisticated approach to the problem of picture-making, but the freshness and openness of these early portraits make them impressive accomplishments for an untrained painter. They reveal above all

23. Portraits of J. T. Birch and his wife, a second portrait of Mrs. Birch, a study for the full-length portrait of Gen. F. P. Blair, and a portrait of Vinnie Ream, all painted after 1870, are the only signed portraits by Bingham known to me at present. At least two portraits painted at Liberty, Mo., in 1835 (those of Col. John Thornton and Col. Oliver Perry Moss) bear the artist's name on the reverse, and one portrait of the same period of an unknown man has a stencil with the artist's name on the reverse, but these cannot be considered true signed pictures.

an individuality that can be shared with no other in their class. These characteristics typify what I regard as the first line of his portrait style.

Although he was unquestionably primarily concerned with form in these early portraits, Bingham also evidently attempted to cope with the infinitely more difficult problem of relating form to recognizable space and atmosphere. To accomplish these effects, he broke up the neutral background by introducing a darker vertical division at right as well as an oblique shadow which cut across the composition near the center. The verticals were without doubt intended to suggest the existence of wall divisions, with the subject seated near the corner of a room where a spatial idea could be more readily established. Although the motif is not convincingly carried out in the various half-length portraits in which it was introduced, its purpose becomes obvious in the single full-length that can be dated close to this period (plate 22).[24]

Of the group of Sappington and Marmaduke paintings, the portraits of the women command special attention. In both the compositions are considerably enhanced by the impression of rich decorative effects achieved by the addition of elaborate costume detail. The portrait of Lavinia Sappington Marmaduke (plate 4) is certainly the more splendid example of the two pictures. Despite the rather metallic handling of such details as the headdress, the portrait combines a delicacy, monumentality, and sense of strong presence that is rarely equaled by most of the artist's more sophisticated contemporaries.

Having gained sufficient confidence in his ability at portrait painting in his home town, Bingham decided to try his new profession elsewhere. Accordingly, we find him established in the early part of 1834 in the town of Columbia, in Boone County, about 50 miles from Arrow Rock.[25] There he opened a studio on Guitar Street and prepared for business. We do not know how much he charged for a portrait, but if we can judge from Harding's first experience, and from a later statement by Bingham himself, a portrait must have cost in the neighborhood of 25 dollars.[26]

Bingham himself is silent on his activities in Columbia at this time, but

24. Portrait of Sarah Helen Rollins, 1837.
25. Columbia was considered an "up and coming" town by that time. It could boast of about 300 inhabitants by 1830, including four ministers, five lawyers, four doctors, and three druggists. Business houses included dry goods, grocery and general stores, and three taverns (History of Boone County Missouri... [St. Louis, Mo.: Western Historical Co., 1882], p. 801).
26. Letter, May 6, 1837 (MHR, XXXII [1937], 7). Bingham's price for a portrait evidently advanced considerably during the next few years. One of his patrons in Fayette, in 1839, recalled many years later that the artist "reduced the price from fifty to forty dollars." In all probability this was a special price Bingham set for a group of portraits commissioned at one time, which would seem to apply in this instance (letter, David Kunkle [A68] to Mrs. George B. Harrison, Craigsville, Va., Sept. 4, 1899). And a receipt for a portrait of Col. Edward Cresap McCarty (A240), dated Dec. 12, 1855, indicates payment of $50. The artist had obviously set a standard price of $50 for a portrait as early as 1839.

a remarkable document in the form of a reporter's discussion of a visit to the artist's studio is especially revealing of the local interest taken in his work.[27] The young painter's work was said to show "undoubted creative genius," which was further underlined when it was realized that "not since he reached the stature of manhood, has he been East of the Mississippi" and "except for those of his own execution, he never saw a portrait painted in his life." The reporter, who seemed to have at least a smattering of knowledge of art, went on with mounting enthusiasm. Bingham's pictures were favorably compared with those of Harding, Catlin, and Jouett, and he even went so far as to attempt to relate his style to the old Italian schools of painting! The only adverse criticism was rather gently composed: "the pencil of our artist might be permitted occasionally, a stroke or two more of flattery, with advantage. In some instances too faithful a copy of features is unfavourable to effect." Although the writer hastened to add that he might be "mistaken" in his opinion, it is entirely probable that Bingham may have called forth some criticism from some of his subjects for his insistence on realistic detail which was not always flattering. This characteristic was to remain a dominant trait in all of his portrait work.

Bingham probably remained in Columbia until early March, 1835.[28] During this period he executed a number of portraits of the leading men of the town, of which a few fine examples still remain to us.

The hard, sculptural quality of the Marmaduke and Sappington portraits is again seen in the likenesses of James Sidney Rollins (A9; plate 7), Josiah Woodson Wilson (A10; plate 8), and the artist's self-portrait (A11; frontis.). The compositions are identical, including the background treatments where the divisions of space and shadow are clearly visible, as well as the chair as accessory. Despite the similarities, the characteristics of the subjects are carefully reported, giving each a strong individuality.

To the first Columbia period also belong the exceptionally fine portraits of Dr. Anthony Wayne Rollins (A7; plate 5) and his wife Sarah (A8; plate 6). They are similar in composition to the portraits of the men, but the greater awareness of design through the use of costume detail places these pictures among Bingham's most significant productions of the period. The crisp details of the man's pleated shirt front and the woman's elaborate headdress may appear to be of the same texture as the flesh, but the general effect indicates an already well-developed sense of design. The combination of precise realism of representation with an appreciation of decorative values in these portraits is a direct continuation of a style formed during the slightly earlier

27. *Missouri Intelligencer*, March 14, 1835, 3-1.
28. B. to Sarah Elizabeth Hutchison, postscript of letter, Columbia, Mo., Feb. 16, 1835, coll. SHSMo.

Arrow Rock period, although now one senses a better coordination of these values. In this connection the portrait of Mrs. Marmaduke forms an excellent comparison with that of Mrs. Rollins.

Having temporarily exhausted the possibilities of further employment in Columbia, Bingham left the town. He apparently felt encouraged by his early success to try his chances in the big city, for a card published in a St. Louis newspaper on March 24 announces his presence there, offering his "professional services to the citizens" as a portrait painter.[29] Business could not have been very brisk, because by May, or perhaps earlier, he was already back in the provinces. He can definitely be placed in Liberty, Clay County, during that period. The artist undoubtedly had good reason to remember this time, for he contracted smallpox on the way, and it was not until later in May, 1835, that his own words advise us of his condition as well as the fact that he was only then well enough to be able to resume his work.[30]

It is possible to assign with certainty to the short Liberty period at least four portraits now extant: Colonel Shubael Allen (A14), Colonel Allen's wife (A15), Colonel Oliver Perry Moss (A16), and Colonel John Thornton (A17; plate 9). The portrait of Colonel Moss, although in poor state, is stylistically close to that of the Columbia group of young men, as are those of the Allens. That of Colonel Thornton (plate 9), however, is a more unusual example. The composition is similar to the other portraits, characterized by the typical three-quarter placement of the head facing left, and the usual vertical divisions in the background. The severe delineation of the features and the strong contrasts of flesh tones against dark hair almost completely framing the face are again emphasized. The strong presence of the head is, in fact, even more pronounced in this example because it is presented somewhat larger than the other and placed higher up on the canvas. But what makes this portrait an even more unusual one is the inclusion of the hand, although most of it is hidden in the waistcoat, with only the thumb protruding. Nevertheless, it is probably the first portrait in which Bingham attempted to enlarge his composition or to vary the design. The awkward effect of the hand reveals the artist's apparent lack of knowledge of the drawing of such details at this period. The unconvincing modeling and drawing of the ear is another fault found in all of the early portraits.

Without doubt Bingham painted other portraits in Liberty and the surrounding region during the summer months of 1835, but we have no knowledge of his whereabouts in or around Liberty beyond June 5 of that year.[31]

29. *Missouri Republican* (St. Louis), March 24, 1835, 3-2.
30. B. to S. E. H., letter, Liberty, Mo., May 23, 1835, coll. SHSMo.
31. S. E. H. to B., letter addressed to the artist at Liberty, June 2, postmarked Boonville, June 5, 1835, coll. SHSMo.

The winter found him in St. Louis again. It can be considered more than mere conjecture that Bingham felt it to be a matter of the utmost importance that he make a mark for himself in the city. St. Louis was already considered an important commercial metropolis, regarded by some as the "principal nursery of the fine arts, in 'the far West.' "[32] The city, with a population of 15,000, had its first daily mail and a daily newspaper by 1836,[33] and a convention had been held the previous year by representatives of the leading counties of the state to determine what steps to take toward the construction of railroads within the state and particularly to and from St. Louis itself.[34]

The early inhabitants of the city, largely of French origin, brought with them an inherited taste and appreciation of works of art. Since relatively few of these settlers came of wealthy backgrounds, we cannot assume that they brought along any important possessions, although it is entirely possible that modern copies of old masters (a taste then prevalent abroad as well as in this country) were imported in this manner. Once established in their new homes, they continued their artistic interests, creating a new demand for pictures, and particularly for portraits of themselves. By 1821 the first St. Louis city directory could boast that the town had "one portrait-painter, who would do credit to any country,"[35] and by the early 1830's the city was an important station on the route taken by itinerant artists, chiefly portrait painters, who came from the East during the winter months.[36]

The great pride and joy of St. Louis was the Cathedral, which was commissioned in 1831 and consecrated in 1834.[37] Much attention had been given to the decoration of the interior, a considerable part of which being evidently accomplished by the time of Bingham's first visit. An English traveler, seeing it at that time, comments upon the decoration in some detail:

The interior . . . has altogether a pleasing effect. The columns, cornices, pilasters, transparencies, &c. together with two or three pictures were painted by a French artist. I was fortunate enough to obtain him as my cicerone. . . . His object in painting the interior decorations, appears to have been *not* to 'rival all but Raphael's name below' but to put on a given number of yards of paint, and transfer a given number of dollars to his own pocket, in a given number of hours. He, accordingly, completed the whole of his operations within eight months, as he boasted to me! Now the church is very large; every window is covered by a large transparency painted by him; and besides the half-dozen

32. *Missouri Intelligencer*, March 14, 1835.
33. L. P. Powell, *Historic Towns of the Western States . . .* (New York, London: Putnam, 1901), pp. 361-362: "St. Louis had its first daily mail Sept. 20, 1836, and on the same day the *Missouri Republican* commenced the publication of a regular daily edition."
34. *Ibid.*, p. 362.
35. J. T. Scharf, *History of Saint Louis City and County . . .* (Philadelphia: L. H. Everts, 1883), II, 1617 ("Art and Artists" by H. H. Morgan and W. M. Bryan).
36. *Ibid.*
37. A. Wetmore, *Gazeteer of the State of Missouri . . .* (St. Louis, Mo.: C. Keemle, 1837), p. 184.

sacred pictures, there is a great profusion of painting in every part of the building. I have no doubt that, if Michael Angelo, or any of his distinguished pupils, had engaged in the same work, it would have cost more years of labour than it cost months to our Parisian knight of the easel; indeed, I could scarcely keep my risible muscles in due subjection, while he explained to me that he had not worked and plodded at it with a small pencil, as some painters do; but that he had taken a good large brush, and laid on the colour rapidly, broadly, and boldly. Here he waved his right hand to and fro, like a fellow painting a door or a railing: "comme ca- click-click- poof-poof-poof." I was really vexed at the careless folly and vanity which thus marred the performance of a man who possesses considerable talent. . . .[38]

The "Parisian knight of the easel" was Leon Pomarede, who was said to have been brought over from France to execute the Cathedral commissions,[39] although we know now that the statement, calculated to dazzle the reader, was not an entirely accurate one. Besides the decorations so vividly described by the English visitor, the church was also said to possess paintings by Rubens, Raphael, Guido Reni, and Veronese, and others "by the first modern masters of the Italian, French, and Flemish schools."[40] At least one of the pictures was reportedly presented by Louis XVIII himself.[41] The "old masters" were very probably school pieces or copies.[42]

Another collection of pictures was to be seen at St. Louis University, and something of its appearance to an observer in the 1830's is preserved for us in the following description:

The chapel of the institution is a large, airy room, hung with antique and valuable paintings. Two of these, suspended on each side of the altar, said to be by Rubens, are masterpieces of the art. . . . In an oratory above hangs a large painting by the same master; a powerful, though unfinished production. All of the galleries of the buildings

38. Sir C. A. Murray, *Travels in North America During . . . 1834, 1835, and 1836 . . .* (London: R. Bentley, 1839), II, 88. Sir Charles was in St. Louis in 1835.

39. E. Flagg, *The Far West: or, a Tour Beyond the Mountains* (New York: Harper, 1838), I, 139. Leon Pomarede (*ca.* 1807-1892) arrived in America from France in 1830, settling first in New Orleans. He came to St. Louis in 1832, at which time he executed the Catholic Cathedral commissions. Between 1837 and 1843 he was again in New Orleans, but had removed permanently to St. Louis by 1843. Later Pomarede collaborated with Henry Lewis on a panorama of the Mississippi, but apparently nothing came of the project. Instead, both produced separate panoramas of the river. Pomarede's "Panorama of the Mississippi and Indian Life" was first exhibited in St. Louis in 1849, and afterward shown in various parts of the country until its destruction by fire in 1850. Following that venture Pomarede maintained a studio in St. Louis until his death, carrying out commissions for religious and genre pictures, as well as murals for churches, theaters, and other public buildings. (J. F. McDermott, "Leon Pomarede, 'Our Parisian Knight of the Easel,'" *Bull. of the City Art Museum of St. Louis*, XXXIV [Winter, 1949]; J. E. Arrington, "Leon D. Pomarede's Original Panorama of the Mississippi River," *Missouri Historical Society Bull.*, IX [April, 1953], 261-273.)

40. Scharf, *op. cit.*, p. 1617, quoting from the first St. Louis city directory of 1821.

41. Taylor and Crooks, *Sketchbook of St. Louis . . .* (St. Louis, Mo.: G. Knapp, 1858), p. 41.

42. Scharf, *op. cit.*, p. 1617.

are decorated with paintings, some of which have had but little to commend them to notice but their antiquity...[43]

The paintings by Rubens were presumably copies, and the old pictures were obviously of doubtful quality. In addition, however, the University was able to make the practice of drawing part of its curriculum as early as 1821.[44]

Despite the limitations in terms of quality and attribution, Bingham would find a new and eye-filling world of art opening up before him on this first visit to the city. He could see a profusion of pictures painted by Europeans, some reputedly by old masters, as well as good copies,[45] and he could see portraits by American artists trained in the East. It was a new experience for him from another standpoint, too: in the smaller towns of the interior he had been admired and encouraged, and was without real competition, but now he found himself working beside experienced artists from the East. This, together with the chance he now had to observe the work of more mature and better trained painters, must have more than ever revealed his own deficiencies and the urgent need for further study. That his confidence in himself must have been severely tried at this time is shown in a letter he addressed to his future wife Sarah Elizabeth Hutchison:

... Though I am frequently under the influence of melancholy when my prospects appear dark and gloomy before me, yet I have never entirely despaired, and the determination to do my utmost to rise in my profession has ever remained strong in my mind. I am fully aware of my many deficiencies, and though I generally succeed in pleasing others, it is but seldom I can please myself — in fact no work has yet gone from my hands with which I have been perfectly satisfied. Very few are aware of the mortifications and anxieties which attend the work of a painter, and of the toil and study which it requires to give him success and raise him to distinction. Nearly three years have elapsed and I have yet scarsely [sic] learned to paint the human face, after having accomplished which, I shall have ascended but one step toward that eminence to which the art of painting may be carried....[46]

That he did succeed in "pleasing others" with his portraits is revealed in the following sentences:

When I wrote to you before I had not commenced painting, since then I have taken several likenesses which give general satisfaction. Perhaps I shall not suffer more un-

43. Flagg, op. cit., p. 142.
44. Scharf, op. cit., p. 1617.
45. Ibid. Scharf states that the early settlers of St. Louis, of French origin, owned copies of original paintings by celebrated European masters, a taste they cultivated abroad: "Of copies thus called into existence many were brought to St. Louis and the surrounding region by the earlier French settlers. It doubtless happened also that an occasional original picture by a really great artist found its way over, though the fact that few specially wealthy families were counted among these early immigrants reduces such probability to a minimum."
46. B. to S. E. H., letter, St. Louis, Mo., Nov. 30, 1835, coll. SHSMo.

easiness for want of employment. But whether I am patronized or not I shall continue to paint, and if men refuse to have their faces transfered [sic] to canvas I will look out for subjects among the dogs and cats. I can't endure the horrors of inaction....[47]

In yet another letter written to Miss Hutchison from St. Louis, we are given some further details regarding the progress of his work in the city:

Since I wrote to you before I have been painting without intermission. I have completed two portraits, and also a couple of landscapes representing the bufaloe [sic] hunts of our western prairies; they are thought by those who see them to be superior to the original paintings from which I coppied [sic] them. The gentleman who employed me to paint them designs taking them to Louisville....[48]

This is the first knowledge we have that Bingham painted subjects other than portraits during his early years. Although the letter clearly states that the pictures were copies from the originals of another painter, it does indicate the artist's interest in expanding his painting repertory. Whether or not these copies could claim to have any artistic merit, their value as pictorial documents is certainly undeniable as evidence of Bingham's early inclinations toward genre painting. It is important to note that the pictures were of typically western scenes, already suggesting the subjects that we so closely associate with Bingham's name today. The buffalo hunt was a popular subject, although Bingham seems never to have painted an original version of it. It would be somewhat difficult, too, to determine who may have painted the original pictures from which Bingham made his copies, for artists like Peter Rindisbacher and George Catlin, as well as other painters, had depicted scenes of buffalo hunts by this time.

A portrait of an unknown man (A19; plate 10), for some years in the collection of the Isaac Delgado Museum of Art in New Orleans, may date from this St. Louis sojourn. The portrait itself follows the typical pattern of other subjects of the 1834/1835 period in its firm and direct handling. In terms of force of characterization and monumentality it is close to the fine Thornton portrait. The most individual trait of the portrait, however, is not concerned with style; it is the presence of a stencil on the reverse of the canvas (plate 11) which gives the name of the painter and the date of execution of the picture — thus far unique in the Bingham procedure (although in at least two instances already noted [see note 23 to page 19], inscriptions written by hand, indicating names of sitters, the painter's name, and the date, appear on the reverse of portraits originating from Liberty earlier in the year). These identifications on the reverse were apparently the only "signatures" that Bingham allowed

47. *Ibid.*
48. Dec. 16, 1835, coll. SHSMo.

26

himself at this time. The stencil would seem to be the first formal means he had ever attempted in order to more positively relate a work of art to his hand. Perhaps, in assuming a St. Louis provenance for this portrait, the coincidence of some kind of official "trademark" may not seem too far-fetched if one considers Bingham's conscious desire to establish a reputation for himself among competitors in this first attempt to capture some attention in the big city.

There is no evidence to support the suggestion that Bingham took instruction in painting while in St. Louis. His visit to the city was more likely concerned mainly with the business of painting for a livelihood, but there can certainly be little doubt that he took advantage of the opportunity to observe and study the many examples of painting to be seen in the city, such as those in the Cathedral by Leon Pomarede. Observation was certainly Bingham's first school of instruction and so it would continue to be.

An article in a St. Louis newspaper dated January 2, 1836, affords us an intimate glimpse into the artist's activities in the city at this time:

The Fine Arts.—We were much pleased with a visit a day or two since to the Painting Room of Mr. Bingham, on Market-street, where we found some as good portraits of a few of our well known citizens as we could expect to see from the pencil of any artist, as young in the profession as Mr. B.

Mr. Bingham, though not a native of the State of Missouri, has been a resident of Cooper county from infancy. His first efforts in portrait painting were made about two years since in Columbia, Boone county and the success he there met with, induced him to try his fortunes where he could find a wide field for enterprise and better school for instruction. He came to St. Louis a few weeks since, warm with enthusiasm, and full of hope, that with proper instruction and attention, he could distinguish himself in his profession. He has, we are happy to say, found a welcome reception among our citizens, his patronage has been as extensive as he could have wished, and we have but little doubt that if he devotes that time and attention to the profession he has undertaken, which it requires, he will in the event meet the warmest anticipations of his friends. His success in portrait painting is all the result of perseverence and his own genius, no master's hand directed his pencil, no wise head pointed out his faults—he alone designed and executed. His portraits are invariably good, yet there is a want of skill in coloring evinced, which does not disclose a want of genius but of instruction. His portrait of Fanny Kemble from an engraving in "The Gift," is we consider, one of his best efforts. The delicate and beautifully blended tints of the cheek are inferior to but few of the best paintings of the day, and we have no doubt, that with the patronage on the part of our citizens, a due regard to his profession, Mr. B will at no remote time, become an ornament to his profession, and an honor to Missouri.[49]

In all probability the artist himself supplied the biographical details of this article. That his "first efforts in portrait painting were made about two years

49. *Jeffersonian Republican*, Jan. 2, 1836, 4-2 (from *St. Louis Bulletin*).

since in Columbia" clearly indicates that he considered the town the scene of his first professional attempts at partraiture, and the statement that his "success in portrait painting is all the result of perseverance and his own genius, no master's hand directed his pencil, no wise head pointed out his faults" is also most significant in serving further to discount the early connection with Harding.

The engraving of Fanny Kemble (plate 19) published in the annual *The Gift*[50] was executed by John Cheney (1801-1885) after the painting by Thomas Sully. The mention of Bingham's copy is our first hint that the artist was aware of the accomplishments of the Philadelphia painter. It is scarcely possible that he was acquainted with Sully's work at this time other than through the engraved reproduction. The Kemble engraving must have appealed to Bingham, for it showed variety in portrait composition while maintaining the three-quarter pose invariably adopted by the artist from the beginning. The motif of the upraised hand, the suggestion of movement which avoided the sterile mode of the formula to which he was compelled to adhere through lack of experience, the vivacity of expression, and the suggestion of atmosphere in the background, as well as the general painterly quality so well translated from the painting to the print, must have made a strong impression on the young artist. His determination to study in the East may quite conceivably have been fired by the little engraving in *The Gift*, as well as by other prints after Sully and his contemporaries. The criticism here of his "skill in coloring" and elsewhere of his use of "chiaro-scuro" revealed those deficiencies that he must have felt could be eliminated through further study and observation in the eastern art centers.

The stimulation Bingham must have received during his St. Louis sojourn, occasioned certainly by his success in obtaining some commissions, made him more confident of his future career as a painter. A fragmentary letter, now lost, written from St. Louis on February 13, 1836, seems to indicate this optimistic attitude: "[I am more] confident now [of suc]ceeding as a painter t[han] I was before I [came] here, I design next winter to try [what] I can do in the South and wherever I [may] be, I am determined to use every exertion to become distinguished in the profession which I have adopted."[51] This growing self-assurance is further borne out by his determination to go through with his marriage to Sarah Elizabeth Hutchison in April of that year. He evidently now felt sufficiently secure financially to take on the responsibility of a family. The marriage took place in Boonville. Bingham did not

50. *The Gift, a Christmas and New Year's present for 1836. Ed. by Miss Leslie* (Philadelphia: E. L. Carey & A. Hart [*ca.* 1835], frontis.
51. B. to S. E. H., letter (Rusk, *op. cit.*, p. 22).

return to St. Louis until September. On September 19 he addressed his wife from the city: "I have now been engaged just one week, and have four portraits commenced, which can be finished in four or five days. This success is flattering, as but few persons know of my return to the City."[52] In the same letter he reveals his desire to remain in St. Louis until the beginning of the winter. He was certainly in the city as late as mid-December of that year. At that time he received some notice from a local reporter who not only felt that the artist "gives promise of attaining to an enviable celebrity in the profession which he has chosen,"[53] but also underlined the fact that Bingham had the "advantage of being a native of the State," presumably referring to the competition from the presence of artists then in the city who came from other parts of the country.

Bingham's wife had joined him, probably during the fall, and together they left St. Louis for a trip to the South. He had evidently intended going to the East, presumably for study, but poor road conditions forced a cancellation of the plan. The trip south during the winter months was a much-frequented route followed by itinerant painters. A letter written by Bingham to Rollins from Natchez, Mississippi, on May 6, 1837, gives us a glimpse of his activity there: "I have been regularly employed during the winter, at from forty to sixty dollars per portrait."[54] The greater part of the stay seems to have been spent in Natchez, where he set up shop, although he very probably painted portraits elsewhere in the state at this time.

At least three portraits now known (A27, A28, A29) can be ascribed with some certainty to the Natchez period.[55] Since Bingham was traveling as many another itinerant artist, and rarely signed or otherwise inscribed his portraits, his name has been lost in association with any other paintings that may still remain in the region.

In the letter addressed from Natchez, Bingham also indicated his intention of leaving for Missouri "in a few days" and spending "the best part of the summer there." He evidently planned it as a business trip and hoped to include a stopover in Columbia: ". . . if you could procure me subscribers for a dozen portraits at $25 I should be glad to remain with you six or eight weeks previous to making a trip eastward."[56] Undoubtedly Rollins got him

52. B. to S. E. H., letter, St. Louis, Mo., Sept. 19, 1836, coll. SHSMo.
53. *Missouri Republican* (St. Louis), Dec. 13, 1836, 2-1:
54. Letter, May 6, 1837 (*MHR*, XXXII [1937], 6).
55. The photographs of the portraits available to me were inadequate for detailed study, and the portrait of David Hunt (A29) was obviously in a very poor condition at the time the photograph was made. But all three portraits still reveal stylistic characteristics that are closely identified with Bingham at this period.
56. Letter, May 6, 1837 (*MHR*, XXXII [1937], 7).

the desired commissions, for Bingham is known to have painted a number of portraits in Columbia at this time. Rollins was married on June 6 and it is entirely possible that Bingham was on hand for the occasion. Shortly afterward, he painted a portrait of the bride.

His pictures now reveal a considerable advance over the earlier ones. Although the color scheme remains much the same, he shows a greater technical skill in the handling of his medium, and a decided tendency toward a more sophisticated pictorial effect. We now see the results of his stay in St. Louis, with the opportunity it afforded him of seeing other works of art, including paintings by his more experienced contemporaries.

The portraits are still three-quarter view, looking out toward the spectator, but there is now an attempt to relate the figure more directly to the background. Contours are softened slightly and features modeled so that the stiff formality of the earlier portraits is somewhat less pronounced. The artist is also now interested in textural effects as well as decorative detail.

Two outstanding portraits of this Columbia period are those of Judge Warren Woodson (A36) and General Richard Gentry (A33). The portrait of Woodson (plate 13) has been dated 1834 by Rusk, but the greater sophistication in the handling, with the corresponding interest in the softer modeling of features, and the attempt to relate the figure to the background in a true pictorial sense suggest the later dating. The awkward background divisions so typical of the 1834/1835 period disappear in the 1837 pictures. The painting of the ear, troublesome in the first portraits, is now handled with greater assurance. In the Woodson portrait the modeling and drawing evidences the growing maturity. Even the earlier metallic treatment of the hair, with its sharp break at the hairline, has been replaced by a greater sense of texture and by softer, more natural transitions.

The portrait of General Gentry (plate 12) is one of the most striking painted by Bingham at this time. Here again the artist reveals clearly the results of his developing powers of observation and continuing study. The drawing is still decisive but the modeling against shows a decided advance in terms of a deeper understanding of tactile values and subtler transitions of tone.

Among the other portraits of men in this period are those of Col. Caleb Smith Stone (A30), David Steele Lamme (A31), Priestly Haggin McBride (A42; plate 15), and Roger North Todd (A35). The portrait of McBride reveals a particularly close stylistic relationship to that of Judge Woodson. A small portrait of Thomas Miller (A44; plate 14) was also probably painted during this second Columbia sojourn; it may have been the first true miniature executed by the artist.

30

In all the portraits painted by Bingham since his first efforts, the heads are modeled in full light, not depending on strong shadows for dramatic effects. Only a slight shadow appears along or under the right side of the nose of the sitter, and a highlight is placed at the tip of the nose so frequently as to be almost a signature of the artist. This scheme of modeling in the light is, of course, typical of the English school of Lawrence and Hoppner, and is found carried over to this country in the works of Stuart and Sully.

The poses of the figures are usually kept very simple, with no movement suggested. A slight variation from the usual system occurs in the portrait of John Woods Harris (A41), in which Bingham places the subject's arm over the back of his chair. This attempt at creating a more casual movement is not happily effective in this portrait, although the motif was one frequently adopted by other artists of the period.

A number of portraits of women also date from this period. These also show the painter's decided technical advance. The new facility in the rendering of textures is displayed to good effect in the portrait of Mrs. William Johnston (Rachel Spears) (A45; plate 16). Although the portrait has hitherto been placed at a much earlier date, the softness of contours and the rather convincing execution of the lace cap and collar cannot possibly date before 1837.

The portrait of Mrs. Anthony Wayne Rollins (Sarah [Sallie] Harris Rodes) (A38; plate 17) is the second painted by Bingham of his friend's mother. It is severe in characterization and the artist has obviously made no attempt to disguise that quality. The head is also masculine, the lines of the mouth firmly set, the chin square, and the cheeks angular. The triangular collar and stiff headdress serve to emphasize the firmness and strength of the portrayal. The cast shadow on the left side of the face and the oblique shadow along the nose, as well as on the collar, help to form a forceful and decorative whole. The portrait contrasts in every way to that of Mrs. Johnston, where the artist strives to create a truly feminine effect.

A portrait with which Bingham must have taken special pains is that of Mrs. James Sidney Rollins (Mary Elizabeth Hickman) (A39; plate 18), probably painted shortly after her marriage. The head is shown almost full-face, the figure turned toward the left. Although not a forceful or expressive portrayal, it is one of the most decorative from the point of view of costume and accessories; and the three-quarter length figure is unusual for Bingham at this period.

The double portrait of Mrs. David Steele Lamme (Sophia Woodson Hickman) and her son (A32; plate 20) is of interest from several points of view. It is the earliest Bingham portrait of the type now known, as well as being

31

one of his earliest portrayals of a child. It is also without doubt his most ambitious undertaking in portraiture up to this time. Most important of all, it represents the artist's determined attempt to depart from his usual scheme, probably stemming from his realization that his customary procedure would be somewhat ineffectual in this instance. The innovation also suggests a possible desire to demonstrate to his patron (the mother-in-law of his friend James S. Rollins) how much he had benefitted from his St. Louis experience.

For its design he adopted a composition that ultimately derived from Raphael's "Madonna della Sedia," which he could have known through engraved reproduction. Many painters, including West, Trumbull, and Vanderlyn among Americans, had previously produced portraits that reflected the famous composition, either directly or through some intermediate source. Bingham could have referred to Raphael, as did his predecessors, or he might also have been in contact with a more contemparary interpretation of the composition. In this instance, it is more than conceivable that he might have been attracted to the well-known portrait of Lady Dover and her child, by Sir Thomas Lawrence (plate 21), readily available through engravings by that time.[57] Apart from the composition, Bingham would have found the poses of the heads of even greater importance at a moment when he must have been seeking some variety of design possible within his still restricted repertoire. But Bingham was obviously unable to cope with the problem on a level with the English master. Still somewhat restricted by his own technical limitations, he rearranged the figure of the woman so that she assumed his familiar scheme, and avoided the complicated pose of the child, although he sought to express the movement contained in the sharp turn of the head toward the observer. The artist fails completely, however, to create anything like the desired effect. Although the child's arms are seemingly around his mother's waist, and hers envelop the boy, the painter is somehow unable to develop the action necessary to give his composition its proper dimension, nor has he been able to recreate even the mood of the original.

Apart from the composition itself, however, and within Bingham's still slender area of development, the heads of Mrs. Lamme and her son show a decided step forward in style over his earlier efforts. The softer modeling of the forms, the treatment of hair, and the textures of lace and cloth all display improvement based on constant study and observation; but such details as hands still obviously present a serious problem to the artist.

---

57. The portrait, painted by Lawrence in 1828, was engraved by James Henry Watt in 1830, and by Samuel Cousins in 1831. Evidently a well-known picture, it was illustrated in publications as late as the 1840's: S. C. Hall, *Gems of European Art: the Best Pictures of the Best Schools...* (London: G. Virtue, 1846-[1847]), ser. 2, p. [75].

32

It can be safely assumed that the difficulties Bingham encountered in the course of this commission, such as his inability to cope with the composition in terms of what he must have certainly intended, and his realization generally of his several limitations, both large and small, must also have made him even more acutely aware of those deficiencies that impeded his progress. The problem he faced in this portrait must have brought home to him more than ever his need for professional contacts and guidance, and the feeling that the time was at hand to seek out such assistance if he was indeed to do "the utmost to rise in [his] profession."

Curiously enough, many years later, Bingham was to return again to the special problem posed by the mother-and-child group, and to adopt once more the same compositional motif that had defeated him in his youth.[58]

In the same category of particular interest among the portraits of the period about 1837 is the full-length figure of Sarah Helen Rollins (A40), youngest sister of his friend James Sidney. Bingham evidently extended himself to prove his growing facility in the field of portraiture at this time, clearly visible in the variety of composition he attempted in the portraits of the various members of the Rollins and related families.

The large portrait of Sarah Helen (plate 22) is an especially ambitious project, and as in the portrait of Mrs. Lamme, Bingham seems to have sought out sophisticated source materials for inspiration and guidance. Perhaps by coincidence, Bingham appears to have had more than passing reference to an engraving after a painting by the same artist who may have inspired the Lamme composition — Sir Thomas Lawrence's portrait of Emily Anderson as "Little Red Riding Hood" (plate 197). Although rather obvious liberties have been taken in the arrangement and with details, probably to allow for the difference in subject connotation, there still remain clues significant enough to relate the design to the Lawrence picture.[59] It is also of interest to observe that Bingham was to have an even more positive reference to the same Lawrence composition at a later period in his career.

The interior background has been substituted for the forest landscape generally associated with the story of Red Riding Hood. The corner of the room, suggesting the setting, is completely visible here, making more con-

---

58. See p. 212.
59. Lawrence's painting of Emily Anderson as "Little Red Riding Hood," now in the Henry E. Huntington Art Gallery at San Marino, California, executed *ca.* 1821/1822, was engraved several times. An engraving by Richard Lane was published in 1824, and another engraving appeared in an American gift book, *The Atlantic Souvenir* for 1828. The artist could have seen an engraving in reverse of the original, which could account for the changes in the position of hands and feet, or he may have deliberately attempted the reverse arrangement himself to vary his design from the Lawrence original.

33

vincing the explanation for the use of the vertical divisions so often used by the artist in his earliest bust-length portraits.

The placement of the figure in a comprehensive three-dimensional space appears to occupy the artist's attention, visible particularly in the decided emphasis on cast shadows, from the presentation of the figure itself with relationship to the floor, to the strong shadows cast by the upraised hand and the drawstring bag she carries.

The turn of the child's head and the steady concentration of gaze are characteristics of Bingham's style which can be considered most typical of the period. The tipping-up of the floor evidences the painter's still rather uncertain knowledge of perspective, and the rigidity of the figure manifests Bingham's inability to cope with the subtleties of the Lawrence composition. The result, at first glance, gives the spectator much the impression of a so-called "primitive," and even the careful attention to the details of the elaborate costume seems to emphasize that impression, despite the fact that the strength in handling of the head obviously draws a firm line of distinction between this portrait and those belonging to the limner tradition.

IV

STUDY IN PHILADELPHIA (1838)

Despite the encouragement afforded him by regular employment as a portrait painter, Bingham must have felt ever more strongly the need for improvement in his work, both technically and artistically, at this stage of his career. In a letter to his friend Rollins, written from Natchez on May 6, 1837, he speculates along this line:

I cannot foresee where my destiny will lead me, it may become my interest to settle in some one of the eastern cities. The greater facilities afforded there, for improvement in my profession, would be the principle inducement. There is no honourable sacrifice which I would not make to attain emminence [*sic*] in the art to which I have devoted myself. I am aware of the difficulties in my way, and am cheered by the thought that they are not greater [than] those which impeded the course of Harding, and Sully, and many others, it is by combatting [*sic*] that we can overcome them, and by determined perseverance, I expect to be successful.[1]

This is the first and only documentary reference Bingham ever made to Chester Harding, that artist with whose name he was so often to be linked in the years following his death. Sully's fame as an artist was a national one, and Harding himself held an enviable position in the field of portrait painting by this time. Bingham's knowledge of the struggles that beset Harding, Sully, and others—a knowledge that seemed to help him realize that it was only through "determined perseverance" that one could hope to overcome obstacles and gain desired success in one's chosen field—was without doubt acquired from the accounts of the lives of those artists included in Dunlap's *History of the Rise and Progress of the Arts of Design*, published in 1834. Since Harding was better known in Missouri,[2] Bingham must have given special attention to the account of his early professional struggles, compiled

1. Letter, May 6, 1837 (*MHR*, XXXII [1937], 7).
2. W. Dunlap, *History of the . . . Arts of Design . . .*, II, 291. Harding was in St. Louis *ca.* 1820-1821.

by the author from the artist's own notes. Indeed, the unusual coincidence that compel our consideration of the Harding–Bingham parallels can be more conclusively dealt with once we realize Bingham's immediate source of communication with Harding.

It may well have been Harding's account of his visit to Philadelphia about 1820 that decided Bingham to follow in his footsteps. Certainly the circumstances that brought Harding to the city were identical. A self-taught artist, he had gained what skill he had from an observation of the work of other itinerants, and at the time he left Kentucky for Philadelphia he must have also believed he could improve his chances through the advantages afforded by the facilities available to the art student there. In his autobiographical notes in the Dunlap account, Harding said that he "passed five or six weeks in looking at the portraits of Mr. Sully, and others, and then returned to Kentucky."[3] Later in life he added his impression that "one good effect of my visit to Philadelphia was to open my eyes to the merits of the works of other artists."[4] Bingham may have felt that Harding's implied "advice" might serve him well at this critical point in his own career.

Certainly the notion that his immediate "destiny" lay in the East, where the "greater facilities" for his development were to be found, was deeply implanted in Bingham's mind by May of 1837, but it is more than likely that he did not take the step until March of the following year and that he very probably spent the winter of 1837/1838 painting portraits to help finance the trip.

The biographical sketch prepared slightly over a decade afterward informs us that "in 1838, he spent three months in Philadelphia, and obtained a little knowledge of color by looking at pictures which before he had no opportunity of studying."[5] This is a significant statement from more than one standpoint. As the earliest notice affording us any knowledge of the all-important trip, we can safely assume that its details closely follow information supplied to the author by Bingham himself. This assumption can be tested by the accurate dating of the trip, now borne out by documentary evidence, although all later accounts place Bingham in Philadelphia a year earlier.[6]

3. *Ibid.*
4. M. E. White, ed., *A Sketch of Chester Harding, Artist; Drawn by His Own Hand* ... (Boston and New York: Houghton Mifflin, 1929), p. 24.
5. *Bull. AAU*, II (Aug., 1849), 11.
6. Davis and Durrie, *An Illustrated History of Missouri* ..., p. 469. Apparently the first account to give the 1837 date. Bingham may have supplied the misleading date himself, for his memory could understandably have failed him after a lapse of almost 40 years. Rusk, *George Caleb Bingham* ..., pp. 26, 129, accepted the earlier date for the visit, and attempted to explain away the divergence in dating found in the 1849 and 1876 accounts by stating that "he may have made more than one trip to Philadelphia in these years" — a statement that cannot now be accepted.

The early sketch also significantly avoids any mention of a formal program of study undertaken by Bingham in Philadelphia; it merely indicates that he spent his time "looking at pictures,"[7] a statement which we recall closely echoes the experience described by Harding. There is apparently no conclusive evidence to bolster the assertion of later biographers that the artist attended the school of the Pennsylvania Academy of the Fine Arts;[8] the Academy's records of students enrolled at that period are not extant.[9]

It is far more plausible to assume that very probably Bingham, like Chester Harding, did not come East with a formal study plan in mind. Not only would he have been unable to spare the time for any prolonged period of instruction —the usual procedure of the academies involving a slow progression from the antique to the life class—but even were he prepared to take advantage of such instruction, there is sufficient evidence to indicate that the Philadelphia academy would probably have been unable to fill the requirements. John Sartain, describing the Pennsylvania Academy as it appeared about 1830, stated that it was in "anything but a prosperous condition. Located as it was far out on Chestnut street beyond Tenth, it stood in a kind of solitude, and paying visitors were few and far between."[10] Judging from the institution's seeming poverty, it would appear that the school could ill afford to employ the necessary instruction for a long-range plan of study, and there was probably little more available to the student than the collection of casts after the antique from which he could sketch, as well as some study of anatomy by a qualified instructor.

That the benefits to be gained through formal instruction were indeed slight may perhaps be more conclusively deduced in terms of Bingham's own evaluation of the situation as expressed briefly by him in a letter he addressed to his wife from Philadelphia on June 3, 1838, written just prior to taking his final departure from the city: "I have just been purchasing a lot of drawings and engravings, and also a lot of casts from antique sculpture which will give me nearly the same advantages in my drawing studies at

7. *Bull. AAU*, II (Aug., 1849), 11.

8. In none of Bingham's correspondence or other extant writings, either of this period or afterward, do we discover any mention of his studying at the Pennsylvania Academy. Although Bingham seems to have prepared a statement of the "prominent incidents" of his life in connection with the Davis and Durrie publication, we do not know how far his friend Rollins went in making the "alterations" he may have deemed necessary in preparing the material for inclusion in the publication as his "own production" (B. to R., letter, Kansas City, Mo., June 25, 1876, *MHR*. XXXIII [1939], 368-369). The statement that the artist "studied for a time in the Philadelphia Academy of Fine Arts" appears for the first time in the Davis and Durrie account.

9. If such records did exist, they were probably destroyed in the Academy fire in 1845 (Mrs. Barbara S. Roberts, PAFA, to author, letter, Jan. 28, 1948).

10. J. Sartain, *The Reminiscences of a Very Old Man, 1808-1897 ...* (New York: D. Appleton, 1899), p. 144.

home that are at present to be enjoyed here."[11] Revealing as the statement is of the artist's inferred appraisal of the "advantages" he discovered in Philadelphia during his short stay, it is even more important in giving us a direct insight into those secondary influences and directions to which he felt he could turn for the desired instruction to achieve "nearly the same" benefits at home. Let us now examine those opportunities which the enterprising artist had available to him at this period, and to which he could turn for self-instruction.

Bingham specifically mentions his purchase of engravings for study purposes, but he was well aware of the value of such reference material even before the visit East. We have been told that he copied engravings from his childhood days, and we can also recall the praise that was given his copy of the engraving of Fanny Kemble in 1835.[12] Indeed, it was almost a standard method of self-training adopted by painters in America before him. It was, in fact, a means of communication among artists everywhere from the moment that impressions of designs were first produced on paper. The vast quantities of reproductive engravings made during the early decades of the nineteenth century made them the obvious and simplest means available for study and inspiration. In his biography of Thomas Cole, Dunlap quotes that artist's account of his early experience: "My first attempts were made from cups and saucers, from them, I rose to copying prints, from copying prints to making originals."[13] And from the same source we learn that John Vanderlyn's inspiration to paint was received from an examination of the engravings he saw during the time he was employed in a print-importer's shop in New York City.[14] So common was the procedure that an artist's instruction book of the period did not hesitate to advise: "A portfolio of prints, scrupulously selected, is highly advantageous, if not absolutely necessary, as a means of acquiring valuable ideas. It is not disgraceful to art, nor derogatory even to its advanced professors, to accept assistance from the works of others, if they but kindle and assimilate with their own powers."[15] Yet the same source also warns its readers: "The greatest caution ... must be exercised 'in the selection,' and every example which is not excellent, should be rejected, as whatever is continually seen, unavoidably vitiates or improves the taste, for such is the force of habit, that where wrong impressions have once been admitted, the light of

11. Letter, coll. SHSMo.
12. *Jeffersonian Republican*, Jan. 2, 1836, 4-2.
13. Dunlap, *op. cit.*, II, 352.
14. *Ibid.*, II, 32.
15. S. Prout, *Hints on Light and Shadow*...(London: M. A. Nattali, 1848), p. B.2(3). First published in London in 1838; appeared on Carey and Hart's lists in 1839.

improvement may strive in vain to pierce the cloud which intercepts its rays."[16]

Of course, it would be immensely valuable to know the contents of Bingham's portfolio of prints, but this collection, if such it was, probably no longer exists. It is possible, however, to estimate that reproductive engravings after the works of other artists had a considerable influence on his work, that he studied and gathered ideas from them in a manner closely resembling the instruction book's advice, and that he continued to make use of such materials for inspiration to the end of his painting days. As we progress to an analysis of individual pictures we shall have a better opportunity to gauge the full extent of the influence, and in this way we may also deduce something of the contents of his portfolio.

In this connection, one valuable source of inspiration in engraved form consisted of those prints that appeared as illustrations in the gift books and annuals that were produced in large quantity in this country and abroad during this period. The inspiration afforded the artist through the engraved plates that appeared in these elaborate little publications can scarcely be overestimated. For many artists developing their talents in rural communities, some of them never having seen a painting, the stimulation developed by the engraved illustrations in these books must have been considerable. For most beginning artists, the basis of any knowledge of what their eastern contemporaries were accomplishing was derived from prints reproducing their pictures.

The great vogue for the gift book began in America as early as 1825, but the publishing of such volumes was preceded by its European counterparts. The idea was to bring together between the covers of a book the best popular prose and verse, combining such literary efforts with the finest illustration obtainable. In their elaborately tooled bindings, these compilations were attractively prepared for presentation as suitable gifts for every possible occasion. The title page almost always clearly indicated its purpose: *The Gift, a Christmas and New Year's Present*; *The Offering of Beauty, a Present for All Seasons*; *The Opal, a Pure Gift for the Holy Days*; and so forth. There were many others, too, as the taste for these books increased — birthdays, weddings, remembrance of friendship, and "tokens of affection." The prolific publication of the volumes is certainly worthy of further study. As the demand grew, so did the competition among publishers. At first the literary sections were selected with some care, and some of Edgar Allan Poe's works made their first appearances in these books, but later the greater emphasis was given over to the embellishment, both in illustration and in binding.

16. *Ibid.*

Without doubt, the gift books marked the finest achievement of the book-maker's craft in this country up to that time.

Some of the best known print-makers of the day were employed for the engraving of the illustrations. Asher B. Durand's work appeared in *The Atlantic Souvenir*, John Cheney's in *The Gift* and *The Token*, and John Sartain, who engraved some of Bingham's pictures in later days, made a livelihood from this kind of work for many years. At the beginning, most of the illustration was engraved after well-known paintings—the publisher's patronage benefiting both the artist and the engraver. But when one of the publishers, Edward L. Carey of Philadelphia, became a patron of contemporary American painters, many of the illustrations that appeared in the annual he published, *The Gift*, were engraved from pictures in his own collection. The portrait of Fanny Kemble by Thomas Sully, copied earlier by Bingham from the engraving in *The Gift*, was one of Carey's pictures. Reproductions made from other paintings in this collection included the work of Americans of established reputation as well as of those still comparatively young and little-known—Stuart, Inman, Huntington, Mount, Page, Clonney, Comegys, and Doughty—representing a cross section of painting of the time. Other private collections were drawn upon too; the owners were requested to lend their paintings for reproduction purposes. And artists also submitted pictures, receiving a fee for permitting their use. In later years the design was frequently the work of the engraver himself, which can account for the conspicuously marked decrease in the quality of the work by that time.

Most of the gift-book publishing was accomplished in the East—in New York, Boston, and Philadelphia—but the books apparently found a ready market in all parts of the country. It was this widely popular distribution that enabled the gift books to fill a need that had probably not been considered by their publishers, namely that of making it possible for young artists to see good reproductions of the works of their contemporaries. And the artists evidently eagerly awaited the appearance of those books for this reason, that is, if we accept as evidence the fact that Bingham copied Sully's picture from an edition of *The Gift* which had appeared only shortly before reaching his hands.

Bingham's letter from Philadelphia in which he specifically advises his wife about the various materials he was then in the process of gathering for use during his further studies at home, gives us a direct clue to yet another source that he evidently considered important for his future efforts—namely, his purchase of "casts from antique sculpture." The artist had probably never seen examples of classical sculpture before he came to Philadelphia, although he could have been familiar with published illustrations of them, which, of

40

course, would not have brought home to him their full meaning and impact. More importantly, he also evidently learned firsthand the value of the study of drawing from the cast as an essential step in a student's program toward a knowledge of the living form, especially valuable if he hoped to become a figure painter. The academies considered the proportions and even the poses of the classical figures as universal and ideal, and as such of primary value for the student's concentrated attention. How conscientiously Bingham followed this line of thought and studied the antique figures, and how deep an impression his study of them made upon his mind, we shall have an opportunity of determining during our future observations of his work.

In fact, the artist was able to put into words his continuing firm belief in the value of study from antique models when, much later in life, it became his turn, as a teacher, to consider the primary materials he deemed essential for use by his students at the University:

A number of plaster casts from antique statuary should be found as models for pupils in Art. They are indeed indispensable, as without them the mind of the student cannot be properly imbued with those ideas of grace, elegance and truth which form the basis of genuine art. These casts are not very costly, and may perhaps be obtained in St. Louis I[t] will be best for me to give my personal attention to their selection.[17]

Early in his stay in Philadelphia Bingham must have come to know the large collection of casts after the antique which was owned at that time by the Pennsylvania Academy, a collection exhibited annually along with its paintings as an important part of the permanent holdings of the institution. He probably acquired his first taste and appreciation of the value of the observation of the antique for his figure studies from an examination of this collection. The annual exhibition of the Academy in 1838 included casts after a majority of the best-known antique works, and originals and casts after Canova, Houdon, and Chantrey, as well as Americans Rush and Morse.[18] But Bingham obviously concentrated on the classical antique examples for his study purposes.

In addition to an early realization of the values of the accumulation and study of engravings after the old masters—which not only afforded him a ready reference to their pictorial methods in terms of composition and style, but also made him familiar with the various schools of painting and their chief exponents—Bingham must have become familiar with yet another source of self-instruction. Instruction books that told of the painting methods of the masters were already in use during the later Renaissance, and drawing books

17. B. to R., letter, Boonville, Mo., Sept. 9, 1877, coll. SHSMo (MHR. XXXIII [1939], 381-382.
18. Catalogue of the Twenty-seventh Annual Exhibition of the Pennsylvania Academy of the Fine Arts, 1838.... (Philadelphia: William S. Martien, printer, 1838).

intended primarily for the amateur were well known before the nineteenth century, but it is doubtful whether any greater demand for publications dealing with self-instruction in the ways and means of drawing and painting had existed in America much before Bingham's time.

The best of the books on the subject were published in England from about 1810 onward, although a variety of them appeared in this country also during the same period. We have only to read booksellers' lists to understand something of the eagerness with which these volumes were sought after by young artists earnestly seeking to learn something substantial in the way of method and approach to the rudiments of their craft. There was little system in the art education practiced by the academies, even for those fortunate enough to be able to spend some time in them. And the number of artists who could plan to study European methods on the spot were few indeed. Thus the technical instruction books that contained progressive lessons on ways to paint landscapes, portraits, and figure compositions, including "hints" on chiaroscuro and color, most of them illustrated by examples after the masters, enjoyed their heyday in this country for many years as works indispensable to the enterprising student. It would have been possible, one can suppose, for a young hopeful in the field of portrait painting to follow the instructions of one book that contained plates, colored by hand, displaying the palettes he should use for each progressive setting of his subject, accompanied by descriptions of procedure for each successive phase of the work.[19] One can readily understand how any young artist would eagerly grasp at the straws of valuable information contained in these books, especially one living away from a center of art activity where even consultation with a fellow artist was certainly not always possible. In Bingham's case we again have no documentary evidence in the form of his own library to indicate the books he may have made use of, and we are therefore once more compelled to extract our evidence from other sources, as well as from an examination of his work. This we shall attempt to do in succeeding chapters. At this point we can only indicate the availability of such material and attempt to evaluate other more or less circumstantial evidence.

We know, for instance, that William Sidney Mount, a close contemporary of Bingham, one whose work undoubtedly made a great impression on him and whom he may have known personally,[20] made extensive use of instruction books for his own study and investigation.[21] A notation in a perspective note-

19. J. Cawse, *Introduction to the Art of Painting in Oil Colours....* London: R. Ackermann, 1822.
20. B. to Goupil & Co., letter, St. Louis Mo., Jan. 31, 1852, coll. M. Knoedler & Co., N.Y. Postscript: "please present my best regards to Mr. Mount when you see him."
21. M. B. Cowdrey, and H. W. Williams, Jr., *William Sidney Mount, 1807-1868...* (New York: published for the Metropolitan Museum of Art by Columbia University Press, 1944), p. 11.

book dated 1836 indicates that Mount based his sketches on information contained in Edward Edwards' *Practical Treatise of Perspective on the Principle of Dr. Brook Taylor*, published in London in 1806.[22] We are told by Mount's biographers that it was "through books on the history of the technique of painting, notably those by Mrs. Merrifield and Charles L. Eastlake, he studied the methods of the old masters."[23]

Booksellers in the East actively imported the latest instruction books from England. During his Philadelphia visit Bingham could well have had his eyes opened early to the variety of books on the subject then appearing in the art center. Carey and Hart's catalogues included all the latest books on the technique of painting and drawing, some of them being on their lists within a year of their publication abroad. This bookseller's list for 1839[24] included Howard's *Colour as a Means of Art*, published the year before; Prout's *Hints on Light and Shadow, Composition &c.* (for whose precepts the claim was made that "As maxims of expression, they deserve to be written in letters of gold");[25] and Burnet's *The Principles of Practical Perspective*. Other books listed by the firm included books on drawing, as well as various illustrated volumes such as the complete works of Hogarth.[26]

The statement that Bingham spent his time "looking at pictures" can be considered indicative enough to merit our examination of it with relationship to those opportunities for "looking" as they actually existed at the time.

By the 1830's Philadelphia was the country's second city in population and second to none in terms of its progressiveness, scientifically and artistically. It was justly proud of its factories, bridges, fine public buildings, and the waterworks at Schuylkill. The appearance everywhere of comfort and affluence immediately impressed the visitor, and it was perhaps not without good reason that the city was called the "Quaker paradise."[27] Intellectually and culturally, Philadelphia seemed well in advance of her neighbors, causing at least one English traveler to state unequivocably that "the public institutions, such as libraries, museums, and the private cabinets of Philadelphia, are certainly very superior to those of any other city or town in America, Boston not excepted."[28]

22. *Ibid.*
23. *Ibid.* Mrs. Mary Philadelphia Merrifield (d. 1877); Sir Charles Lock Eastlake (1793-1865).
24. *Carey & Hart's Catalogue of a Valuable Collection of Books, in the Various Branches of Architecture, Engineering and Science....* Philadelphia [1839].
25. *Ibid.*
26. *Carey & Hart's Catalogue of Choice, Rare and Valuable Books, Forming the Most Complete Collection of English Editions Ever Imported....* Philadelphia [1839].
27. T. Hamilton, *Men and Manners in America*... (Edinburgh: W. Blackwood; London: T. Cadell, 1833), p. 237.
28. F. Marryat, *A Diary in America*... (Philadelphia: Carey & Hart, 1839), I, 146. Captain Marryat visited Philadelphia *ca.* 1837.

Apart from its scientific interests, the city had been one of the first art centers in the East, and for many years had the best and only museum, Peale's Museum, owned and operated by Charles Willson Peale. It was also Willson Peale who first realized the needs for American artists and worked tirelessly on their behalf, in the formation of the Columbianum, an association of artists in Philadelphia, and as the moving force behind the Pennsylvania Academy.

The Academy was inaugurated in 1803 and opened to the public in 1807.[29] It held annual exhibitions, but the content of the shows did not change very much from year to year, comprising principally its accumulation of casts after the antique, as well as its collection of pictures, including those lent for the purpose by the Academy's subscribers. Few, if any, contemporary paintings appeared in these annuals. The visitor in 1838[30] could see, however, a number of important American pictures such as Washington Allston's "Dead Man Restored to Life," purchased by the Academy in 1816; Benjamin West's "Death on a Pale Horse," acquired in 1836; Charles Robert Leslie's "Murder of Rutland by Lord Clifford," presented by the artist's family in 1831, but exhibited by the Academy as early as 1816; John Neagle's "Pat Lyon at the Forge"; and a full-length portrait of Washington by Gilbert Stuart, probably the Lansdowne portrait received in 1811. There were also portraits by Thomas Sully, Henry Inman, Charles Willson Peale, Charles Bird King, and landscapes by Thomas Doughty. Among the old masters listed were landscapes attributed to Salvator Rosa, from the Academy's collection, interior scenes said to be by Ostade and Teniers, and a portrait by Sir Henry Raeburn. Some of the Dutch pictures were lent by John Hare Powell. Despite its limitations in point of time, the Academy's exhibit was one that could easily have opened the eyes of a young painter "to the merits of other artists." He would have to look elsewhere, of course, if he wished to see what artists of his own age were doing.

The domination of the Academy by amateurs rather than artists and its restricted exhibitions led early to a reaction on the part of the artists who felt that the "state of arts in this country demanded the establishment of a society on enlightened and liberal principles, in order to collect, as it were, into a focus the various talents and resources of artists."[31] In 1810 there was therefore formed the Society of Artists of the United States, which held exhibitions in 1812, 1813, and 1814, but its name had disappeared by 1815. It was not

29. A. W. Rutledge, comp. and ed., *Cumulative Record of Exhibition Catalogues: The Pennsylvania Academy of the Fine Arts, 1807-1870; The Society of Artists, 1800-1814; The Artists Fund Society. 1835-1845* (Philadelphia: American Philosophical Society, 1955), p. 1.

30. *Catalogue of the Twenty-seventh Annual Exhibition of The Pennsylvania Academy of the Fine Arts....* 1838.

31. Rutledge, *op. cit.*, p. 2.

until 1824 that another society appeared, founded in similar lines—The Artists' Fund Society of Philadelphia. This new society held annual shows from 1835 to 1845 which were concerned mainly with the works of contemporaries. Here the visitor could see recent pictures by some of the better-known painters, although the representation was limited, for the most part, to residents of the city. The exhibitions were opened to the public in April of each year and remained open for eight or nine weeks.

The 1838 exhibition, on view during Bingham's stay in Philadelphia, included portraits by Sully and Neagle, as well as by younger men such as William E. Winner, John Carlin, and Joseph Kyle; landscapes by Thomas Birch, Joshua Shaw, Thomas B. Ashton, and George R. Bonfield; and there were two genre pictures by John Gadsby Chapman, one of historical connotation.[32] Apart from the large shows, Benjamin West's showpiece "Christ Healing the Sick" was to be seen at the Pennsylvania Hospital. It was a famous painting at the time, and was very probably one of the first pictures to which Bingham had access that involved the grouping of many figures composed in the grand manner.

It was also possible to see many more pictures, although mainly those attributed to old masters, as they were brought up for sale at auction. Both Philadelphia and New York were already active markets in the buying and selling of pictures. A sale held in Philadelphia in May 1838,[33] which Bingham could have attended, included works said to be by Ostade, Teniers, Van Dyck, and Rubens; drawings attributed to Greuze, David, Watteau, Michelangelo, Rembrandt, and Dürer; prints after Claude, Teniers, and Poussin. John Neagle is supposed to have made a large purchase of drawings at this sale.[34]

The picture dealers and galleries also held exhibitions which were open to the public. Sully and Earle's Gallery was one of the best known in Philadelphia. Sartain recalled years afterward that the gallery "was filled with pictures of fairly good quality," and that because of Sully and Earle, "those who enjoyed viewing works of art were not obliged to go so far west as Tenth Street, to the Academy of the Fine Arts."[35]

In this account of the availability of works of art, we must not discount the fact that the studios of the artists themselves were also possible areas open

32. *Artists Fund Society of Philadelphia. Catalogue of the Fourth Annual Exhibition. 1838.* Philadelphia: C. Sherman & Co., printers, 1838.
33. *Fine Arts. M. Thomas & Son. Will Sell at Auction...The Elegant Paintings, Drawings, Etchings & Engravings* [of William Carey, London]...[Philadelphia, 1838]. The sale, held May 2, 1838 in Philadelphia, included 359 lots, of which 39 were paintings and the remainder drawings and engravings.
34. *Ibid.* An old inscription on the copy of the catalogue in the Frick Art Reference Library, N.Y., states that Neagle purchased about 150 drawings at the sale.
35. Sartain, *op. cit.*, p. 164.

45

to the student who might wish to consult with the master and examine pictures in the making. The student could usually gain such entree through a letter of introduction or by application. Established artists such as Sully received many young artists who sought their advice, although at the time of Bingham's visit Sully was in England painting the portrait of Queen Victoria. [36] Aside from the younger artists then resident in the city, there were established painters such as John Neagle, Bass Otis, Joshua Shaw, and Thomas Birch. [37]

Finally, there were the private collectors of the city who frequently lent their pictures to public exhibitions. Conceivably, the interested student could see such collections in their entirety on occasion. Two of the best-known collectors were Edward L. Carey and Colonel Cephas C. Childs, both publishers and patrons of American artists. As we have already noted, many of Carey's pictures, like the portrait of Fanny Kemble by Sully, were engraved and used as illustrations for his gift annuals. His paintings by American artists included genre pictures by Mount, Inman, and Chapman, as well as other subjects by Huntington, Leutze, Page, Stuart, and Sully. Colonel Childs' collection contained landscapes by Cole, Bonfield, Doughty, western scenes with buffalo by Peter Rindisbacher, and portraits by Sully, Inman, and Stuart.

In writing about Bingham's activity during this period, one biographer has further stated: "It is known that in 1838 he spent some time in New York City, where he probably again studied." [38] The statement seems without substantiation from any other source, although the artist may indeed have paid at least a brief visit to the city at the time, if only to view the current exhibition at the National Academy. At the New York exhibition he could have seen a large selection of pictures by American artists, and probably nowhere else could he have received a more definite impression of the kind of painting that was then receiving favorable criticism in the press.

The annual exhibition of the National Academy opened in May of that year with a collection of 337 works of painting, sculpture, and engraving. [39] A large

36. Thomas Sully sailed for England on Oct. 10, 1837, and did not return to Philadelphia until Sept. 15, 1838. From "Journal of Thomas Sully's activities May 1792-1793, 1799–December 1846; includes paintings executed by him, financial affairs, visitors received, calls made, trip to England and France, 1837-38," p. 120 (typescript in New York Public Library, Manuscript Division).
37. Listed in *M'Elroy's Philadelphia Directory, for the Year 1837....* Philadelphia: printed by Rackliff & Jones, 1837.
38. Christ-Janer, *George Caleb Bingham ...*, p. 29. The statement seems without foundation, and there is no evidence to indicate that Bingham stayed in New York at this time. It is entirely conceivable, however, that he took advantage of the city's proximity to visit exhibitions there, and it is with that idea in mind that the possibility is considered. But the statement that he "spent some time in New York City, where he probably again studied" points to a prolonged stay and period of study which seems beyond our consideration in view of the lack of any positive supporting evidence.
39. *Catalogue of the Thirteenth Annual Exhibition. 1838.* New York: printed by E. A. Clayton, 1838.

46

number of young artists were represented, but older established artists like Allston, Morse, Sully, Harding, and Doughty were strangely missing. One critic, reviewing the pictures one by one in a series of articles running through several issues of his paper, was inclined to see a distinct danger in this absence of the older men, proclaiming that

if this course prevails in future exhibitions, a serious injury will result both to the arts and the artists; for, without works of older and abler hands, the desire of young artists to produce a flashy effect by superficial means, and the approbation which such works will receive from the publick [sic] will immediately become visible in future exhibitions. Honest and impartial criticism may do much toward correcting this evil.[40]

Nevertheless, the same critic was able to write favorably of portraits by Huntington and Inman, as well as of others by Page, Neagle, Dunlap, Ingham, and Cranch. One of Thomas Cole's landscapes received special attention: the artist himself was advised "not to expect to rival Claude or Salvator Rosa" in terms of his color and design, but he was assured that "as a true lover of his own native lands, as a faithful and bold delineator of all her wild scenery, he stands, and will ... continue to stand, unrivalled and alone"[41] — high praise indeed for the thirty-seven-year-old painter. But the highest praise was reserved for an even younger artist, William Sidney Mount, and if Bingham saw the review, he might have been greatly encouraged. Mount had two pictures in the big exhibition: "Fortune-telling," described as unfinished, and "The Tough Story" (also known as "The Long Story") (plate 93). The reviewer was evidently completely taken with the artist's work, for he was complimentary without reservation, although he had been just the opposite in his criticism of many of the other artists. He began by saying: "If we may be allowed a preference, this artist is our favourite. He has, certainly, more original powers of mind than any other artist in the country." But of special interest to us was his impression of "The Tough Story":

Here we have the jewel of the exhibition — original, characteristick [sic] and full of life and meaning. To this end, colour, light and shade, and composition, are all made to blend. And there is no greater mistake, we might almost say insult, than to call him the American Wilkie. ... The truth is, he is a child of nature — a vigorous, untaught and untutored plant, who borrows from no one, imitates no one, and should be compared to no one.[42]

If we accept the statement that Bingham went to New York in 1838, a visit to the Academy show would unquestionably have been his principal reason for coming, and there he would have made his first important contact with

40. *New-York Mirror*, IV (May 26, 1838), 382.
41. *Ibid.*, XV (June 2, 1838), 390.
42. *Ibid.*, XVI (July 7, 1838), 15.

47

original examples of Mount's genre subjects, which he could hitherto have known only through reproduction. In this particular field Mount had almost no competition in the exhibition, certainly none that could have overshadowed him, if we eliminate pictures such as Charles Deas's "The Turkey Shoot" (which Bingham may have recalled at a later date) and Albertis D. O. Browere's "Capture of Fort Casimir," which appears to have been more of a composition approaching historical genre and had been described by the New York critic as "a singular combination of humour, extravagance, and caricature."[43]

A visit to New York could well have proved to be an important experience for Bingham at this particular time, and possibly one marking a turning point in his career. A chance to see the work of Mount, already recognized as America's chief exponent of the storytelling picture, might easily have inspired him to develop his own talents in the same direction. As a point of fact, in support of the strong possibility of such a visit having taken place and its subsequent influence, it would appear highly significant that Bingham's first public showing, a picture entitled "Western Boatmen Ashore" exhibited at the Apollo Gallery in New York during the fall of the same year,[44] was also, insofar as we now know, his first recorded painting of a genre character. That the exhibition setting was New York and was held within a few months of the Academy show seems hardly mere coincidence, but rather an indication of some on-the-spot prior contact. The choice of the subject itself, with its special western connotation, leads to speculation along another line, which we shall have occasion to discuss in another connection.

Apart from a possible visit to New York at this period, the short stay in Philadelphia, when he looked at paintings and prints as well as drawing from casts, had a maturing and significant influence on Bingham, judging by the developing painterly sense that can be observed in his work during the period immediately following. In portraiture, the opportunity to see a profusion of sophisticated productions by Stuart, Sully, Neagle, and Inman, among others, must have proved a revelation to him, for soon afterward the stiff formality of his earlier portraits began to give way to a generally more relaxed and varied system of composition. The hard outlines and brittle modeling that characterized his previous work began to dissolve into softer tones and edges, allowing the subject to take its place within a three-dimensional background rather than being seemingly mounted against a flat backdrop.

43. *Ibid.,* XV (May 26, 1838), 382.
44. *Catalogue of the First Fall Exhibition of the Works of Modern Artists, at the Apollo Gallery, no. 410 Broadway, New York, 1838*... (New York: J. M. Marsh, printer, 1838), #237.

V

PORTRAIT PAINTING: MISSOURI AND WASHINGTON, D.C. (1838-1844)

~

If it can be assumed that Bingham was able to follow the schedule he described in the last letter he addressed to his wife from Philadelphia, he left the city at the end of the first week in June, fulfilled his "engagement" in Baltimore, and returned to his home in Boonville "on the first boat that goes up the river in July."[1]

By the early fall of 1838 Bingham must have been again busily at work painting portraits, canvassing the small towns and outlying districts of his home state. It is possible to trace his route, partly on the basis of claims by current owners of family portraits, indicating that he painted a number of pictures in Glasgow, Fayette, Boonville, and near Gilliam at this time. One portrait, conveniently bearing an inscribed date, places the artist in Saline County late in 1838, or early in 1839. The painting, a likeness of Mrs. Thomas Shackelford (Eliza Chives Pulliam) (A51), is of further importance because it also serves as a key to Bingham's development as a portrait painter following his Philadelphia period.

Mrs. Shackelford's portrait (plate 23) reveals in many ways a distinct advance over his previous efforts. It can be regarded as one of the artist's more ambitious portrait projects following his largely unsuccessful effort in the case of Mrs. Lamme. It represents a single figure, but he has also shown the subject seated in three-quarter length, and with both hands visible. The sitter is turned toward the left, still typical of his earliest portraits, but she is now displayed almost full-face, a complete departure from anything Bingham appears to have attempted before. Light enters the picture at the left, rather than from the right as in almost all of the earlier pictures, and

1. B. to S. E. B., letter, Philadelphia, June 3, 1838 (coll. SHSMo).

49

the right half of the face is cast in soft shadow. The expression of the eyes is gentle, unlike the fixed frontal stare of the first portraits. The coördination of the features, with the half-smile in the eyes, echoed in the slight curve at the corners of the mouth to catch a fleeting expression, is an idea Bingham must have developed through a careful examination of the work of other artists. The softer contours of the face and the considered transition from the skin to the hairline is felt with a greater sureness than was evident in his work before he went East. And the figure now seems to occupy a well-defined place within the setting—a neutral yet airy background which gives the figure its proper dimension.

In a variety of ways, both general and specific, Bingham demonstrates in this portrait, perhaps for the first time, a growing awareness of the possibilities of his medium which reveals itself in a certain ease and even a subtlety of handling that clearly distinguishes the itinerant delineator of faces from the professional portraitist. On the other hand, the artist still struggles with the painting of textures of cloth and lace, and the handling of the folds of drapery is awkward and uncertain. The hands give him trouble, too, revealing a lack of understanding of their basic structure.

The artist's developing ability to capture the individuality of his subject and to catch the underlying subtlety of expression, as well as his growing appreciation of these elements that go into the making of a successful portrait, is also shown in another group of pictures that can be assigned stylistically to this period. But of the pictures available for study, none is so impressively composed as the portrait of Mrs. Shackelford; the others are all the usual half-length figure, and all have three-quarter heads turned toward the left—Bingham's favorite pose. But there the resemblance ceases, if we compare these pictures with those produced between 1834 and 1837. Enough of the former crispness is retained to mark a recognizable line of development, but the modeling of the features is far less rigid and the outlines are softer, the transitions from hair to flesh to cloth conceived with a technical skill not understood before. The starkness that marked Bingham's portraits of 1834 is gone, yet he has lost none of his individuality. There is a vitality about some of these portraits which may yet single them out as being some of his best productions in the field, despite obvious crudities. Such expressive portraits as those of Judge Henry Lewis (A63; plate 25) and his wife (A64; plate 26), Jacob Fortney Wyan (A57; plate 27), and Mrs. Thomas Eddens (Elizabeth McClanahan Harrison) (A76) date from this period.

Of particular interest is a group of portraits, all except one still extant, that can be placed in Bingham's studio in Fayette at this time. Documents by the artist's contemporaries are relatively rare and are not always trustworthy, but in this instance there are two statements made by participants in an event in Bingham's studio in Fayette in 1839 which evidently excited enough interest to allow it to be recalled with accuracy many years later. The portraits of Lewis Bumgardner (A65) and David Kunkle (A68) and their wives (A66, A69; plate 29), as well as those of Samuel Grove (A67), Thomas Erskine Birch (A71; plate 28), and Joseph Davis (A70) were displayed in the studio (of these, the Davis portrait is the only one of the group yet unlocated). One of the statements, by James Bumgardner, Jr., affords a rare glimpse of Bingham's studio and adds a bit of color to a little-known corner of the artist's early career as an itinerant painter:

One of my earliest recollections is of George Bingham, the Painter. I was born and lived until I was five years old in Fayette, Missouri. During that time Mr. Bingham painted the portraits of a number of the citizens of Fayette and vicinity. His studio or work room was a room over the Court House. I was taken one day by David Kunkle to the studio and quite a number of portraits, either completed or nearly completed, were leaning against the walls. I was taken to each one and asked to tell who it was. Among the portraits I distinctly remember those of my father, Lewis Bumgardner, of my mother, Hetty Ann Bumgardner, David Kunkle and his wife, Sallie Kunkle, Samuel Grove, Joseph Davis. Mr. Bingham was in the room at that time, and seemed to be highly gratified by the fact that the likeness, in each case, was recognized by a small child.[2]

All of the portraits of this period bear a striking "family" resemblance in composition and handling, unlike some of the earlier portraits executed in Columbia in 1837. For the moment, at least, Bingham seemed to have lost any incentive to experiment with new ideas; he relaxed instead into the usual pattern of pot-boiling productions, at so much per head, although a decided character and developed technical facility are visible in these portraits. In his portrait of Sarah Ann Cooper Kunkle (A69), Bingham departs from his usual pattern. Perhaps for the first time, the pose of the figure is reversed, shown turned toward the right instead of the usual left, to face the companion portrait of David Kunkle (A68). The artist must have realized the greater effectiveness of this new scheme, for by the mid-1840's he adopted the procedure consistently in a series of companion portraits.

Another departure from his routine manner can be seen in at least one portrait that can be placed within the 1838/1839 period—the painting of Richard Henry Robinson (A61; plate 32). Although the "standard" Bingham

2. From typescript of statement made by James Bumgardner, Jr., signed and dated March 24, 1915. James Bumgardner, Jr., was the oldest child of Lewis and Hetty Ann Bumgardner, whose portraits were painted by Bingham in Fayette.

A letter written by one of Bingham's Fayette patrons, David Kunkle, to Mrs. George B. Harrison from Craigsville, Va., Sept. 4, 1899, mentions all of the subjects named by Bumgardner, except Joseph Davis, substituting that of Thomas Erskine Birch. He states that there were "in all six" portraits. If we accept both statements as accurate, there were actually seven portraits.

composition is maintained, there is at least one significant difference which brings this portrait into the ranks of the unusual among Bingham's paintings. The former static arrangement of neutral background elements has been replaced by a lively effect of clouds parting to admit light in a halo-like fashion about the head of the subject. This is perhaps the earliest painting in which Bingham made use of outdoor elements to enforce his growing interest in achieving atmospheric effects, and it serves to announce a period immediately following in which he proceeds in that direction with even greater freedom.[3]

By mid-May of 1839 Bingham was again in St. Louis,[4] devoting his time chiefly to portraits, but without doubt willing to take on any other painting commission that might come his way, as he had done earlier. However, strong public notice of Bingham during this period was still evidently confined to his portrait painting, certainly his chief stock-in-trade. A St. Louis reporter could nevertheless now emphasize not only Bingham's Missouri background but also his obvious improvement due to his study visit to the East during the preceding year:

Portrait Painting—Those who have a taste for examining the efforts of genius should call at the studio of Mr. Bingham, no. 62, Main-street, up stairs, and look at some specimens of his skill. He has transferred to the canvass, the likeness of several of our citizens with a fidelity and taste which every one who will examine them, must commend. Mr. B. is already favourably known to many of our citizens, but he has much improved of late. He has visited the East, studied with assiduousness and is now as all must admit. a superior artist. Call and see his work, which is the best evidence of his merit.[5]

It is likely that the portrait of Mrs. John Fletcher Darby (Mary M. Wilkinson) (A78; plate 24), usually assigned a much later dating, was painted during this period in St. Louis. The portrait bears a strong stylistic relationship to that of Eliza Pulliam Shackelford, probably executed just a few months earlier in Saline County. The general arrangement of the figures —shown three-quarter length, seated, turned fully toward the spectator—the relaxed placement of the left hand, the half-smile motif, and the evident weakness in the handling of the textures of materials are all elements common to both pictures. To the St. Louis reporter, however, such a portrait as that of Mrs. Darby could only be dramatized as one of "fidelity and taste," and

3. The inspiration for the sky-filled background could also have come as a direct result of his stay in Philadelphia. The motif often occurs in the works of Thomas Sully.
4. The arrival of the artist in the city was noted by the local reporter, who, probably with deliberate intent, emphasized Bingham's Missouri background, undoubtedly as a means of attracting local support and attention. The notice of the painter's presence appears under the banner "Native Talent." *Daily Missouri Republican* (St. Louis), May 16, 1839, 2-1. A letter, S. E. B. to B., dated May 31, 1839 (coll. SHSMo), was addressed to him in St. Louis.
5. *Daily Missouri Republican*, June 6, 1839, 2-2.

the obvious elaboration of the artist's style beyond his earlier work attributed to his recent sojourn in the East.

St. Louis newspaper accounts also inform us that Bingham left town during the summer months of July and August, but he was supposedly back in his studio awaiting business by early September.[6] He was undoubtedly there when a St. Louis paper reported the exhibition, for raffle purposes, of two works by the Canadian painter Paul Kane, who was then in the city.[7] Chiefly interested in the portrayal of the North American Indian, Kane was evidently at that time attempting to earn enough in the States to finance a trip abroad for further study. Like Bingham, he was almost completely self-trained, and supported himself by painting portraits. However, the two pictures he exhibited in St. Louis were described as "a family of emigrants encamped by a stream" and "a dog fight." The painter himself was dubbed "an artist of considerable attainment and a young man of much worth."[8] Although at no time does Bingham refer to Kane in his writings, it is interesting to speculate as to whether the paths of these almost precise contemporaries crossed at this point in their careers. Both men were destined to become recognized as foremost illustrators of the western scene, and both were already exhibiting their early attempts in this special field.

As was his custom, Bingham left St. Louis early in the winter. A fire that destroyed his studio and its contents was reported on December 12, and the artist was said to have "gone to the country," leaving his painting room in the hands of another painter, whose own productions had also gone up in smoke at the same time.[9] By "the country," the reporter was evidently referring to Bingham's itinerant haunts, since by February 15, 1840, the artist was mentioned in the press as being in Fayette, "transferring to canvas the countenances of some of the good citizens of the place."[10]

The painter may have returned to St. Louis after he had exhausted the possibilities of commissions in Fayette and the surrounding area. It could have been at that time, or during the previous fall in St. Louis, that he executed the portraits of Marbel Camden (A73) and his young daughter, Sallie Ann (A74), and that of Leonidas Wetmore (A86; plate 30). The portrait of Sallie Ann Camden (plate 33) was in all probability the most important

6. *Ibid.*, July 25, Aug. 19, 1839, 2-4; professional cards, evidently inserted by Bingham as portrait painter, announce his intended return to the city on Sept. 5. A short account in the issue for September 10 (2-1) informs the public that he has returned "to his stand on Market Street."
7. *Ibid.*, Sept. 28, 1839 (reprinted in *MHR*, XXXII [1937], 122). (Paul Kane, b. 1810; d. 1871.)
8. *Ibid.*
9. *Daily Missouri Republican* (St. Louis), Dec. 12, 1839, 2-1. Among the "number of life-drawn likenesses" by Bingham destroyed in the studio fire, the reporter lists "our own pretty face." The reporter could have been the editor himself, Col. Adam B. Chambers.
10. *Missouri Saturday News* (St. Louis), Feb. 15, 1840.

53

portrayal of a child attempted by the artist since the portrait he painted of Sarah Helen Rollins some three years earlier. The child is represented full-length, seated within a landscape that spreads out into the background. In a manner characteristic of other portraits of this period of the artist, the subject faces the spectator, gently smiling. Unlike the stiffly formal representation of the Rollins child, which so clearly displayed those limitations that prevented Bingham from affording much variety to his compositions, he now appears capable of developing a design in which a considerable impression of movement and atmosphere is achieved, as well as a clearly improved ease of handling. Of course, there are still some rather obvious technical limitations in the treatment of drapery and the definition of landscape elements, but the work marks a distinct advance over the production of the earlier period—an "improvement" that was duly noted by his contemporaries.

By far the most compelling Bingham portrait of this time—in which the use of landscape elements assumes important dimensions—is that of Leonidas Wetmore (plate 30), only recently rediscovered in the St. Louis art market. In this portrait the landscape actively vies with the subject in claiming the attention of the observer and already shows much of the character we find in the backgrounds of the painter's genre subjects and pure landscapes of later years. Bingham obviously lavished much of his attention on this portrait and certainly there is no precedent for it among his previous pictures. Wetmore, dressed in elaborate buckskins and carrying his rifle, is to a large extent a forerunner of the Daniel Boone prototype. Very early in his career, Bingham had portrayed this prototype on a tavern sign, but it was to take on a far more dramatic character as part of a larger figure composition a decade later. The Wetmore picture is thus something more than a portrait. Although the pose is an academic one, the placement of the figure within a setting of rich foliage, lake, and distant mountains—all shown against an atmospheric sky—gives the painting a strong storytelling quality. The idea for the portrayal of heroic figures in settings intended to be descriptive of their lives and achievements was not an original one with Bingham. It would seem obvious, in fact, that he had direct reference in this instance to an engraving after Robert Walter Weir's well-known portrait of "Red Jacket" (plate 31; painted in 1828) for both the archetype and the pose of the figure.

It is also conceivable that the portrait of Colonel Samuel Bullitt Churchill (A60) was painted during the same period. As in the portrait of Sallie Ann Camden, the painter opens up the background, introducing landscape elements and a large expanse of sky leading the eye into the distance. In this picture, too, the artist shows a developing interest in atmospheric effects, with a consequent softening of his older manner, while such problems as the

54

rendering of textures of materials and of landscape details are still much in evidence.

Bingham was evidently still in Missouri in June, 1840, reportedly taking an active part in the Whig convention at Rocheport, executing a processional banner for Saline County,[11] as well as becoming involved in local political affairs. In all probability he did not leave the state until late in the year. In the account of his life published by Dunlap in 1834, Chester Harding is quoted as saying: "In the autumn after I left St. Louis, I made my debut in Washington. I painted a few heads for exhibition; so that by the time congress met, I made something of a display. I was successful beyond my most sanguine expectations. I painted something like forty heads, during this winter and spring."[12] And again it may have been Harding's words that encouraged Bingham to emulate yet another step in the older artist's early career.

For the artist, a move to the nation's capital could have meant nothing more than a bid for prestige—the privilege of painting the portraits of the distinguished politicos of his time. Such portraits could be exhibited, thus helping immeasurably to establish him as a portrait painter of some substance, especially on home ground.

Certainly Washington could offer the enterprising artist and student nothing in the way of inducement as a cultural center, although some paintings were already permanently placed in the Capitol, and temporary exhibitions were also permitted in the building. English visitors, however, visiting the city in the years just prior to Bingham's trip, could say little to commend the place. Harriet Martineau was in Washington in January, 1835, describing the city as "no place for persons of domestic tastes. Persons who love dissipation, persons who love to watch the game of politics, and those who make a study of strong minds under strong excitement, like a season at Washington...."[13] She described the physical appearance of the city as being "unlike any other that ever was seen, straggling out hither and thither, with a small house or two a quarter of a mile from any other, so that, on making calls 'in the city,' we had to cross ditches and stiles, and walk alternately on grass and pavements, and strike across a field to reach a street."[14]

11. *Daily Commercial Bulletin* (St. Louis), June 22, 1840, 2-1. Also recounted by C. B. Rollins in "Some Recollections of George Caleb Bingham," *MHR*, XX (1926), 469.
12. Dunlap, *History of the ... Arts of Design ...* (1834), II, 291.
13. H. Martineau, *Retrospect of Western Travel...* (London: Saunders & Ottley; New York: [sold by] Harper & Brothers, 1838), I, 143.
14. *Ibid.*, p. 144. Miss Martineau visited Washington early in 1835, but the city apparently changed very little within the next few years. Bingham's wife, writing to her mother-in-law from Washington, Jan. 11, 1841, reported: "I was a little disappointed in the appearance of the City, it is not as prety [sic] a place as St. Louis, there is but one street paved, which is the one we live on."

Captain Marryat, who came to Washington about two years later, found the city little changed in appearance, but believed it to be "an agreeable city, full of pleasant clever people who come there to amuse and be amused."[15] He discovered that books were readily available at the library in the Capitol, describing that section as "open to all" and being the "best lounge in Washington," noting, however, that many valuable volumes were then in poor condition, specifically mentioning a copy he saw there of "Audubon's Ornithology."[16]

By January of 1841 Bingham had a studio in the Capitol,[17] a privilege that was enjoyed by a number of artists who came to work in Washington. This placed him conveniently in the center of things and in the most likely area for business, although he was not immediately given recognition. The Capitol studios could apparently become rather lively centers of activity other than art, as Miss Martineau reported when she sat for her portrait in 1835. The artist's studio was a place where "much amusement was picked up," and where "members and strangers dropped in, and the news of the hour circulated."[18] Bingham appears to have kept aloof from this sort of thing, however, concentrating entirely on the work that brought him to Washington. In a letter written to Rollins a month after he took up quarters in the Capitol, he said:

Though I have a painting room in the Capitol, I know less of the proceedings of Congress than if I were in Missouri . . . I have not felt sufficient interest in what was passing to attend the debates in either house this winter. . . . I am a painter and desire to be nothing else, and unless another corrupt dynasty, like the one that has just been overthrown, shall again arouse the energy of the whole people in behalf of a suffering Country I shall be content to pursue the quiet tenor of a painters life, contending only for the smiles of the graces, while the great world may jog along as it pleases.[19]

Letters written by Bingham during his Washington years rarely refer to his work, and our only direct references to pictures in progress are to those he painted for pleasure, such as the portraits of his wife and her friends. For any indication of his more formal efforts, we must turn to a fragmentary letter written by the artist's wife in 1844, in which she mentions that Bingham had painted the portraits of Robert Tyler, the son of the President, and of Wise (in all probability Henry Alexander Wise, the Virginia Congressman), and that he had "succeeded admirably in both."[20] From another contem-

15. Marryat, *A Diary* . . . . I, 163.
16. *Ibid.*, p. 166.
17. S. E. B. to Mary (Amend) Bingham, letter, Washington, D.C., Jan. 11, 1841, coll. SHSMo: "Mr. B. has a room in the Capitol where he spends the most of his time in painting."
18. Martineau, *op. cit.*, I, 146.
19. B. to R., letter, Washington, D.C., Feb. 21, 1841, coll. SHSMo (*MHR*, XXXIII [1937], 11-12).
20. S. E. B. to M. B., letter, Washington, D.C., March 3, 1844, coll. SHSMo.

porary source we learn indirectly that he had also painted a portrait of the Postmaster General, Charles Anderson Wickliffe.[21]

Bingham is said to have painted a number of portraits of the great men of his time during his long stay in Washington, among these being Daniel Webster, Henry Clay, John C. Breckenridge, Andrew Jackson, John C. Calhoun, Robert J. Walker, James Buchanan, Martin van Buren, John Howard Payne, and John Quincy Adams.[22] Although no contemporary evidence now exists to bear out the later statements that he did indeed portray all of these men, there can be little doubt that the artist sought to obtain as many important commissions as possible during this period, having in mind the full realization of the prestige value of such commissions. Thus far, however, only the three portraits of John Quincy Adams, the small watercolor of John Howard Payne (A98), and, of late, the portrait of Daniel Webster (A113) have come to light. In later years Bingham painted official portraits of Henry Clay and Andrew Jackson for the Missouri State Capitol, and it is conceivable that he was then able to make use of preliminary studies he had made from life at this time.

Two of the three Bingham portraits of John Quincy Adams (A112, 210, 211) may have been painted after the Washington period, although probably based on one version known to have been painted from life. Adams himself fortunately recorded his sittings to Bingham in his invaluable diary. Adams mentions the artist's name for the first time on May 14, 1844, when he writes: "From half past 9 o'clock I sat to Mr. John Cranch and Mr. Bingham who occupy jointly the painting room for my portrait."[23] The diary entry for the previous day had recorded details regarding Cranch's request to paint his portrait, including a description of the "hut or shanty at the foot of the capitol hill" to which he came for his first sitting. It is conceivable that Cranch made more convenient and hospitable arrangements for his distin-

21. Washington newspapers of June, 1843, report with enthusiasm the appearance of a mezzotint by John Sartain based on Bingham's portrait of Wickliffe. The portrait, undoubtedly executed in Washington sometime earlier, "was pronounced by those who visited his [Wickliffe's] study, to be as near perfection as gifted artist could make it." The painting has not been located and I have not yet been able to discover an impression of the Sartain print said to have been based upon it. (*The Daily Madisonian*, June 22, 1843, 2-1; *Daily National Intelligencer*, June 26, 1843, 3-5.)
22. Shannon Mountjoy, "Missouri's Great Painter...Gen. George C. Bingham...," *St. Louis Globe-Democrat*, Nov. 6, 1904; Rusk, *George Caleb Bingham...*, p. 29.
23. John Quincy Adams Diary, MSS. coll. Massachusetts Historical Society, Boston, Mass. Some of the material, in which some of the Bingham data are recorded, has already been published: C. F. Adams, ed., *Memoirs of John Quincy Adams. Comprising Portions of His Diary from 1795 to 1848*... (Philadelphia: J. B. Lippincott, 1874-1877), XII, 32, 35.
John Cranch (1807-1891) was b. Washington, D.C.; d. Urbana, Ohio. He was a student of Charles Bird King, Chester Harding, and Thomas Sully. Adams mentions in his diary entry of May 13 that Cranch had asked for sittings for the portrait at the request of his father Judge William Cranch, a cousin of the former president.

guished subject by May 14 which could have involved an agreement to share Bingham's studio in the Capitol itself, providing the artist from Missouri might also take advantage of Adams' presence by painting a portrait of him at the same time. This would have been indeed an opportunity that Bingham could not afford to miss.[24]

Adams described further sittings to Cranch and Bingham, each of an hour's duration, on May 21, 23, 24, 27, and 28. On May 21 he added his firm opinion that "neither . . . is likely to make out either a strong likeness or a fine picture." Cranch had additional sittings on several occasions until June 7, but Adams indicated on May 29 that "Bingham had already finished" his portrait.

The President did not have anything further to report in his daily commentary which might indicate that he had in any way changed his preliminary impressions about the possibilities of success of the two artists. But Adams had been badgered so much by artists[25] during his long career that he appears to have long since soured on the subject and he certainly had already made up his mind which of his portraits he considered the best likenesses. He described the subject at some length in his diary some months earlier when he complained that he had sat to portrait painters about 45 times and questioned "whether another man lives who has been so wofully [sic] and so variously bedaubed as I have been." He wrote that "from the age of 16, when I was cariacatured [sic] by Mr. Schmidt for four ducats, down to this my 77th year, when Mr. White has lampooned me in oil scarcely a year has passed away without a crucifixion of my face and form by some painter engraver or sculptor." He considered Copley's portrait painted in 1796, Stuart's of 1825, and Durand's of 1836 among the only paintings of himself "worthy of being preserved."[26]

It is my belief that the small portrait on panel owned by the Rollins family (plate 34) is the earliest of the three portraits of Adams, and very probably the one he painted from life in May, 1844. It is certainly the most convincing of the group, the only one that has caught something of the vital quality of a fleeting expression. The artist has gone further, too, in capturing the more

24. The "bible story," evidently a tradition in the Rollins family, in which it was said that Bingham "worsted" Adams during a discussion on biblical matters, and the notion that the former president simply "stopped in one day at the studio" of the painter, do not appear to coincide with the facts of the matter (Rusk, *George Caleb Bingham . . .*, pp. 29-30).

25. The diary records sittings in April and May, 1844, to James Reid Lambdin (1807-1889) and to one Gilbert (probably Grove Sheldon Gilbert, 1805-1885), the same period in which Adams was being painted by Cranch and Bingham. In August of the previous year he sat for the portrait painter Franklin White, whom he declared "could scarcely claim to be called an artist" (Diary, Aug. 15, 1843).

26. *Ibid.*

general impression of stern obstinacy, coupled with the gentility, which was so descriptive of the sitter's appearance in life. So penetrating and lively a portrayal is rarely accomplished without direct contact with the model.

The head is enclosed in a painted oval, broadly modeled in terms of light and shade; and the detail is limited to the eyes, which look out sternly to the right. The head itself is turned only slightly away from the spectator, toward the left. The approach and the final effect in terms of portraiture is a radical departure from anything Bingham had attempted before and may well have been an experimental scheme.

From the beginning Bingham had strictly avoided sharp contrasts in light and shade in his portraiture, usually modeling his heads almost entirely in the light in the manner of the mature period of Gilbert Stuart and his followers. A slight change in the artist's approach appears in the period following his Philadelphia visit, and may have its roots in observations he made there both from the works of his colleagues and from instruction books. However, the bolder experimentation with the dramatic possibilities of the use of strong light and shade seem not to have blossomed forth in his work until the Washington years.

In the small portrait of Adams the background forms an almost concave spatial effect, with a light area, having no visible source, appearing directly behind the shadow side of the head, throwing it into bold silhouette. To interrupt the light at the far right Bingham once more introduces the vertical division we recall from his earliest portraits. The outline of the head on the light side is greatly softened in an attempt to relate the form to the background. It is especially interesting to observe how the painter strives to cope with the problem of the background. Evidently fearing to lose some of the importance of the head by allowing the shadow area to merge into the background shadow, he introduces a light behind the figure which, although successful in bringing the head forward, affords the spectator a rather unhappy view of the outline of that form. And the vertical break is meaningless, as always, and even more disturbing in this example. That the artist himself must have realized his own shortcomings and sought to correct them is seen in a copy he made several years later, now in the collection of the Detroit Institute of Arts (plate 35). This time he deals more knowingly with the problem, modeling the head within a simplified neutral background. Here, the shadow at right merges into the darker background, allowing only a slight reflected light to appear behind the figure to bring the outline of the jacket into relief and cast a shadow beyond it. The artist has also slightly varied the pose of the original; the head faces the spectator almost frontally with the eyes staring ahead. Above all, a comparison with the Rollins version

59

reveals how much of the lively quality of the original has been dissipated through duplication.

The large portrait of Adams (plate 36) is also perhaps the least effective of the group. The sitter is shown in the usual three-quarter pose, the head turned toward the left. The painter has modeled broadly, using ruddy flesh tones, with the light moving in from the left to cast the right side of the face in shadow. Outlines are subdued and the figure appears in bold relief within its setting. A reflected light, similar to the method used in the Detroit picture, appears behind the figure at the right to bring out the outline of the coat and reduce the depth of the shadow on the head. A cast shadow at far right gives a greater three-dimensionality to the figure. A maturing ability to handle the technical problem of lighting which is similarly evident in the Detroit portrait would seem to relate these two versions closely, dating them later than the Rollins painting. The same dullness of expression shown in the Detroit paint-ing would seem once more to point to a loss of vitality through copying. Although varying the pose of the head to form what he always considered a "proper" official portrait, Bingham must have used the original small portrait as his model.

The portrait of Daniel Webster (plate 37), which turned up in recent years at a Washington auction, bears a contemporary presentation inscription (it may well be in the artist's hand)[27] on the reverse side which ascribes the picture to Bingham in 1844. There can be no doubt that the picture is the work of the artist at this period. Unlike the small experimental Adams portrait, the only one of the three I am inclined to place within the Washing-ton period, the portrait of Webster may very probably have been executed as a commission, and is therefore important to us for displaying the artist's "public" style at the time.

As a formal half-length figure, the sitter assumes the artist's usual pose. The strong head is firmly modeled, chiefly in the light, the deep eye-sockets cast in strong shadow, with softer shadows on the face at left, thus reducing the rugged outline and marking a not unhappy transition to the neutral background. The artist has caught the familiar determined, almost fierce presence of the statesman-orator, a quality he could only have caught through actual contact with his subject and a quality that Bingham almost always lost in duplication, whether from his own original or from some less direct means. The handling of the texture of cloth and other accessories, formerly a weak point in the artist's work, now takes on a more knowing

27. "[To] my friend Chas. Wilkes / Wash. D.C. 1846 / Likeness of Dan¹ Webster / From Life by George C. Bingham / 1844." The recipient was apparently the same Charles Wilkes who was also awarded in the same year a "Landscape with Cattle" by Bingham at the annual distribution of the American Art-Union (*Transactions*, AAU, 1845, #131).

60

handling through observation and constant application, obvious in this and other examples produced during these years in the East.

Before leaving for Washington late in 1840, and giving St. Louis as his address, Bingham submitted six paintings for inclusion in the annual exhibition of the National Academy of Design in New York,[28] the first time any of his pictures were shown by the institution. At least three of the paintings were obviously genre in character: "Pennsylvania Farmer," (A91) and two versions of "Tam O'Shanter" (A72, A90) based on the well-known poem by Robert Burns. These subjects, all very probably conceived and executed at least a year before, possibly in St. Louis, may have been intended by the artist for his debut at the National Academy in the belief that they would have a more immediate appeal to the desired eastern audience than would the Western Boatmen picture which had apparently gone unnoticed during its showing at the Apollo Gallery in New York in 1838.

We have some further knowledge about one of the pictures. Both the artist and his most recent effort in a new field evidently attracted the considerable attention of at least one St. Louis reporter, who not only took time out to relate the story of Bingham's self-imposed determination to overcome all obstacles to become an artist (a fact that the artist seems to have taken every opportunity to underline himself, as did so many of his American contemporaries), but also described in some detail one of the "Tam O'Shanter" pictures, affording us a somewhat vivid impression of the appearance of the painting:

Mr. Bingham is a native Missourian, and like many of the distinguished lights of his profession, commenced his career under apparently very unpromising circumstances. By the aid of a strong will and a deep-felt enthusiastic attachment to his art, he has overcome many of the obstacles that beset the career and depress the spirit of the aspirant to fame. He has been quite happy in some of the portraits that he has taken of our citizens. ... A design from 'Tam O'Shanter' executed by Mr. Bingham is really felicitous. The moment chosen by the artist is when Tam approaches the kirk; and his horse stands in rooted terror, refusing to advance an inch toward the haunted sanctuary. The terror of the animal is most admirably depicted; and the maudlin, mixed expression of alarm and defiance, which covers the face of his rider, is well suited to the character and situation of Tam.[29]

The emphasis placed by the reporter on the emotional impact of the picture is important in that it clearly reflects Bingham's interest in problems of expression and physiognomy and its importance to him in his picture-making, which was actually to become a conspicuous characteristic of his figure pic-

28. *Catalogue of the Fifteenth Annual Exhibition, 1840*... (New York: E. A. Clayton, Printer, 1840), # 88, 96, 249, 257, 293, 303.
29. *Daily Evening Gazette* (St. Louis), June 26, 1839, 2-1.

tures throughout his career. The moving description of "Tam O'Shanter" is perhaps even more significant in its indication that the artist was aware so early of the value of expression in painting, an ideal that had long been recognized as an essential pictorial ingredient by his European counterparts.[30]

Bingham's fourth picture in the exhibition was a "Landscape" (A89), and the other two were apparently portraits: "Group, Two Young Girls" (A88) and "Sleeping Child" (A92).[31] The artist seems not to have attempted group portraits until after his first St. Louis period. The earliest such composition extant, and probably his most elaborate effort, was the portrait of Mrs. Lamme and her son, already discussed at some length.[32] There are no further indications of group compositions until the Washington sojourn, at which time Bingham is known to have painted the double portrait of two family friends, Jane Hood Shaw and Eliza Robison (or Robertson) (A105),[33] and also the portrait of his wife and young son Newton (A97; plate 38). An analysis of the latter picture, still in the possession of the artist's descendants, may perhaps afford us some impression of the style of the other paintings, as well as indicating what progress if any the artist had made in the handling of the more complex type of portrait composition. In the portrait of his wife and son, he appears to have shaken off much of his former awkwardness and has developed a fairly harmonious organization. He has also managed to create an intimate relationship between the two figures which he had been unable to effect in the Lamme group. The mother leans her head gracefully against that of her child and his hand rests lightly on hers. In the Lamme portrait the child seems an afterthought in the development of the composition, although such was obviously not the artist's intention. Mrs. Lamme's gaze meets the spectator's and the child stares out of the picture, too, both seemingly unaware of each other. The painter's attempt to establish a more than physical relationship between the two figures, following a masterly conceived prototype, must be considered a failure. Technical limitations can

30. A further picture inspired by the poem "Tam O'Shanter" was painted by the well-known English artist Abraham Cooper, and an engraving after it was published by George Virtue in 1839, precisely at the time Bingham also felt the urge to pictorialize the subject. Although the description in the St. Louis paper clearly indicates that Bingham was not in any sense copying Cooper's design, the expressions of the "terror of the animal" and the rider's "mixed expression of alarm and defiance" are elements equally descriptive of the central figures of the Cooper composition. Bingham was evidently already impressed by the work of his English contemporaries and it seems entirely conceivable that this engraving could have been in his mind, if not his hands, at this time.
31. The elimination of the names of specific sitters, especially when of no social or political prominence, and the substitution of titles of slight genre connotation, was a not infrequent procedure among portrait painters exhibiting during this period. Portraits as such were rapidly becoming anathema to gallerygoers.
32. See above, pp. 31-33.
33. Present location unknown. Described by the artist to S. E. B., letter, Washington, D.C., Nov. 28, 1842, coll. SHSMo.

undoubtedly be said to account for the major part of the difficulty in handling the problem at that time.

In this portrait of his wife and son, however, painted in the years following his Philadelphia experience, Bingham has obviously overcome some of the technical limitations he encountered earlier. He is now able to vary the positions of the heads, giving him a greater freedom in the arrangement of the figures and hence a certain amount of fluidity in the composition as a whole. To be sure, there are still some disturbing factors present: the head of the child seems large in proportion when compared to that of the mother; the right contour of his figure is cut off, lacks dimension, and is somewhat awkward in its outline; and the mother's hands lack structure, although the child's visible hand does show careful study. To the artist's credit is his obvious increased knowledge and interest in problems of light and shade, in this example revealing a growing ability to cope with the intricacies of cast shadows and reflected lights. The figures take their places within the setting, and we note that the textures of skin, hair, and cloth are handled now with a far greater understanding than was formerly evidenced in his work. The arrangement within an oval was probably conceived as such from the outset, and is a further indication of the painter's growing sophistication through an observation of contemporary pictorial trends.

The "Sleeping Child," entered in the Academy show, could have been a portrait of the artist's son Newton, who would have been two or three years of age at the time. This picture seems to be no longer extant, but there is still in the possession of Bingham's descendants a portrait of a sleeping child (A111; plate 39) which has been called, by family tradition, a portrait of the artist's second son, Horace. It is said to have been painted in Bingham's Washington studio, and the age of the subject and the style of the painting would appear to indicate a dating about 1843/1844,[34] although we may perhaps assume that the earlier Academy version was not dissimilar in composition.

Along with the small Rollins portrait of Adams, the portrait of Horace Bingham represents another experimental study by the artist of the effects of the use of strong light and shade. The painter seems completely absorbed with the problem, apparently intrigued by the dramatic play of pattern it was possible to achieve. In this picture the head of the child is almost entirely sunk in shadow, as are the legs. Bingham was conscious of light effects on

34. Rusk, *op. cit.*, p. 30. Rusk accepted information given by Miss Laura Rollins King which indicated that the subject was portrayed in Washington at the age of six years. This is obviously incorrect, judging by the apparent age of the child in the portrait and the period of the sojourn in the capital. Horace Bingham, b. 1841, could not have been more than three years old at the time the picture was executed.

textures, too, utilizing the checked pattern of the child's dress to lend variety to the composition. The background elements are submerged in shadow, allowing the figure to dominate the scene as well as to take its proper place within its setting. A picture of great charm, notable especially for its natural-ness and ease of pose, it also marks a distinct advance in the artist's ability to cope with a variety of technical problems.

The "Landscape" sent by Bingham to the Academy exhibition marks the second indication we have recorded of his activity in this branch of painting. We recall that he mentions his landscape work while describing his efforts in St. Louis in 1835. None of these early recorded landscapes has as yet come to light.

While in Washington, although without giving his address, Bingham sub-mitted another entry to the Academy which was exhibited there in 1842—a genre picture called "Going to Market,"[35] which appears to have been keyed in the same tempo to those he sent to New York two years earlier. No one seems to have pointed to his picture as the work of an artist worthy of notice, nor had anyone done so at the 1840 show. Alfred Jacob Miller, freshly returned to the United States from his studies abroad, made some notes about the Academy show when he saw it in June, 1842: "Chapman is advancing backward, Elliott is about the best portrait painter in Gotham, between Durand and Cole in landscape it is 'nip and tuck,' to quote a Texan writer, Edmonds is promising finely. There is a 'screw loose' in Cropsey, Mount has nothing this season, Rothermel ditto, Weir ditto."[36] One cannot help feeling that perhaps Bingham was fortunate to escape the attention of this critic.

Attributed to the Washington period are two Bingham portraits that, perhaps more impressively than in the other examples discussed so far, dis-play his growing strength through almost constant study and application. Like the "Sleeping Child" and the group portrait of his wife and child, these paintings also were probably executed for his own pleasure and experiment, and possibly for exhibition. Both were radical departures from those com-missioned works we have examined, all of which had been kept within the pattern familiar to us from his earliest pictures. The paintings, said to be portraits of his wife, were conceivably painted within a short time of one another, since Elizabeth did not remain with her husband throughout his stay in Washington. The two pictures were originally three-quarter length

35. *Catalogue of the Seventeenth Annual Exhibition. 1842 . . .* (New York: E. A. Clayton, Printer, 1842), #166.
36. B. De Voto, *Across the Wide Missouri . . .* (Boston: Houghton Mifflin; Cambridge: The River-side Press, 1947), pp. 409-410.
Alfred Jacob Miller (1810-1874), b. and d., Baltimore, Md. Studied under Thomas Sully, 1831; in Paris, Rome, Florence, 1833-1834; visited England and Scotland, 1840-1842.

portraits, but one now exists only in fragmentary form, although we still have a daguerreotype taken from it (A104; plate 40), which fortunately affords us a clear impression of what the composition was like. The original fragment is in the hands of the artist's descendants. The second portrait, "The Dull Story" (A110; plate 43), is now in a private collection.

The former example represents the subject seated in profile. There is certainly no precedent for the pose in his work and he does not seem to have retained it in his repertoire thereafter. The portrait was possibly intended as an experiment, or as an exhibition piece. The additional accessories of hands and elaborate dress form a decorative composition of an unusually high quality and outrank anything of the kind he had attempted up to this time. As in the Lamme portrait, Bingham may again have used as inspiration an engraved composition known to him. In fact, an engraving after a composition by an English artist, William Fisher (plate 41), bears a striking resemblance to Bingham's composition. This resemblance also shows Bingham's more sophisticated approach through selection as well as revealing a technical ability which he so sadly lacked when he tackled the engraving after Lawrence for the Lamme group.

The artist's ever-increasing interest in light and shade and textures is again brought into focus in this portrait, visible even in the daguerreotype photograph. The entire figure is carefully composed in terms of a studied light and shade which plays up the portrait in an unusually dramatic fashion within its setting. The dress of the sitter is no longer simply an accessory, but is given the same amount of attention as the head. The resultant effect of the original must have been a wholly satisfying one to the painter.

"The Dull Story" presents an even more radical departure in Bingham's style at this period. Miss Rusk quite correctly describes this picture as one that "might quite as well be considered in the class of genre works as in that of portraiture."[37] It obviously belongs to the group of portraits bearing titles other than the names of the actual sitters which he exhibited earlier at the National Academy. In this large figure composition the artist is attracted more by the decorative and varied technical aspects of the pictorial problem than by mere likeness. For the head he adopts a more stylized portrayal somewhat reminiscent of the Sully formula, which he would have had a greater opportunity of studying at close range by this time. The high pitch of the color is also related to the method of the Philadelphia master. The dozing figure is well composed, with light, color, and textures all utilized to form one of the artist's richest and most attractive designs. As in the instance of the profile portrait of his wife, he evidently did not repeat the composition

37. Rusk, *op. cit.*, p. 28.

again. The subject idea was not necessarily an original one with Bingham, however, and may indeed have occurred to him once more through the engraved reproduction. An engraving called "Love Asleep," based on a painting after Gilbert Stuart Newton, which was probably published in a gift annual, a source of reference already used by Bingham,[38] reveals much the same motif and a very similar composition.

At least one published account of the Washington period gives us a fascinating glimpse of Bingham's activity in an area quite unrelated to portraiture:

He [Bingham] is a portrait painter of fine promise, but occasionally throws off fancy pictures of great merit. Among these is his Ariadne on canvass, of the kit-kat size.

This copy is made from a beautiful engraving of Durand, after the celebrated original of Vanderlyn, and does great credit to Mr. Bingham's capacity. He has caught the spirit of the history of Ariadne ere she wakes from her sweet dream of love and confidence in her Athenian lover. I would advise all admirers of sweet painting to call at his room in the basement story of the Capitol, where this picture is at present exhibited.[39]

Although John Vanderlyn's "Ariadne," and Asher B. Durand's engraving based upon it, were already well known to the art public, it seems conceivable that the reporter's somewhat inspired description of the picture and its subject still could have drawn many curious sightseers from the upper floors of the Capitol. Perhaps this was exactly what the painter had in mind when he painted this "fancy" subject, the original of which, owing to the nude condition of the central figure, having become one of the most sensational pictures of its kind in America. Bingham occasionally made sketches of the nude female figure, generally derived from classical and Renaissance sources, but insofar as we know, painted only one other picture in which the nude played a leading role.[40] Such occasional forays into this special field seem never to have been destined for anything more than purely private exhibition.

38. *The Atlantic Souvenir; a Christmas and New Year's Offering, 1829* (Philadelphia: Carey, Lea & Carey [*ca.* 1828], opp. p. 20.
39. *Daily National Intelligencer* (Washington), Feb. 17, 1841, 3-5.
40. A "Bathing Girl," described as "a girl at the side of a forest stream ready for a bath" *(Kansas City Star*, March 18, 1893) and in an inventory of the artist's estate as "Musidora about to take a bath," was in the Bingham studio at the time of his death in 1879. It could have been, like the "Ariadne," a copy after Asher B. Durand's engraving of "Musidora," but it was more likely a version by Bingham of the popular subject, executed for his own pleasure. There is evidently considerable precedence for this private practice: in 1835 Thomas Sully completed a copy of a nude "Musidora" (coll. Metropolitan Museum of Art) which was based on C. R. Leslie's copy made after Benjamin West's original version of the subject. The Rollins scrapbook (coll. SHSMo) contains several drawings of the nude by Bingham, including one obviously based on the classical Venus de' Medici, and a similar classic figure type shown seated "at the side of a forest stream," conceivably "ready for a bath," either of which, or both, could have been preliminary thoughts for the now lost "Musidora." In the same collection are a nude "Danae," after Titian, and two studies of a sleeping, reclining figure. Most of these sketches were in all probability derived from drawing books which contained several nude models, taken from Classical and Renaissance sources, intended to serve the artistic needs of students of all ages.

Despite his occasional excursions into other fields, Bingham still devoted his major energies to portrait painting during this period. The taking of likenesses was, after all, his one sure means of a livelihood. In this connection, the American Art-Union biography informs us that Bingham spent four years in Washington "with the exception of six months passed in Petersburg, Virginia."[41] A Petersburg reporter brings us closer to the situation, both in terms of date and purpose of the visit: "Mr. Bingham, Portrait Painter, from Washington City, has executed some uncommonly happy likenesses here. His room is at Sycamore Street, near Swan's Bookstore. Those who have a taste for the fine arts, will do well to call and look at Mr. Bingham's work—some of his likenesses are inimitable."[42]

Among those "inimitable" likenesses are a group of portraits of the Heath family which were unquestionably painted in Petersburg at this time. The finest of the group is that of Mrs. Hartwell Peebles Heath (Elizabeth Anne Cureton Rives) (A100; plate 42), in which the artist develops a highly decorative and somewhat original composition within a formal pattern that is still reminiscent of such Missouri portraits as those of Eliza Pulliam Shackelford and Mary Wilkinson Darby. The portraits of the Heath children show an increased understanding of the special problems involved in painting the very young. The oval portrait of Anna Rives Heath (A103; plate 44) has a particular charm in its representation of a child in fancy dress holding a basket of flowers. The artist's obvious concern with the problems of light and shade and color used to effect a deepening impression of three-dimensionality is clearly in evidence here.

41. *Bull. AAU*, II (Aug., 1849), 11.
42. *Statesman* (Petersburg), June 18, 1841.

VI

GENRE PAINTING: THE EMERGENCE OF "THE MISSOURI ARTIST" (1838-1857)

How Bingham came to choose the local scene for his chief artistic direction is not known, nor do we get any clue from his letters or other writings. Contemporary and more recent biographers of the artist seem not to have considered the matter. We must therefore resort to conjecture, but happily this important point can be considered, and perhaps even resolved, from one or more viewpoints.

There is certainly no pictorial evidence extant to demonstrate that the artist seriously considered painting the local scene, or entering any other area of painting except portraiture, prior to his visit to Philadelphia in 1838. From the practical standpoint, there had been no encouragement for him to try his talents in other directions. He had to earn his livelihood by painting the type of picture most in demand in his part of the country, namely portraits, and he had to develop his skill in that field. There was little time to experiment, although he must have been aware of the developing interest in genre pictures in the East through the engravings then available after paintings by Wilkie, Leslie, and Hogarth, as well as by seventeenth-century Dutch masters. Copies of Dutch genre pictures were also to be found in St. Louis, and at least one Missouri contemporary, Pomarede, painted the local scene. Bingham himself reported from St. Louis as early as December, 1835, that he had painted, as a commission, copies of pictures of buffalo hunts,[1] our first indication that he had ever executed anything except portraits up to that time.

Nevertheless, it was the stay in the East that seems to have stimulated him to turn to genre painting. The opportunity to observe the work of his contemporaries at close range must have given considerable impetus to his

1. B. to S. E. H., letter, St. Louis, Mo., Dec. 16, 1835, and p. 26 above, note 48.

68

change in subject matter. William Sidney Mount had already established a reputation for himself as a painter of the local scene and was being hailed as the "American Wilkie." Mount transferred to canvas in a lively and skillful way those scenes which were most familiar to him, mainly scenes associated with the day-to-day existence of the Long Island farmer. The generally enthusiastic criticism in the press that greeted each new Mount production, as well as the accompanying praise accorded him by his fellow painters, could have played a strong role in bringing Bingham's attention to this as yet unexplored area in his own work. Portrait painting was, and would always continue to be, "pot-boiling" for him, and if he was to develop in his profession, it would have to be in an area that was far less competitive.

Mount's simple storytelling pictures of a life he loved and with which he was most familiar must have touched off the spark in Bingham's own imagination which led to his own concentration on subjects equally beloved by him—subjects indelibly stamped in his memory from childhood and actual experience and through an already rich tradition of folklore. Mount's subjects depicted farming people at work or play; they were anecdotes simply told, always slightly humorous, but never controversial, and never satirical. In this approach Mount was close to Wilkie, although Wilkie tends to veil his storytelling with a play of sentiment which seems to complicate the central subject. Mount takes over Wilkie's understanding of the value of the gesture and expression in storytelling, although he limits his theme more than his English counterpart, as he does his approach to composition and technique. Although Mount seems to have paid special attention to the work of Hogarth, that artist's bitterly critical commentary on life of his time was an approach completely foreign to the genial Mount.

Bingham's work was to become more controversial as he developed, for his was the kind of personality that must have understood at once the weapon his brush could easily become, but it may have been the sight of the gay and relaxed types portrayed by Mount that touched a sympathetic chord in his imagination, starting a trend in his work which was to become the artistic contribution for which he would be best known.

In his genre subjects it was only natural for Bingham to turn to those themes that depicted the life he knew best. It was also the right moment for him to proceed freely in this direction. With the rise of the Jacksonian democracy in the 1830's, accompanied by the growth of a comfortable bourgeois class, came an interest in art beyond mere face-painting—one that looked more to a portrayal of American history and life. Pride was taken in seeing illustrated, for all the world to see, those everyday aspects of life, the individuality of which was so specifically American. Bingham was a

69

product of such an environment and needed but slight encouragement from such a patronage. And he needed little to follow the dictates that Mount had set for himself: "Follow the bent of your own mind—do not paint to order. Please yourself as to subject. When I painted to please myself I was myself—when one paints to order he sells his birthright."[2]

Bingham's earliest impressions as a backwoods frontier boy were of the boatmen, traders, and trappers. When he sought to turn from portraiture to a new field of self-expression, it was natural that he would seek to depict on canvas the life he knew and understood so well. His was a deeply rooted urge to illustrate those characteristics of western frontier existence that were basic and typical rather than to give a portrayal of those more melodramatic moments, so often bordering on the fictional, that were depicted by some of his fellow artists. In this attitude he was akin to William Sidney Mount, whose chief and enduring quality was his ability to represent the rural life he loved in a simple and characteristic fashion. Like Mount, Bingham's individuality and strength lay in the virile realism he was able to bring to his portrayals of the local scene, and like his eastern counterpart, he was also able to avoid the sentimental vein that is so frequently a trademark of the genre painter of the period. In this, Mount's credo could well have been his own. "I shall endeavor to copy nature as I have tried to do with truth and soberness. . . ."[3]

It was the right moment, too, for the appearance of Bingham's honest and lively depictions. The reading public had been prepared for it through a growing literature on the West which began to appear during the late 'twenties and early 'thirties. Some of the country's leading writers—Irving, Cooper, Whittier, and Longfellow—had described Indian life and border warfare in prose and verse. Bryant's *Prairies* had been described as a "prophetic prelude to the march of mankind toward the lands of the setting sun."[4] John J. Audubon, Edmund Flagg, Timothy Flint, and Basil Hall were among those who recorded aspects of western life from the standpoint of the reporter, which could have helped to persuade Bingham that the time was at hand to take the step of translating the written word into the pictorial dimension. Indeed, in discussing Bingham's contribution, it was recently stated that his pictures "might have been illustrations for the *Episodes* of Audubon."[5]

2. M. B. Cowdrey and H. W. Williams, *William Sidney Mount, 1807-1868; An American Painter . . .*, p. 10.
3. *Ibid.*
4. S. G. W. Benjamin, *Art in America; A Critical and Historical Sketch . . .* (New York: Harper, 1880), p. 88.
5. Van Wyck Brooks, *The World of Washington Irving* (New York: Dutton, 1944), p. 370.

We have already noted that Bingham's first excursion into the field of western genre was a picture he painted during his stay in Philadelphia in 1838. It was also his first recorded appearance in a public show. The painting was exhibited at James Herring's newly established "permanent Gallery for the exhibition and sale of Paintings, Statuary, and Engravings in the City of New-York,"[6] and appeared on the walls of the Apollo Gallery during October of that year. The picture, entitled "Western Boatmen Ashore," suggests by its title a type of composition not too far removed from the boatmen scenes the artist was to develop in the future, although seven years were to elapse before another of the series was to make its appearance in a public exhibition. Instead, as we have observed, the artist apparently deliberately avoided the western scene, preferring to send less picturesque genre and landscape efforts to New York's National Academy of Design. The Apollo Gallery picture does not appear to have received critical notice and probably did not find a purchaser. This lack of encouragement, together with the strong possibility that his own lack of facility was brought home to him in this first experience in competition with artists already eminent—men such as Thomas Birch, John G. Chapman, Daniel Huntington, Emanuel Leutze, Rembrandt Peale, Thomas Sully, and John Trumbull—could easily have halted his efforts in a special line for the time being.

We have as yet no specific indication, through available documentation, of the immediate impetus that started Bingham on his career as a painter of the western scene. We can only make some general observations based upon the circumstances of the time that would have encouraged a creative talent. Certainly Bingham's personal attitude toward his work must now have been one of greater confidence in his ability to handle the varied technical problems of painting beyond the limited field of portraiture which, up to this time, had so actively determined an American artist's way to success. In speaking of the period following the Washington sojourn, the biographical account of 1849 tells us that "having returned to Missouri, he was induced to attempt those delineations of western life, as exhibited among boatmen and pioneers."[7] Elsewhere in the same account, discussing the "material assistance" the Art-Union afforded the artist, we are informed that "indeed,

6. M. B. Cowdrey, *American Academy of Fine Arts and American Art-Union* (New York: New-York Historical Society, 1953), I, 98.
7. *Bull. AAU,* II (Aug., 1849), 11. Bingham's return to St. Louis was duly noted in newsprint. He was already dubbed "The Missouri Artist." Although mention was made of "some fancy sketches, and some paintings which demonstrate the possession of a high order of talent" in an area other than portraiture, the reporter's enthusiasm was nevertheless reserved for his work as a portrait painter—Bingham being described as "one of the most faithful delineators of the human face we know of." To his work in "another line" (presumably genre) it was believed that he had not yet "devoted a large share of his time" *(Daily Missouri Republican* [St. Louis], June 4, 1845, 2-2).

according to his [Bingham's] own statement, if it had not been bestowed, he would never perhaps have attempted that peculiar class of subjects which have given him all his reputation."[8]

Certainly Bingham could in all sincerity acknowledge his "indebtedness" to the American Art-Union as the "first patron of his higher efforts, and his main-stay in all attempts beyond the line of portraiture."[9] The first paintings depicting western scenes and manners which were conceived and executed by him during the latter part of 1844 and the early months of 1845 were submitted to the Art-Union for sale. The Union readily purchased them for the 1845 distribution and, in the years that followed, until its dissolution, continued to encourage Bingham by its patronage. By 1847 the Art-Union had honored him by engraving one of his pictures for distribution to its vast membership, thereby affording him an opportunity for national recognition. And his fame on a national scale was also furthered somewhat through the special notices given him in the Art-Union's *Bulletin*—the kind of publicity he was able to earn hitherto in a limited way only, on home ground.[10]

The American Art-Union, with its headquarters in New York City, was formerly known as The Apollo Association, which was in turn an outgrowth of the Apollo Gallery to which Bingham sent a picture for exhibition in the fall of 1838. The Gallery's system of demanding no commission from the artists and no fee "to keep specimens before the public,"[11] inviting them to contribute only the loan of their paintings until they were sold from the walls of the gallery, brought an immediate and popular response from the artists themselves, who readily appreciated the chance the gallery gave them for unlimited exhibition and the possible sale of their work. The idea was to promote and widen patronage for the artists and to provide increased opportunities for sale. These were benefits the founder of the gallery understood only too well, being an artist himself. The National Academy's system arranged for an exhibition that lasted "about eight weeks,"[12] but most of the works were lent from private collections, and it has been estimated that "hardly more than fifty"[13] works a year were listed in the catalogues as being for sale. Unfortunately, however, the Apollo Gallery's enterprising

8. *Bull. AAU*, II (Aug., 1849), 10.
9. *Ibid.*, II (Oct., 1849), 12.
10. Bingham evidently placed considerable value on such notices and carefully scrutinized the *Bulletin* for mentions of his work. On one occasion, however, he took so great an exception to an unfavorable notice that he threatened to bring suit (Bingham to A. Warner, Corresponding Secretary of the AAU, letters, St. Louis, Mo., Jan. 31 and March 1, 1852; Warner to Bingham, letter, New York, Feb. 16, 1852, coll. NYHS. Re article: W., "Development of Nationality in American Art," *Bull. AAU* [Dec., 1851], 137-139).
11. Cowdrey, *American Academy . . .*, I, 98.
12. *Ibid.*, p. 96.
13. *Ibid.*

plan did not bring the ready sale to the works of art on exhibition that was hoped for, and the sales of admission tickets failed to keep up with running expenses. It was at that point that James Herring, knowing of the success of the Art-Union plans abroad, called a meeting at his gallery early in 1839, "for the purpose of considering a plan of operation for the promotion of the Fine Arts in the United States."[14] Thus was formed The Apollo Association.

The organization, later called the American Art-Union, sincerely devoted itself to "a philanthropic and patriotic desire to foster American Art through (1) the financial and moral encouragement of producing artists and (2) the aesthetic education of the public."[15] In a more specific way the Constitution of the Art-Union provided that:

The net funds of the institution (accumulated through membership subscriptions of five dollars a year) shall be applied *first*, to the purchase or production of fine Engravings, or other Works of American Art, annually, which shall be distributed equally to all members for each year respectively. Second, to the purchase or production of Works of American Art [principally paintings] to be distributed publicly at the annual meeting among all members for the year, by lot, each member having one share for every five dollars paid by him. By works of American Art, are meant the works of Artists resident in the United States, or American Artists abroad.[16]

The Art-Union went further than the Apollo Gallery in not only affording the artist a chance to exhibit and sell his work but giving his situation a greater dignity and stability through a definite patronage which could now encourage his further efforts, provide him with direction in terms of his life and work, and help to establish his position for the future, as well as benefiting the buying public. The security gained through the Art-Union's patronage gave many an artist the encouragement he sorely needed to develop his talent, which might otherwise have remained dormant, or even been destroyed. For Bingham, the encouragement that greeted the first efforts he submitted to the organization persuaded him to lay aside his "pot-boiling" portrait activities and to progress in a direction closer to his heart.

POLITICAL BANNERS

Although not to be considered within the central core of Bingham's production as a painter of genre, at least one area of his work, designed by him primarily for political propaganda purposes, bears enough of the subject character that suggests genre to be considered in that context, if only at the perimeter. Chronologically, it appears just ahead of his most prolific period

14. *Ibid.*, p. 100.
15. *Ibid.*, p. 103.
16. *Charter and Constitution of the American Art-Union; and By-Laws of the Committee of Management* (New York: G. F. Nesbitt, Stationer and Printer, 1848), pp. 7-8.

as a genre painter, thus serving as a valuable keynote to the important decade to follow.

This field of work was the painting of processional banners for political conventions held in Bingham's home state. Our first indication of such activity has already been noted in connection with a Whig banner he is known to have executed for Saline County for the presidential convention held at Rocheport, Missouri, in June, 1840.[17] Of this earlier work we have only a description,[18] but it includes sufficient detail to illustrate the artist's serious and conceivably deliberate attempt to demonstrate in such public display his developing ability to cope with varied aspects of painting beyond portraiture. The elaborate design obviously included, aside from the portrait of the candidate with accompanying inscription and symbols testifying to his virtues, a large landscape of specific western character, as well as vignettes in which elements of genre connotation were included. Despite the temporary character of these commissions, Bingham evidently devoted considerable effort to the work, without doubt realizing full well the prestige potential of such an outdoor exhibition. This can be readily borne out by the considerable attention given to the banner in the public press. The reporter not only described the work in terms of its content but took special note of the quality of the execution, giving full credit to the artist as well.

Four years later, when Bingham was commissioned to paint banners for the Whig convention to be held at Boonville in October, 1844, in favor of Henry Clay for president, he was thus entirely familiar with the requirements of the work. With the benefit of some years of painting experiences in the East behind him, he could now enter with much greater confidence than before into the competition that must have existed among the various artists employed by the counties represented at the convention. One can assume that the ability of an artist was certainly put to the test to produce an effective and eye-catching design, and that his standing in the community and state could very well depend upon the amount of care and skill he expended in

17. See chap. v, note 11.
18. *Daily Commercial Bulletin* (St. Louis), June 22, 1840, 2-1: "Most of the delegations bore appropriate banners but those from Saline and Lafayette counties appeared to excite the most interest. One of the banners from Saline, was gotten up by Mr. Bingham, well known in this city as an artist of great talent, and its whole execution reflected the highest credit on his genius. Upon its front was a portrait of Gen. Harrison, mounted upon a marble pedestal, inscribed, Commerce, Agriculture and the Arts, in union we will cherish them; at the base of the pedestal lies the Constitution, with mechanical and artists instruments. On the left is the battle of the Thames, Harrison and his aids [*sic*] occupying the foreground. On the right is a log cabin boy with his plough, and a log cabin in the back-ground. In the rear, a river of the West with a canoe: surmounting the six feet square of canvass, waves a banner inscribed with the words 'our country.'"

these productions. In a revealing letter to his friend Rollins regarding a banner for his delegation, Bingham clearly indicates his concern with the quality of his work, significantly developing his ideas less in terms of the temporary character than from the aesthetic viewpoint, emphasizing primarily his desire to use a more permanent material to ensure "an effective picture," and then intimating the value of his effort in terms of possible future conservation:

... With reference to the banner which you desire for your delegation to the convention, I can merely state, that I shall be happy to execute it, provided you allow me to paint it on linnen [sic], the only material on which I can make an effective picture.

I am now just beginning one for Cooper, and one for Howard, each 7 by 8 feet—on one I shall give a full length portrait of Clay as the Statesman with his American System operating in the distance, on the other I shall represent him as the plain farmer of Ashland—each of them will also have appropriate designs on the reverse side, and will be so suspended, as to be eisily [sic] borne by four men walking in the order of the procession. The cost will be from fifty to sixty dollars each.

They will be substantial oil pictures and may be preserved as relics of the present political campaign. If your delegation would be pleased with a similar banner as "Old Hal" is already fully appropriated, I would suggest for the design as peculiarly applicable to your county, old Daniel Boone himself engaged in one of his death struggles with an Indian, painted as large as life, it would make a picture that would take with the multitude, and also be in accordance with historical truth. It might be emblimatical [sic] also of the early state of the west, while on the other side I might paint a landscape with "peaceful fields and lowing herds" indicative of his present advancement in civilization.

It should be full as large as those I am preparing for Cooper and Howard and borne in the procession in like manner. If you approve of my suggestions or see proper to make others, write to me as soon as possible, as I shall have but little time to spare....

P.S. On the reverse side of the Howard banner I intended to portray a large buffaloe [sic] just broken loose from his keepers making the poke stalks fly to the right and left in the fury of his unbridled career.[19]

It is interesting to note the rapidity with which Bingham executed the banners, despite the serious consideration he gave to the ambitious designs and the technical handling. With the convention a little more than two weeks away, the artist speaks of "just beginning" one of the banners, a work "7 x 8 feet," while another, of similar size, and yet another, remain to be done. At the same time he is prepared to accept one more commission, to be completed within the same period! This is a characteristic of Bingham which we shall find to be an important consideration in the dating of his pictures, and one to which we shall return again during our discussion of his later works. Once the design was organized in his mind and perhaps worked out as a

19. Letter, Boonville, Mo., Sept. 23, 1844, coll. SHSMo (MHR. XXXII [1937], 13-14).

preliminary sketch, the actual execution almost always proceeded with despatch.

The Boonville Convention was evidently a gala affair. The *Boonville Observer*'s reporter vividly described the events, allowing considerable space to a description of the banners which gives us a further indication of the careful attention given to such works by the spectators:

The 10th and 11th days of October 1844 were days long to be remembered by the gallant Whigs of Missouri, and will be refered [*sic*] to in future as the days on which assembled in *our* city the most glorious Convention that our State has ever witnessed. . . .

As early as the 8th the Delegates commenced coming in, and by the evening of the 9th the City was crowded to overflowing, all the hotels in the city and every private house into which admittance could be obtained, were literally cramed [*sic*]. On the morning of the 10th at an early hour, the thundering of the cannon commenced. At sun rise the National salute was fired; and shortly after the crowd commenced being swelled by the pouring in of new delegations from all quarters, and in the course of a few hours the streets presented an almost solid mass of people.

On the 9th the streets were very dry, the dust was almost beyond enduring and all were wishing for rain. When they arose in the morning to their surprise they found their wishes gratified with a fine shower which had fallen during the night.

The rain continued to fall during the morning of the 10th, which caused some delay in forming the procession, but towards noon it cleared off and the procession was formed and passed to the stand in the southern skirts of the city, in the following order as nearly as we can remember; First, the splendid band of music from the Jefferson Barracks. Next the Pilot Grove and Pisgah Rangers, an independent cavalry company.

Then the immense delegation from Howard, bearing a most splendid banner, on one side of which our noble champion is represented advocating the "American System." "All the great interests" of America are here represented. On one hand is a fortress with our National flag waving above it; on the other, and to the rearward is the ocean, crowded with shipping, and farther in the front is a farmer with his plough, a railroad, a number of dingy manufacturing establishments, the capital and other national buildings, while Mr. Clay, with his hand extended towards them, exclaims in his own impressive manner, "All these great interests are confided to the protection and care of government!"—The portrait of Mr. Clay as well as the entire picture, is an admirable specimen of painting, and both as to design and execution is highly creditable to the artist. On the reverse side of the banner is represented a prairie, in its uncultivated state, with a herd of buffalo roving across it. . . .

Next came the Washington Delegation bearing a beautiful banner, on one side representing the miners working their iron and lead mines. On the reverse side is a representation of commerce, manufacture and agriculture, with Henry Clay in the midst. . . .

The Boston delegation came next, bearing quite a humorous banner. A coon is represented snugly seated on a limb of a sturdy old Ash, while a crowd of men below are vainly endeavoring to beat him down with poke stalks. . . .

Next came the Boone delegation, bearing a handsomely painted banner.—Device:

on one side a large fat coon, rolling a ball over a cluster of poke stalks; on the reverse side: a waggon [sic], driven by Polk, containing three individuals, including the driver, and drawn by a poor old horse that is just ready to break down; over which is inscribed, "Bound for Texas." . . . And finally came the Ashland Club—composed of the young men of Boonville—and the Boonville Clay Club. The Ashland Club bore decidedly the most beautiful banner we have ever seen. On one side was represented the plain, unaustentatious [sic] but noble farmer of Ashland on his farm; on the reverse side is an Eagle perched high on a firm, immovable rock. The banner is without lettering—save the name of the Club—the devices alone being sufficiently significant. The Juvenile Club also bore a most beautiful banner; on one side of which is repre sented a mill-boy riding merrily through the slashes of Hanover to mill; on the reverse side is a little fellow carving the name of Henry Clay. A mere description of the devices on these banners, however, conveys no idea of their real beauty. They, as also the Howard banner, were painted by Mr. Bingham, a noble young artist of this city.[20]

Bingham was thus responsible for half of the pictorial display used in the procession. As the Boone County banner was not attributed to Bingham by the convention reporter and his description of it does not fit the subject Bingham suggested for it in his letter to Rollins, we must assume that the Boone County commission was awarded to another painter.

The disposition and fate of the banners executed by Bingham at this time has been investigated by local historians through the years. A report con cluding that all of the paintings had been destroyed by fire[21] may be at least partly true, for the Howard and Cooper County Ashland Club banners are now lost. That the Howard banner suffered a fate other than burning on the night after the procession is reported in the same issue of the *Boonville Observer*:

On last Friday night [October 11] some villain went into the courthouse where the whig banners were placed, and cut several gashes in the portrait of Mr. Clay, on the Howard banner. One gash, several inches in length was cut across the throat. Our opponents must be very much pushed for some method of venting their spleen against Mr. Clay and the Whigs when they resort to such meanness. . . . Mr. Clay was repre sented as delivering one of his most eloquent and patriotic speeches in behalf of the American interests; and while so doing he is now represented as being assassinated![22]

Within recent years, however, a chance discovery of mine in a private collec tion in Columbia, Missouri, brought to light a painting by Bingham which closely adheres to the description of the Boonville Juvenile Clay Club banner and is without doubt one of the long-sought campaign pictures (A116; plate 45). The picture represents Henry Clay as "a mill-boy riding merrily through the slashes of Hanover to mill" and is painted on canvas, following the

20. *The Boonville Observer*, Oct. 15, 1844, 2-1.
21. C. B. Rollins, "Some Recollections of George Caleb Bingham," *MHR*, XX (1926), 471.
22. *The Boonville Observer*, Oct. 15, 1844, 2-3.

provision required by the artist in his letter to Rollins. When I first examined the canvas it was crudely mounted on stretchers, and in a torn and grimy state, revealing through overlaps above and below that it had been cut down at some later period, although still of substantial dimensions. It has since been restored.

More important to us than even the interesting historical connotation of the picture is its position as perhaps the first Bingham painting bearing in its subject and treatment those characteristics we usually assign to genre. It is the earliest key, other than documentary, that remains at present to indicate the painter's ever-growing technical competence and preparation for the very special problem of the storytelling type of picture.

From a technical standpoint "The Mill Boy" affords us a glimpse of Bingham's achievement which would not have been exposed on an academy exhibition level because of its apparent lack of "finish." From our standpoint, however, it affords us an extremely valuable impression of his basic development at that time. The painting, treated in terms of broad masses of tone and colors, is left without that final layer of paint which eliminated all traces of the underlying brushwork, a phase of procedure that was almost a requisite of the American and European "salon" painter. Undoubtedly the pressure of work for the Convention made it impossible for the artist to carry his pictures to their final phase, nor was it practical or necessarily a requirement to create the desired effect.

"The Mill Boy" reveals the tremendous strides the artist had made since his early Missouri years. The constant application and observation, more acutely developed since his study in the East, and the possible contacts he may have been able to make with some of his contemporaries, together with the greater awareness of the value of published technical source material, all obviously played their parts in bringing the painter toward a maturity in the field. His own awareness of his early deficiencies and his deliberate attempts to overcome them have been clearly visible in our examination of his work. He was especially conscious of the intricate problems of light and shade, and we have already seen how he attempted to deal with their varying aspects from the first steps taken at Philadelphia to the more dramatic effects he exploited at Washington. That the artist had developed a more knowing and mature painterly approach to the problem becomes immediately visible in "The Mill Boy."

The little figure of the boy, moving toward the observer on his pony, is painted almost completely in shadow, the light striking him from the upper left and slightly behind him. All about the lone figure on horseback appears a broad landscape, with only the briefest indications of foliage and a section

78

of fence or stile to suggest locale. Not even a cloud appears to interrupt the bold silhouette of the central subject against its air-filled background. The almost impressionistic light and the artist's unhesitant and knowing handling of the problem is immediately brought home to the observer, particularly in the direct and bold brushwork of the head.

The charming head of the boy (plate 46) gives us no clue to the individualistic types Bingham was to affect in his genre subjects within the year to follow. This head is still reminiscent of Thomas Sully's types and, curiously enough, there is an undeniably close resemblance to Sully's "The Torn Hat" (plate 47) in both subject and the treatment of light.

One cannot say that "The Mill Boy" prepares us for the series of paintings Bingham was to produce so shortly afterward, but it does fill in a gap left by the now vanished recorded work of 1838, 1840, and 1842 in the field of genre and landscape. It also permits us to form a clearer impression of his increasing ability to deal in a mature way with the work that was to set him apart in his profession.

Fur Traders and Trappers

A large proportion of Bingham's genre subjects touched upon scenes of activity on the Mississippi and Missouri rivers, particularly those emphasizing the role of the boatman in his most picturesque and varied everyday capacities. The artist undoubtedly knew river life well through personal experience, and desired to record those aspects of it that he recalled as a boy—a vivid life which was fast disappearing by the mid-forties along with the development of steamboat traffic. Such subjects were bound to be popular with the public, for by that time a considerable amount of literature had already appeared which described in detail the peculiar characteristics of those people who depended on the river for their livelihood. We must not discount the facts that the artist was also conscious of the public interest in western lore and there was likely to be a popular demand for accurate illustrations of those scenes and characters described by travelers.

Of the four pictures that Bingham submitted to the American Art-Union in 1845, all purchased and distributed by the Union late in December of that year,[23] two were western genre subjects, one a river scene depicting two figures in a dugout entitled "Fur Traders Descending the Missouri" (A136; plate 50). The latter painting had been acquired by the Art-Union for $75 and was awarded to Robert S. Bunker, a member from Mobile, Alabama. It afterward descended in the family of the original owner until 1933, when

23. *Transactions of the American Art-Union, for the Year 1845* (New York: printed at the Office of the Evening Post [1846], #93, 95, 98, 102.

it was acquired by the Metropolitan Museum of Art. The painting is particularly significant to this study as one of the earliest in a long series of
representations of western subjects that Bingham sent to the Art-Union for
sale and public exhibition. It was with this picture and its companions that
the artist was to announce his entrance into the art world of the East as a
mature painter, taking his place beside his contemporaries, and, perhaps
more specifically, as a factual illustrator of the western scene.

It had been only a few years since Washington Irving had written and
published his fascinating book *Astoria*,[24] a work based largely on the records
of the American Fur Company, the documentation for which had been made
available to him by John Jacob Astor. In the book Irving had noted that
"singular aquatic race that had grown up from the navigation of the rivers—
the 'boatmen of the Mississippi,' who possessed habits, manners, and almost
a language, peculiarly their own, and strongly technical."[25] His description
of the French fur traders and the colorful anecdotes of their lives and
exploits, interspersed with the history of the fur company, present an
intriguing picture of a race of unusual characters dating from a transient
era in western history which called forth the illustrator. Indeed, Bingham's
"Fur Traders Descending the Missouri" could have served as an illustration
for *Astoria*.

Irving described at length the lives of the French traders at St. Louis,
particularly those who had intermarried with the Indians. He presented a
lively picture of Dorion, a fur trader whose father had been with Lewis and
Clark and whose mother was an Indian, himself married to a Sioux squaw
and raising a large family of his own. Bingham could actually have had this
story in mind when he executed the picture. At any rate, the painting was
sent to the Art-Union for consideration under the pointedly significant,
although less appealing title: "French Trader and his Half-breed Son."[26]

It can be assumed that, by selecting the fur-trader motif as his first bid for
Art-Union patronage and for a subsequent appearance before the New York
art critics, Bingham was aware of the probable popular appeal of the subject
and that the way was clear for a factual illustrator of the western scene. He
must have been conscious of the immense appeal of Catlin's accurate pictorial
recordings of the Indian, and, like him, may have realized that his great
opportunity for public recognition lay in making full use of his visual
experience to present the typical aspects of western life and manners and to

24. W. Irving, *Astoria, or Anecdotes of an Enterprise Beyond the Rocky Mountains....* Philadelphia:
Carey, Lea, & Blanchard, 1836. 2 vols.
25. *Ibid.*, I, 141.
26. AAU minutes of meeting, Dec. 8, 1845, coll. NYHS.

depict the unusual characteristics of those individuals who inhabited the rivers, prairies, and inland towns. From the beginning he deliberately avoided presentation of the single or fleeting action of the hunt or the attack; instead, he concentrated always on the more usual and descriptive. Perhaps the Art-Union itself had indicated this direction. In one letter of advice to an artist, the Corresponding Secretary pointed out that the Art-Union was more inclined toward pictures, "taken from the every day scenes of life, those that are not suggestive of, or create painful emotions. . . . Anything, however, that illustrates our country; history or its poetry. . . ."[27]

Apart from the attention that Bingham must have given to the presentation of the picture from the point of view of its reception as a subject, we are even more consciously aware, upon examining it, of the consummate care he took in the preparation of his composition in an effort to create the proper concentration and mood. The considered plotting of every line, which was to remain the dominant characteristic of all his genre painting, is never more effectively realized than in the Metropolitan Museum's "Fur Traders Descending the Missouri." In this picture he has gained a harmony of mood through a happy coördination of line and color which even masters of the craft seldom achieve.

The composition presents a dugout moving downstream, with an old French trader paddling in the stern. His son is shown amidships, leaning on the cargo. A captive fox is chained to the bow. All three are turned to face the spectator, a characteristic the artist was to use consistently in his genre pictures and one which recalls his early portraits (it is also somewhat reminiscent of one of Marcantonio Raimondi's best-known engravings after Raphael[28] and of paintings by the brothers Le Nain[29]).

Concentration within the composition is held entirely to the figures of the fur trader and his son, the inclined backs of the pair combining to suggest a triangle or pyramid. The lines thus obtained are echoed in the movement of the trader's paddle and the shapes are reëchoed in the water's reflections. The vertical line formed by the fox and its enforced reflection seems to create the desired balance at left. The figures are decisively drawn and appear

27. A. Warner to Frederick E. Cohen, letter, New York, Aug. 12, 1848, coll. NYHS. Cohen was active in Detroit from 1837 to 1855. Two of his pictures were purchased and distributed by the AAU in 1848.

28. The group at right in the "Judgment of Paris" (B. 245). The classical balance of the group recalls compositions by Bingham, and variations of the poses of the figures at right and left are also found in his pictures, although the inspiration may not have been a direct one. The same detail was to have a much more direct influence on Edouard Manet's "Le Déjeuner sur l'Herbe," 1862-63 (Musée du Jeu de Paume, Paris).

29. For example, paintings by Louis Le Nain (d. 1648): "The Truck" and "The Forge" (Louvre, Paris).

81

in bold relief against the suffused landscape backdrop. Indeed, the bright light that illuminates and brings the figures into such sharp focus that even the striped shirts are clearly defined is in direct conflict with the impression of the hazy atmosphere that hangs over the scene. The artist, still concerned with the study of light, was as yet unable to unite his figures and landscape in terms of an atmospheric light, a characteristic failing that was to dominate his work during this early period. The palette he adopted is high-pitched and generally warm, with pinks and light blues in the ascendant.

The care given this composition suggests that it is not only highly likely that Bingham studied the works of his contemporaries and referred to engravings after old masters but that he also took to heart some of the more important published treatises on the subject. The integration of the two figures into a pyramidal form cannot be considered accidental here; and later, more deliberate instances, will bear out clearly the artist's adherence to a formula he could have learned from the instruction books. One of the best known of such treatises, by Samuel Prout, had stated: "*Triangular* or *pyramidal* composition, has been selected . . . as exemplifying a principle easily understood. It is applicable to almost every variety of subject, and is perhaps, hardly ever unpleasant to the eye; it may be adapted to advantage where the subject will admit of it, but as there cannot be any general rule, the taste of the artist will be the best and sufficient guide." [30]

An interesting parallel to the Bingham composition of the "Fur Traders," and an ideal pendant to it, is William Sidney Mount's "Eel Spearing at Setauket" (plate 49), completed the same year but not exhibited until the year following. [31] The aims of the two men were never closer in terms of mood and concentration, as well as in characterization. There are similarities in composition, too, with Mount also attempting to fix the spectator's attention on two figures in a small open boat by making use of the triangular or pyramidal motif to unify the pair. He uses the device, however, in a bolder manner than his still unpracticed western contemporary—the lines of the long pole and the oar forming the more obvious geometric shape which is enforced through the reflections in the water. We have already noted Mount's reliance on information contained in the instruction books. [32]

Bingham was consciously a craftsman and, like Mount, must have made many preliminary trial studies for his compositions. As evidenced in the

30. Samuel Prout, *Hints on Light and Shadow, Composition* . . . (London: M. A. Nattali, 1848), p. 11.
31. Exhibited at the National Academy of Design, 1846, #131, as "Early Recollections of Early Days—'Fishing Along Shore.'"
32. See chap. iv, notes 21-23. A more immediate inspiration to Mount, both in terms of the organization of the composition and for the dominant standing figure, could have come from an engraving after John Singleton Copley's well-known "Brooke Watson and the Shark."

82

"Fur Traders," nothing is left to chance in any of his pictures: all indications point to an elaborate and even constructive planning, with the balance of each line, form, and color precisely measured with a view to achieving the desired effect. But once these problems were accomplished, and we can assume that they were reached in terms of color notes and sketches, the actual painting was begun and completed quickly. Unfortunately, none of Bingham's preliminary efforts has come down to us. What does remain, however, is the splendid series of drawings comprising the John How Collection, now in the St. Louis Mercantile Library Association, which are powerfully executed studies for the individual figures of his various compositions. This series of drawings actually served as the artist's pattern book, one from which he could build his figure compositions. It also comprised a record of the pictures that had already passed from his hands, recalling for him figural types already used, but on which he might call again, either for variations of the same theme or for transposition into other compositions. The "Fur Traders" is a typical example in which the procedure was followed. Two of the figure studies in this collection (S26, S35) were undoubtedly prepared in connection with this subject and later put to use for "The Trappers' Return," actually another version of the "Fur Traders." The artist certainly must have thought of his drawings as models for the development of future subjects and so he carefully preserved them. Even their reverse sides, frequently bearing tracings of sections and details of figures on the obverse, seem to have served the artist on those occasions when he desired reverse poses of some of these studies in connection with new compositions. Bingham allowed himself a fairly limited repertoire of posed figures and, within that limitation, attempted to create a variety by turning over the figure, or by slight alterations to fit the new need.

In "The Trappers' Return," (A222; plate 48), painted six years after the "Fur Traders," Bingham has varied the figures only slightly in terms of characterization and detail, but considerably altered his emphasis on the figures by moving them closer to the spectator. The triangular composition of the group has been maintained, although perhaps slightly more knowingly enforced in the deliberate importance given to the boy's rifle, the oblique sweep of which parallels the line of the figure grasping it. The contours of the figures have been softened, and details such as the patterns of the garments have now been eliminated in an attempt to relate the figures more effectively to the landscape background. The suffused aspect of the earlier landscape has been sacrificed, however, in favor of a more precise and descriptive delineation of rock and foliage. The little fox has given way to a creature more closely resembling a bear cub, but whose awkward silhouette no longer

83

offers anything like the sensitive line of balance we were able to discern in the 1845 version. According to the prevailing taste of the time, the later picture must be considered the more highly finished treatment of the subject from a technical standpoint; in it the artist also reveals his growing ability to relate the figures to the setting in terms of light, but the subject itself has been somewhat coarsened in the translation, and the delicate balance of line and form so admirably achieved in the earlier painting has somehow been dissipated in the process.

BOATMEN ON THE MISSOURI

A picture entitled "Boatmen on the Missouri" (A145), probably completed by Bingham only a few months before he executed the first of his "Jolly Flatboatmen" compositions,[33] forms, from the standpoint of style, a logical link between the earlier "Fur Traders" (1845) and "The Jolly Flatboatmen"; it is a painting that certainly marked an important turning point in his early career as a genre painter. It was submitted to the American Art-Union for sale before May 29, 1846,[34] and was purchased by its committee of management on July 6 for 100 dollars.[35] It was distributed at the annual meeting of the Art-Union on December 18 of that year to J. R. Macmurdo, a New Orleans member.[36]

This painting, long lost, came to light in a private collection in California as this book was about to go to press. The composition had been recognized for some years, however, through an anonymous copy now in the Henry Francis du Pont Winterthur Museum (G489). The present illustration (plate 51), made after much surface grime and earlier restoration had been removed from the picture, clearly demonstrates those positive qualities of drawing, composition, and high-pitched color scheme which are, among others, such distinctive trademarks of Bingham's style.

There are two drawings by Bingham for this composition — one in the Mercantile Library for the central figure (S95), and another, now in a private collection, for the figure at left[37] (S111; plate 52).

33. Probably one of the four paintings completed by late March, 1846, which were among those "western scenes" regarded as making a "brilliant reputation" for the artist by a St. Louis reporter. *Weekly Reveille*, March 23, 1846.
34. One of two pictures by Bingham listed in a "memorandum of pictures to be recommended for purchase," May 29, 1846. AAU, Letters, vol. 6, coll. NYHS.
35. AAU, minutes of committee of management, July 6, 1846, coll. NYHS.
36. *Transactions of the American Art-Union, for the Year 1846* (New York: G. F. Nesbitt, Stationer and Printer, 1847), #14.
37. The study for the figure at right was reportedly in a private collection some years ago, but has not been relocated.

The woodboat motif, used in this picture for the first time, was to be developed in later years into a subject of greater literary connotation for the observer. As presented here, it could not have held any particular interest, although for Bingham, the boatmen subject, with a central figure in action, offered pictorial possibilities which must have superseded, at least for the moment, any extension of the storytelling idea.

The somewhat more refined solution of the angular composition that had been developed in the "Fur Traders" moves ahead toward a more positive assertion in the "Boatmen on the Missouri." The line of the boat, which parallels the picture plane, serves as a base for the simple pyramid composed of three figures rising above it. The lines of the sides of the boat itself, carried to their vanishing point, meet in the central figure, a method of picture planning that could not have been an accidental one, if any conception of Bingham's logical and deliberate self-training is to be understood. The construction is an obviously simple and direct one, a solution that remained to be carried logically to its next step, the much more complex "Jolly Flatboatmen." The particular motif of the oars spreading beyond the boundaries of the picture is a key to the following period in which it persists, although there developed in a more monumental and positive way, as indeed is the entire conception.

The prominence given to the figures is perhaps the only contradictory element of the composition, occurring as it does in a period when the painter apparently sought to effect a closer integration of figures with landscape — usually by moving the figural motifs away from the immediate foreground and by reducing their scale. In other respects, however, the picture follows a pattern already well developed by Bingham. The landscape, rolling into the distance, is clearly intended to serve as a background for the figures. In this respect the painting is closely related in artistic intention to the "Fur Traders," particularly in the specific mood achieved in placing a group of figures modeled in monumental relief against a highly atmospheric landscape.

THE JOLLY FLATBOATMEN

Without doubt the support afforded Bingham by the Art-Union through its purchase of his paintings for the 1845 distribution, and particularly by its selection of his western subjects, must have persuaded him to continue along that line. Financially, too, the Art-Union's patronage enabled him to devote less of his time to portraits and more to genre subjects. One of those subjects was for a composition depicting the flatboatmen of the Mississippi, an idea that must have occurred to him from the beginning of his thinking as a

85

painter of the western scene. His "Western Boatmen Ashore," exhibited in 1838, could well have depicted flatboatmen types, but there is no more direct evidence of that, nor of the contention that Bingham painted the "Jolly Flatboatmen" motif before 1846.[38] He apparently had not completed the canvas acquired by the Art-Union under that title much before the actual date on which the Committee of the organization recommended its purchase — October 9, 1846 — for 290 dollars (including the frame!).[39]

As with the "Fur Traders," the subject of the flatboats was one that struck a romantic note among the writers who traveled west and had observed in particular the appearance of "that singular race of men who were their navigators."[40] The flatboats and the men who operated them were, like the fur traders, fast disappearing in the wake of steamboat traffic, but accurate descriptions of the boats were given by observers such as Audubon, Flagg, Flint, and Hall, who described their crews in vivid and picturesque terms. After first recalling the many dangers that were the boatman's lot, Timothy Flint went on to describe the typical appearance of a flatboat and its crew:

All the toil, and danger, and exposure, and moving incidents of this long and perilous voyage, are hidden, however, from the inhabitants, who contemplate the boats floating by their dwellings on beautiful spring mornings, when the verdant forest, the mild and delicious temperature of the air, the delightful azure of the sky of this country, the fine bottom on the one hand, and the romantic bluff on the other, the broad and smooth stream rolling calmly down the forest, and floating the boat gently forward, present delightful images and associations to the beholders. At this time there is no visible danger, or call for labor. The boat takes care of itself, and little do the beholders imagine, how different a scene may be presented in half an hour. Meantime one of the hands scrapes a violin, and the others dance....[41]

The writer concludes his remarks on the note that "These scenes and those notes ... have a charm for the imagination, which although heard a thousand times repeated, at all hours and in all positions, present the image of a

38. MHR, XXXIII (1939), 511, note 11 (C. B. Rollins): "In 1844, when Bingham was in Washington City, he painted 'Jolly Flatboatmen,' which was his first genre picture. A copy of an engraving of this 'Jolly Flatboatmen' appeared as the frontispiece in the Transactions of the American Art Union for 1846." This statement was accepted by Christ-Janer (George Caleb Bingham ..., p. 35). Rusk asserted that the picture "must have been painted as early as 1845, for a copy of an engraving of the painting appears as a frontispiece in the American Art-Union Transactions, for the Year 1846" (Rusk, George Caleb Bingham ..., p. 33). The AAU Transactions for 1846 were published after the annual meeting of the year, which took place on Dec. 18, 1846; hence the announcement of "The Jolly Flatboatmen" could have been (and was) based on a decision made in the latter part of 1846.
39. AAU, minutes of executive meeting, Oct. 9, 1846, coll. NYHS.
40. E. Flagg, The Far West...I, 30.
41. T. Flint, The History and Geography of the Mississippi Valley... (Cincinnati, O.: E. H. Flint & L. R. Lincoln, 1832), I, 153. A first edition was published in Cincinnati in 1828 under the title A Condensed Geography and History of the Western States.

tempting and charming youthful existence, that naturally inspires a wish to be a boatman."[42]

This colorful picture of the flatboatman in his happiest aspects was repeated in a similar vein by other authors.[43] And, as with the "Fur Traders," it could have served Bingham as inspiration for his painting, so closely does his own portrayal of the typical appearance of the flatboatman fit the details of the description. Indeed, an exact quotation from the Flint description, republished in 1847 in connection with an article on John Banvard's panorama of the Mississippi, was actually illustrated by a woodcut after Bingham's "Jolly Flatboatmen."[44]

It was a decidedly opportune choice of subject-matter by the artist, from several viewpoints. The picture was well received by the Art-Union, which purchased it for the 1847 distribution, placing it first in their *Transactions* for the year[45] and also selecting it, along with a work by the distinguished Daniel Huntington,[46] to be engraved for their membership. It was through this picture, too, that the painter earned his reputation as "The Missouri Artist."

The original painting, awarded by the Art-Union on December 24, 1847, to Benjamin van Schaick, a New York grocer, was known to students for many years only through the large engraving by Thomas Doney. It was located again within recent times in the collection of Senator Claiborne Pell in Washington, D.C. (A146; plate 53). This fortunate occurrence affords us an opportunity to study this important picture on a basis not formerly possible. Its remarkably good state of preservation actually enables us to judge the painting along with the contemporary critic.

The composition, obviously constructed in terms of a monumental pyramid, is formed of six figures in the immediate foreground and two others filling out the distance. The flatboat faces the spectator squarely, its bottom parallel to the picture plane. The two long oars resting atop the arched roof of the boat are also placed parallel, extending beyond the limits of the picture, left

42. *Ibid.*
43. There was even a popular song called "The Jolly Raftsman," copyrighted as early as 1844 by C. H. Keith, Boston; H. Dichter, *Handbook of American Sheet Music* [Philadelphia, 1951], #1614: "My raft is by de shore, she's light and free,/To be a jolly raftsman's the life for me,/ And as I pole along, our song shall be, / O darlin Dinah I love but thee." Bingham may have shrewdly seen the value of adapting the title of his picture after that of the popular song.
44. Headpiece to the article "John Banvard's Great Picture, Life on the Mississippi," *Howitt's Journal of Literature and Popular Progress*, II (Sept. 4, 1847), 145.
45. *Transactions of the American Art-Union. for the year 1847* (New York: G. F. Nesbitt, Stationer and Printer, 1848), #1.
46. "The Sibyl." Daniel Huntington (1816-1906) was an Associate Member of the National Academy in 1840; a Member from 1841 to 1906; President of the Academy from 1862 to 1870 and from 1877 to 1890.

and right. Serving as a base for the pyramid, the angles are held below by two figures seated on the oars. The upper step in the geometric pattern so meticulously planned by the artist is formed by two music-making figures on a crate, one placed slightly higher than the other, obviously to avoid a static effect. The apex of the pyramid is held by a flatboatman dancing on top of the crate facing the spectator. To further break an appearance of rigid regularity the dancer is placed slightly off center, to the left, the artist filling the void with the two figures partially seen in the background. A reclining, strongly foreshortened figure fills out the center of the pyramid below. Indeed, the deliberate architectonic enforcement of the composition is visible in almost every line.

Following the instruction book's advice that "groups of figures without some appearance of geometric form apparent to the eye, would produce a confused effect upon the spectator,"[47] Bingham adapted the classic formula for a pyramidal composition, applying it to suit his own needs. One critic, however, took him to task for his strict adherence to the form in this instance: "In composition, Mr. B. should be aware that the regularity of the pyramid is only suitable to scenes of the utmost beauty and repose, that when motion and action are to be represented, where expression and picturesqueness are objects sought for, proportionate departures must be made from this formal symmetry. A little study of the compositions of the great men of old, would do much towards correcting the artist's faults in this respect."[48] But Bingham was not aware of any restriction on an artist's use of the form. Prout had specifically recommended its use as one "applicable to almost every variety of subject ... it may be adopted to advantage where the subject will admit of it, but as there cannot be any general rule, the taste of the artist will be the best and sufficient guide."[49]

We can recall that in the "Fur Traders" and in "Boatmen on the Missouri" Bingham attempted to fix the spectator's attention to his figures by adopting the simple pyramid and by having his chief actors look out directly toward the observer. With the larger and more complex structure of "The Jolly Flatboatmen" he apparently uses, for the first time, a mode or presentation that adheres to a plan deriving ultimately from Italian Renaissance masters and brought home to Bingham probably via the instruction book and the engraved reproduction.

By analyzing the means Raphael used in attaining the greatest concentra-

47. J. Burnet, *An Essay on the Education of the Eye with Reference to Painting* ... (London: J. Carpenter, 1837), p. 41.
48. *The Literary World,* II (Oct. 23, 1847), 377-378.
49. Prout, *Hints on Light and Shadow* ..., p. 11.

tion within a figure composition, Burnet, in one of his treatises for artists, apparently quotes from the master's own notes on the subject, and appends his personal explanation of the basic idea (added below in brackets):

It is to be observed, that the first thing to be considered . . . is where the point (*id est*, the spectator or spectator's eye) is to be placed, whether in the middle of the work or on one side, and as to determine its situation that the important figures be distinctly visible. . . . It is my opinion, confirmed by the practice of the most skilful [*sic*] men . . . those figures which are nearest to the point should present their backs, those further removed their sides, and so on in perspective, as if a circle were drawn and figures ranged round it. . . .
[In illustration of the above, supposing an action to be represented in a circle, which would be quite natural if the object of attention were in the centre, the spectator might view it so as to be himself without the circle, or be supposed within it. In the latter case, the nearest figures would have their sides towards him, in the former their backs. Thus, when the spectator sees a semicircle, he completes the circle by his forming a part. This arrangement was adopted by the early Italian painters in their sacred subjects, and from its fitness was never abandoned by Raffaello. . . .] [50]

In a manner closely following the words of the master, Bingham concentrates attention on the central figure of the dancing boatman, arranging all the subordinate figures in a way that affords the strongest effect. The eye of the observer, viewing the scene from a place outside the composition, is led from the central foreground figure with his back turned, to those seen from the sides in varying aspects, to the dancing flatboatman shown *en face*, thus forming a circle in perspective with the figures arranged within it. The base of our old pyramid has now become circular, and the combination of the two forms assumes a cone.

Although the pyramid-cone form, which Bingham seems to have first adopted here, was not specifically described by such treatises on composition as that of Burnet, the combination of angular and circular compositional devices was one that was at least encouraged by suggestion. Burnet pointed out that in nature, "all her varieties emanate from a straight line and a curve,"[51] and further amplified his remarks to the artist by advising that "by making the principal heads depend on one mode of arrangement, the general appearance of the group on a different mode, the background on a third, and so on with the minor points (provided they all tend to the assistance of one

50. Burnet, *An Essay . . .* , p. 44.
51. J. Burnet, *Practical Hints on Composition in Painting . . .* , p. 29, in *A Practical Treatise on Painting. In Three Parts. Consisting of Hints on Composition, Chiaroscuro, and Colouring. The Whole Illustrated by Examples from the Italian, Venetian, Flemish, and Dutch Schools* . . . (London: Printed for the Proprietor, and Sold by James Carpenter & Son, 1828). First published in 1826; a fifth edition appeared in 1838. The "Parts" were evidently published separately at first—that on composition in 1822.

another), his composition will not only have intricacy without confusion, but that variety which is so characteristic of nature."[52]

It might be well to observe at this point that Bingham, in the obviously sincere and painstaking approach to what he had come to consider proper form was, in fact, only following a procedure that had already been laid down by the classicists more than a century earlier. They had attempted to synthesize the heritage of the past, much as the Carracci and their school had done before them, as a means of achieving "correctness" of form and harmony of composition. The instruction books of the nineteenth century, which Bingham apparently referred to, simply continued the tradition by repeating most of the old recipes. There can be little question that Bingham sought to develop a system of rules which he could readily adapt in his work. Once they were found and assimilated with his style, they were always to be closely obeyed, as we shall be able to observe by the repetition of specific formal features in the pictures analyzed here and in the following pages.

The New York reporter who found fault with Bingham's use of the pyramidal form in "The Jolly Flatboatmen" also added that he found the composition "artificial" and the subject itself a "vulgar" one, regretting its choice by the Art-Union as a subject to be engraved for its membership. He then proceeded to discuss the painter's use of color and handling of textures in both the "Flatboatmen" and the "Raftsmen Playing Cards" (also included in the Art-Union's distribution for 1847), stating that "in color they are disagreeable, a monotonous, dull, dirty pink pervades every part; and in texture there is the same monotony. Flesh, logs, and earthen jug have the same quality of substance, the same want of harmony."[53]

The predominantly pink tonality and the sameness in the handling of textures observed by the critic were limitations the artist himself may have realized. In addition there is still present, as noted in the "Fur Traders," the lack of atmospheric unity between figures and landscape. The figures are sharply outlined against the sky and the pattern of the garments carefully delineated, while the landscape just behind them suggests a softer, more suffused mood. Indeed, so decisively are the contours enforced that on placing the Doney engraving beside a black-and-white photograph of the painting it is difficult to tell the two apart.

The "Jolly Flatboatmen" motif must have proved a popular one with the public, for the artist returned to it again and again. The carefree, light-hearted note it suggested was one that appealed to the romantic sensibility of the period. And again, Bingham seemed always to seek out the typical aspect

52. *Ibid.,* p. 28.
53. *The Literary World,* II (Oct. 23, 1847), 377-378.

of the western scene in almost the same way that William Sidney Mount portrayed similar interpretations of the Long Island scene. Perhaps Mount's "Dance of the Haymakers" (plate 55), sometimes alternatively titled "Music is Contagious," comes closest to serving as a pendant to "The Jolly Flatboatmen." The intimate glimpse of farmers enjoying a moment of relaxation after a day's toil—two of them dancing while another plays the fiddle—appears almost identical in mood and action to the flatboatmen. The Mount picture was painted in 1845, a year earlier than Bingham's, and a lithograph produced after it may have appeared shortly afterward. Mount had previously used a similar motif in his "Breakdown," dated 1835, in which a dancing figure was also the central subject.

The tendency to avoid the more melodramatic interpretation of these subjects, which may be said to be characteristic of both Bingham and Mount, was evidently early recognized and appreciated by contemporary critics. Although the following statement was extracted from a review of other Bingham paintings, it could actually serve to describe any of his genre subjects:

He has not sought out those incidents or occasions which might be supposed to give the best opportunity for display, and a flashy, highly colored picture; but he has taken the simplest, most frequent and common occurrences on our rivers—such as every boatman will encounter in a season—such as would seem, even to the casual and careless observer, of very ordinary moment, but which are precisely those in which the full and undisguised character of the boatman is displayed.[54]

There can be little doubt that Bingham was also well aware of the work of the Scottish painter Sir David Wilkie, if only through the engraved reproductions then available of his more important pictures. In fact, it would seem more than conceivable that he owned such a reproduction of at least one of Wilkie's subjects, "The Blind Fiddler" (plate 54), for that particularly celebrated composition had been engraved and even copied by other artists over and over again. Not only would the rustic setting of the picture, and its musical motif, have set the mood for his own work, but the carefully organized pyramidal composition would have also offered pictorial demonstration of the instruction book's ideas on the subject. And the picture had actually served just such a purpose in John Burnet's essay on composition, to which we have already made some reference.

Wilkie's more sophisticated handling of "The Blind Fiddler" reveals a composition that is, by comparison with "The Jolly Flatboatmen," far less consciously confined to the formal geometric structure that Bingham set for

54. *St. Louis Republican*, April 21, 1847, 2-1. The review evidently referred to Bingham's pictures in a general way, but was prepared at the time his "Raftsmen Playing Cards" and "Lighter Relieving a Steamboat Aground" were on exhibition in St. Louis.

91

himself. Yet the probability of his knowledge of the Wilkie composition gains undeniable meaning once we realize that those key elements which set the tempo and serve to unify the group—the fiddler and the smiling man who snaps his fingers in time to the music—are the same elements that Bingham utilizes to set the pace of action and mood in "The Jolly Flatboatmen." Even the fiddler keeps time with his foot in a manner very much like that of his Scottish counterpart.

At least five drawings for figures in the Mercantile Library collection were unquestionably prepared in connection with this picture (S10, S11, S14, S23, S55).

As an interesting sidelight, Bingham's flatboatmen, as presented in this picture, reappeared only slightly altered in two lithographs published by Currier and Ives in 1865 and 1870.[55] In both examples the flatboat, with its dancing and music-making figures, was unmistakably borrowed from the Bingham composition, in all probability using the Art-Union engraving as the immediate source of inspiration. Charles Wimar, a Bingham contemporary, who was active in St. Louis and certainly must have been familiar with the artist's work, painted a scene of "Jolly Flatboatmen by Moonlight" in Düsseldorf, in 1854.[56] Despite obvious alterations in arrangement and detail, the composition was undoubtedly inspired by Bingham's first "Jolly Flatboatmen," although Wimar also probably knew only the engraved copy of the picture.

A second version of "The Jolly Flatboatmen" (A157; plate 56) was included in the administrator's sale of Bingham's estate which was held in Kansas City some fourteen years after his death. This painting is still in the possession of the family of the original purchaser, Thomas Hoyle Mastin. We know little about its history beyond the fact that it was apparently retained by the artist from the time it was executed. The picture is an important one for our study, primarily because it reveals so eloquently the artist's constant effort at self-improvement through study and observation, not only of the works of others, but also by a critical analysis of his own compositions.

In point of time the painting can be dated stylistically about 1848. Although related to the Art-Union painting of the same subject, its differences are

55. "The Mississippi in Time of Peace," 1865, after drawing by Frances Flora Bond Palmer (Peters, #3949); "Bound Down the River," 1870, after Palmer (?) (Peters, #3940). Checked in H. T. Peters, *Currier and Ives.* ... New York: Doubleday, 1931.

56. Charles (or Carl) Wimar (1828-1862): b. Siegburg, Germany; d. St. Louis, Mo. Wimar came to America in 1843, settling in St. Louis, where he became a pupil of Leon Pomarede some three years later. He had his own studio there in 1851, but went to Düsseldorf the following year to further his professional studies, working under Emanuel Leutze. He returned to St. Louis in 1856. (G. H. Groce and D. H. Wallace, *The New-York Historical Society's Dictionary of Artists in America* ... [New Haven: Yale University Press; London: Oxford University Press, 1957], p. 695.)

marked in the artist's development in terms of a firmer grasp of the pictorial problem involved.

The flatboat is still placed parallel to the picture-plane, but its scale has been reduced to permit a larger sense of air and space on both sides and to allow the eye to travel more freely into the background. The oars have been pulled in, too, breaking the strong barrier of horizontals which held the spectator's attention fast to the action in the foreground in the earlier version. The scale of the figures has been reduced as well, also permitting the observer more freedom and a greater sense of the distance as something other than a backdrop for the group.

The central composition has been retained, with the six foreground figures occupying the same positions as in the Art-Union picture, conforming to the cone-shaped pattern noted in the earlier painting. The most significant change occurs in the dancing figure. The strict frontality has been altered; the figure is now turned on its axis toward the right, his raised right leg and arm forming an oblique line which creates a far more effective impression of movement. The silhouette created by the figure is freer and more effectively succeeds in catching the attention of the observer than its precursor in the 1846 version, which appears stilted and pictorially limited by comparison. The arrangement of the new figure also enabled the painter to simplify the background group by eliminating one of the boatmen. Details detracting from the central composition have also been simplified, so that many of the objects formerly occupying the area in front of the figures have been removed, that section now being cast into strong shadow. Minor details of costume have been changed, and the seated figure at left now smokes a pipe instead of merely resting his right hand against his cheek.

There is a greater intensity in the general technical handling of the picture, marking the artist's transition from his first composition to his later, more developed style. The sharp and incisive modeling of the earlier figures, the sameness of textures, and the considered though uncoördinated treatment of lights and darks now give way to a broader and more mature understanding. The contours of the figures in the Mastin picture are softened, and a general and decisive handling of lights and shadows unites the group, affording them space occupancy within the setting. Textures are handled more knowingly, with details such as patterns of cloth eliminated almost entirely; only the striping of the dancing boatman's vest remains to remind us of a characteristic that can be considered almost a signature of Bingham's first genre pictures.

The gaily dancing figure at the apex of the composition holds added interest for this study; its pose reveals the artist's continuing observation and use of the antique model, in this instance paralleling in pose and movement a

Hellenistic figure of a dancing satyr (plate 57). (This classical figure was actually well known in small-scale reproductions which must have ornamented many a parlor in Bingham's time.) The motif of the handkerchief that the boatman waves as he dances brings to mind a similar motif used in Géricault's "The Raft of the Medusa" (plate 58), a painting Bingham could conceivably have known through engraved reproduction.[57]

The third composition, "The Jolly Flatboatman in Port" (A265; plate 61), is by far the most ambitious extant treatment of the subject by the artist, and rightly marks the final step in the series. It was completed during the fall of 1857 in Düsseldorf, Germany,[58] and can also be said to indicate his final important effort in the field of pure genre.

Bingham evidently thought well enough of the painting to submit it to two important exhibitions on his return from Europe: The Pennsylvania Academy of the Fine Arts in Philadelphia[59] and the first show of the Western Academy of Art in St. Louis,[60] both in 1860. Two years later he placed it on indefinite loan to the St. Louis Mercantile Library Association.[61] The picture was purchased by John How in 1865 for eventual display in the O'Fallon Polytechnic Institute of St. Louis,[62] and soon afterward removed from the Library,[63] to be returned to the institution when presented by John H. Beach in 1879[64] for its permanent collection. The painting passed into the possession of the City Art Museum of St. Louis in 1944.

Although "The Jolly Flatboatmen in Port" belongs in point of time and place to another phase of Bingham's career, it is more properly included within the present consideration as marking the culmination of his progression and developing maturity in the study of composition, color, and light, using this special theme.

57. A lithograph after "The Raft of the Medusa" was produced by Géricault and Charlet, *ca.* 1820, and a lithograph by Charles Etienne Motte was made to illustrate Alexandre Correard's *Naufrage de la Frégate La Meduse...*, published in Paris, *ca.* 1821. It was also engraved by Alphonse Alexandre Leroy (by 1847 [?]).

58. B. to R., letter, Düsseldorf, Oct. 12, 1857, coll. SHSMo *(MHR*, XXXII [1938], 357): "I am now fiinishing my 'Jolly flat-boatman in Port,' it is a large picture, containing 21 figures."

59. *Catalogue of the Thirty-seventh Annual Exhibition of the Pennsylvania Academy of the Fine Arts. 1860 ...* (Philadelphia: Collins, printer, 1860), #141.

60. *Catalogue of the First Annual Exhibition of the Western Academy of Art ...* (St. Louis, Mo., 1860), #12.

61. *Seventeenth Annual Report of the Board of Directors of the St. Louis Mercantile Library Association, January 13, 1863* (St. Louis, Mo.: McKee & Fishback, 1863), p. 18.

62. *Twentieth Annual Report ... Mercantile Library Association (1865)* (St. Louis, Mo.: Printed for the Association, 1866), p. 22.

63. *Twenty-second Annual Report ... Mercantile Library Association, 1867* (St. Louis, Mo.: Printed for the Association, 1868), p. 14.

64. *Thirty-fourth Annual Report ... Mercantile Library Association, 1879* (St. Louis, Mo.: Printed for the Association, 1880), pp. 18-19.

The subject differs from the two earlier known versions in that the flatboat and its occupants are no longer represented in the peaceful occupation of drifting downstream on the river, following the romantic descriptions of the early writers. The boat is shown tied to the wharf, its cargo discharged, and its occupants actively celebrating the completion of a successful voyage by dancing, playing music, and drinking. The crew has been joined by dock workers who fill out the central group, and additional figures such as the two businessmen and the two children are introduced.

The core of the original composition has been retained—the dancing flatboatman at the apex of the pyramid, flanked by the two figures playing musical instruments and the three onlookers in the foreground. The poses of the two players and the dancer remain almost unchanged, the dancer taken over directly from the Mastin example, but showing a better understanding now of the movement of the body and the turn of his head—both closer to the pose of the antique satyr than its predecessor.

The painting is composed of twenty-one figures, with the central group made up of fourteen figures instead of seven or eight, but the artist nevertheless seeks to use the same solution as formerly, despite the greater complexity of the problem. The same deliberate approach is visible, and despite the complication of the scheme through the addition of many supplementary figures and accessories, the careful plotting of the lines is still very much in evidence. The old pyramid-cone, although once more the underlying framework of the picture, no longer recalls the obvious, naïvely conceived composition of the earlier versions. The approach is a more sophisticated one in which the desired elements of the idea are retained, but the action is no longer sublimated or limited by the basic framework. There is now a far more fluid, less contrived movement felt throughout which reveals the mature artist. It is interesting at this point to compare the Pell and Mastin versions with the later composition. In the Pell painting we see the rather symmetrically conceived framework, the central figure facing the spectator, and the entire action concentrated within the limits of the pyramid-cone, adhering rigidly to the letter of the instruction book. Perhaps realizing the restrictions of the form, and attempting to offset its stiltifying effects, while still retaining its effectiveness, Bingham turns the central figure on its axis away from the vertical in the second version. However, although the change reveals the result of study and self-criticism, the underlying influence of the instruction book still remains.

The third composition, on the other hand, evidences a tremendous change in Bingham's experience and understanding. His study of engravings after

95

the old masters must have taught him much about figure composition, but he no longer appears bound by any restrictive formulae. And we realize that by this time he had also benefited by his observation of original paintings by the masters in European galleries, and by his experience at Düsseldorf. One wonders, for instance, how great an impression Géricault's "Raft of the Medusa" might have made on Bingham's concept of composition. He certainly could have known it previously through the engraved reproduction,[65] and he may have seen it on his visit to the Louvre during the fall of 1856. With its underlying pyramidal framework, the figures pushed toward the observer, making him a participant in the action, the diagonal placing of the raft, the equal number of figures, even to the figure at the apex waving a cloth — all are parallels which seem to point to more than a coincidental relationship.

While retaining the essential elements of the pyramid-cone, and the key-notes of figural types developed more than a decade earlier, Bingham now creates a new composition of greater character and forcefulness. Along with these ideas he may have learned from Géricault's masterpiece, he places new emphasis on the importance of the spectator's role in the action. With obvious aforethought, the observer is led into the picture from the left through an opening between two rings of figures, progressing without interruption to the main action. Only then is the eye permitted to travel to the secondary action in the background and to the right. The landscape, formerly assuming a competitive role, now takes its place merely as a setting.

Three of the drawings in the Mercantile Library collection are of figures undoubtedly prepared in connection with the picture (S2, S41, S54), and at least four others were readapted, with slight alteration, from their previous appearance in older subjects such as "Raftsmen Playing Cards" (1847), "The Stump Orator" (1847), and "In a Quandary" (1851) (S12, S63, S87, S104). Variations somewhat further removed from their original sources are discoverable in other figures, although obviously derived from motifs used in earlier genre compositions.

During his last years Bingham apparently returned once more to the subject that had brought him his first recognition as a painter of western genre. Among his latest letters to Rollins is one written from Washington, D.C., in February, 1878, in which he indicated that he was "about finishing" a painting of "The Jolly Flatboatmen."[66] The picture was evidently afterward in his studio in Columbia, for during the summer of that year Bingham wrote again to his friend asking him to arrange for its shipment to Kansas City where

---

65. In *Illustrated Magazine of Art*, II (1853), 284; undoubtedly not the earliest published reproduction of the subject (see note 57).
66. B. to R., letter, Washington, D.C., Feb. 22, 1878, coll. SHSMo (*MHR*, XXXIII [1939], 511).

he intended exhibiting it at the Kansas City exposition together with other of his paintings, "with a view to taking the premiums offered."[67] It was therefore probably included in the "collection of pictures" that he displayed at the show. Whether this fourth version of "The Jolly Flatboatmen" was sold at this time, or by his widow during the years following the artist's death, is not known, but the painting itself has not yet come to light.

CARD PLAYERS

Along with his first representation of the flatboatman in a typical aspect of dancing and music-making, Bingham soon afterward depicted another class of boatman, the raftsmen of the Mississippi. The "Raftsmen Playing Cards" was not necessarily a motif that belonged specifically to this special branch of western life, nor was it by any means a theme that originated with the artist. Bingham's inspirational adaptation of the popular subject of the cardplayer may indeed have come in part from a personal observation of that leisure-time activity aboard a raft, but he must also have been aware of the many engravings after paintings of the subject by the Little Dutch Masters of the seventeenth century, as well as of those after Caravaggio and his followers in Italy. It was still a universally popular subject among artists and public alike during the first half of the nineteenth century, as evidenced by the many engravings after pictures including the motif which appeared at the time. Among more contemporary works, reproductions had appeared of David Wilkie's "Card Players" (plate 59), painted in 1808[68] and still regarded in the 1840's as a work of the first importance. An American contemporary, Richard Caton Woodville, painted a version of "The Card Players" in 1845 which later became well-known through the engraving made from it for distribution to the membership of the American Art-Union.[69]

In all probability Bingham completed "Raftsmen Playing Cards" (A152; plate 62) during the early months of 1847 and placed it on view in St. Louis, together with another picture, at the establishment of Mr. Wool,[70] where it was seen and described by a local reporter.[71] Shortly afterward Bingham submitted the painting for sale to the American Art-Union in New York. The organization purchased it for $300, and awarded it at its annual meeting in December of that year to Edwin Croswell of Albany, New York, a distinguished editor.

67. B. to R., letter, Kansas City, Mo., Aug. 25, 1878, coll. SHSMo (*MHR*, XXXIII [1929], 513).
68. Not only was the picture engraved but painted copies were evidently also in demand. A copy by Alfred Thomas Derby was in the Edward L. Carey collection at Philadelphia.
69. Richard Caton Woodville (1825-1856). Engraved by Charles Burt in 1850 after the painting then in the collection of William J. Hoppin (now Detroit Institute of Arts).
70. Francis Wool (or Wooll), listed as a carver and gilder, at 112 N. 4th St., St. Louis (1848).
71. *St. Louis Republican*, April 21, 1847, 2-1.

The painting was on exhibition at the Art-Union before the distribution and appears to have had an immediate popular appeal, if one can judge by the opinion of one New York critic:

It is truly American, (we always award this compliment with pleasure), and decidedly original; and when we remember that the painter thereof is a statesman by profession, we think it is a remarkable production. The scene represents a large plank raft floating down the Mississippi upon which the artist has placed a number of raftsmen. Two of them are playing cards on a wooden bench, while two of the party are looking on watching the progress of the game, one individual is seated on a plank examining his injured foot, while another is in the rear, hard at work managing the raft. . . . The power of expression displayed in these figures is indeed remarkable, nearly, if not quite equal to Mount.[72]

The composition once again conforms to the pyramid form. The central triangle, composed of the two seated card players and the figure standing behind them, is enforced by the standing figure at right, the line of his bent back paralleling one side, and by the angle developed by the pole of the raftsman in the background at left, forming the other. The raft, shown in strong perspective, is placed parallel to the picture plane, but moved forward so that the spectator partakes of the action. The observer's eye is led through the center of the composition, however—the sides of the raft that spread out and beyond the picture to left and right being closed off by the converging angles created by the ax and the plank. In the manner typical of the artist's compositions of the period, the landscape background is prominently placed, and the spectator's attention is drawn away from the figures to the great distance beyond. The figures themselves appear to be acting within their surroundings rather than dominating the scene.

The outlines of the figures are decisive, and details such as the patterning of the garments are typical of the artist's handling of this picture, and reminiscent of the first "Jolly Flatboatmen." The sharp relief of the central group is maintained in opposition to the soft, hazy landscape surrounding it, a characteristic of Bingham we have noted in all his pictures of the period.

The warm, high-keyed color is again present, with the pinks and yellows prominent. The contemporary critic was "disposed to complain" of the color, although he still felt that Bingham was "the only man in this country who has it in his power to rival Mr. Mount.": "The flesh tints are all too heavy, and not in keeping with the surrounding effects of sunlight; the lights of the picture are too heavy and dead-like; and all the deeper shadows are nearly of one hue."[73] The critic rightly noted the lack of atmospheric unity between figures and landscape, adding that he found the sky "tame and uninteresting."

72. *Jefferson City Metropolitan*, Aug. 17, 1847 (from *New-York Express*).
73. *Ibid.*

98

The flat, undramatic sky is almost a hallmark of the artist's pictures of the period.

Bingham undoubtedly had available many engravings after paintings representing the cardplayer motif,[74] some of which may have afforded him inspiration for his own composition. Among contemporary pictures, David Wilkie's version (plate 59) could have suggested at least a mood, if not the motif, of the standing spectator at right who can be related in pose so strikingly with Bingham's onlooker at center. Certainly Louis-Léopold Boilly's composition, lithographed in 1825 (plate 60), is an example that appears to offer something more than a mere coincidental similarity. The poses of the two card players and the way the cards are held and displayed, particularly those in the hands of the player at right, are very close indeed, suggesting strongly that Bingham made reference to the print in constructing his own composition.

In 1852 Goupil and Company published a lithograph after a painting by Bingham entitled "In a Quandary." Closely related to the Art-Union painting just discussed—its central subject portraying raftsmen playing cards—it also took over, with but slight change, the group of the two seated players and the standing onlooker at right. It was a smaller, more compact composition, showing four figures instead of the six of the Art-Union painting, and with a much reduced background area.

Both Rusk and Christ-Janer, comparing the Art-Union version and the Goupil lithograph, together with the St. Louis reporter's impressions of the composition "Raftsmen at Cards" in 1847[75] in which he described four figures, were convinced that the painting adapted for the lithograph was the one so described.[76] The conviction was somehow bolstered by the belief that the more elaborate composition, the Art-Union picture, had to be the later one. Of course, this pattern does not necessarily always follow, and certainly not with Bingham. The reporter was actually discussing the Art-Union picture, choosing to discuss only those key figures that had attracted his attention.

The reduction of the importance given to the landscape background and the moving forward of the figures to emphasize their position are elements we have discovered to be more typical of the artist's mature style. Of course, the lithograph could not offer for study those other technical characteristics that distinguish Bingham's later work, and it was not until 1939 that the painting on which the print was based came to light, signed and dated 1851 (A220; plate 63). At present in a private collection, the later version is much smaller in size than the Art-Union picture.

74. Including, in particular, those after Teniers and after the school of Caravaggio.
75. *St. Louis Republican*, April 21, 1847, 2-1.
76. Rusk, *op. cit.*, p. 42; Christ-Janer, *op. cit.*, p. 42.

The pyramidal group of figures is composed with greater concentration on the central action than in the earlier picture. An upright figure leaning on a pole now occupies the position between the two cardplayers, giving a more organized monumentality to the group. It seems conceivable that Bingham adapted an organization similar in terms of the pyramid to that used by Raphael in the "Holy Family" (Canigiani), in which the figure of St. Joseph forms the vertical axis of a majestically conceived composition. Indeed, the pose of St. Joseph, leaning heavily on his staff, seems rather close to the motif used by Bingham, however far removed the subject and inspiration is in every other respect.

We have already noted that landscape ideas are by this time reduced to a secondary position so that the eye of the spectator is concentrated on the action of the figures. The arrangement of lights is now better understood and used to accentuate that concentration, although it is also a more suffused light which seeks to relate the figures to their surroundings. The figures themselves are brushed in broadly, details are reduced, patterning of garments eliminated. A detail of one of the cardplayers (plate 64) reveals the softened outlines, permitting a unity of one figure with another and with the background, and the obviously greater painterly quality of the whole.

The sketches for the five principal figures of the 1847 version of the "Raftsmen Playing Cards" are contained in the Mercantile Library Collection (S4, S5, S6, S63, S87); three of them were re-used in the smaller picture painted four years later (S4, S5, S6). Another drawing (S104) was probably executed in connection with "In a Quandary," and repeated, with some alteration, in "The Jolly Flatboatmen in Port" six years later.

BOATMEN: LIGHTER RELIEVING A STEAMBOAT AGROUND

The second painting exhibited with "Raftsmen Playing Cards" at the gallery of Mr. Wool in St. Louis in April, 1847, which was seen and admired by the local reporter was a subject we now know as "Lighter Relieving a Steamboat Aground" (A150). Because of later confusion with regard to the identification of this picture, on the basis of the reporter's review, his description is included here:

Mr. Bingham gives a view of a steamboat, in the distance, aground on a sandbar. A portion of her cargo has been put upon a lighter or flatboat, to be conveyed to a point lower down the river. The moment seized upon by the artist is when the lighter floats with the current, requiring neither the use of oar nor rudder, and the hands collect together around the freight, to rest from their severe toil. One is apparently giving a narration of his adventures at *Natchez under the hill*, some where else, and the rest are listening—whilst a few others are seeking more congenial enjoyment in the jug.

100

pipe, &c. The characters grouped together on the lighter, their dress, expression of countenance, positions, &c., are true to the life.[77]

The artist had evidently intended sending the painting east, together with "Raftsmen Playing Cards," for consideration by the American Art-Union in New York, but it was purchased beforehand by a local collector, James E. Yeatman of St. Louis. This owner allowed the painting to be shown at the first annual exhibition of the newly formed Western Academy of Art in St. Louis, in 1860,[78] and possibly at the Mercantile Library as late as 1871, but it afterward dropped out of sight. At the time of Miss Rusk's publication, in 1917, she surmised that it might be the same painting awarded by the Art-Union in 1847 under the title "Watching the Cargo,"[79] on the basis of the rather similar description accompanying the latter picture: "A group of boatmen on the Missouri River, keeping watch over the cargo of a boat which has been wrecked. A box has been opened and its contents spread out to dry."[80]

Unfortunately, some of the confusion in identification between the two subjects was perpetuated in 1940.[81] By that time "Watching the Cargo" was known, and its divergence from the description of the Yeatman picture, as well as from the typical style of the earlier period, was such that the two pictures could no longer be identified with one another.

A recently discovered daguerrotype of the painting (plate 65), probably made shortly after its completion, bears the unmistakable stamp of Bingham's style and technique both in the strength of the drawing of individual figures and in the atmospheric breadth of the river landscape. These features had become veritable trademarks of the artist's style by this time. There is also a painting, now in a private collection, that has long been identified with the original picture. It is unquestionably the same subject, but the clearly visible weaknesses (when seen in 1946) that separate the painting from the daguer-rotype compel me to reserve any further identification of the two, at least until such time as a more scientific analysis is made possible.

The picture shows a raft in midstream laden with cargo which has been removed from the steamboat visible in the distance aground on a sandbar. A landscape spreads out in the background. Seven figures are on the raft itself, arranged to form a compact pyramidal group. The figures are seated or standing at different levels to establish the sides of a carefully planned

77. *St. Louis Republican*, April 21, 1847, 2-1.
78. *Catalogue of the First Annual Exhibition of the Western Academy of Art*, #105.
79. Rusk, *op. cit.*, p. 41.
80. *Bull. AAU*, II (Oct., 1849), #227.
81. Christ-Janer, *op. cit.*, p. 41.

101

pyramid, a method we have already observed in the artist's designs for the first and second versions of "The Jolly Flatboatmen," although in this picture he has varied the position of the apex figure by representing him standing on the floor of the boat, as a large figure whose head looms above the others. The tall pole he holds is used as a device to enforce the central axis of the angular form.

In many respects the composition is closely related to the first "Jolly Flatboatmen" in its construction, and must have been conceived and executed very shortly after the completion of that painting. Those typical characteristics of the flatboatmen composition—the boat placed parallel to the picture plane, but moved beyond the spectator; the figures occupying space within a landscape setting instead of dominating the scene; the strongly centralized perspective—all indicate a closer relationship to that picture than to "Raftsmen Playing Cards." The last-named work points to a second phase in the artist's development which was actually an outgrowth of the two pictures.

In other respects, however, Bingham has attempted to improve on the first "Jolly Flatboatmen." The oars that in the earlier painting spread horizontally beyond the picture frame, paralleling the lines of the flatboat, are now eliminated, and the monotonous effect is reduced by means of the planks and the oar set at angles to the line of the boat. The strict frontality of the old figural arrangement is also deliberately altered by placing the central raftman with his back to the spectator. The general placement of the other figures is decidedly Binghamesque; they look out toward the observer in a manner very reminiscent of the "Flatboatmen." The young raftsman leaning on the salvaged cargo, at upper right, recalls the pose of the Fur Trader's son.

Six of the drawings of figures in the Mercantile Library can be identified with this composition (S33, S46, S56, S97*b*, S61, S103*a*). That individual character of the figures and the severely linear manner of drawing, both very positive qualities of Bingham's style at the time, were translated into the painting, is clearly evident in the contemporary photograph of the picture.

BOATMEN: WATCHING THE CARGO

The painting entitled "Watching the Cargo" (A162; plate 67), related in subject to the picture discussed above, was executed some two years later, and submitted to the American Art-Union for sale on August 1, 1849.[82] It was purchased by the organization on the following day[83] for the price asked

82. B. to AAU, letter, New York, Aug. 1, 1849, coll. NYHS.
83. AAU, minutes of meeting, committee of management, Aug. 2, 1849, coll. NYHS.

102

by the artist — $200 — and at the annual meeting of the Art-Union on December 21, 1849, it was awarded to Stephen E. Paine of New York.[84] It now forms part of the collection of the State Historical Society of Missouri at Columbia.

The subject presents three boatmen temporarily stranded on a sand bar, guarding the cargo that had been removed from the wrecked steamboat visible as a shadowy form in the background. The composition is broadly and forcefully organized, revealing the great strides Bingham made in the short period since he painted "Lighter Relieving a Steamboat Aground" and other pictures of the years 1846/1847.

Characteristic of his developing compositional style, the foreground is brought forward so the observer participates in the action; the figures themselves assume the dominant role. The centralized figure group of old, so obviously constructed of many parts to form a pyramid, is now completely changed. The story is told in simpler terms: the composition is made up of three figures grouped as a triangle, whose sides are echoed in the bend of the leg of the foreground figure and in the arrangement of the pieces of wood beside him, one of which, with its shadow, repeats the form of the group itself. The accent of the composition is shifted to the left, and the landscape no longer surrounds the figures or acts in competition with them. The artist knowingly controls the observer's eye, leading it into the picture at left to confront the actors, and only subsequently permitting it to move into the distance stretching off to the right.

The painter's understanding of light and shadow, of textures, and of color has also developed since the days of the first "Jolly Flatboatmen" and "Raftsmen Playing Cards." Light and shade is now used to clarify the figural group, as well as to relate it to the surroundings. The figures are skillfully massed into a single plastic group. Although the contours are still sharply defined, the brittleness of the line has been greatly reduced. Textures of draperies are softer and more supple, the old patterning giving way to a broader and more painterly quality. Colors are warm and rich both in the figures and in the background. The previous pink and gray tones are replaced by a more dramatic palette. At this period, too, Bingham concentrated more on an achievement of unusual and complex cloud effects, in direct contrast to the flat treatments found in his earlier pictures.

The drawings for the two central figures are found in the St. Louis Mercantile Library (S48, S57) and are certainly among the most powerful drawings in the collection. It is especially interesting here to note the artist's

84. *Transactions of the American Art-Union, for the Year 1849* (New-York: G. P. Nesbitt, printer. 1850). #227.

103

ability to translate his designs from the graphic to the oil medium without losing any of the force and character of the original.

WOODBOATMEN, FISHERMEN, AND SQUATTERS

Six pictures executed by Bingham between 1850 and 1854—"The Wood-Boat," "The Squatters," "Fishing on the Mississippi," "A Mississippi Fisherman," and two night scenes of western boatmen—all slightly varied in subject matter but closely related in design, afford us an interesting means of study of the painter's stylistic development during this period.

The first painting, "The Wood-Boat" (A191; plate 66), first exhibited in St. Louis in October, 1850,[85] was submitted by the artist to the American Art-Union for sale on November 19, priced at $200.[86] It was rejected for purchase at that time,[87] and again when brought before the committee for reconsideration on February 20, 1851.[88] The picture was finally accepted by the Art-Union on March 20, 1851, for $125,[89] and was later included among the paintings auctioned during the dispersal of the organization's property in December, 1852.[90] At that time it passed into the possession of John J. Herrick, who successfully bid $95 for it.[91]. The picture is unsigned and undated but undoubtedly is one of those painted by Bingham in 1850.

In his letter to the Art-Union accompanying the painting, Bingham described "The Wood-Boat" as representing, "...a group such as the traveller daily sees upon the navigable waters of the west. The wood for sale is conveniently placed in a flat boat, while the hardy choppers await a purchaser in some approaching steamer."[92] The artist's custom of depicting the typical aspect of the western scene is indicated in his description of the design as showing a view "such as the traveller daily sees upon the navigable waters of the west," and one such traveler, Basil Hall, did indeed describe a similar scene for which Bingham's painted version could have served as illustration:

As the Steam-Boats on the Mississippi, and indeed all over America, burn nothing but wood, it becomes necessary to make occasional stops to replenish their stock of fuel.

85. *Daily Missouri Republican* (St. Louis), Oct. 11, 1850, 2-2.
86. B. to AAU, letter, New York, Nov. 19, 1850, coll. NYHS.
87. AAU, minutes of meeting, committee of management, Nov. 19, 1850, coll. NYHS.
88. *Ibid.*, Feb. 20, 1851.
89. *Ibid.*, March 20, 1851.
90. *Catalogue of pictures and Other Works of Art, the Property of the American Art-Union. To be Sold at Auction...the 15th...16th, and...17th, December, 1852...* [New York, 1852], #352.
91. Cowdrey, *American Academy...*, I, 297: Addendum, Sale of Art-Union holdings, 1852.
92. B. to AAU, letter, New York, Nov. 19, 1850, coll. NYHS. The particular subject-matter implication of the picture was also underlined by the St. Louis reporter who described it in considerable detail while it was on exhibition in the city (*Daily Missouri Republican*, Oct. 11, 1850, 2-2).

Accordingly, on the banks of the great rivers—which are now all covered with these vessels—many settlers find it a profitable occupation to devote themselves exclusively to preparing stacks of firewood, close to the bank, ready for the boats as they pass. either by day or night. . . . The price per cord varies from a dollar and a half, to three dollars.[93]

The earlier "Boatmen on the Missouri" was, in all probability, the artist's first depiction of a woodboatmen motif, although the reference in that instance was obviously of only secondary interest. And at least two other recorded compositions by Bingham, "Woodyard on the Missouri" and "A Boatman," both as yet unlocated, also appear to refer to a similar subject matter.[94]

The second painting in this group, "The Squatters" (A192; plate 68), was another subject of specific western connotation. It was submitted to the American Art-Union for sale at the same time as "The Wood-Boat."[95] It was similarly priced at $200 framed and was also declined, but subsequently purchased for $125.[96] Like its companion, it reached the auction block in December, 1852,[97] when it was sold to W. T. (or N. P.) Hood for $85.[98] It is now in a private collection.

The background of the subject was described by the artist in his letter to the Art-Union, November 19, 1850:

The Squatters as a class, are not fond of the toil of agriculture, but erect their rude cabins upon those remote portions of the National domain, when the abundant game supplies their phisical [sic] wants. When this source of subsistence becomes diminished in consequence of increasing settlements around, they usually sell out their slight improvement, with their "preemption title" to the land, and again follow the receding footsteps of the Savage.[99]

93. B. Hall, *Forty Etchings, from Sketches Made with the Camera Lucida, in North America, in 1827 and 1828* . . . (Edinburgh: Cadell & Co.; London: Simpkin, Marshall, and Moon, Boys, Graves, 1829), accompanying plate xxxii, "Wooding Station on the Mississippi."
94. Contemporary descriptions of the pictures indicate that "Woodyard on the Missouri" represented "a broad stretch of the Missouri . . . over which hangs that hazy atmosphere peculiar to it. In the foreground is a woodyard. Two men have discovered a boat in the distance, and are watching for the signal indicating that wood is wanted. A third lounges on the bank with his feet hanging over the water, smoking his pipe. The accessories of the wood piles, axes, whisky jug, &c., go to make up a scene that cannot be mistaken by any one who has travelled on the western waters" (WAU, *Record*, I [June-Oct., 1849], #150); "A Boatman" represented "a figure seated beside a pile of wood, on the banks of the Missouri" (*Bull. AAU*, II [Oct., 1849], 43, #241).
95. B. to AAU, letter, New York, Nov. 19, 1850, coll. NYHS. Together with "The Wood-Boat," this painting, titled "The Squatter's Settlement," was among those pictures exhibited by Bingham in St. Louis before sending them East for consideration by the Art-Union *(Daily Missouri Republican,* Oct. 11, 1850, 2-2).
96. AAU, minutes of meetings, Feb. 20, March 20, 1851, coll. NYHS.
97. *Catalogue of Pictures . . . the Property of the American Art-Union. To be Sold at Auction . . . December, 1852, #162.*
98. Cowdrey, *American Academy* . . . , I, 297.
99. B. to AAU, letter, New York, Nov. 19, 1850, coll. NYHS.

Bingham obviously sought to depict that special class of emigrants to the west who were not generally looked upon with favor by the regular settlers. The squatter types had no desire to settle permanently on the land they occupied, but found the public lands simply a place of temporary refuge and planned to move on to the next frontier once their land was opened for settlement. They were regarded as among the socially unfit, the men being described as indolent and untrustworthy, and the women inclined to be timid and queer. Their homes were one-room cabins, crudely built, almost completely barren of furnishings, and occupied at all times by several people crowded together.[100] Bingham's design displays little of these unwholesome conditions, however, but shows us instead a quiet, simple scene in which only the external elements are presented.

The third painting, "Fishing on the Mississippi" (A221; plate 69), was also submitted to the American Art-Union by the artist. It was received by the organization on March 13, 1851, purchased for $100,[101] and in December, 1852, was sold at the Art-Union property auction to James C. McGuire of Washington, D.C., for $150.[102] It was on the art market in 1933 and soon afterward acquired by the William Rockhill Nelson Gallery in Kansas City. Signed and dated 1851, the picture may have been executed in New York during the winter of 1850-51.

In more recent years, chiefly as the result of an exhibition listing in 1935, the picture was erroneously entitled "Fishing on the Missouri," causing at least one writer to speculate as to whether there were actually two versions of the subject.[103] There can be no doubt that the Kansas City painting is the Art-Union's "Fishing on the Mississippi," and the existence of another picture under the variant title should be discounted.

A fourth painting in this group, "Mississippi Fisherman" (A206; plate 73), was long in the possession of the family of Eliza Thomas Bingham. The single figure is unusual, although Bingham appears to have produced at least two other pictures of the kind, one the now lost painting of "A Boatman" —which was described as "a figure seated beside a pile of wood, on the banks of the Missouri"[104] when it was listed among those pictures to be distributed by the American Art-Union in 1849—and the other a "Mississippi Boatman" (recently discovered), described as "an old man smoking his pipe at the river-

100. H. M. Anderson, "The Evolution of a Frontier Society in Missouri, 1815-1828," *MHR*, XXXIII (1938), 299. Based on a description in H. R. Schoolcraft, *Scenes and Adventures in the Semi-Alpine Region of the Ozark Mountains of Missouri and Arkansas...* (Philadelphia: Lippincott, Giambo & Co., 1853).
101. AAU, Register of Pictures, coll. NYHS.
102. Cowdrey, *American Academy...*, I, 157.
103. Christ-Janer, *op. cit.*, p. 56.
104. *Bull. AAU*, II (Oct., 1849), #241.

side"[105] when it was in the hands of the Philadelphia Art Union in 1851. The three single-figure pictures are clearly related; all were executed within the same period and all have a dominant motif based on figure types such as those which appear in Bingham's drawings, prepared with larger compositions in view, but obviously also intended for more modest efforts. "Mississippi Boatman" (A194), dated 1850, is evidently a typical example of his procedure. The subject repeats the central figure of "Watching the Cargo," painted a year earlier, for which a drawing still exists in the Mercantile Library album (ML 48). Changes have been made only in physiognomical features, color, and the choice of background accessories. Although the same procedure cannot now be traced so readily in the undated "Mississippi Fisherman," this picture bears an undeniable relationship to "Mississippi Boatman." Stylistically, the monumental figure is also related to the larger, more plastically realized forms that are typical of Bingham's paintings of the early 1850's.

The fifth subject, entitled "Woodboatmen on a River" (A234; plate 74) by its present owner, might more properly be recognized as a night version of an older Bingham subject, "Western Boatmen Ashore." The provenance of the painting indicates that it apparently remained in private collections in St. Louis from the time it left the painter's hands until its sale in 1944. The picture belongs to the latest of the group presently under discussion, and it is signed and dated 1854.

Even more recently, another painting has been discovered that is very closely related in subject, mood, and period to "Western Boatman Ashore by Night"; even more importantly, it points up a culminating pictorial accomplishment by the artist at this particular moment in his career. The painting, in recent times called "Raftsmen by Night" (A235; plate 72), but which seems more likely to represent a night version of "Watching the Cargo," was virtually unknown before it turned up on the New York market during the past few years. Like "Western Boatmen Ashore by Night," to which it might well have served as a pendant, it is signed and dated 1854.

These six compositions are characteristic of a pictorial means developed by Bingham before 1850, a phase of which we were able to observe as already well formed in his "Watching the Cargo" of 1849. In each, the story is simply and decisively told, the central subject usually composed of three or four main figures forming the now familiar pyramid, although the persistence of the angular form no longer appears so forced or so obvious as of old. In five of the examples cited above a single figure forms the central axis of the pyramid, always emerging as a distinctly vertical element which is accented by the placement of a tall pole in his hands, or by an

105. Philadelphia Art Union, *Catalogue of Prizes to be Distributed on December 31, 1852,* #58.

arrangement of the figure well above all the others. In "The Wood-Boat" and "Western Boatmen Ashore by Night," the standing boatmen are closest in pose, appearing between two seated or reclining figures.[106]

The pattern follows. In "Fishing on the Mississippi" the standing fisherman is related to his boatman colleagues, with a slight variance in pose as well as in arrangement. With the composition reduced to two principal figures, he occupies a central position between a reclining figure and a prominently placed tree stump, the oblique lines of which suggest the opposite side of a pyramid.

In "The Squatters" the pose of the standing figure of the old man leaning heavily on his stick is in turn related to that of the fisherman holding his rod. In this composition the angles of the pyramid are formed by the seated figure at left and the dog to the right.

A slight variation occurs in "Watching the Cargo by Night," in which the central figure is seated, although he is, as in all these paintings, placed well above his comrades, and behind him a tall pole or signpost serves to emphasize the desired total pyramidal effect. The specific compositional organization of the picture seems to recall the original "Watching the Cargo" of 1849 in a manner that may have been an intentional one on the part of Bingham. This seems to be demonstrated not only by the massing of seated figures but also by the rather deliberate repetitions of triangular patterns formed by the figures themselves, the peaked arrangement of the cargo in the left background, and finally, in a fashion so peculiarly reminiscent of the 1849 picture, by the small angular form developed by the box with the stick resting against it at the right, together with its reflections in the pose of the legs of the man seated beside it.

In all of the group of compositions discussed, the main subjects are moved forward, confronting the observer, placed either to the left or right within the picture frame. The eye is led directly to the main subject action and only afterward into the landscape background. Although we sense, as always, the skillfully laid-out design, we are perhaps less pointedly aware of the artist's elementary intentions. There is now a somewhat more sophisticated under-standing of the compositional idea, and thus a relaxed handling of the pic-torial problem, however positive and fixed certain specific notions still remain visible.

Light and shadow and general atmospheric effects take up more and more of Bingham's attention during this period. It is in this direction that we must turn to note the area marking the most significant developments in his style.

---

106. The standing boatman leaning on a tall pole also appears in "In a Quandary," a picture already discussed, and dated within the same period.

This group of pictures reveals perhaps more importantly than others the varying phases of that development.

"The Wood-Boat" of 1850 shows little change beyond "Watching the Cargo," painted a year earlier, in its handling of light and shadow. There is the same sense of atmospheric unity between figures and background, and a similar clarity in the organization of the figures in terms of light and shade. The still well-defined outlines of the figures nevertheless show an obvious attempt to give a plastic meaning to the edges turned toward the light.

"The Squatters" of 1850 and the slightly later "Fishing on the Mississippi" disclose a decided softening of the contours of figures, and of rocks and distant foliage as well. There seems an increased atmospheric unity now, and a greater related tonality, between figures and backgrounds.

The two night scenes of 1854 reveal the final development of the painter in his ever-increasing effort to achieve more unified and more fluid effects of atmosphere in terms of light and shadow. Both are experiments in the use of a night light in which the figures are illuminated by campfires, a pictorial means not specifically new to the artist.[107] But now the painter appears to be almost entirely concerned with the problems of light; he reduces all details and suffuses the usually hard edges of his figures to achieve the desired effects. Distant moonlight is used to create backlighting which serves to develop the figures in relief, as well as to form an impression of infinite space. A detail of the figures of "Western Boatmen Ashore by Night" (plate 70) clearly reveals a unity of central mass in terms of light and shadow, together with a new and richer painterly breadth than Bingham had hitherto been able to achieve. In the two night pictures the artist seems to have finally conquered the problem of the unity of form and atmospheric space which had evidently been a conscious concern from his early years as a figure painter.

Although the fishing motif forms the central theme of two of the pictures we have discussed, a little figure quietly seated in the background, patiently waiting for a "bite," occurs in three other paintings in this group. The musical motif in "Western Boatmen Ashore by Night" recalls the mood of "The Jolly Flatboatmen," one that can be said to express a very typical aspect of Bingham's approach to such subjects. The use of the jew's-harp as a means of music-making, replacing the fiddle for the moment, appears to be a unique instance here. It may have been suggested by an engraving after the painting "The Jew's Harp" by David Wilkie (plate 71), in which the same motif forms both its title and main subject concentration. That Bingham

107. "Captured by the Indians" (1848) and "The Belated Wayfarers" (1852) are earlier Bingham experiments in the use of outdoor night light. See pp. 111-112.

was undoubtedly well aware of the work of this well-known Scottish genre painter, whose works had been repeatedly reproduced by this time, should be regarded as fact and no longer as mere supposition.

Among the drawings in the Mercantile Library are figures related to all but one of the compositions discussed: "The Squatters" (S44), "The Wood-Boat" (S51, S94, S101), "Fishing on the Mississippi" (S22, S50), "Western Boatmen Ashore by Night" (S105 and [with some alteration in pose, gesture, and costume] S101), "Watching the Cargo by Night" (S33, S103a [both adapted from figures used in an earlier composition], and S15 and S34, the last with slight changes).

INDIANS

Of the three paintings to be discussed under this heading, only "The Concealed Enemy" and "Captured by the Indians" can be considered as specifically Indian subjects. The picture "Belated Wayfarers" is introduced into the group because it was obviously executed by the artist as a companion to the second subject and, as such, must be considered stylistically inseparable from it.

The Indian theme was a highly popular one during the first half of the nineteenth century, and artists such as George Catlin, John Mix Stanley, Seth Eastman, Charles Bird King, and James Otto Lewis earned their reputations by their portrayals of Indian life. Bingham, undoubtedly well aware of the welcome reception generally accorded such subjects, nevertheless rarely adopted the motif in his own work. He probably did not find himself on sufficiently familiar ground with a theme that required an intimate knowledge of tribes and customs. His own experience afforded him little contact with the Indian, and he apparently had no yearning to develop the kind of contact that brought Catlin his fame. And, unlike Charles Deas and Charles Wimar, Bingham was not imaginative enough to be strongly attracted to the more fictional storytelling aspects of Indian deeds and exploits.

Although we have observed that Bingham made copies of paintings of buffalo hunts as early as 1835, which might conceivably have included Indian figures as well, we know of only two examples of his contribution to the field, neither of which can be claimed to give him an important place among the painters of the Indian.

The first painting, "The Concealed Enemy" (A137; plate 75), was, with "Fur Traders Descending the Missouri," among the earliest figure subjects the artist submitted to the American Art-Union. It was purchased by the organization[108] on December 8, 1845, for $40, and was afterward awarded to

108. AAU, minutes of meeting, Dec. 8, 1845, coll. NYHS.

110

James A. Hutchison of Pittsburgh, Pennsylvania.[109] In recent times it was part of the collection of David I. Bushnell of Washington, D.C., who presented it to the Peabody Museum at Harvard University in 1946. The subject, representing the single figure of a crouching Indian, partially concealed by the shadow of a large rock and tree formation, suggests the tension of a moment just preceding an action and indicates more of the imaginative story-telling aspect than is usual with Bingham.

Perhaps some clue to a possible inspiration for the subject and its treatment can be offered by a painting by Joshua Shaw, "The Reedy River Massacre" (plate 76). The crouching Indian, with the mound rising behind him, serving as a means of concealment, as well as the handling of the foliage, recall Bingham's association of similar motifs, although the compositions vary on other points. Shaw's painting is obviously the more sophisticated one, both from a technical standpoint and in the richer illustrative approach to the subject. Bingham's use of theme and composition was necessarily limited by the frontal pyramid construction which appears to have been the one sure means he could command with some conviction during this early period of his career as a figure painter. It is not suggested that Bingham knew this painting by Shaw, but he certainly could have come into contact with other similar pictures by the artist during his stay in Philadelphia in 1838, and afterward through engravings taken from them. We shall have reason later to pursue further a possible connection with Shaw during this period of Bingham's investigation of areas other than portrait painting.

The second picture, "Captured by Indians" (A154; plate 78), is signed and dated 1848. The painting has no documented provenance, and appears to have always been in private ownership. Its attribution, and that of its pendant, "The Belated Wayfarers," was questioned by Rusk because it was said to bear the artist's signature and date, and she was not aware at that time of any other similarly marked paintings.[110] She also had not seen the pictures. Christ-Janer questioned the paintings because of their uncertain history.[111] But the old doubts can no longer be maintained. Stylistically the

---

109. *Transactions of the American Art-Union, for the Year 1845,* #95.
110. Rusk, *op. cit.,* p. 48. Of course, other paintings signed by Bingham have turned up during the years since Miss Rusk questioned the authenticity of this signature. The form of signature, "Geo. Bingham," followed by the date, which occurs in both "Belated Wayfarers" and "Captured by the Indians," is undoubtedly the more unusual form. Until very recently this form was known only on these two paintings. Bingham customarily signed his pictures with the formal "G. C. Bingham." Within recent times, however, two further pictures have come to light, "Guarding Their Master's Hat" and a small Colorado landscape—said to have been presented by the artist to a favored pupil during the late 1870's—which also bear the less familiar "Geo. Bingham" signature. I would venture to suggest that the artist used the less formal signature on those few occasions in which gifts or private commissions were involved.
111. Christ-Janer, *op. cit.,* pp. 71-72.

pictures belong completely within the artist's development. The Osage Indian type adopted by Bingham in "The Concealed Enemy" is repeated in "Captured by the Indians" (plate 78), and the approach to the subject is also similar in mood: the quiet, though tense and suspenseful moment, is again suggested. The work is composed of few figures, the dominant role being given to the figure of the captive white woman and her sleeping child, with the light from the campfire seeming to enforce the drama and imaginative storytelling quality of the scene. Technically, there is breadth and decision in the handling of the subject. The figures are moved forward to confront the observer and take a dominant role in the design. The seemingly casual construction of the central group is evidence again of Bingham's growing maturity in his understanding of the pictorial problem. The Indian figures act as foils for the figures of the mother and child, the latter group forming a strong triangle set slightly off the central axis of the picture frame.

Nevertheless, Bingham seems not at his best in the special type of genre subject to which "Captured by the Indians" can be said to belong. In this particular work he may actually have derived his inspiration from a similar subject by John Gadsby Chapman[112] called "The Rescue" (plate 77), which he could have known through an engraving. The campfire, the captive mother and her sleeping child, and the Indians are all there, although Bingham developed a more formally organized composition in which the secondary elements formed by the additional figures in the background of the Chapman picture have been eliminated.

The third painting, "Belated Wayfarers" (A231; plate 79), a companion design to "Captured by Indians," is not an Indian subject, but is closely related to it in mood and intention, as well as in design, setting, and lighting. The outdoor night scene affected by the artist in this pair of pictures must be considered among the more unusual experiments in dramatic effects of light and shade attempted by him during this period. The scenes are tightly enclosed, the figures appearing in strong relief against a landscape setting which itself has no real depth and is only distinguished by the light striking the elements of trees and foliage. The more advanced compositions of this type, "Western Boatmen Ashore by Night" and "Watching the Cargo by Night," both painted in 1854, introduce moonlit backgrounds to develop the effect of distance, while the campfire is concentrated on the figures in the foreground. The diffused outlines of the figures themselves indicate the more highly developed understanding of atmospheric values and relationships.

112. John Gadsby Chapman (1808-1889), Honorary Member, professional, National Academy, 1832-1836; member of the Academy, 1837-1889.

INTERIOR SCENES

Such subjects as "Country Politician," "Feeding Time," "Daybreak in a Stable," "Old Field Horse," "Interior with Figures," and "The Puzzled Witness" may be discussed together because of their general relationship in terms of the indoor scene, although the pictures themselves are somewhat diverse in theme.

Since the topographical aspect so often plays a significant role in representations of the western scene, interior settings can only rarely be said to adequately describe a specific locale of the kind with which Bingham's name was invariably linked in his lifetime. This may well be one of the main reasons for the infrequent appearance of interiors among the artist's genre subjects. Certainly none of his paintings of interiors reveals characteristics that can be related specifically to any particular area. Indeed, they are compositions that are actually descriptive of a rural life that might describe many sections of the country during the period in which they were executed.

The first record of an interior view by Bingham occurs in a brief American Art-Union memorandum, dated May 29, 1846, which mentions a painting that had evidently been submitted by him for consideration by the organization.[113] The picture was indicated only by the title "Interior," with no further description. It had been "recommended" to the purchasing committee, but it appears not to have been approved and nothing more is known about the subject or its later history.

A possible clue to the subject may perhaps survive in a painting of an "Interior with Figures" (A151; plate 80), here reproduced for the first time. Although very probably dating from a slightly later time (1846/1848), it seems conceivable that the earlier "Interior" might have concerned itself with a similar figure subject, reflecting an interest in the rustic "cottage scenery" motif which occurs in at least one of Bingham's known landscapes of the same period. The distinctive feature of the extant version, however, is the artist's apparent preoccupation with the problem of strongly contrasted effects of light and shade as demonstrated in scenes illuminated by artificial light.

The special area of the night scene was evidently one that had occupied Bingham's attention for several years, beginning with the earliest dated outdoor subject painted in this manner, "Captured by Indians," of 1848, and culminating in the two outdoor subjects of boatmen, both dated 1854. Since "Captured by Indians" already evidences a maturing phase of this develop-

113. Letters, AAU, vol. 6, coll. NYHS: a "memorandum of pictures to be recommended for purchase" by the Committee of Management of the AAU, May 29, 1846.

ment, one might surmise that Bingham was not without some prior experience in this area of painting. Of the surviving pictures, however, "Interior with Figures" is the only known interior scene by the artist in which a true nocturnal effect has been developed, but it also belongs stylistically to the period of "Captured by Indians."

The origins of the night scene can be traced to the early part of the seventeenth century when that special genre began to gather momentum as a result of the precedent set by Caravaggio, which was exploited by his many followers in Italy and Northern Europe. The night scene was still a popular means of expression among figure painters in the late eighteenth and early nineteenth century, particularly in England and Holland.[114] In America, night scenes appeared rarely before the nineteenth century,[115] and seem never to have had an enduring influence on the native painters.

"Interior with Figures," in its quiet, pensive mood, reflects a sense of timelessness which can be said to be typical of Bingham's pictorial method. In the particular area of the night picture, a somewhat similar mood is also reflected in "Captured by Indians," a composition that is closest to it in point of dating. The subject of the "Interior" is concentrated on the central pyramid of three figures arranged around a table. Both in the rather deliberate placement of the figures and in the source of the light, Bingham displays an already sophisticated understanding of the means by which an artist achieves a positive impression of pictorial dimension. The play of silhouette, strongly modeled contrasts, and cast shadows make this picture one of his most unusual compositions.

Another well-documented interior subject by Bingham, entitled "Country Politician," was an American Art-Union selection in 1849. The painting,

114. In eighteenth-century England in the work of Joseph Wright of Derby, probably known here through the mezzotint engravings of William Pether after his "Philosopher Reading a Lecture on the Orrery," published in 1768, and of Valentine Green after "A Philosopher Showing an Experiment on the Air Pump," published in 1769. Other mezzotint engravings by Green and his school reveal a distinct preference for night scenes, possibly because the medium could best exploit its potential in such pictures. In nineteenth-century England in the work of Sir David Wilkie, such as "The Rabbit on the Wall," painted in 1816, known popularly through engravings in S. C. Hall's *Gems of European Art* (London, 1847) and in *The Wilkie Gallery* (London and N.Y., 1848/1850). In Holland in the work of G. A. van Merkestijn, P. van Schendel, J. Rosierse, and others, who painted night scenes by mid-nineteenth century.

115. John Greenwood's "Sea Captains Carousing at Surinam," *ca.* 1755 (City Art Museum, St. Louis) and Charles Willson Peale's "Staircase Group," 1795 (Philadelphia Museum of Art), are rare instances of the early period. In the nineteenth century Henry Sargent (*ca.* 1770-1845) did interiors with figures, such as "The Dinner Party" and "The Tea Party" (both in the Museum of Fine Arts, Boston); S. F. B. Morse's (1791-1872) "The Old House of Representatives," painted 1821/1822 (Corcoran Gallery of Art, Washington, D.C.); John (Johann) Mongles Culverhouse (act. 1851-1891), of Dutch extraction, painted night scenes, interiors and exteriors, in the manner of his Dutch contemporaries which were exhibited at the National Academy in 1852 and at the American Art-Union from 1849 onward.

still unlocated at this writing, will be discussed under the heading "Election Series."[116]

Farming scenes, typically represented by subjects such as "Feeding Time" and "Daybreak in a Stable," also belong among the interiors of the 1849/1850 period in the painter's career. Of this group, "Feeding Time" (A166) was probably the most important composition. It was purchased from the artist by the Western Art Union by September, 1849,[117] and awarded to Joseph M. Dana of Athens, Georgia, at the Union's annual distribution held in December of that year.[118] The painting was described as showing "the interior of a stable, horses tied in their stalls, a groom feeding them, while another sleeps in the sunlight by the door. With these, the chickens, farming tools &c., he [the artist] has made up a large and pleasing picture."[119]

The description indicates another typical farming scene, but a design in which contrasts of indoor and outdoor atmospheric effects have been juxtaposed, a means frequently adopted by William Sidney Mount. Bingham undoubtedly knew Mount's works in this vein and was attracted to the idea in connection with his own experimentation with the various aspects of light and shade as a pictorial problem. In a similar direction Bingham must also have been familiar with engravings after the works of George Morland, an English painter whose rustic scenes had earned him a distinguished reputation. The popularity of paintings representing interiors of stables in which animals and other forms of farm life form the central subject evidently reached its crest in America by mid-century. And Bingham, always alertly aware of the changing tides of public taste in art, must have felt encouraged to execute a number of such pictures at this time. "Daybreak in a Stable," also called "Cattle at Daybreak: Stable Scene" (A204), certainly belongs to this series. It was submitted to the Philadelphia Art Union in 1850 and listed for sale at $50 in connection with the Union's plan of distribution. It was selected by Joseph Weir of Philadelphia,[120] but its location is now unknown.

The "Old Field Horse" (A213; plate 81), up to the present time the only extant example of Bingham's activity in this special area, affords some impression of what "Feeding Time" and "Daybreak in a Stable" were like. It was at one time in the collection of James C. McGuire of Washington, D.C., a well-known collector of American art who also purchased Bingham's "Fishing on the Mississippi" at the American Art-Union sale in December, 1852, and who also evidently owned several of Bingham's drawings. We

116. See pp. 137-139.
117. Western Art Union *Record*, I (Sept., 1849), #58.
118. *Transactions of the Western Art Union, for the Year 1849* (Cincinnati, O.: Printed at the Daily Times Printing Office, 1849), #14.
119. WAU, *Record*, I (Sept., 1849), #58.
120. PAU *Reporter*, I (Jan., Feb., May, Dec., 1851; Jan., 1852).

have no knowledge about the "Old Field Horse" before 1867, when it already formed part of the McGuire collection under that title.[121] There can be little question, however, that it was painted during the 1850's. The composition is a very simple one. An aging horse is shown standing in profile, his drooping head shown in the shadows of the stable interior, while a shaft of warm sunlight throws the rest of his body into strong relief. If one can trust the accuracy of all known details about Bingham's other pictures of the period, such as "Feeding Time" and "Daybreak in a Stable," there is certainly a similar preoccupation here with the study of atmospheric effects of juxtaposed indoor and outdoor lighting.

"The Checker Players" (A193; plate 83) was one of several genre subjects that Bingham probably executed in New York during the winter of 1850 with a view toward an ultimate sale to one of the art unions. He submitted the picture for consideration by the American Art-Union between January and February of 1851,[122] but it was declined, and he evidently did not attempt to offer it to them again. He mentioned that he had been unable to sell the painting when he wrote to Rollins on March 30, and it was evidently still on his hands in late October, 1851, when it was seen in his Columbia studio by a visiting reporter.[123] Nothing further was known of the painting's history until it turned up again in 1952 and passed into the collection of the Detroit Institute of Arts.

The mood of the picture, the general expression and attitude of the figures, recalls Bingham's "Raftsmen Playing Cards," although the outdoor aspect of the latter composition, with its additional interest in terms of western illustration, gave the motif a new connotation despite the lack of originality of the idea. In its interior setting, "The Checker Players" takes its place more readily within the long line of "gaming" pictures that can be traced back to the later seventeenth century in Italy and Holland. Bingham was undoubtedly familiar with engravings after the school of Caravaggio and Dutch masters like Teniers in which tavern scenes depicting intimate "gaming" scenes are especially familiar.[124]

121. H. T. Tuckerman, *Book of the Artists*... (New York: Putnam; London: Sampson Low, 1867), p. 632.
122. AAU, minutes of committee of management, Feb. 20, 1851, coll. NYHS.
123. B. to R., letter, New York, March 30, 1851, coll. SHSMo (*MHR*, XXXII [1937], 21); *Missouri Statesman*, Oct. 31, 1851 (copied in *Bull. AAU* [Dec., 1851], 151) painting called "Chess Players").
124. A painting of "The Card Players" (1845) by Richard Caton Woodville, now in the Detroit Institute of Arts, was engraved as one of the prints to be distributed to American Art-Union members in 1850. The subject and compositional relationships to Bingham's "Raftsmen Playing Cards" and "The Checker Players" should actually be considered more in terms of related artistic sources rather than by any assumption of a contact between the two artists. It seems unlikely that Bingham could have known Woodville's painting before he painted his "Raftsmen Playing Cards" in 1847, and the appearance of "The Checker Players" at the Art-Union at about the time the engraving was being prepared for distribution can be regarded as probable coincidence.

116

Bingham's means of storytelling is accomplished by concentrating all of the spectator's attention on the tightly woven group of figures, which is moved even closer to the picture plane than is usual and which, for the first time, is actually cut by the frame. The tendency to move his figures ever more forward, allowing the observer to partake of the main action, is one we have noted before as a progressive development in Bingham's genre subjects after 1849. But the idea of bringing the spectator into closer contact with a subject of intimate interest by allowing the figures to be cut by the framing lines, although new to Bingham, is not an original conception with him. It may have occurred to him through Mount's "Raffling for a Goose," in which a very similar means is adopted, and in which a not dissimilar organization of the central group is developed. Both artists, in turn, must also have been familiar with engravings based on pictures after Italian and Dutch masters.

The latest interior composition by Bingham now extant is "The Puzzled Witness" (A363; plate 184), painted in 1874. Although it is a design made up of many figures, the concentration is on the foreground group composed of the two opposing lawyers and the witness. The emphasis on the horizontal line of the table facing the spectator, echoed by the line of the judge's bench on the higher plane beyond, recalls the underlying pattern used in "The Checker Players" of 1850. In another sense the general conception of mood is also similar, for here Bingham reveals again his realization of the pictorial value of a psychological unity in the organization of a multiple figure composition. This painting will be discussed further in another connection (pp. 239-240).

SHOOTING FOR THE BEEF

Subjects that can be termed "sporting pictures" are rare among Bingham's known works. In his series of western illustrations, only fishing as a sportsman's activity appears as a frequent motif. Hunting scenes as such evidently held no attraction for him, and even guns only occasionally find a place in his paintings. "Shooting for the Beef" (A195; plate 86), while not concerned with hunting, can still be said to come within the special category of the "sporting" subject that gained great popularity in American genre from the 1840's onward.[125] Yet even in this instance, Bingham's approach to the theme is very different from the ordinary run of sporting pictures followed by

125. Subjects depicting duck, turkey, and snipe shooting, as well as the hunting of rabbit and deer, were popularized in painting by William Ranney (1813-1857), Arthur Fitzwilliam Tait (1819-1905), and Thomas Hewes Hinckley (1813-1896). In 1852 Nathaniel Currier (1818-1888) published his Long Island series of lithographs of *Game Bird Shooting*, based on the designs of Frances (Fanny) Palmer (ca. 1812-1876), and later the firms of Currier & Ives published many of Tait's hunting subjects.

artists of his time, which tended usually toward portrayals of the actual hunting and shooting of game. Bingham's "Shooting for the Beef" involves simply a marksmen's contest, the target being merely a bull's-eye marker; it is a quiet composition which, like all of his genre subjects of the period, tends to avoid any note of violence or cruelty. The subject is one of specific western connotation, depicting one of those typical scenes so favored by the artist. As such, it could well have served as an illustration for another of Edmund Flagg's descriptions in *The Far West*:

As I rode along through the country I was somewhat surprised at meeting people from various quarters, who seemed to be gathering to some rendezvous, all armed with rifles, and with the paraphernalia of hunting suspended from their shoulders. At length, near noon, I passed a log-cabin, around which were assembled about a hundred men; and, upon inquiry, learned that they had come together for the purpose of "shooting a beeve," as the marksmen have it. The regulations I found to be chiefly these: A bull's eye, with a centre nail, stands at a distance variously of from forty to seventy yards; and those five who, at the close of the contest, have most frequently *driven the nail*, are entitled to a fat ox divided into five portions. Many of the marksmen in the vicinity, I was informed, could drive the nail twice out of every three trials.[126]

The subject appears to have been an original one with Bingham, although a possible inspiration may be found in the turkey-shooting pictures of decidedly eastern derivation. There seems to be no pictorial precedence for the subject among Bingham's contemporaries, nor was it afterward popularized. The unusual theme was duly recognized when it was first seen by a St. Louis reporter:

Mr. George C. Bingham, "the Missouri Artist," at his studio, in this place, is about completing, for George W. Austen, Esq., of New-York, Treasurer of the American Art-Union, one of the choicest specimens of Art with which we have met. It is of rare conception and most graphically delineated. The painting represents a Western scene— *Shooting for Beef*—and presents a group of characters with life-like fidelity. There are seen the eager marksmen, in the attire of the backwoodsmen; the log cabin at the cross roads, with sign above the door lintel, *"Post Office Grocery"*; the prize in contest, a fat ox, chained to the stump hard by; a beautiful landscape in perspective,—but a description is impossible. The painting is thirty-six by forty-nine inches. Every feature on the canvas is instinct with life. Indeed it seems an incarnation rather than painting, and gives us reason to exult in the genius of Bingham, a native artist of our own State.[127]

This suggests that Bingham was either given a commission, or at least some encouragement, to paint the subject with the promise of a ready sale to the American Art-Union. The idea of some prior understanding seems the more plausible in view of the unusual size and importance of the composition.

126. E. Flagg, *The Far West...*, Vol. II, pp. 58-59.
127. *Bull. AAU*, Series for 1850 (July, 1850), 64-65 (from a "St. Louis paper.")

Most of Bingham's pictures that were produced during this period with a plan of sale to the Art-Union were of modest dimension and limited in number of figures. Instead of the usual three or four figures, "Shooting for the Beef" includes twelve figures, exclusive of four dogs, the horse, and the bull.

The painting was received by the Art-Union by February 1, 1851,[128] and the artist was paid $350 for it.[129] However, owing to the dissolution of the institution, the picture was never distributed in the usual manner, but later sold at the auction of its art properties to one Isaac Townsend at a price somewhat below that paid to Bingham.[130] It then passed out of sight until recent times, when it reappeared in the collections of Stephen C. Clark and Francis P. Garvan. In 1940 the picture was acquired by the Brooklyn Museum in New York.

Certainly in the growing conception of its role in the development of a so-called "national school of art," this painting could have served as an example that amply fulfilled the Art-Union's ideals along lines relating to "native subject matter," "American simplicity and freshness," as well as the more technical aspects of "careful preparation" to achieve "breadth of mass, of light and shade," and "higher finish and accurate drawing."[131] To be sure, Bingham's works were still looked upon as having "certain faults in color-handling," although even those "faults" were regarded as "much less conspicuous than his want of advantages would have led one to expect."[132]

Stylistically, the painting reveals those developed characteristics we have already noted in Bingham's compositions after 1849. The skillful organization of the figures and the knowing use of light and shade are especially significant in this composition. A rigid pyramidal formula has given way to less tightly woven figural arrangements, which, however, still maintain the basis of the old idea—as evinced by the central group of marksmen in which the angle formed by the rifle at the right, together with that formed by the arm of the figure standing to the left and the partially visible rifle at the apex, develop a well-defined triangle, which is in turn echoed by a smaller triangle of figures in the distance. The spectator's eye is led into the main action through the open area in the foreground, flanked by the two seated marksmen, then carried to the figure aiming his rifle, and finally along the line of perspective formed by the rifle-barrel itself into the distance.

128. AAU, Register of Pictures, coll. NYHS.
129. AAU, minutes of meeting, March 20, 1851, coll. NYHS.
130. *Catalogue of Pictures ... American Art-Union ... To be Sold ... December, 1852,* #221; Cowdrey, *American Academy ...* I, 297 (sold for $190).
131. Cowdrey, *ibid.,* I, 164-168.
132. *Bull. AAU,* Series for 1850 (Dec., 1850), 157.

119

The painting was executed during a period in which the artist was also occupied with a series of "landscapes with cattle," and thus the more than usual accent on the landscape setting is noteworthy, as is the possibility of a further clue to the cattle motif within the subject itself. In a general way the design recalls a painting by Charles Deas of a more typical American sporting subject, "The Turkey Shoot" (plate 82), which can be dated about 1836. The painting was on exhibition at the National Academy of Design in 1838 at the time Bingham is said to have visited New York.[133] But the coincidental appearance of some of the best of William Ranney's popular sporting paintings at the American Art-Union during the 1849/1850 period could have supplied the more immediate impetus for Bingham's entrance into the field at the same time.

Two studies for background figures of "Shooting for the Beef" are included in the Mercantile Library collection (S96, S107), and a third (S100) is a study for the man loading his rifle in the left foreground.

THE EMIGRATION OF DANIEL BOONE

This painting (A219; plate 87), which might be considered Bingham's earliest extant historical-genre subject, was painted in New York City during the early spring of 1851. First mention of the picture was made by the artist in a letter to Rollins, written on March 30 that year: "You wish to know what I am doing. I am now painting the *emigration of Boone* and his family to Kentucky. I do not know whether I will sell it to one of the Art Unions, or have it engraved with the expectation of remunerating myself from the sale of the engravings. The subject is a popular one in the West, and one which has never yet been painted."[134] Bingham's statement that the subject was "one which has never yet been painted" seems strange in view of the fact that a large and important painting by William Ranney called "Boone's First View of Kentucky" had been included in the American Art-Union's distribution in December, 1850,[135] and must have been on exhibition at the Union gallery during the fall at the time of Bingham's arrival in New York.[136]

---

133. Charles Deas (1818-1867) was later best known for his paintings of Indian and frontier life, and spent some years in St. Louis in the 1840's. His work must have been known to Bingham, with whom his name was sometimes linked by contemporary art critics.

134. Letter, March 30, 1851 (*MHR*, XXXII [1937], 21).

135. *Distribution of Works of Art, by the American Art-Union . . .*, Dec. 20, 1850, #2. The Art-Union painting (54 x 36), now in a private collection, is signed and dated 1849. Ranney also painted a second version of the picture during the same year, (F. S. Grubar, *William Ranney, Painter of the Early West* [New York: Clarkson N. Potter (1962)], pp. 32-33, #38, 39.)

136. Arrived in New York by Nov. 19 (Letter to AAU of that date, written in New York, accompanied pictures Bingham submitted to the Union for the 1850 distribution, coll. NYHS).

Furthermore, the Art-Union Bulletin for May, 1850, contained an engraving made after the picture.[137]

In any event, Bingham did not choose a particularly propitious moment to think of the American Art-Union in connection with the sale of his version of the Boone subject, following so closely as it did on the heels of Ranney's painting. He submitted it for purchase to the Union on April 14, 1851, but it was declined.[138] Failing in this, he evidently proceeded with his alternate idea of having it engraved. He was already on familiar terms with Goupil, who had already commissioned two of his other western subjects for publication, so we can assume that he soon brought this new picture to the firm's attention, possibly with a notion of having it published himself. What actually occurred was that Goupil purchased the copyright privilege to the painting, publishing it in lithographic form during the following year (plate 84).

When Bingham returned to St. Louis from New York in May, 1851, it was reported that the copyright to the picture had already been sold to Goupil, and that the painting itself had been sent to Paris to be engraved.[139]

We hear next about the painting in late October, 1852, when Bingham placed it on exhibition in the Grand Jury Room of the Courthouse in Columbia, along with his "County Election."[140] In an evident attempt to make his subscription appeal for the prints of the County Election picture especially attractive, he proposed to give each subscriber a share in the Boone painting, preparing to dispose of it by lot. The picture was valued by the artist at $600 and the successful subscriber was offered the alternative of the full cash value in place of the painting, if he so preferred. The Goupil lithograph had been already published by this time.[141]

With the raffle idea still in view, the picture was shown in Glasgow,[142] and probably elsewhere as well, during the weeks that followed. In early March, 1853, when Bingham was about to leave St. Louis for New Orleans with the "County Election," he advised Rollins of his plans: "I leave the 'Emigration of Boone,' in charge of Mr. Philips, the Piano forte merchant. He thinks he will be able to dispose of all the tickets in the course of two or three weeks,

---

137. *Bull. AAU*, Series for 1850 (May, 1850), opp. p. 17; engraved by Alfred Jones (1819-1900). William Ranney, like Deas, was recognized as a painter of frontier life, and there would seem little doubt that Bingham probably kept himself equally well informed about the work of this competitor in his own chosen field. It would, in fact, seem more than mere coincidence that Bingham should select this moment to enter the historical field with his version of the Daniel Boone saga, as well as to compete in the sporting picture category ("Shooting for the Beef"), certainly a field in which Ranney had obviously already achieved an enviable reputation.
138. AAU, Register of Pictures, coll. NYHS.
139. *Missouri Statesman*, May 23, 1851, 3-1 (from *St. Louis Republican*, May 13).
140. *Missouri Statesman*, Oct. 29, 1852, 2-5.
141. *Ibid.*
142. *Weekly Tribune (Glasgow)*, Nov. 11, 1852.

and will then see that the drawing is properly conducted."[143] The raffle had not taken place by October, however, when Goupil expressed a desire to publish "another and more costly engraving"[144] of the painting, and by February of 1854 the drawing was still "expected to take place in a short time."[145] But evidently the raffle had not been held by late May when the artist wrote to Rollins that "whether it shall be raffled or not, I expect to get possession of it when I reach St. Louis."[146] Goupil was still interested in republishing the picture, and Bingham, stating that the "mistake" in the production of the lithograph had "resulted from the want of proper information," could announce that the firm was then preparing to "engrave a large steel plate from it in the style first contemplated by me" as soon as the painting was again available.[147]

The Goupil firm had been making extensive use of the more modern method of reproduction—lithography—in its print-publishing activities. It was certainly a much faster means of reproduction, and a more economical one, than the engraving methods. By the early 1850's lithography had become a popularly accepted medium in France, where all of Goupil's prints were being produced. Lithographic presses were also active in America from 1820 on, but the medium was used principally for the illustration of books and periodicals. Engraving was still regarded by many connoisseurs, and by the print-buying public, as the more aesthetic means, however, and it is also evident that Bingham always thought of engraving when he first considered publishing his own pictures. This would seem to have been the case when he decided to publish his "Emigration of Daniel Boone." When Goupil offered to take over publication of the painting, Bingham had every reason to believe that it would be engraved in the manner he knew best. He had not yet seen impressions of his "In a Quandary" which Goupil had already undertaken to publish, and he obviously thought that it, too, was to be engraved. It actually was being lithographed. Therefore, the publication of the "Emigration of Daniel Boone" in lithographic form was clearly a misunderstanding between Goupil and the artist. And, in order to appease the painter (very probably subscribers already secured by Bingham had been promised an engraving), Goupil cut short the edition and promised to republish the picture in the "more costly" engraved form in the "style first contemplated" by Bingham.

143. B. to R., letter, St. Louis, Mo., March 9, 1853, coll. SHSMo (*MHR*, XXXII [1937], 29).
144. B. to R., letter, Philadelphia, Oct. 3, 1853, coll. SHSMo (*MHR*, XXXII [1938], 165).
145. B. to R., letter, Philadelphia, Feb. 1, 1854, coll. SHSMo (*MHR*, XXXII [1938], 178).
146. B. to R., letter, Philadelphia, May 29, 1854, coll. SHSMo (*MHR*, XXXII [1938], 185).
147. *Ibid.*

The history of the picture is not clear from that time until it was presented in 1890 to Washington University, St. Louis, by Nathaniel Phillips of Boston. It was said in later years that the painting came into the possession of a Boston man (possibly Phillips) after it was sold to him "by the Federals during the [Civil] War after its confiscation at an auction house on Fourth Street, in St. Louis."[148] It is not known whether the raffle was ever held, or whether Bingham was able to take possession of the painting on his return to St. Louis; but in any event, the second version of the print was never published.

The place of Daniel Boone as a symbol of the pioneer spirit of western migration, as well as his stature as a folk hero, seems to have inspired Bingham from his early years as a genre painter.[149] We can also recall that Boone himself spent his last years in Missouri, dying in 1820 not too far from the place where Bingham was then living with his family.

In the fall of 1844, when the artist was busily engaged in executing Whig banners, he suggested "old Daniel Boone himself engaged in one of his death struggles with an Indian, painted as large as life" as a subject suitable for a banner, one that he believed would not only "take with the multitude, and also be in accordance with historical truth" but also "might be emblimatical [sic] . . . of the early state of the west."[150]

In later years, Bingham, hoping for a commission from his home state, intimated that the "emigration of Boone upon a large scale" would be appropriate, although he could not be sure that the state was "ripe"[151] for a subject of this kind. While in Düsseldorf in June, 1857, the idea of painting another version of the Boone subject loomed up again in his mind. Writing to Rollins, he confided: "I have it in contemplation to paint, while we remain here, a life size figure picture of the Emigration of Boone, with the expectation of selling it to Congress and deriving also a profit from its exhibition."[152] By October of the same year, he announced his intention of beginning the work soon, that it would be "12 by 18 feet" and it could, when completed, be exhibited together with the already commissioned state portraits of Washington and Jefferson, "to form a very popular exhibition in the Western States especially, and thus amply repay me for the labor bestowed upon it."[153]

148. Bryan Obear to Jesse P. Crump, letter, St. Louis, Mo., Oct. 23, 1918, coll. Kansas City, Mo., Public Library.
149. As a youth Bingham was said to have painted a tavern signboard which had as its central subject "old Danl Boone in a buckskin dress with his gun at his side" (W. Adams, to J. S. Rollins, letter, Boonville, Mo., Mar. 20, 1882 [*MHR*, XXXIII (1939), 207, note 8]).
150. Letter, Boonville, Mo., Sept. 23, 1844 (*MHR*, XXXII [1938], 14.)
151. B. to R., letter, Philadelphia, Jan. 12, 1855, coll. SHSMo (*MHR*, XXXII [1938], 187).
152. B. to R., letter, Düsseldorf, June 3, 1857, coll. SHSMo (*MHR*, XXXII [1938], 353).
153. B. to R., letter, Düsseldorf, Oct. 12, 1857 (*MHR*, XXXII [1938], 353).

Nevertheless Bingham had evidently not begun any actual work on the proposed new picture by July, 1858,[154] perhaps hesitating to enter into so large an undertaking without more practical encouragement. At that time, however, he returned once again to his original notion of bidding for a government commission.[155] With Emanuel Leutze[156] living close by in Düsseldorf, Bingham was now in a good position to learn more about that artist's long-standing ambitions in that direction.[157] As early as April, 1852, Leutze's name had been brought to the attention of Congress in connection with a national commission,[158] and he had continued to maintain contact in government circles through the years that followed.[159] Bingham knew about an authorization obtained by the Committee of the Library of the Capitol to spend $20,000 for the purchase of works of art, presumably for the Capitol extension, and he had heard privately in Düsseldorf that Leutze had been *indirectly* assured through some of his own personal friends near the seat of Government" that he would be honored with a $10,000 commission as soon as funds were available.[160] Leutze was evidently not aware of his neighbor's similar aspirations, nor did Bingham reveal them even to his family when he

154. B. to R. letter, Düsseldorf, July 18, 1858, coll. SHSMo (*MHR*, XXXII [1938], 365).
155. *Ibid.*
156. Emanuel (Gottlieb) Leutze (1816-1868), Honorary Member, Professional, National Academy. 1844-1860; Member of the Academy 1860-1868. Born Gmünd, Würtemburg, Germany; d., Washington, D.C. Came to the United States when young; educated in Philadelphia. Studied art in Philadelphia under John Rubens Smith, later at Düsseldorf under K. F. Lessing (1841). Maintained a studio at Düsseldorf, 1845-1859. Visited United States in 1851; worked in New York and Washington, 1859-1868. (Groce and Wallace, *Dictionary of Artists in America* ..., p. 395.)
157. Letter, Düsseldorf, July 18, 1858 (*MHR*, XXXII [1938], 365): "I receive the information through an intimate acquaintance of Leutze, who gives it to me without being questioned, not dreaming that I am indulging similar aspirations."
158. C. E. Fairman, *Art and Artists of the Capitol of the United States of America* ... (Washington, D.C.: U.S. Government Printing Office, 1927), pp. 135-138.
159. *Ibid.*, p. 201.
160. Letter, July 18, 1858 (*MHR*, XXXII [1938], 365). Although Bingham believed it was through Maryland Senator James Alfred Pearce, head of the Library Committee of Congress, that Leutze had received assurance that he would be honored with a large government commission, it was apparently Capt. Montgomery C. Meigs, a West Point-educated engineer appointed superintendent of the Capitol extension in March, 1853, who had been in active contact with Leutze. As early as January 12, 1854, Meigs had written to Leutze, indirectly encouraging him to submit a design for a fresco for the new building. (He had been particularly impressed by Leutze's work and had formed unfavorable impressions of the work of leading artists of the day such as Weir, Rothermel, and Healy. In a letter to Gouverneur Kemble, Feb. 8, 1854, he said that "all the others [among Americans] are either portrait or landscape artists.") Meigs had also advised Leutze of his lack of faith in the abilities of American artists at home; significantly, in his reply, Feb. 10, 1854, Leutze assured him: "... scarcely an American artist who has come abroad has not stood, wthout a nation's applause for his award, most bravely along side of his contemporaries and competitors in the schools of Europe ....Give us a chance, and my word on it, we will do what Europe cannot do even with her best artists and I can say so because I know them all, most of them personally. *We* will paint *American pictures!*" Leutze was born in Germany, but spent his youth in America. He returned to Germany in 1840 and settled there for the next twenty years. The last decade of his life was spent in America. Most Americans, including Meigs, probably looked upon him as a foreign painter, but Leutze obviously always considered himself an

wrote to Rollins on July 18, 1858, in the hope that he would see fit to use his influence in bringing his name to the attention of the Committee.[161] Whether or not Bingham was also aware of any specific ideas that might then have been in Leutze's mind relative to subject matter is not known, but the first part of the following statement would appear to contain at least an inference pointed in the direction of the German-born artist's ambitions:

As there is yet no work of Art in the Capitol, properly illustrative of the history of the west, it seems to me that a western artist with a western subject should receive special consideration from this Committee, and also from Congress in the first appropriations which may hereafter be made for such works.

I would be very willing to undertake such a commission upon terms similar to (price excepted) those which you obtained for me from the legislature in regard to the pictures I have just completed. I would be willing to present to a committee authorized to contract for such a work, a small and complete study for the emigration of Boone, or any other subject of equal interest, for their approval and if they should approve it, contract to finish it upon a large scale, to be again subject to their approval before receiving pay for the picture. I think this is the plan which in all cases should really be pursued, and that any artist who has not sufficient confidence in his own powers to undertake a commission upon such conditions, should not be employed.[162]

However, the government's award for a national picture "illustrative of the history of the west" eventually went to Leutze, who was commissioned on July 2, 1861, to paint, for $20,000, the work we know as "Westward the Course of Empire Takes its Way."[163]

Despite Bingham's ambitious plans for a monumental painting of the subject, he seems never to have received encouragement to proceed beyond the version of the "Emigration of Daniel Boone" that he completed in New York during the spring of 1851. We have already noted that it was undoubtedly a subject that held much attraction for him. But unlike most of his other genre subjects, it was one that lacked the element of personal experience. Apart from his political banners, such as the one of the "Mill Boy" representing Henry Clay as a boy riding the slashes of Hanover, Bingham had never executed a subject of historic connotation. His approach to his various genre

American. (Meigs-Leutze correspondence, Library of Congress; letter, B. to R., Düsseldorf, July 18, 1858 [*MHR*, XXXII (1938), 365]; Fairman, *Art and Artists of the Capitol*, p. 149.)

161. Letter July 18, 1958 (*MHR*, XXXII [1938], 365).

162. *Ibid*. Leutze, in a letter written to Capt. M. C. Meigs, Feb. 10, 1854, submitting ideas for a large painting for the Capitol, included "Emigration of the West" as a suitable subject. Earlier, Henry Inman (1801-1846) had selected "The Emigration of Daniel Boone to Kentucky" for his Capitol commission, but the work was not carried beyond a preliminary sketch at the time of his death (Fairman, *op. cit.*, pp. 158-159, 159 n. 2).

163. Fairman, *op. cit.*, p. 202. Contrary to Bingham's notions regarding payment for national commissions, Leutze's contract called for a large payment following completion of the design, as well as monthly installments during the progress of the actual painting.

125

subjects was characterized by its typical aspect, but here he must have realized that it was the opposite quality, the choice of the moment of the most dramatic significance, that determined the successful historic composition. Thus, for his "Emigration of Boone" he selected what was perhaps the most important, as well as the most dramatic incident in Boone's life—namely, the episode that represented him bringing his family and little band of settlers through the Cumberland Gap, the gateway to Kentucky, in 1775.

Although he must have known about Daniel Boone's exploits from his childhood on, Bingham's habitual concern for accuracy of detail must have suggested consultation of published source material. One contemporary reporter said that the design was "taken from Marshall's History of Kentucky,"[164] although an examination of that source indicates that the author was apparently little interested in the background elements of the Boone story. If we accept Marshall's history as the painter's sole inspiration, it would seem more than likely that one fact alone therein described actually served as the guiding motive for his composition—the statement that in bringing his family into the western country, "his [Boone's] wife, and daughter, were the first white women ever known in Kentucky."[165] The importance of this motif for Bingham's interpretation of the Emigration is further emphasized when we note that the Goupil lithograph produced from the painting bears a dedication to "The Mothers and Daughters of the West." The location of the figures of Rebecca and Jemima Boone at the apex of the pyramidal group adds further to our concept of the significant part played by the two women in the composition.

The "Emigration" is unusual among Bingham's extant works in still another aspect: It is probably the only picture he altered extensively after its completion.[166] In fact the picture was evidently repainted after the original composition had been lithographed (P6; plate 84). We can thus assume that in all probability the changes were made by the artist before the end of October, 1852, at which time the painting was on exhibition in Columbia in connection with the announced raffle. It certainly does not appear likely that it was altered after March 1853, when it had been placed in the hands of Mr. Philips, the "Piano forte merchant" of St. Louis.

The rather considerable repainting was confined mainly to the background, the comparatively meaningless and topographically commonplace selection of

---

164. *Missouri Statesman*, May 23, 1851, 3-1. Referring to Humphrey Marshall (1756-1841), *The History of Kentucky. Exhibiting an Account of the Modern Discovery; Settlement; Progressive Development; Civil and Military Transactions; and the Present State of the Country....*, Frankfort. Ky.: G. S. Robinson, Printer, 1824. 2 vols.
165. Marshall, *The History of Kentucky...*, I, 22.
166. The "ghosting" of the first painting is visible upon close examination of the picture.

landscape elements being replaced by a forbidding aspect of high mountains and deep passes rendered in startling effects of light and dark against a dramatic sky, somewhat reminiscent of the landscapes by Thomas Cole. This was certainly more characteristic of the terrain through which Boone and his family must have had to make their way. Perhaps Bingham realized as much and had even read Boone's own description of the place by that time:

We had passed over two mountains, Powell's and Walden's, and were approaching Cumberland mountain.... These mountains are in the wilderness, in passing from the old Settlements in Virginia to Kentucky, are ranged in a south-west and north-west direction, are of great length and breadth, and, not far distant from each other. Over them nature hath formed passes less different than might be expected from the view of such huge piles. The aspect of these cliffs is so wild and horrid, that it is impossible to behold them without terror.[167]

Since no portraits exist that depict Daniel Boone as he appeared at the time of the migration, one must assume the artist portrayed him ideally. For the all-important central figure of Rebecca Boone, however, he may indeed have taken special pains. A document written some years ago seems to indicate that Bingham copied her features from a supposed portrait of her.[168]

The general aspect of the composition reveals, as always, Bingham's careful and deliberate organization of forms. The pyramidal group of figures occupies a central position in both versions. During the later repainting Bingham added two new heads on either side of Jemima Boone, probably in an effort to solidify the angular line formed by the group. This filling-in of voids and deliberate solidification of figure masses we will observe repeated in the alterations the artist made in the second version of "The County Election," painted within the same period. The greater bulk developed by the figures in shadow in the left background serves to emphasize the relief quality of the forms in light. The large masses, composed of mountains and foilage to left and right, act as effective foils in the later version, serving further to enhance the dramatic effect of the incident represented—an effect not realized in the original picture.

The artist's growing understanding of light and shade at this period is again evidenced in the painting. A shaft of light enters the picture at left, striking the chief actors in the manner of a stage spotlight and etching in light the wings formed by the tree trunks at either side in the foreground. The distance is effectively held in retreating planes of half-light, middle tones, and deep shadows.

167. *Life and Adventures of Colonel Daniel Boon, the First White Settler of the State of Kentucky ... Written by Himself* ... (Brooklyn, N.Y.: Printed by C. Wilder, 1823), p. 15.
168. B. Obear to J. P. Crump, letter, Oct. 23, 1918 (source in note 148 above).

127

Beyond the inspiration of the subject, Bingham may have drawn from other sources once the central theme was established. An engraving by Sartain after a design by Peter F. Rothermel (1817-1895), probably known to the artist, also reveals a central group of a pioneer family finding their way through a narrow pass in a rugged wilderness setting (plate 85). Details of tree-stumps and even the way the man holds his weapon bear striking resemblances to Bingham's composition, painted two years after the Rothermel subject, titled "The Pioneers," was published in a gift annual.[169]

Bingham's strong sense of the classical as the ideal figural type, as well as his early studies made from the antique, reveals itself in the poses of two of his pioneers. Daniel Boone himself strides forward like the Greek "Doryphorus" (plate 89), although the position of the legs is reversed and the original balance of the figure is lost in the translation. The companion at left ties his moccasin in the manner of his ancestor the "Jason" or "Cincinnatus" (plate 88).

Sketches for the figures of the guide (S102B) and Flanders Callaway (S3) (the pioneer at Boone's side) are included in the Mercantile Library collection.

THE ELECTION SERIES

As "The Missouri Artist," whose fame even in his own day seems to have been based on his scenes illustrating life in the west, it was inevitable that Bingham should one day turn to a representation of a familiar aspect of Missouri life that held a special meaning and attraction for him—the political scene. Just as his personal observation of the boatmen at play had inspired some of the finest genre subjects of his early years, the reflections of his ever-increasing interest and personal contact with politics in his home state are to be discovered in the most important works of his mature period.

Bingham's lively interest in politics is revealed in many of his early letters, and we have already observed that he painted political banners as early as 1840.[170] But his actual translation of the political scene to canvas seems not to have seriously developed until his own appearance in the role of politician made him acutely aware of its artistic possibilities.

In a bitter contest in 1846, which ended in his defeat, Bingham ran for office as a State Representative. His opponent, Erasmus Darwin Sappington, contested the results of the election which had shown a small margin in favor of the artist and was able to have the affair decided in his own favor.[171]

169. *The Opal, A Pure Gift for All Seasons* (New York: J. C. Riker, 1849), opp. p. 143.
170. See above, pp, 73-79.
171. *Missouri Statesman*, Dec. 25, 1846, 1-4; *Liberty Weekly Tribune*. Jan. 2, 1847, 3-3.

Bingham, feeling that the ultimate result derived from political maneuvering, appeared before the Legislature and "salted down the whole Sappington family,"[172] and, as one newspaper reported with relish, "cast the hot shot in every direction."[173] At the following election for the same office, in 1848, Bingham was again Sappington's opponent, but this time he was elected by a decisive margin.[174]

Without doubt, the artist's close contact with politics, during which he must have taken to the stump himself, brought home the realization of the rich store of pictorial subject-matter available. Indeed, his sketches for his first recorded picture of a political subject, "The Stump Orator," were probably made at the precise moment he was an active participant in a similar action. The painting was completed within a month of the election.

As an artist consciously aware of his position as an illustrator of the western scene, Bingham obviously lost little time in taking advantage of the fertile pictorial possibilities of the subject matter. Yet we must realize that he was undoubtedly cognizant of the works of his predecessors in the field. As we shall later be able to observe in greater detail, he was certainly familiar with William Hogarth's series of election pictures through the engraved versions, and in a similar fashion knew David Wilkie's "The Village Politicians." Among American paintings, he could have come into contact with subjects depicting politics in action by John Lewis Krimmel, William E. Winner, Manuel J. De França, John C. Hagen, and James G. Clonney, whose depictions of such scenes were exhibited in New York and Philadelphia between 1838 and 1845.[175]

The Stump Orator

"The Stump Orator" (A153) was completed by late in November, 1847, and placed on exhibition at Mr. Wool's store in St. Louis where Bingham had shown his "Lighter Relieving a Steamboat Aground" and "Raftsmen Playing Cards" earlier in the same year. It would seem conceivable to assume that the very good press reception accorded his paintings on the previous occasion, as well as the subsequent quick sale of one of them to a prominent local collector, encouraged him to exhibit the picture at Mr. Wood's establishment.

172. *Boonville Weekly Observer*, Mar. 11, 1847, 1-6.
173. *Ibid.*
174. *Missouri Statesman*, Aug. 11, 1848, 2-1.
175. In Philadelphia: John Lewis Krimmel (1789-1821), engraving by Alexander Lawson after his "Election Day in Philadelphia," PAFA (1843); William E. Winner (b. *ca.* 1815), "Election Night," AFS (1843). In New York: Manuel J. De França (1808-1865) "The Red-Hot Politician," Apollo Association (1838, 1839); John C. Hagen (active 1838-1882), "The Politicians" and "The Stump Candidate," NAD (1839, 1841); James G. Clonney (1812-1867), "The Political Argument," AAU (1845).

But the painting did not sell, although lavishly reported by at least one St. Louis newspaper,[176] and it was soon afterward shipped to New York, where Bingham hoped to dispose of it to the American Art-Union.

As he had evidently done in the past, Bingham submitted the picture to the Art-Union for sale through Robert F. Fraser, the superintendent of the Union, believing that he was following a standard procedure in such matters.[177] Fraser, however, actually acted as agent for the artist, and charged a commission on the sale price, although as it later turned out, neither he nor any other officer of the Art-Union was permitted to receive any compensation for the handling or sale of any artist's works submitted to the organization.[178]

Fraser offered the picture to the Art-Union at the painter's asking price of $400, and at the meeting of the Executive Committee on April 20, 1848, it was "resolved that $400 be offered for Mr. Bingham's picture 'The Stump Orator' framed, payable 1 Nov. next."[179] But the resolution must have been overruled shortly thereafter, for we are later told that it was not immediately purchased, "on account of the price."[180] Still representing the artist as agent, Fraser then sent the picture to the National Academy of Design,[181] where it appeared in its annual exhibition, listed as "for sale."[182] We can probably assume that the exhibition took place, as usual, during May and June of 1848. The painting was not sold during the course of the show, and it was afterward once more submitted by Fraser to the Art-Union.[183] On October 5, when the Committee met, a reduced offer of $350 was made[184] and accepted,[185] the picture then being included among the works of art to be awarded at the annual distribution that year. On December 22 "The Stump Orator" was awarded to William Duncan, a leading cotton merchant of Savannah, Georgia,[186] who was fortunate enough to receive yet another picture award from the Art-Union at the next distribution.[187]

176. *Daily Missouri Republican*, Nov. 30, 1847, 2-1.
177. B. to AAU, letter, Arrow Rock, Mo., Oct. 18, 1848, coll. NYHS.
178. A. Warner to B., letter, New York, Nov. 2 [1848], coll. NYHS (letterpress copy).
179. AAU, minutes of meeting, executive committee, April 20, 1848, coll. NYHS.
180. Warner to B., letter, Nov. 2 [1848].
181. *Ibid.*
182. *Catalogue of the Twenty-third Annual Exhibition of the National Academy of Design ...* (New York: I. Sackett, Printer, 1848), #226.
183. Warner to B., letter, Nov. 2 [1848].
184. AAU, minutes of meeting, committee of management, Oct. 5, 1848, coll. NYHS.
185. B. to AAU, letter, Oct. 18, 1848.
186. *Transactions of the American Art-Union, for the Year 1848* (New York: G. F. Nesbitt, Printer, 1849), #212.
187. William Duncan was awarded "Canal Scene—Little Falls (N.Y.)" by William R. Miller in the 1849 AAU distribution.

Although the painting has been lost since it passed into the hands of Mr. Duncan in 1848, its place among Bingham's more important genre works, and particularly as one setting the keynote for the election series, compels its special consideration in this study. Certainly the fact that the price the artist had originally set on his picture was higher than any previous one would indicate to some extent the relative importance he gave to this work. In addition, the more than usual amount of extant contemporary description and criticism appears to attest to a picture of outstanding appearance. Fortunately, we are enabled to get a good over-all impression of the composition through this special attention. And the fortuitous discovery, as this book was about to go to press, of a daguerreotype of the painting (plate 89) probably made shortly after its completion, now enables use to consider this important composition on much firmer ground than has been possible before.

A St. Louis reporter's observation of the painting, describing its various parts in vivid detail, affords us our first impression of the picture through the eyes of a contemporary:

Paintings—We yesterday called to see the efforts of two of our Western artists, and only regret that our familiarity with the art does not enable us to do justice to the merits of the painters.

The painting by *Mr. G. C. Bingham*, better known as the Missouri artist, is at the room of Mr. Wool in Glasgow's row, on Fourth street. It represents "Stump Speaking," as seen in the west. For vitality, freshness, grouping, shade and light, and costume, we have never seen anything equal to it. It is no carricature [*sic*] nor an attempt at carricature [*sic*], but a picture which may be seen at any of our respectable political meetings in the west. The artist has fixed the scene at the moment of time, (late in the evening,) when the orator is arriving at the climax of his argument. The speaker is evidently well pleased with the impression which he is making. He is mounted on the *stump* of a fresh cut tree. In front of him, "whittling a stick," sits his "opponent", with his brows knit, and the blood veins swollen, mouth compressed, and rage and opposition depicted in his countenance. Around and along the trunk of the prostrate tree are congregated the sovereigns, comprising about sixty figures, in the attitude of listening to the orator—some pleased, some displeased, and some without any idea at all of what he is saying. We could occupy a very considerable space in sketching the varied countenances, the changes of expression, and the predominant feeling, which the artist has given to each individual of the group; but no description could do justice to the talent, skill and study, which it displays. It is a painting which may be studied by the hour—every face may be critically examined, and yet in every one there is evidence of a deep, thoughtful and comprehensive understanding, on the part of the painter, of the feelings, motives and impulses which act upon crowds and on individuals. As we have said, it is not an attempt to carricature [*sic*], but an effort to draw an unexaggerated representation of an assemblage which is familiar to every one in the west. The postures—the dress, as clean and neat as the humble means of western life will justify—the little knot of busy politicians around the finely dressed

131

Demagogue, in the back ground—the idiotic expression of an unfortunate inebriate behind the speaker—the joy of the zealous partizan—the cool, calculating aspect of the more reflecting citizen—the half stare and half incredulity of another—the man with his coon skin cap and rifle—the side bar dialogue at the end of the circle—the tavern, and unfinished log house in the distance—the mellowed landscape and autumnal evening scene—give to the whole a merit, a richness and a beauty, to which ordinary language cannot do justice. No part of the picture is more happy, nor in any part of it has the artist displayed more skill, than in the ease and naturalness with which he has grouped this large number of figures together, upon a small canvass—preserving all the characteristics of dress and countenance, and, what we conceive the most difficult part of the painting, the usual posture of those who attend such meetings.

We could indulge in our admiration of many other points of the picture, but, after all, give to the reader no idea of its excellence. It must be seen and *understood*, to be appreciated. The artist, himself, has been on the stump, and gone through a hot and exciting canvass. Whilst he disclaims every thing personal—and we know he is above anything of the sort—we think we can recognize in the group many well known political characters. Of this, they ought not to complain for they have here the best—almost the only chance of immortality.

The painting will be sent, in a few days, to New York, to the exhibition of the Art Union. Those who desire to enjoy the luxury of examining it, should at once call Mr. Wool's rooms. . . .[188]

The composition was unquestionably the most ambitious undertaken by Bingham up to that time. He had experimented with figure subjects since he first began to devote himself seriously to genre, some two years before, but none had contained more than eight figures. In this painting he bravely launched a design including "about sixty figures," a composition in which he evidently attempted to incorporate all possible varieties of pose and expression in his repertoire. His sketchbooks were without doubt filled with sketches of the various types he had observed during his own recent experience on the stump. The St. Louis critic was able to discover, upon a closer examination of the individual figures, "an unexaggerated representation of an assemblage which is familiar to every one in the West," even fancying that it was possible to "recognize in the group many well known political characters." As in other instances, Bingham had obviously chosen the familiar aspect of the western political scene he knew, giving some individual figures those characteristics of physiognomy which seemed not only typical but also familiar enough to suggest identification with known personalities. Indeed, various so-called keys to Bingham's election pictures have been suggested through the years. This is the first indication of that kind of resemblance, and we note that at the first hint the reporter also said the artist "disclaims every thing personal" in his portrayal of "The Stump Orator."

188. *Daily Missouri Republican*, Nov. 30, 1847, 2-1.

Although Bingham's earlier figure pictures clearly evidence an interest in the study of character and expression, this interest seems not to have been thoroughly exploited by him until this time. Certainly the many-figured composition encouraged this kind of exploration, and the effect was noted by the St. Louis reporter. He specifically describes the "varied countenances" and "changes of expression," and even more pointedly underlines the fact that "every face may be critically examined, and yet in every one there is evidence of a deep, thoughtful, and comprehensive understanding, on the part of the painter, of the feelings, motives and impulses which act upon crowds and on individuals." All of this leads us to wonder whether Bingham had attempted, like some of his predecessors and contemporaries among American painters, to apply a study of phrenological science to his art.

The search for reality in both portrait and genre painting, which involved the necessity of achieving a wide variety of emotional expression, had led many artists into intensive studies of interpretive physiognomy and phrenology. Such studies were widespread in Europe and America by the 1840's. Johann Caspar Lavater's *Essays on Physiognomy* had long been available in English, the first American edition having appeared in Boston in the 1790's. The *Physiognomical System of Drs. Gall and Spurzheim*, the work of Johann Gaspar Spurzheim and Franz Josef Gall, had been published in England in 1815, and American editions of Spurzheim's *Phrenology in Connection with the Study of Physiognomy* had appeared by 1834 following his death in Boston the previous year while on a lecture tour. By 1820 John Wesley Jarvis, the portrait painter, was said to have "entered into the view of the phrenologists most enthusiastically" after having read a copy of Gall and Spurzheim which had been brought to his attention, noting afterward that it "elevates our art to a science" and "renders the artist the phrenological delineator."[189] William Sidney Mount reportedly owned a copy of Sir Charles Bell's *The Anatomy and Philosophy of Expression* in 1846,[190] a book that was first published in London in 1806 and ran into many subsequent editions. It hardly seems conceivable that Bingham would not have had recourse to such studies in connection with his own work. Certainly it was just that stamp of character and expression which had attracted the St. Louis reporter to "The Stump Orator," a quality for which his later Election pictures became best known to a public already versed in pseudoscientific studies of phrenology and physiognomy and thus well-equipped to recognize and appreciate those specific characteristics of his works.

189. Dunlap, *History* . . ., Vol. II, pp. 77-78. Further discussion in Harold E. Dickson, *John Wesley Jarvis, American Painter* . . . (New York: The New-York Historical Society, 1949), pp. 206-207.
190. M. B. Cowdrey and H. W. Williams, Jr., *William Sidney Mount* . . ., p. 10, note 54.

133

The concentration on expression is particularly well demonstrated by the collection of Bingham's drawings in the Mercantile Library. At the same time the strongly individual character of so many of the figures also suggests that Bingham must have had direct reference to models in his work. The recurrence of the same facial types would seem to enforce that impression, as well as the fact that none of the drawings seem to be casual, on-the-spot sketches, but are evidently carefully posed and precisely delineated.

On the technical side the contemporary observer was able to declare that "for vitality, freshness, grouping, shade and light, and costume, we have never seen anything equal to it," pointing especially to the "ease and naturalness with which he has grouped this large number of figures together, upon a small canvass." But, for the most part, the reporter preferred to dwell on the subject itself, regretting that his "familiarity with the art" (or lack of it!) did not permit him to "do justice to the merits of the painters" (referring to Bingham and Seth Eastman, both of whose paintings were then on exhibit at Wool's store).

The artist's style was more likely to receive special critical attention by the New York critics, and so it did when the painting was placed on public exhibition at the National Academy of Design several months later:

> Mr. Bingham's picture, *The Stump Orator* ... makes one's eyes ache to look at it. All the laws of chiar' oscuro are set at defiance, so that the eye is distracted and carried all over the canvas, without a single resting-place. He has evidently no idea of the value of light, and how sparingly it should be used in a picture. In color it is unmistakably bad; its only merit is in the broad exaggerated characters of the heads, which look as if painted from daguerreotypes.[191]

Later in the year, when the picture had passed into the hands of the American Art-Union, and was on exhibit at its gallery, newspaper critics were able to state simply that "this highly wrought and multitudinous picture is full of both merits and faults,"[192] or that it was "executed with the nicety of a daguerreotype but with a monotony also,"[193] with the additional comment that "every separate part ... is a picture in itself, replete with strong character; so that one recovers, on closer examination, from the unpleasant impression the first glance may have made upon him."[194]

The painting, referred to as "highly wrought," with "every part ... a picture in itself,"[195] can be said to be accurately described as we now see it

191. *The Literary World*, III (June 3, 1848), 350-351.
192. *Bull.* AAU, I (Nov. 25, 1848), 29 (from the *Evening Post*).
193. *Ibid.*, p. 30 (from the *New York Courier and Enquirer*).
194. *Ibid.*
195. *Ibid.*, 29.

134

through the contemporary photograph. The composition is painstakingly organized, with individual figures and groups of figures carefully placed to form part of the whole. On a less ambitious scale, the "Raftsmen Playing Cards" and "Lighter Relieving a Steamboat Aground," both exhibited earlier in 1847, reveal a classicizing organization as their outstanding characteristic. Bingham's experience with figure compositions had been limited up to this time to small groups that could be held together by the simple expedient of the pyramidal form, which the instruction book had assured the artist would give the desired sense of "order and regularity" to the design.

However, the same instructor had also pointed out that the "form of a composition is best suggested by the subject or design"[196] and had indicated that, as an alternate to the geometric mode, the circular form be regarded as "applicable to the highest walks of art from its simplicity and extensive sweep."[197] For compositions of outdoor scenes, it was considered as often the only arrangement in which the artist could obtain the "mass of shade so necessary to the group in a pictorial point of view."[198] Raphael was most frequently illustrated for the best examples of the use of the form. Although Bingham had already learned how to make use of the circular mode in combination with his geometrically evolved figure groups, he was yet to evolve a composition that reflected the pure use of the form prescribed in the instruction manuals. "The Stump Orator" afforded him an excellent opportunity to adopt that form, chiefly because the many-figured subject also demanded a new solution to the problem of design.

A close analysis of the photograph of the composition clearly indicates how carefully Bingham plotted his pictorial plan, with the large group of figures tightly organized into a circle that is dominated by the elevated figure of the orator at left. Following the example of Raphael demonstrated in the instruction book ("The Death of Ananias"), the figures are shown "gradually declining from the sides to the centre of the circle in the foreground."[199] The tight massing of figures to left and right encloses the composition securely within its frame, as well as increasing the required sense of "order and regularity." While the foreground ring of figures not only carries the richest concentration of the subject in terms of variety of posture and expression, the dense row of figures in the background somewhat detracts from the total effect, although it was probably introduced to enforce the structure of the composition. The rigid, heavily populated area, with its evenly arranged figure heights, not only offers no relief to the observer insofar as the play of

196. Burnet, *Practical Hints on Composition* . . . , p. [7].
197. *Ibid.*, p. 24.
198. *Ibid.*, p. 25.
199. *Ibid.*, p. 24.

135

light and shade distribution is concerned, but creates that sense of "monotony" which at least one critic observed in the picture. As a compositional feature, the figures also unfortunately block off any progression into the landscape in the far distance.

Using "Raftsmen Playing Cards" as probably the most typical example of Bingham's style at the time, we can also observe that those characteristics we have already discussed would also describe the outstanding points of "The Stump Orator." A decisive outlining of the figures and an emphasis on detail, with the figures set in sharp relief against a more atmospheric landscape, must almost certainly have been among those specific elements that defined the style of the picture. The "strong character," which partially distracted the *Courier* critic from what he considered less agreeable impressions, probably resulted from the artist's decisive delineations of the figural types and those accompanying details that added to the painting's undoubtedly great storytelling power.

The heaviest criticism leveled against the picture was on the basis of its color and use of light and shade. It was much the same criticism that had previously confronted "Raftsmen Playing Cards" and "The Jolly Flatboatmen." Earlier, Bingham's color had been termed "disagreeable" and "monotonous";[200] now it was described as "unmistakably bad."[201] The warm, high-pitched color that marked his palette in the raftsmen and boatmen subjects was very probably repeated in "The Stump Orator." Bingham was still struggling with the varying problems of light and shade and its use as a unifying force in his compositions. The restless, dissonant quality of light and dark values is clearly visible in the old photograph of "The Stump Orator." In dealing with a subject involving so many figures, the disturbing lack of organization in terms of light and shade must have indeed made "one's eyes ache to look at it."[202] Assuredly the painter took such severe criticism to heart, for he did not undertake so "multitudinous" a composition again until he felt himself in far better control of the problem. In any event, at least five years were to elapse before he attempted a large figural subject again, and seven before he undertook to paint another version of "The Stump Orator."

Twelve of the sketches of figures in the Mercantile Library collection can be closely identified with this composition (S9, 20, 36, 42, 43, 45, 67, 70, 80, 81, 88, 103*b*), and others were very probably prepared in connection with it (S12, 59, 74, 83). The drawing for the political opponent (S20),

200. *The Literary World*, II (Oct. 23, 1847), 377-378.
201. *Ibid.*, III (June 3, 1848), 350-351.
202. *Ibid.*

136

shown "whittling a stick," seated "with his brows knit, and the blood veins swollen, mouth compressed, and rage and opposition depicted in his countenance," is one of the most powerful examples of Bingham's draughtsmanship. A drawing for a figure in the collection of the William Rockhill Nelson Gallery, in Kansas City (plate 91), previously unidentified with any known subject, can now be associated with this picture.

Country Politician

Bingham's second recorded political subject, "Country Politician" (A158) was first brought to the attention of the public when it was seen and described by a St. Louis reporter[203] who may have viewed it at the artist's studio in the city during April, 1849. The painting was first placed on formal exhibition in June of the same year in Cincinnati, where it was listed as "for sale" in the gallery of the Western Art Union.[204] When it evidently did not find a ready buyer in Ohio, the painter brought it to New York, offering it to his old patron the American Art-Union, priced at $200.[205] The picture appears to have been immediately purchased by the Art-Union for the price asked,[206] and at the annual distribution in December, the Union awarded it to John Boyd of Winsted, Connecticut.[207] The subsequent history of the picture is unknown.

As with "The Stump Orator," it is the St. Louis reporter (perhaps the same one) who affords us our most revealing impression of the picture. Discussing it, along with two other Bingham compositions, he describes the subject as "a scene in a bar room" in which the group is most perfect life-like. The jolly old landlord, smoking his pipe; a politician, most earnestly discussing to a very indifferent looking farmer, the Wilmot Proviso; whilst a boy, with coat-tail turned up to the stove, is reading a showbill."[208] The description that accompanied the picture when it was listed by the American Art-Union was briefer, and less colorful: "Three men are seated around a stove, one of whom is arguing some knotty point with an old traveller. Behind the stove a man is standing warming his back with his coat-skirts lifted."[209]

With both published references as a basis for identification, we can perhaps venture to relate at least three of the Mercantile Library sketches to this composition: the country politician himself (S65), "arguing some knotty

203. *Daily Missouri Republican,* April 17, 1849, 2-1.
204. WAU *Record,* I (June 1849), #151.
205. B. to AAU, letter, [New York] Aug. 1, 1849, coll. NYHS.
206. AAU, minutes, committee of management, Aug. 2, 1849, coll. NYHS.
207. *Transactions of the AAU, 1849,* #232.
208. *Daily Missouri Republican,* April 17, 1849, 2-1.
209. *Bull. AAU,* II (Oct. 1849), #232.

point," the "indifferent looking farmer" (S90), or other variants of the figure (S66, S89), and the "jolly old landlord, smoking his pipe" (S102A). Both S65 and S102A were used, with slight alteration, in a later Bingham composition, "Canvassing for a Vote" (plate 102).

A painting of modest dimensions (20 x 24) and composed of only four figures, the "Country Politician" is nevertheless unusual among Bingham subjects in presenting an interior scene. The artist seemed generally to prefer outdoor settings, which enabled him to make use of landscape elements and to represent landmarks of a typically western connotation. Pictures portraying local political scenes, some undoubtedly set within interiors, were not uncommon among the works of Bingham's contemporaries. Wilkie's "Village Politicians" had great fame at the time and we can assume, with little doubt, that Bingham knew at least one engraving made from it (plate 92). The rustic interior, the village characters listening to the alehouse politician, the participants registering varying degrees of interest and intelligence—all are reminiscent of the approach adopted by our artist in his own pictures. And the gesture of the politician himself is especially familiar in its close parallel to a specific Bingham type.

The descriptions of "Country Politician" suggest an even more immediate connection with one of William Sidney Mount's compositions, "The Tough Story" (or "The Long Story") (plate 93), so much so that, with perhaps the addition of one figure, they might serve to describe the latter as well. The Mount subject, representing a country tavern interior, shows two seated figures, one being a "kind of Barroom Oracle"[210] who is explaining some debatable point to the landlord, who smokes his pipe while listening. Between them is a stove with a young man standing behind it warming his back. Bingham could have seen this painting when it was exhibited at the National Academy of Design in New York in 1838.[211] In any event, he must at least have been familiar with the picture through the popular engraving of it that appeared in *The Gift* for 1842.[212] Mount's painting was considered the "jewel" of the 1838 exhibition, where it was admired because the artist seemed free of that "strict adherence to the rules" which the *Mirror* critic saw as Wilkie's weakness.[213] Yet Mount made use of instruction books in his studies, and the pyramidal form of this composition would suggest his deliberate use of that

210. M. B. Cowdrey and H. W. Williams, *William Sidney Mount....*, p. 18: quoting from a letter of Mount to Robert J. Gilmor, describing the picture.
211. This possibility has already been discussed, p. 47.
212. *The Gift, A Christmas and New Year's Present for 1842. Ed. by Miss Leslie* (Philadelphia: Carey & Hart [*ca.* 1842], opp. p. 99.
213. *New-York Mirror.* XVI (July 7, 1838), 15. See p. 47 above where this review is partially quoted.

form of organization. Bingham's own adherence to the rules of the instruction book, and more specifically to the angular type of composition, must have inevitably led him to make special note of Mount's adaptation of the form in "The Tough Story."

The contemporary critic did not enter into a discussion of Bingham's style as displayed in the "Country Politician," but those characteristics of a developing style that we noted in our study of another composition, "Watching the Cargo," can also be considered as descriptive of the picture. Both paintings must have been executed at about the same time, and both were submitted to and purchased by the Art-Union on the same day. A writer for the *Bulletin* of the Art-Union at precisely that time, discussing Bingham's life and work at some length, made special note of the artist's obvious development in the following significant terms: "It is pleasant to see . . . that observation and study have already corrected, to a considerable degree, those defects of color, in the distribution of light and shadow and in specific form, which formerly diminished the value of his works; while the higher qualities of character and expression and general form which first attracted the attention of the Committee are still preserved."[214]

The County Election

The third, and by far the most important of Bingham's political subjects up to this time was "The County Election" (A229; plate 94), which became extremely popular among the artist's contemporaries, largely through the engraving made after it. The painter himself, after several years of painstaking study of the many technical problems involved in the making of a large figure composition of this kind, and no doubt benefiting from the criticism leveled against his earlier attempts in that direction, very likely considered "The County Election" his crowning effort up to this time. His friend Major Rollins regarded the picture as "Unquestionably the 'master piece' of his [Bingham's] life,"[215] and the press appeared no less enthusiastic, one such observer going so far as to state that "it is one of the most admirable pictures that ever came from the artist's brush or brain."[216]

His most ambitious picture in terms of size, it was, nevertheless, executed for the most part during a three-month period, with final touches, and perhaps slight alterations, being made from time to time during the few months that followed. The original version of the picture was painted in Bingham's studios

214. *Bull.* AAU, II (Aug. 1849), 10.
215. James S. Rollins to A. Warner, AAU, letter, Columbia, Mo., Jan. 11, 1852, coll. NYHS.
216. *Daily Louisville Times,* May 14, 1853, 3-3.

in Columbia and St. Louis,[217] begun in August, 1851,[218] and completed by early February of the following year,[219] although it must have been already well in hand by late October, 1851, when it was seen and described in detail by a Columbia reporter.[220]

The idea of having the painting engraved had been put forth as early as January, 1852, by Major Rollins, who even took it upon himself to address the American Art-Union in the hope of persuading the Union to purchase and reproduce the picture.[221] The Union declined, however, pointing out that it would be an impractical idea for their purposes, considering the excessive length of time it would take to produce an engraving involving so many figures, although it agreed that the subject would "no doubt be a popular work for Engraving."[222] When that plan failed, the artist, evidently with his friend's further encouragement and necessary financial assistance, set about having the picture engraved himself. During June, 1852, while Bingham was in the East as a delegate for the eighth district to the Whig national convention at Baltimore, he obviously took advantage of this chance proximity to Philadelphia to visit the city and consult with engravers,[223] afterward continuing to New York for the same purpose. These consultations included two of the best-known American engravers of the time, Alfred Jones and John Sartain. We know now that Bingham would probably have awarded the commission to Jones, but the printmaker was evidently unable to guarantee completion of the engraving within a "reasonable period," and so it was given to Sartain, who was, however, not spared the knowledge that he was the artist's "second choice."[224] The engraving was contracted for on August

217. Bingham's letters and the reports of visiting reporters, referring to the painting, emanate from Columbia and St. Louis. According to C. B. Rollins, "Bingham painted 'The County Election' in Arrow Rock" (*MHR,* XXXII [1937], 25, note 35), but there appears to be no evidence at the basis of the statement.

218. *Missouri Statesman,* Oct. 31, 1851, 2-4: "The painting has engaged the artist constantly for three months." The picture was probably begun in Columbia during the summer of 1851, and was still in progress there by late October of the same year. The artist took it to St. Louis in November (*The Western Journal,* VII [Nov. 1851], 145) and completed work on it during his winter sojourn in the city.

219. *Weekly Missouri Statesman,* Jan. 9, 1852, 3-2 (from *St. Louis Intelligencer*): speaks of the painting as "not quite finished," but Bingham, in his letter to Goupil & Co., St. Louis, Jan. 31, 1852, mentions the picture as one "I have had on hand."

220. *Missouri Statesman,* Oct. 31, 1851, 2-4.

221. Rollins to Warner, letter, Jan. 11, 1852.

222. Warner to Rollins, letter, New York, Jan. 29, 1852, coll. NYHS (letterpress copy).

223. B. to R., letter, Philadelphia, June 27, 1852, coll. SHSMo (*MHR,* XXXII [1937], 24-25).

224. Bingham first consulted with Sartain and another engraver in Philadelphia before going to New York for further discussions with Jones and possibly other printmakers then active in the city. When he wrote to Rollins from Philadelphia on June 27, 1852 (*MHR,* XXXII [1937], 24-25) he expressed particular interest in the low terms proposed by Sartain, who was obviously anxious to obtain the commission ("He [Sartain] agrees to finish the plate in the best Style of line and Mezzotint for

24,[225] with the completion of the plate set for precisely fourteen months from that date.[226] But, owing to a variety of circumstances which Bingham described in some detail in his letters to Rollins, he was not to see his work in engraved form until the latter part of May, 1854.[227] It is thus likely that the painting also remained in Philadelphia until the work was completed.

The history of the first "County Election" from May, 1854, to January, 1860, is somewhat clouded, although we can probably safely assume that it remained in Bingham's studio, along with the two succeeding scenes of the Election series, during most of that period. He evidently had it in mind to eventually dispose of the series, and this idea seems to have finally taken active form early in 1860 when he addressed his friend Rollins from Washington, D.C.: "I will have my election pictures here in a few days and will endeavor to dispose of them to the Library Committee of Congress, though such is the depleted state of the treasury, that my hopes of success are not very sanguine at present."[228] His surmise was obviously an accurate one, for the Election series was soon on view at the annual exhibition of the Washington Art Association in the capital, described as "for sale."[229] Before returning to Missouri, the paintings also were shown at the Pennsylvania Academy's annual exhibition.[230] And when they arrived in Missouri, they were lent to the first exhibition of the newly founded Western Academy of Art in St. Louis.[231]

In 1862 the Election pictures, together with "The Jolly Flatboatmen in Port," were placed by Bingham on indefinite loan to the St. Louis Mercantile Library Association. The report of the Board of Directors of the Library, issued in January, 1863, stated that the paintings, "will probably remain in their present position, as Mr. Bingham has intimated to us that he will never

two thousand dollars"). By the time Bingham wrote to Sartain from New York on July 19 (coll. MHS, St. Louis), he had evidently received an even better proposition, or perhaps a better impression of competence, from Jones, but the time element had become the decisive factor in favor of Sartain.
225. MS., contract between Bingham and Sartain, coll. Historical Society of Pennsylvania.
226. B. to R., letter, Philadelphia, Nov. 7, 1853, coll. SHSMo, Columbia (*MHR*, XXXII [1938], 166).
227. B. to R., letters, New York, May 17 and Philadelphia, May 29, 1854, coll. SHSMo (*MHR*, XXXII [1938], 181, 184).
228. Washington, D.C., Jan. 8, 1860, coll. SHSMo (*MHR*, XXXII [1938], 494). Bingham undoubtedly referred to the Joint Committee on the Library, a committee which had almost unlimited authority in connection with the purchase of works of art by the government. They exerted supervision over works of art offered to the Capitol, the White House, and for placement in public areas throughout Washington.
229. *Catalogue of the Fourth Annual Exhibition of the Washington Art Association, 1860* (Washington: Henry Polkinhorn, Printer, 1860), #6, 7, 8.
230. *Catalogue of the Thirty-seventh Annual Exhibition of the Pennsylvania Academy of the Fine Arts* (Philadelphia: Collins, Printer, 1860), #246, 273, 330. "The Election" was described as "Engraved."
231. *Catalogue of the First Annual Exhibition . . .*, #24.

remove them."[232] But the artist probably also hoped that the Library would somehow find a donor who would secure the group for the gallery.

In 1865 John How, President of the O'Fallon Polytechnic Institute of St. Louis, purchased the pictures from Bingham, planning to place them in the Institute's new building, then under construction.[233] They remained on view in the Mercantile Library until 1867[234] when How removed them, presumably to the Institute. Yet, sometime between that date and 1879, the pictures were once more returned to the Library, and in the latter year were made its permanent property through the gift of John H. Beach,[235] who had served as the Library's chief officer from 1862 to 1863. During recent times the four paintings were on long-term loan to the City Art Museum of St. Louis, and were finally dispersed by sale in 1944, "The County Election" becoming part of the museum's collection.

When Miss Rusk's monograph was published, in 1917, this was the only known version of "The County Election." Owing to conflicting information then available concerning the ownership of the painting, she felt compelled to question whether it was the original version or a replica,[236] going so far as to imply the probable existence of more than one such replica—an opinion that was to be partially substantiated in later years by the discovery of a second picture.

In his more recent publication, Christ-Janer related that C. B. Rollins had long suspected that the painting, then on exhibition at the City Art Museum, was not the "initial" picture, and he described in some detail how Mr. Rollins finally located what he considered to be the original version of the subject, eventually acquiring it for his personal collection in 1937.[237] This was the painting that was afterward purchased from the Rollins estate by the Boatmen's National Bank of St. Louis.

The existence of at least one replica would have been a logical assumption, from at least one important viewpoint. Bingham undoubtedly realized the necessity of promoting the sale of his proposed engraving by advance subscription. To accomplish this end, the painting itself had to be displayed. Yet the engraver's work also had to proceed, and for that purpose the painting was required, too. And so a replica (A230; plate 95) was quickly produced to meet an urgent need; it was executed in Columbia during the six-week

232. *Seventeenth Annual Report . . . , January 13. 1863*, p. 18.
233. *Twentieth Annual Report . . . , 1865*, p. 22.
234. *Twenty-second Annual Report . . . , 1867*, p. 14.
235. *Thirty-fourth Annual Report . . . , 1879*, pp. 18-19.
236. Rusk, *op cit.*, p. 59.
237. Christ-Janer, *op. cit.*, pp. 62-63.

142

period between mid-August and early October, 1852.[238] The "original" version was the painting that was shipped to Sartain immediately afterward.[239]

The painting that was exhibited in Columbia, Glasgow, and elsewhere in Missouri during the fall of 1852[240] was unquestionably the so-called replica, and it was also the same picture that accompanied the artist as far south as New Orleans in the spring of the following year during his active campaign to raise subscriptions for the sale of the engraving.[241] It is not known whether Bingham carried through his plans to give lectures on art as a further inducement to potential patrons,[242] or whether the picture served to speak for itself. In any event, one Robert J. Ward of Louisville saw the painting in New Orleans, possibly during the time it was on view in the window of a music store there, and persuaded the artist to part with it for $1,200,[243] exactly the amount that Bingham was required to pay Sartain while work on the engraving was in progress.[244] The price set on the painting seems to have been no more coincidence, since Bingham had to borrow that sum and was prepared to mortgage his Arrow Rock farm to do so.[245] Bingham could scarcely afford to refuse so tempting an offer, although it was made with the understanding that the artist might retain the painting, at least through the summer months, in order to continue his efforts to add to the engraving subscription list.

From mid-May through July the painter continued his tour. He traveled through Kentucky, exhibiting the painting in Louisville, Lexington, Danville, Frankfort, and Harrodsburg, and probably in Paris and Richmond as well.[246] It is not known whether he was able to carry through his announced intention to "try [his] fortune among the Hoosiers and Buckeyes west of the Ohio."[247]

The second "County Election" remained in the possession of the Ward

238. Bingham to Sartain, letters, Columbia, Mo., Aug. 16 and Oct. 4, 1852, coll. MHS, St. Louis.
239. Bingham to Sartain, letter, Columbia, Mo., Oct. 4, 1852, coll. MHS, St. Louis.
240. *Weekly Missouri Sentinel* (Columbia), Oct. 28, 1852, describing the painting as "a copy of the *original*, which is now being engraved..."; *Weekly Missouri Statesman* (Columbia), Oct. 29, 1852, 2-5; *Weekly Times* (Glasgow), Nov. 11, 1852.
241. B. to R., letter, St. Louis, Mo., March 9, 1853, coll. SHSMo (*MRH*, XXXII [1937], 29). See also *Daily Picayune* (New Orleans), March 18, 1853, calling the picture "a copy by the artist of his own original."
242. Letter, St. Louis, March 9, 1853, coll. SHSMo (*MHR*, XXXII [1937], 29).
243. *Daily Louisville Times*, April 6, 1853, 2-1.
244. B. to R., letter, Philadelphia, June 27, 1852, coll. SHSMo (*MHR*, XXXII [1937], 25).
245. *Ibid.*
246. B. to R., letter, Lexington, Ky., May 22, 1853, coll. SHSMo (*MHR*, XXXII [1937], 31), *Daily Louisville Times*, May 14, 1853, 3-3; May 19, 1853, 3-1: underlining the fact that "*the original*, of 'The County Election' is yet the property of the artist, and is now in the hands of Sartain, who is engaged in engraving the picture. The painting now in our city, which was purchased by Robert J. Ward, Esq., is a *duplicate* of it." Apart from the letter written from Lexington on May 22, indications of Bingham's activity in the town appeared in the press: *Kentucky Statesman*, May 24, 31, 1853.
247. Letter, Lexington, Ky., May 22, 1853, coll. SHSMo (*MHR*, XXXII [1937], 31).

family during the years that followed. In 1873 the picture was lent by Mrs. Ward to the Industrial Exposition at Louisville,[248] to which Bingham himself had sent two of his later works. Some time afterward she sold it, and from that point on the history of the picture can be clearly traced to the present owners.

First public notice of "The County Election" was taken by a reporter who saw it in the artist's studio in Columbia, late in October, 1851, some time before Bingham had put his final touches to the work. Together with other pictures on view, it was noted as "the most prominent" among them:

This picture has engaged the artist constantly for three months, occupies canvass about three by four feet, and is composed of upwards of sixty figures. Prominently on the right, on the main street of a western village, we have the place of voting, the court house, in the porch of which the clerks and judges are assembled—one of the judges, a thick pussy looking citizen, being engaged in swearing in a voter, a well-set Irishman in a red flannel shirt. Near by is a political striker, a distributor of tickets, *very* politely tendering his services in that regard to an approaching voter. Around and in front is the crowd, composed of many large and prominent figures—some engaged in earnest conversation, some drinking at a cake and liquor stand, some smoking and some hearing a paragraph read from a newspaper. But we cannot give a description of this painting. Several hours would not suffice fully to examine it, so numerous and life-like are the characters. Indeed it is full of reality, a seeming incarnation, prominent in figure, grouped and colored with admirable skill and effect. Persons of highly cultivated taste in the fine arts, and critics in general, will accord to it a remarkable degree of genius and merit.[249]

A month later, in St. Louis, the reader of *The Western Journal* was told that Bingham, " 'par excellence' the American Artist" and "one of the New Masters" had produced "the Election Scene" as "one among many evidences he has produced going to maintain this position."[250] The writer urged "every friend of Art to pay it a visit," adding that he would be "richly repaid in the refined pleasure it affords."[251]

Certainly no observer was more enthusiastic about Bingham's new painting than his friend Major Rollins, whose special appraisal of its merits deserves repetition at this point. It was given in a letter to the American Art-Union early in 1852, with the view of interesting the Union in the picture:

It is preeminently a *National* painting, for it presents just such a scene, as you would meet with on the Arrostock in Maine, or in the City of New York, or on the Rio Grande in Texas, on an election day. He has left nothing *out*, the courtier, the politician, the

248. *Catalogue of Paintings and Sculpture, with a Classification of the Natural History Department,* 1873 (Louisville, Ky.: J. P. Morton and Co., 1873), #39.
249. *Missouri Statesman*, Oct. 31, 1851, 2-4.
250. *The Western Journal* . . . , VII (Nov., 1851), 145.
251. *Ibid.*

144

labourer, the sturdy farmer, the 'bully' at the poles [sic], the beer-seller, the *bruised* pugilist, and even the boys playing 'mumble the peg' are all distinctly recognized in the group. The painting is composed of perhaps *fifty* characters. As a mere work of art a delineation of character it is superb. But this is not the point of view in which its excellence is to be regarded. The elective franchise is the very corner stone, upon which rests our governmental superstructure and as illustrative of our fine institutions, the power and influence which the ballot box exerts over our happiness as a people, the subject of this painting was most happily chosen, and executed with wonderful skill by its gifted author, When I saw Bingham last several months ago, the picture was not quite finished. I urged upon him, to have it engraved, which he said he would do. . . . From its character and its style of execution, it would arrest the attention of every class of our population it would be admired alike by an exquisite connoisseur in the arts, the most enlightened statesman, and the most ignorant voter, and such a picture *engraved* would be equaly [sic] sought after, to decorate the walls of a palace, and those of a log cabin!

Such is my poor opinion of this superior work of art and viewing it, in this light, it would certainly have a great run over mere fancy pieces or even historical works, which cannot be well made to have such a direct bearing upon the most practical as well as the most important duty, belonging to the citizen under our government. . . .[252]

During the months that followed, the picture still commanded attention wherever it was shown. In October, 1852, "A Friend of Genius" predicted that it was "destined to become one of the most popular paintings ever produced on this continent."[253] While exhibiting the replica of the painting in Kentucky during the late spring of 1853, Bingham was able to write to Rollins from Lexington that "while my picture remained in Louisville the press was profuse in its commendations, and without a dissenting voice, it was pronounced superior to anything of its kind which had yet been seen in America."[254]

Indeed, Bingham, who was now forty-two and had been painting for some 20 years, had every reason to believe that he had "arrived" in his profession. The painting, evidently preceding the artist to Louisville, was placed by its owner on display in a store window for a few days. There it became "all the rage with the community,"[255] attracting throngs of people. The press entered into an enthusiastic description of the picture, calling it "one of the most exquisite and entertaining triumphs of the brush," and a painting "sufficient of itself to immortalize the man who achieved it."[256]

All of Bingham's genre subjects we have discussed manifest his painstaking attention to ideas of compositional construction, based on a scrupulous

252. Rollins to Warner, letter, Jan. 11, 1852.
253. *Weekly Missouri Statesman*, Oct. 29, 1852, 2-5.
254. Letter, May 22, 1853 (*MHR*, XXXII [1937], 31).
255. *Daily Louisville Times*, May 14, 1853, 3-3.
256. *Ibid.*, April 6, 1853, 2-1.

145

observation of the works of the masters, as well as on a consideration of those ideas and principles laid down in the instruction books of his day; but in none of his paintings are these precepts displayed more obviously than in "The County Election." Even the most casual observation of the Election composition makes one feel certain that Bingham was following Prout's counsel that "the whole design must be clearly conceived before the picture is begun: nothing should be admitted or omitted at random. Each object has, in truth, a place proper for itself, and all that is introduced should be with an intention."[257] And certainly the following advice from the same source could have held a special meaning for him:

... a picture may consist of many parts, and possess a variety of interest; but, instead of being a display of 'boastful art,' distracting to the eye, the painter skilfully [sic] marshals every feature, and prevents the obtrusion of one object to the prejudice of the other; creating that unity of design, that essential breadth which constitutes real excellence, whether it be in composition, or color, or light and shadow.[258]

He could recall that the strongest criticism that greeted his earlier large figure composition, "The Stump Orator," was that it apparently lacked pictorial unity and was "distracting to the eye." Bingham, always sensitive to criticism, evidently sought to avoid a repetition of it by an even greater effort to improve himself.

The unusual amount of contemporary interest in the picture was, however, actually centered in the subject itself, and in the variety and character of the figures and groups, all of which were felt to be "instinct with life and expression."[259] As he had previously displayed in his scenes of boatmen and fur traders, Bingham's firsthand experience of the subject enabled him to extract and represent the typical and life-giving aspects of such events. It was just that ability to present the familiar that appealed so much to the public, and compelled at least one admirer to note that "whoever looks at it seems to recognize at once some old acquaintance in the various groupings, and is disposed to fancy that the portrait was taken from the life."[260] On the basis of this type of reaction, we can easily understand how the various so-called keys came to be put forth through the years that followed, each in its way attempting to identify the figures with actual persons,[261] although it is unlikely that the artist ever intended a deliberate caricature of his political associates, however strong the temptation may have been.

257. Prout, *Hints on Light and Shadow* ..., p. 10.
258. *Ibid.*
259. *Weekly Missouri Statesman*, Sept. 10, 1852, 1-7.
260. *Jefferson City Inquirer*, Jan. 17, 1852, 1-6 (from *St. Louis Intelligencer*).
261. Address of Thomas Shackelford before the Missouri Historical Society, St. Louis, in 1901, re "The County Election" (W. B. Stevens, *Centennial History of Missouri* ... (St. Louis & Chicago:

146

Strangely enough, the public's interest in the painting was so concentrated on the subject itself that I have been able to discover only one contemporary critic who in any way attempted to discuss the composition on more technical grounds, although he was actually basing his judgment on the Sartain engraving, thus eliminating the all-important element of color, as well as the many aspects that can only be understood on contact with the painting itself. He was, however, able to appreciate the organization of the composition:

... the chief group occupies nearly the center of the picture, and imparting the title to the work contains the main interest and action, while other subordinate assemblages contributing to the life and character, glide naturally into the ruling current of thought and purpose. They add greatly to the beauty and completeness of the entire composition, in an artistic point of view, increasing the force, harmony, and variety.[262]

The observer is indeed immediately struck by the artist's considered plotting of the structure of his composition. In it he has obviously attempted to incorporate those ideas of arrangement he was able to absorb from the instruction books as well as from those lessons taught by his careful observation of engravings after paintings by the old masters. By this time he was fully aware that the spectator's attention could not be held by a mere gathering together of familiar characters and motifs within a recognizable setting, and that the painter had to direct and control that interest through the pictorial means available to the artist as developed by the masters. Burnet had stated as much in his instructions relating to composition:

A knowledge of arrangement enables us to yet further heighten the gratification of the spectator, by engrafting upon the work those forms found in the compositions of the most celebrated masters. A knowledge of arrangement enables the artist to follow up and extend lines and forms only hinted at in nature; those parts which possess a local character, he preserves as leading points to an harmonious assemblage of lines, while portions possessing beauty he enshrines in masses of repose, or surrounds them with forms and colours, which add to their effect upon the spectator.[263]

The instruction books frequently illustrated their ideas with examples taken from the old as well as contemporary masters, and in a similar fashion, Bingham took what he needed from examples of all periods. Perhaps in no

S. J. Clarke, 1921), I, 614): "The man administering the oath in the picture is the likeness of Col. M. M. Marmaduke, brother-in-law of Darwin Sappington who stands to the left and has his hat off bowing to the voter who is casting his vote for him. The man with the stoop shoulders is O. B. Pearson, trying to get the voter to vote for his friend Sappington. The man with his head tied up was a well-known character of whom alcohol got the better. The others are well-known characters of that day."
262. *Boonville Weekly Observer*, Sept. 30, 1854, 1-7 (From *The Philadelphia Register*, Sept. 7).
263. Burnet, *An Essay ...*, p. 55.

other painting is this more clearly visible than in "The County Election." Arthur Pope was the first modern critic to observe that Bingham must have learned much from engravings after Renaissance and Baroque masters; he noted in Bingham's pictures a consistent use of compositional forms and devices acquired from earlier sources.[264] Pointing specifically to the organization of compositions such as "The County Election," in which an architectural screen at one side is used as a setting for the main action, while the remainder is left open for background, Pope saw a relationship with the method begun by the masters of the High Renaissance and continued by painters of the seventeenth century such as Poussin and Claude.[265] There can be little doubt that Bingham was familiar with the works of those masters through engravings, and that he readily made use of them, as we have repeatedly demonstrated. For the general arrangement and descriptive details of the setting of this composition, however, the artist seems to have been inspired by sources closer to his own time. The political subject would have inevitably drawn him to the series of election subjects by William Hogarth — in this case, to an engraving in reverse of "Canvassing for Votes" (plate 96), from which Bingham apparently took over the stagelike architectural background, to say nothing of such motifs as the refreshment-stand in the left foreground, the seated drinker, and the group of three figures at center (at right in "The County Election"). Bingham probably also had reference to an engraving after David Wilkie's "Chelsea Pensioners Reading the Gazette of the Battle of Waterloo" (painted 1822), which is also indebted to Hogarth's composition both in general disposition of setting and in details. In this instance Bingham would have been attracted to Wilkie's handling of the many-figured subject, although Bingham's solution is obviously much more consciously composed from the standpoint of monumental visual effect. There are also recognizable points of similarity between Bingham and Wilkie in the specific arrangement of buildings and trees, and in the interplay of the negro servant and the smiling man seated beside him.

Hogarth's story is easily made with few figures, the main action being held in the central foreground with everything else subordinated to it to better emphasize the moral implication. Bingham's point, like Wilkie's, is a purely descriptive one, and the picture depends on its many characters to achieve the greatest storytelling effect. After taking his setting from his predecessors,

264. *George Caleb Bingham, The Missouri Artist, 1811-1879 . . .* (New York: The Museum of Modern Art [1935]), p. 15.
265. *Ibid.* Virgil Barker also saw in Bingham's compositions a classic spirit comparable to Poussin, and noted the probable influence of engravings in his procedure (*American Painting, History and Interpretation . . .* [New York: Macmillan, 1950], p. 474).

148

Bingham turned to other sources for direction and procedure. As the instruction book had advised:

Having decided upon his general form of composition, the several portions of the design next claim his attention; those portions of the most consequence to the illustration of the story are to be brought into notice, while other parts are made subservient, by being thrown into shade or more interrupted by other situations; action and repose, masses convex or concave, lines regular or picturesque, spaces diminishing or increasing, are all combined in producing an harmonious result upon the eye and mind of the spectator.[266]

Here, that portion of the composition that can be deemed of the "most consequence to the illustration of the story" includes the figures pointing to the voter in the act of exercising his prerogative—the motif that gives title to the subject. While the two main performers—the voter and the oath-giver—are given prominence by their position within the framework of the portico, the figure of the voter is further emphasized through his placement at the apex of the large pyramidal mass composed of many figures.

Using a circular ground plan, the main group or pyramid is placed on the inner rim, its position with relationship to the spectator being made more prominent by the arrangement of the figures on a stepped elevation. The area leading to the group is left free of distraction, but is flanked in the foreground by two small wings, left and right, composed of smaller subordinate groups of figures which descend toward this "corridor" and serve to point the observer toward the main action. Bingham had adopted a compositional scheme derived from a close observation of the works of Renaissance and Post-Renaissance masters, and, as we have pointed out earlier, could also have had his attention drawn to the values of the circular form of composition by way of the instruction book. Burnet had recommended this form for large figure subjects and, following classical precedent, used illustrations taken from Raphael to point out that "in the design, a strict adherence to the plan laid down . . . secured a decided character to the picture."[267] Bingham tended to avoid the strict symmetry of Raphaelesque compositions in his later works, although we have seen that the important subjects of his earlier years, particularly those painted in 1846 and 1847, were undoubtedly influenced by such designs.

The problem of light and shade was one that must have taken up much of the artist's attention during his maturing period, for the lack of breadth in his handling of light and shadow had brought forth some of the severest

266. Burnet, *An Essay . . .*, p. 46.
267. Burnet, *Practical Hints on Composition . . .*, p. 24, In *A Practical Treatise.*

149

criticism of his pictures. One in particular has a special bearing on the present discussion—"The Stump Orator," in which, a critic had complained, "all the laws of chiar'oscuro are set at defiance" and that "he [the artist] has evidently no idea of the value of light, and how sparingly it should be used in a picture."[268] It is entirely conceivable that during the long interval that elapsed between the painting of "The Stump Orator" and "The County Election," the painter expended more than a little effort in laboring to overcome this serious deficiency. An instruction book counseled that "a judicious management" of light and shade was necessary to achieve what was termed an effect of "relief, harmony, and breadth" such as one could discover in "the best pictures of the Italian, Venetian, and Flemish Schools."[269] The same book contained a warning that might have been directed at Bingham himself:

... breadth of light and shadow is a quality too much neglected and too little felt, without which the highest finishing and the most laborious detail will always fail to prove the master mind or hand; the excellence of light and shadow mainly depend on breadth. It is evident that many artists in the treatment of their subjects (if it may be called treatment) have been unwilling to unite objects as a *mass*, but give to each separately its proportions of light and shadow, so that they form *pictures of parts*, the very opposite of breadth, and frequently, from an erroneous idea that beauties are sacrificed, by being thrown, as it were, under a cloud.[270]

It was added, however, that "the exact quantity of light and shadow cannot be suggested, as different subjects require different proportions; neither is a fixed division at all necessary. The best practice is to form *one broad mass*— to keep other masses quite subordinate, and particularly to *avoid equal quantities*."[271]

In the first "County Election" Bingham chose to bring his large central group forward as "one broad mass," casting his strongest light upon it. The subordinate mass of figures in the background and the more distant figures are thrown gradually into half-shadows and full shadow, serving their purpose as foils for the central group. The smaller foreground masses receive only partial light. The artist apparently labored energetically to develop tonal unity and balance in the picture, striving to heed the warning to "avoid equal quantities" of light and shade. To a large extent he succeeded in avoiding the old distractions to the eye by his careful arrangement of masses, although there is still evident a lack of the total control required to achieve complete breadth. He still lingers over individual parts and figures, particularly in the background, perhaps under the impression (despite the instruction book's

268. *The Literary World*, III (June 3, 1848), 350-351. Review quoted, p. 134.
269. Burnet, *Practical Hints on Light and Shade* ... , p. 2, in *A Practical Treatise*.
270. *Ibid.*, p. 13.
271. *Ibid.*

150

admonition of the erroneous notion of the idea) that "beauties are sacrificed, by being thrown, as it were, under a cloud." As a result, the picture is tight and somewhat hard in effect, with various discordant notes in the overall pattern of tonal values. These harsh notes tend to offer little rest to the spectator seeking to follow the meaning and direction within the vastly populated composition spread out before him.

Since Bingham was obviously well aware of all aspects of the pictorial problem by this time, he was also in a good position to observe his own shortcomings, and in the second version of the subject, he appears to consciously attempt to improve upon the first, while retaining all those salient identifiable features that were to appear in the engraving. Although one might take the trouble to point out the various niggling details that mark differences between the two pictures, or seek to establish the seeming importance of priority of execution between them, such efforts would be of little value here. The essential variations between the two pictures are those that indicate the still developing artistic impulses of the artist. Such obvious changes in the second version as the new hat for the boy in the right foreground and the variations in the tree groupings and cloud formations in the background, as well as the slighter alterations, are of the kind one might expect, even in terms of a close replica. The elimination of the two figures that had originally appeared between the voter and the trio conversing beside the building at right should be considered as perhaps the only physical change of any significance. The figures appear to have been included at first to close what might have been thought to be an undesirable gap in the area, while the head of the figure standing against the rail of the portico also served to complete a strongly defined side of the central pyramid. Yet the painter must have soon realized that the figures were actually without meaning in terms of the chain of communication, both external and internal, that existed to a large degree within the over-all composition. The exclusion of the figures in the second picture afforded a far greater clarity of spatial values in the area they formerly occupied, and in a larger sense also played a role in establishing a sharper definition of the organization of planes within the composition. But by far the greatest difference between the two painted versions of the subject lies in the treatment of light and shade, the problem that was occupying the artist's main attention during this period.

Bingham's reluctance to sacrifice detail can be said to have resulted in the considerable loss of structural emphasis and unity visible in the first Election composition. That he must have realized as much is revealed in the important changes he made in the second version. Manipulating his lights and darks in broader terms, he succeeded in developing a decidedly more effective and

151

dramatic picture, despite the fact that the alterations in its physical appearance are minor ones.

In the second version he achieves at last something closely approaching the ideal of compositional balance through an understanding of the proper handling of light and shade which the instruction books hinted at, but obviously could not give a precise recipe for, since "different subjects require different proportions." Only in the form of simple diagrams could the textbook[272] attempt to bring its ideas closer to its readers. One such diagram (plate 99) appears to bear a startling relationship to the problem involved in the Bingham composition. In a manner similar to the final effect achieved in the second "County Election," Prout has demonstrated how a composition made up of a multitude of figures can be developed in simple and direct terms through a broad manipulation of lights and darks. A shaft of light brings the foreground groups into strong relief, while the background mass, in deep shadow, unites the two architectural wings.

The various planes are more knowingly handled in the second version, so that the spectator can now more readily comprehend the composition. The jarring notes have also been largely eliminated, resulting in a picture that is actually quite different from its predecessor. A greater ease and fluidity of handling also characterizes the second version. A comparison with the Sartain engraving quickly reveals that Bingham carried over all those "improvements" into the graphic medium, so that although the engraver almost certainly worked from the first version, the painter evidently made sure, during the time he supervised the work beside his printmaker, that the richer qualities of the second version were also incorporated. The print necessarily reproduced most of the details of the first picture, but in a larger way it is a composite of both versions, including as it does the more important figure change and the more knowing handling of the system of light and shade.

The Mercantile Library collection of drawings contains many studies for single figures, as well as groups, that Bingham incorporated into "The County Election": S8, 17, 18, 25, 27, 30, 39, 40, 49, 53, 72, 82, 86, 97*a*, 98. At least two of the figures—the men standing beside the man taking notes—are recognizable as variants of types that had been previously used in the 1847 "Raftsmen Playing Cards" (S6, S63). It is also conceivable that other figures had been similarly adapted from earlier subjects still unlocated.

The drawings of the sketchbook are scrupulously translated, almost line for line, into the final composition. It is interesting to note that each figure, even when drawn individually, was always developed in terms of its possible arrangement within a group—a method Bingham seems to have adopted in

272. Prout, *Hints on Light and Shadow . . .* , p. 13.

forming the figure designs of subjects such as "Watching the Cargo," "The Wood-Boat," and "The Squatters." For the Election picture, he also executed studies of pairs of figures that appear in the sketchbook as masses complete in themselves (S17, S82), although obviously intended for incorporation within an established scheme involving many other figures.

These preliminary sketches enable us to observe the painstaking means adopted by the artist in his approach to the problem of a figure composition of this size. Undoubtedly following a preconceived general layout, the single figures, or pairs of figures, are joined with other figures to form small closely-knit groups, which are in turn adjusted to take their places within the complex of the larger design. In "The County Election" the painter maintained his inclination toward the pyramid as an ideal means in an organization of figures, developing each group as a small pyramid, with the smaller forms gradually forming segments of larger pyramids. It is a conscious and deliberate approach to the problem; yet in no way does the effect seem a labored or artificial one as it did perhaps in the first "Jolly Flatboatmen" and the 1847 "Raftsmen Playing Cards." Throughout the picture there is visible a keen awareness and controlled handling of the special problem of balance and proportion between the smaller groups of figures and the general mass of the over-all composition. Perhaps Bingham recalled the words of at least one commentator on the problem:

The groupe [sic] is that close kind of arrangement which combines two or more figures in a single mass, and when finely treated, has always been considered the most perfect mode of composition, indeed it comprises all its principles, and is an epitome of beautiful and effective combination; for the groupe [sic] should be subdivided by harmonious lines and well-balanced quantities, and should contain a portion of variety and contrast, intricacy or simplicity, as may best agree with the character of the subject. A composition, according to its extent, may consist of several groupes [sic], or be limited to one; but however numerous, they must be conducted on the same principle, and still be proportionate parts of the whole.[273]

Bingham must also have known engravings after Raphael's "School of Athens," often used by the instruction books as an ideal example of a subject in which single groups are balanced by the larger mass of the composition. The organization of the individual groups and the variety of expression could well have offered suggestions for his own work. Perhaps the figures of the detached group of the "Sceptic" and "History" in the fresco offer a more direct connection in their similarity with the figures of the man taking notes and one of the onlookers in "The County Election."

As we have already noted, the artist often drew from various sources out

273. H. Howard, *A Course of Lectures on Painting*... (London: H. G. Bohn, 1848), p. 211.

of the past for his figures and motifs in his ever-continuing search for correctness in the classical sense. In this picture, apart from the larger considerations, we have already observed the obvious relationship between the trio of figures beside the portico with a group in Hogarth's "Canvassing for Votes." And one wonders whether it is mere coincidence that the clerk shaping his quill, at upper right (S97a), bears so close a resemblance to the figure in an engraving after a painting by Frans van Mieris (plate 97), or that the boy in the left foreground, playing mumble-the-peg (S25), resembles the pose of a classical sculpture (plate 98) that was especially popular in Bingham's time, both in engraving as well as in small scale reproduction.

In Bingham's art "The County Election" undoubtedly represents a major step in the development of a monumental conception of painting that is a rare phenomenon in its time in America. In terms of the artist's self-training, and particularly of the means he had available to him for study, the accomplishment would be nothing short of extraordinary in any place or time. This is true regardless of any shortcomings which, to the painter's credit, he obviously recognized and sought to overcome. As we shall see, in the years to follow, he was to continue to pursue the problem, constantly striving to improve his procedure and technique, seeking to attain a harmony of form and expression which he seems to have realized was at the basis of the achievements of the old masters he consistently referred to as his guides.

Canvassing for a Vote

On March 30, 1851, writing from New York, Bingham advised his friend Rollins that he had been commissioned to paint a picture by Goupil & Co., who proposed to publish a print taken from it. Earlier in the year the artist had painted a small version of his "Raftsmen Playing Cards" for the same firm which was already in the hands of a printmaker, and afterward appeared under the title "In a Quandary." Bingham was evidently pleased to be favored with such commissions, realizing as he did that "their publication by such a firm will be calculated to extend my reputation, and enhance the value of my future works."[274]

The subject "Canvassing for a Vote" (A228; plate 102) was well in hand by late October of that year when a reporter saw the picture in the painter's studio in Columbia and described it as a "political scene of great originality and conception and beauty of finish."[275] At that time Bingham was still hard at work on his "County Election," and both subjects were in the studio. He

274. Letter, coll. SHSMo (*MHR*. XXXII [1937]. 21).
275. *Missouri Statesman*, Oct. 31, 1851, 2-4.

154

had intended to take them later to St. Louis to be completed during his winter sojourn in the city, but the busy schedule of work that developed for him there caused a further delay in bringing the small picture to completion. Writing to Goupil from St. Louis on January 31, 1852, he attempted to explain away the situation:

I trust you will excuse my remissness in not having written to you before this. Since I saw you last Spring, a considerable portion of my time has been employed in portraiture, which, together with *"The County Election,"* a rather extensive composition which I have had on hand, has caused me to delay the completion of your picture, the *"Canvassing for Votes."* I hope, however, that I will be able to forward it to you shortly, and that you will find it much improved by *time,* and the additional touches it has received since you saw it.[276]

The painting is signed and dated 1852. We can therefore assume that it was completed shortly after the letter was addressed to the New York art dealer, although it may not have been delivered until later in the summer or early fall. The September number of the *New-York Mirror* reported having viewed the picture "a few days since," while it was being unpacked, describing it as "a small cabinet piece of some four or five figures, forming an out-of-door group, which is composed of the candidate or his friend electioneering for him, endeavoring to circumvent an honest old countryman, who has by his side a shrewd old fellow, who cannot be readily taken in. The picture is a faithful study from life, and full of character."[277]

The lithograph by Régnier was published in 1853, but the painting itself had disappeared from view for more than a hundred years before it turned up in a private collection in Florida in 1954 and soon afterward acquired by the William Rockhill Nelson Gallery of Art in Kansas City. Curiously enough, the lithographer has taken several liberties with the original composition, both in detail as well as in its general impression. Probably most significant is the printmaker's reduction of the setting to move the figures forward, supposedly in an effort to further emphasize their position. The spectator has been afforded a close-up view of the conversation group, with a consequent loss of many of the additional details of the building at left on which the artist had expended so much labor in the painting. Some of the individual character of the original has been lost, in the handling of other details, such as the large tree enframing the background, which in the print assumes a feathery quality quite unlike Bingham's usually crisp treatment of foliage. The sky has also been altered. The lithographer further elected to change the pose of the politician, elongating his torso and avoiding the artist's deliberate

276. Letter, coll. M. Knoeder & Co., New York.
277. Copied in *Weekly Missouri Statesman*, Sept. 10, 1852, 1-7.

155

foreshortening, as well as turning the head so that it appears in a more decidedly three-quarter view.

The painting is characteristic of Bingham's style at this period, a style already discussed in some detail in connection with the "County Election," which was in process of execution at precisely the same time. In common with the latter work, it is a carefully controlled and organized composition, both in its general construction and in the consciously balanced treatment of light and shadow. The central subject, made up of four closely related figures, is so composed as to form a tall pyramid whose apex converges on the vertical line of the building behind them. The standing man is placed off-center, affording both height to the form of the group and also developing the sweep of the left side of the pyramid, thus avoiding the stiff centralization that characterized so many of his earlier pictures. The crouching posture of the politician serves not only to emphasize the speaker's energetic activity, almost caricatured to act more effectively as a contrast to the relaxed and casual attitudes of his companions, but also allows the exaggerated bend to his back to form the right side of the pyramid. (The lithographer has not carried this construction into the print in the same telling way.) Developing the background in shadow, with only a half-light on the building at left, Bingham casts his strongest light on the central group, thereby focusing the observer's attention on the aspect that gives title to his subject. The figures themselves are modeled in high relief, with the outlines softened to blend with the general atmospheric effect yet controlled to maintain their force and presence. The lithographer has lost much of the drama of the original in his translation; his tendency was to soften and spread out the light. Regrettably, the final effect is pedestrian indeed in comparison with the painting.

As with the small "Raftsmen Playing Cards," also commissioned by the Goupil firm for publishing purposes, it is conceivable that Bingham did not attempt to develop an entirely new composition for this picture, but saw fit instead to borrow elements from one of his older subjects, probably one with which his patron was already familiar and which had already proved itself a popular one with the public. There are, in fact, several indications that point to the 1849 "Country Politician" as the immediate precursor of "Canvassing for a Vote." Retaining the essential motif of the earlier composition, and re-using the figures of the politician and the "jolly old landlord," he would seem to have altered the two remaining figures and their grouping, and changed the setting from an interior to an exterior of an inn. Both subjects are essentially four-figure compositions; the partially visible figure in the background of the later picture takes no part in the main action.

Those slight differences noted in the translation of sketchbook studies for

156

the figure of the country politician (S65), shown in the drawing without his top hat, and the landlord, S102A, shown reversed, may indeed exhibit just the changes effected by the artist for the new version of the subject. A new figure (S21) was probably created, however, with this composition in mind.

Although it bears a closer relationship to the "Country Politician," the general motif and arrangement of figures in Mount's "The Tough Story" (plate 93) suggests more than a passing relationship to "Canvassing for a Vote." The rather obvious contact Bingham must have had with the Mount composition in connection with the "Country Politician" is recalled through a contemporary description of the latter, and the similarities between the Mount subject and Bingham's "Canvassing for a Vote" would, in turn, appear to bridge the gap formed by the missing painting. However, I am well aware of the dangers of attempting to develop ties between two pictures within an artist's *oeuvre* when one is unknown except through a short description. Only time alone will be able to judge the reliability of this kind of deduction.

As for the title of his new political picture, Bingham once again must have had before him the engraving of Hogarth's composition of the same subject. And a contemporary English painter's impression of a political scene entitled "Soliciting a Vote" had appeared as an illustration in a well-known gift annual — in the very issue (1836), in fact, from which Bingham copied his portrait of Fanny Kemble some years earlier.[278]

Stump Speaking

Intended as a pendant to "The County Election," the subject "Stump Speaking" (A233; plate 103) was first called "The County Canvass," and was evidently painted by Bingham in Philadelphia during the time he spent in the city supervising the work then in progress on Sartain's engraving of the plate of the earlier election picture. First mention of the new painting was made by the artist in a letter written to Rollins from Philadelphia on November 7, 1853:

As your knowledge of my habits may lead you to suppose, I have not been idle during my sojourn here. I am very buisily [*sic*] engaged upon my companion to the "County Election"—the "County Canvass." I have already completed the drawing and am proceeding rapidly with the painting. As much as you admired the "County Election," I think you will be still better pleased with the present work. I have found less difficulty in the management of the subject, admitting as it does of a much greater variety of attitude, if not expression. Sartain is very much pleased with the drawing and grouping

278. *The Gift ... for 1836*, opp. p. 88. Engraved by G. B. Ellis after R. W. Buss. Curiously enough, another proof of the same engraving reveals letterpress changed by another publisher to "Canvassing." The subject was also published separately on a larger scale, probably during the same period.

of the figures, and surrenders the opinion which he had previously entertained, that I would not be able to surpass the "County Election."[279]

Further in the same letter Bingham speculated: "I expect to have my 'County Canvass' ready for exhibition by the time Sartain terminates his labors upon the election and be obtaining subscribers for *that* while distributing the prints of the other."[280] This was, of course, hopeful planning, although Sartain had assured the artist that the Election engraving would be completed by December 20, the date specified in his contract.[281] The plate was actually still in progress by the middle of May of the following year.[282]

Meanwhile, Bingham bided his time by continuing his work on the "County Canvass," his enthusiasm mounting as he watched it grow under his hand. A letter to Rollins written on November 23 reveals a note of unrestrained confidence in the importance of this latest achievement which is rare among the painter's writings: "I am getting along, fully up to my expectations upon the 'County Canvass,' and flatter myself that I will have it nearly finished by the beginning of the new year. I should like much for you to see it in its present state. I do not think you would counsel any change in the design, and if you did, I scarcely think your advice would be followed."[283]

When he wrote to his friend again, on December 12, Bingham went into more than usual detail about the painting, exhibiting more than ever his increasing satisfaction with this latest effort:

My "County Canvass" will keep me, I think, fully employed until the Election is ready for distribution. *The gathering of the sovereigns* is much larger than I had counted upon. A new head is continually popping up and demanding a place in the crowd, and as I am a thorough democrat, it gives me pleasure to accommodate them all. The consequence, of this impertinence on one side and indulgence on the other, is, that instead of the select company which my plan at first embraced, I have an audience that would be no discredit to the most populous precinct of Buncomb.

I have located the assemblage in the vicinity of a mill, (Kit Bullards perhaps). The cider barrel being already appropriated in the Election, I have placed in lieu thereof, but in the back ground, a watermellon waggon [sic] over which a *darkie*, of course presides. This waggon [sic] and the group in and around, looming up in shadow, and relieved by the clear sky beyond, forms quite a conspicious [sic] feature in the composition, without detracting in the slightest degree from the interest inspired by the principal group in front. In my orator I have endeavored to personify a wiry politician, grown gray in the pursuit of office and the service of the party. His influence upon the crowd is quite manifest, but I have placed behind him a shrewd clear headed

279. Coll. SHSMo (*MHR*, XXXII [1938], 166).
280. *Ibid.*, p. 167.
281. *Ibid.*, p. 166.
282. B. to R., letter, New York, May 17, 1854, coll. SHSMo (*MHR*, XXXII [1938], 182).
283. Philadelphia, Nov. 23, 1853, coll. SHSMo (*MHR*, XXXII [1938], 169-170).

opponent, who is busy taking notes, and who will, when his turn comes, make sophisms fly like cobwebs before the housekeepers broom.[284]

The composition, evidently originally conceived as a subject in which the story could be told in comparatively simple terms, had grown into a picture of far greater dimension as Bingham was swept along by his seemingly ever-increasing delight with its dramatic possibilities. Never before had he revealed in writing an enthusiasm equal to the one he now felt for this subject.

On the following February 1 he advised his friend of his progress and continuing satisfaction with the result: "I am now giving the last touches to my 'County Canvass.' It will be a more imposing and effective picture than the Election, the figures are larger, more varied in character, and also much greater in number. Mr. Sartain thinks that its exhibition will produce quite a sensation here."[285]

The picture must have attracted attention, for it was not long before the artist was approached by Léon Goupil, who then headed the New York branch of the company of that name, with a proposal to engrave the painting. It is interesting to note that there was evidently no longer any mistake in understanding between Bingham and Goupil that the painting was to be published as an engraving rather than by the lithographic method which had so obviously not met with his approval when it was used for "The Emigration of Daniel Boone." Bingham sold the copyright to Goupil on April 14, "upon terms as favourable as any artist ever obtained from a publisher,"[286] the plan being to engrave it in Paris, "in the most superior style."[287] The painting itself was to remain in the artist's possession, "unless sold and accounted for at the price of two thousand dollars."[288]

The title of the painting was changed at an early date to "Stump Speaking" under the publisher's impression that the new title "would aid the sale of the Engraving."[289]

Early in 1860[290] Bingham attempted unsuccessfully to persuade the Library Committee of Congress to purchase the picture, along with the first version of "The County Election" and "Verdict of the People." While the paintings were still in the East, the artist also allowed them to be shown at the annual exhibitions of the Washington Art Association[291] and the

284. Philadelphia, Dec. 12, 1853, coll. SHSMo (*MHR*, XXXII [1938], 171-172).
285. Letter, Feb. 1, 1854, coll. SHSMo (*MHR*, XXXII [1938], 176-177).
286. B. to R., letter, Kansas City, Mo., May 19, 1873, coll. SHSMo (*MHR*, XXXIII [1939], 221-222). The contract was dated April 14.
287. B. to R., letter, Philadelphia, April 16, 1854, coll. SHSMo (*MHR*, XXXII [1938], 178).
288. *Ibid.*, p. 179.
289. Letter, May 19, 1873 (*MHR*, XXXIII [1939], 221).
290. Letter, Jan. 9, 1860, coll. SHSMo (*MHR*, XXXII [1938], 494).
291. *Fourth Annual Exhibition* . . . , #6, listed as "for sale."

159

Pennsylvania Academy of the Fine Arts.[292] And upon their return to St. Louis they were exhibited at the first show of the Western Academy of Art.[293] In 1862 "Stump Speaking" (plate 103) was one of the group sent on indefinite loan to the St. Louis Mercantile Library Association[294] which was purchased in 1863 by John How for the O'Fallon Polytechnic Institute.[295] Later it became the property of the Library through the subsequent purchase of the series by John H. Beach.[296] In more recent years, "Stump Speaking" was on loan to the City Art Museum of St. Louis until acquired by the Boatmen's National Bank in 1941.

The general sense of personal triumph that Bingham felt in the seeming ease with which the subject developed in his hands was not merely the expression of satisfaction a craftsman ordinarily feels in the successful accomplishment of a job he sets himself; Bingham was greatly attracted to the problem of the multiple figure composition, and all of his studies were directed toward a complete aesthetic solution of it in terms of the unity of the design with light and shade and color. In this connection we recall that the first subject he ever attempted which included a large number of figures was "The Stump Orator," painted in 1847. That picture was severely attacked by critics because of its apparent lack of harmony, a criticism that Bingham must have taken to heart, for from that time until the appearance of "The County Election," his subjects were usually made up of very small figure groups, although of course the economic necessity to produce pictures more prolifically could have also proved a compulsive factor in that direction. Yet I feel that the personal, more than normal, excitement that Bingham displayed in his work on this later version of "The Stump Orator" was to a large extent related to an inner sense of victory that could have seemed an annulment of a former defeat.

A comparison of the picture with the daguerreotype photograph of "The Stump Orator" (plate 90) clearly reveals that the basic approach to the subject and to compositional structure has been little altered. Bingham obviously retained the essential elements of the old picture, even repeating several of the figures, with only slight variation. The motif of the orator himself, in his dominant role as conductor of the proceedings, is closely related to the older version, both in placement and in essential gesture, although a new drawing was prepared for the more expressively conceived figure.

292. *Catalogue of the Thirty-seventh Annual Exhibition* ... , #246, called "Before the Election."
293. *Catalogue of the First Annual Exhibition* ... , #348.
294. *Seventeenth Annual Report* ... , January 13, 1863, p. 18.
295. *Twentieth Annual Report* ... , 1865, p. 22.
296. *Thirty-fourth Annual Report* ... , 1879, pp. 18-19.

The compositions betray their family relationship in several ways, even to the point of suggesting once more that the artist sought to include in the painting recognizable political figures of the time,[297] but there are also very important differences between them that show how far Bingham had come in his artistic development during the intervening period. Perhaps the most significant difference between the two compositions lies in the artist's increased control over the varying technical problems involved in the painting of a multiple-figure subject of this kind. This advance is particularly notable in the disposition of the figure groups. Although the circular arrangement of figures in the foreground, with the controlling figure of the orator at the left, still forms the nucleus of the composition, the heavily massed background figures that certainly constituted one of the great "faults" of "The Stump Orator" have been eliminated in favor of carefully placed groups that lead the eye progressively into the distant landscape.

"The Stump Orator" had relied entirely upon a circular compositional design to achieve its purpose. But Bingham had earlier shown his preference for a combination of angular forms within the circular ground plan, and in "The County Election" he demonstrated this predilection on a monumental scale. This method enabled him to gain a dramatic emphasis in the arrangement of his figures which he was evidently unable to achieve in the purely circular design. The conscious pyramidal groupings of figures at strategic points in "Stump Speaking" does, in fact, relieve the monotony of arrangement visible in the earlier version of the subject, and there seems little doubt that the impression of dramatic emphasis has been much enforced by means of the now familiar device.

There can also be little question that much of the effectiveness of the new composition comes through the artist's developing understanding of the use of light and shade as an essential means of structural unity. Whereas in the earlier picture he had been unable to achieve the balance of the three prescribed properties of "relief, harmony, and breadth" in his use of light and shade, he now boldly manipulates the values, enforcing the contrasts so that the chief characters are now more emphatically presented and the dramatic possibilities of the subject are brought into full play. The strongest

297. The suggestion that Bingham had consciously attempted to include recognizable political characters of the time in his paintings was first introduced in connection with "The Stump Orator," and there were also various attempts to identify figures in "The County Election." C. B. Rollins in *MHR*. XXXII (1938), 172, note 13, stated: "There are several so-called keys to 'Stump Speaking.' In them the speaker has been variously identified as James S. Green, former U.S. Senator from Missouri; Darwin Sappington, Bingham's old political opponent, the man taking notes has been identified as Bingham himself, and there is something of a resemblance...." But Rollins seemed inclined to believe, at least on the basis of the artist's own written remarks, that he "had no particular persons in mind when he painted at least the major characters in 'Stump Speaking'."

light is cast on the chief actor, the orator, whose form is silhouetted against the dark background of the foliage. The figures in the shadows below him serve to heighten the dramatic effect. The background groups merge into the atmospheric shadows of the distant landscape, and the clear pattern of undulating lights and darks also plays its part in developing the over-all sense of movement and drama. All of this is in direct contrast to "The Stump Orator," in which the use of light brings forward all the figures in equal intensity—a misuse of "all the laws of chiar'oscuro"[298] that brought about the most serious criticism leveled against one of Bingham's major early efforts.

This composition has been considered in some detail by at least one earlier writer, and I certainly do not wish to enter into any repetitious detail here; but the artist's increased sense of order, balance, and unity as displayed in this composition merits perhaps one further word. One cannot help but feel impressed with the great strides made by Bingham toward a truly sophisticated knowledge of the principles that control formal composition. One senses the artist's ability to select the appropriate means to produce the desired effect. Let us observe, for instance, how the eye is led directly to the main action through the narrow corridor formed by the two reclining figures in the foreground, whose postures and glance seem to assist in developing the spectator's direction. And it can scarcely be accidental that the gesture of the orator, so important in creating the entire suspense and mood of the subject, is repeated and enforced by the shape of the undulating branches of the tree behind him, as is its forward bend an echo of the speaker's own inclined figure.

A number of sketches of figures in the Mercantile Library collection belong to this composition (S28, 36, 42, 45, 52, 60, 64, 67, 78, 79, 88, 91, 99), although some of the drawings had been prepared previously in connection with "The Stump Orator."[299] The characteristics of Bingham's style of draughtsmanship show no change during the intervening period. Certainly the drawings we have been able to associate with certainty to the first picture point to relatively little change in a style and method well established almost a decade earlier.

We have already referred to Bingham's own active participation in political meetings of this kind as possible immediate inspiration for the subject, and we have also pointed out that he must have been aware of some of the productions of his contemporaries which made use of the political motif. It would have been most interesting in this connection, for instance, to know something about John C. Hagen's "The Stump Candidate," which was

298. *The Literary World*, III (June 3, 1848), 350-351.
299. See above, p. 136 (specifically S36, 42, 45, 80, 81, 88).

shown at the annual exhibition of the National Academy of Design in 1841.[300]

The Verdict of the People

The plan to "cap the clymax [*sic*]"[301] to his Election series had evidently occurred to Bingham in Philadelphia about the time he was putting his final touches to "Stump Speaking." By the time he wrote to Rollins from the city, April 16, 1854, his ideas for the subject of the new picture seemed already well formulated:

I have already commenced *thinking* for another large composition, which I will entitle *'The Verdict of the People.'* I intend it to be a representation of the scene that takes place at the close of an exciting political contest, just when the final result of the ballot is proclaimed from the stand of the judges. The subject will doubtless strike you as one well calculated to furnish that contrast and variety of expression which confers the chief value upon pictures of this class. I might very properly introduce into it some of those comically long faces which were seen about Fayette when our friend Claib was so genteelly whipped, last summer.[302]

A month later Bingham was able to advise his friend that he had already begun his preliminary studies for the composition.[303] And by the middle of July he had made enough satisfactory progress on the picture to discuss it with some confidence: " *'The Verdict of the People'* is still growing under my hand and I expect to have it sufficiently completed to exhibit it to advantage by the time I shall be able to leave. It is much larger, and will combine more striking points than either of its predecessors."[304]

The painting (A237; plate 104) was not completed by January, 1855, but it reached that state before he left Philadelphia, probably during the late spring.[305] Without exhibiting it publicly, as he had first intended, he sent the picture off immediately to Goupil in New York with a view toward its publication. Bingham wrote to Rollins, however, that "all ... who have seen it, pronounce it the best of my works."[306] He also intended to go to Paris during the fall, planning to remain there until the engravings of both the "County Canvass" and "The Verdict of the People" were brought to completion.[307] This idea was not carried through, however, and by mid-September

300. *Catalogue of the Sixteenth Annual Exhibition. 1841* ... (New-York: E. A. Clayton, Printer, 1841), #54. See above, p. 129.
301. Letter, May 17, 1854, coll. SHSMo (*MHR*, XXXII [1938], 182).
302. *MHR*, XXXII (1938), 179-180.
303. Letter, May 17, 1854 *(MHR*, XXXII [1938], 182).
304. B. to R., letter, Philadelphia, July 15, 1854, coll. SHSMo (*MHR*, XXXII [1938], 186).
305. B. to R., letters, Philadelphia, Jan. 12, 1855; Independence, Mo., June 21, 1855, coll. SHSMo *(MHR*, XXXII [1938], 187, 188).
306. Letter, June 21, 1855 (*MHR*, XXXII [1938], 188-189).
307. *Ibid.*, p. 191.

163

he was back in Columbia, painting portraits and expecting to show his new Election picture to the public.[308] The painting was afterward on view in his studio in Jefferson City.[309] During early May, 1856, it was on exhibition in St. Louis at Spore's Artist Emporium, where subscriptions were also opened for the engraving.[310] Later that month Bingham took the painting to Louisville, Kentucky, where one firm took a large advance subscription for the prints.[311]

Bingham at first entered into negotiations with Goupil regarding publication of the picture and submitted his terms for release of the copyright to the firm when he reached Paris in the fall, although by that time he was already "strongly disposed"[312] to publish the print himself and therefore made his proposition one that he felt might not be easily acceptable. As he more or less expected, Goupil could not meet his terms, and soon afterward Bingham set about looking for an engraver in Paris to do the work. But in a letter written from Düsseldorf on June 3, 1857, we learn that he was not able to find an engraver in Paris who would have been able to complete a plate within three years, and had then decided to have it published in Germany as a lithograph, a graphic means he had not previously found suitable to his taste. At the time of the writing he was able to report that he had already gone ahead with plans for the work, intending to be "the exclusive proprietor of the print," and he felt the lithograph could be produced in Düsseldorf "in the very best manner."[313] The terms of his contract with the lithographer afforded him the privilege of rejecting the print when completed, if it did not meet with his complete satisfaction. He was to have been supplied with a proof of the print by the end of the year,[314] but by August, 1858, it was announced that the work had not yet been finished "owing to some misunderstanding" between the artist and the printmaker, but "it may possibly be completed in a few months."[315]

It is not clear whether it was merely a lack of understanding between the artist and his printmaker that halted the project, or whether Bingham finally decided that he still could not accept lithography as the proper medium for the publication of his paintings. In any event, Bingham's subsequent publishing efforts were to be confined to engraving. We have no further clue to the eventual outcome, nor any evidence to substantiate a statement made

308. *Missouri Statesman*, Sept. 14, 1855.
309. *Ibid.*, Nov. 23, 1855. The artist was in Jefferson City by November 14, painting portraits and exhibiting his picture in his studio in the Capitol. He remained about a month, speaking at a Whig meeting there on December 1 *(ibid.*, Dec. 14, 1855, 1-6).
310. *Ibid.*, May 16, 1856, 1-5.
311. B. to R., letter, Louisville, Ky., June 2, 1856, coll. SHSMo (*MHR*, XXXII [1938], 196).
312. B. to R., letter, Düsseldorf, Nov. 4, 1856, coll. SHSMo (*MHR*, XXXII [1938], 344-355).
313. *MHR*, XXXII, [1938], 351-352.
314. *Ibid.*, p. 352.
315. *The Crayon*, V (Oct., 1858), 292.

some years ago that the lithograph was eventually produced by Goupil in Paris in 1869.[316] As far as is known, the work never went beyond the two proofs, still extant, which are said to have been the ones submitted to the artist for his approval.[317]

The painting was part of the Election series that Bingham placed before the Library Committee of Congress in 1860[318] in the hope of receiving government patronage, and it was lent during the same year to the exhibitions of the Washington Art Association,[319] the Pennsylvania Academy of the Fine Arts,[320] and the Western Academy of Art,[321] together with "The County Election" (1) and "Stump Speaking." "The Verdict" was also one of those paintings placed on indefinite loan to the St. Louis Mercantile Library Association in 1862[322] which were purchased by John How for the O'Fallon Polytechnic Institute in 1865[323] and later returned to the Library, presented by John H. Beach, in 1879.[324] In recent times the picture was on loan to the City Art Museum of St. Louis for seven years, until 1941, when it was acquired by its present owner, the Boatmen's National Bank of St. Louis.

At least one contemporary writer hailed the final Election subject as the completion of a "series of the most thoroughly and peculiarly American productions that have yet been laid before the public."[325] As with Bingham's other genre compositions, it was the typical aspect of the portrayal that caught the attention of the critic and observer. It was described by one reporter as being

... at once suggestive and illustrative of a scene all have witnessed, with a truthfulness that cannot fail to excite our admiration. .... the genius of the artist has transferred to canvas a *principle* in our government—the exercise of the elective franchise—and submission by the people to the will of the majority, is *colored* true to the requirements of the constitution, and the instincts of our people.[326]

The structure of the composition repeats the general scheme used in "The County Election," the main difference being a reversal of the arrangement so that the courthouse portico with its pyramidal mass of figures is now at

316. C. B. Rollins, *MHR*, XXXII [1938], 179, note 22. Repeated in *Print Collector's Quarterly*. XXVII (Feb., 1940), 107. The story probably originated with the article by Bingham's son, J. Rollins Bingham, in the *Kansas City Star*, Dec. 5, 1909, 13-1.
317. *MHR*, XXXII (1938), 179, note 22 (C. B. Rollins).
318. Letter, Jan. 9, 1860, coll. SHSMo (*MHR*, XXXII, [1938], 494).
319. *Fourth Annual Exhibition* ..., #8, listed as "for sale."
320. *Catalogue of the Thirty-seventh Annual Exhibition* ..., #330, called "After the Election."
321. *Catalogue of the First Annual Exhibition* ..., #253, called "Election Returns."
322. *Seventeenth Annual Report* ..., January 13, 1863, p. 18.
323. *Twentieth Annual Report* ..., 1865, p. 22.
324. *Thirty-fourth Annual Report* ..., 1879, pp. 18-19.
325. *Boonville Weekly Observer*, Sept. 30, 1854.
326. *Missouri Statesman*, May 16, 1856.

165

left. The chief actor, the clerk reading the election returns, is, as in other examples, placed at the apex of the group. The eye of the spectator is led to the central action through a narrow opening in the immediate foreground which is flanked at left by the negro with the wheelbarrow and the fallen drunkard at right. The smaller group at the opposite side balances the larger mass and also serves with it to lead the observer into the background. The distant multitude of figures, filling the area between the two architectural wings, is again close to the setting in "The County Election," as is the effect of distant perspective.

Bingham's broadly conceived treatment of the masses in terms of light and shadow recalls similar effects already achieved in the second verion of "The County Election." The Prout diagram (plate 99) noted previously in connection with the Election takes on an even more convincing significance in its obvious parallels to the system of distribution of lights and darks employed in this composition.

The figures are larger in scale than in the earlier Election subjects, and have a remarkably fresh and vital quality which is revealed particularly in details (plate 101). A close observation of such details indicates Bingham's continuing preoccupation with character and physiognomy, a field he had already richly explored from the time he painted his first subject of political connotation, "The Stump Orator." Many of the elements familiar to us from "The County Election" are again made use of here, in both the setting and the characteristics of individual figures. And again, in a similar fashion, Bingham apparently used the pose of a classical figure to fill the role of a dominant foreground motif: the drunkard takes on a pose probably ultimately derived from the "Dying Gaul," a cast of which he could have remembered from his first Philadelphia years,[327] although small-scale reproductions were also readily available at this time.

In terms of Bingham's total achievement, "The Verdict of the People" can be considered his major pictorial statement in the handling of the many-figured composition. This final subject in the Election series forcefully demonstrates what unusual skill he finally attained in his search for an orderly solution to the special problem involved in the structuring of pictures of this kind. The development of a masterly conception of form can be traced from his ambitious "Stump Orator" of 1847, with its dense massing of forms, to "The County Election" and "Stump Speaking," in which a gradual breadth and suppleness of organization is gradually gained. The "Verdict" displays a total balance of design and narrative which is acquired through a conscious

327. *Catalogue of the Twenty-seventh Annual Exhibition.* PAFA, 1838; in "Antique Statue Gallery," listed as "Dying Gladiator." Small casts of the figure were also produced during this period.

balance of form, content, and technical means that indeed marks a fitting climax to Bingham's career as a figure painter in a special field.

A much smaller version of "The Verdict of the People" (A248; plate 100) was still in Bingham's studio at the time of his death and was afterward included among those pictures in the Administrator's sale of the Bingham estate in 1893; it was purchased at that time by James W. S. Peters of Kansas City[328] and remained in his possession until 1940, when it passed, successively, into the hand of several art dealers. At this writing it is privately owned.

There are considerable differences between this picture and the large original, both in its general aspect and in detail. The entire background has been altered: the solid mass of figures in shadow has been broken up to provide a narrow passage which permits the observer to move into the distance. Details of foliage and architecture have also been shifted and changed. The figure of the negro girl bending over a basket, accompanied by a small boy, has been added to the background group. Details of many of the foreground figures have been changed too: the negro, at left, wears a hat instead of a bandana; behind him the smiling gentleman now wears a jacket and a hat; the drunkard also wears a jacket; at right, the boy with the hoop now sports a hat; and the hat peddler, who in the original version wore all his wares on his head, now appears with only one hat. Minor details such as the billboard and the contents of the wheelbarrow have also undergone alterations.

The entire treatment is, in general, broader in handling than the earlier version of the subject. Boldly manipulating his lights and darks, the artist has subordinated much of the detail formerly used in favor of a more vibrant and dramatic effect. Bingham, ever experimenting, has narrowed the area of light concentration so that the central mass of figures now receives only flickering illumination which falls in spots on the group.

* * *

The series of Election subjects represent Bingham's culminating achievement as a figure painter, and it would appear that he consciously regarded the pictures as his finest efforts up to that time. Certainly they were his most ambitious works in terms of size and composition, and he brought all of his knowledge of picture-making to bear in designing and executing them. The fact that he undertook to have the three large subjects engraved, acting as his own publisher, would also seem to underline the importance he attached to

328. Rusk, *op. cit.*, pp. 107, 122.

the paintings, to say nothing of his attempt to interest the national government in acquiring them.

The subjects were closer to his personal experience than any of the river themes that had first earned him his reputation as "The Missouri Artist," and the richness and variety of expression that he incorporated into each picture brings us closer to an understanding of Bingham as a pictorial reporter than at any other time in his career. He also reveals his artistic intention and method far more convincingly and comprehensively than he had accomplished earlier. He informs the spectator, in no uncertain way, that it is not enough for the artist to paint nature as he sees it unfold before him; life must also be ordered and translated into those concrete terms that had been laid down by the masters in order to make it intelligible. Upon the ability of the painter to be properly selective depended the success or failure of his picture, and Bingham, in taking on the difficult problem of the many-figured composition, had obviously accepted the challenge with the complete assurance of a mature artist. The enthusiastic response of the public to each of the Election pictures must have persuaded him that he had indeed arrived at the height of his profession. He had perhaps already convinced himself of that when he confided to his friend Rollins not long before: "The fact is I am getting to be quite conceited, whispering sometimes to myself, that in the familiar line which I have chosen, I am the greatest among all the disciples of the brush, which my native land has yet produced."[329]

Unlocated Recorded Subjects

Among the most important single subjects by Bingham still unlocated is one called "St. Louis Wharf" or "St. Louis Landing" (A159), which he submitted to the American Art-Union on August 1, 1849, for sale at $350.[330] Its relative significance may to a large extent be determined by the high price set upon it by the artist. The painting was immediately purchased by the Union[331] and awarded at the annual December meeting to Stephen Pell of New York City.[332] When seen in St. Louis in April of that year, it was said to be: ". . . a picture drawn from our own wharf, in which he [the artist] has introduced a true and life-speaking description of some of the scenes which may be daily witnessed there. It is the first painting which we have seen in which the real characteristics of the boatmen on the wharf are truly portrayed."[333] The Art-Union's more concise description actually affords us more specific detail:

329. B. to R., letter, Philadelphia, Nov. 23, 1835 (*MHR*, XXXII [1938], 170).
330. Letter, Aug. 1, 1849, coll. NYHS.
331. AAU, minutes of meeting, committee of management, Aug. 2, 1849.
332. *Transactions of the AAU, for the Year 1849* . . . , #218.
333. *Daily Missouri Republican*, April 17, 1849, 2-1.

"On the wharf are piles of merchandise, upon which are seated boatmen and travellers; behind them are teamsters, and beside the levee is a steam-boat, the 'Kit Carson.' "[334]

"The Drovers" (A168) was exhibited by Bingham in the gallery of the Western Art Union at Cincinnati in September, 1849.[335]

"The First Lesson in Music" (A262) was shown at The Pennsylvania Academy of Fine Arts in Philadelphia in 1857, from the collection of Edward P. Mitchell.[336] Its title suggests a genre subject distinctly apart from the artist's Western series.

Bingham painted a number of variations on the Boatman theme which are still unlocated, including "Raftsmen on the Ohio," "The Wood Yard" or "Woodyard on the Missouri," and "A Boatman."

"Raftsmen on the Ohio" (A161) was purchased by the American Art-Union on July 2, 1849, for $300,[337] which was $50 below the artist's asking price.[338] It was awarded in December, 1849, to James Key of Florence, Alabama.[339] The subject was described as: "A man seated on a box is telling a story to three others, as they are 'floating down the Ohio.' In the foreground on the raft are packs of shingles, boards &c."[340]

"The Wood Yard" or "Woodyard on the Missouri" (A160) was purchased from the artist by the Western Art Union at Cincinnati by June, 1849, and awarded at its December distribution to Miss E. E. Reynolds of Lafayette, Indiana.[341] Its description points to a variant on the Woodboat theme:

In this picture a broad stretch of the Missouri is seen, over which hangs that hazy atmosphere peculiar to it. In the foreground is a woodyard. Two men have discovered a boat in the distance, and are watching for the signal indicating that wood is wanted. A third lounges on the bank with his feet hanging over the water, smoking his pipe. The accessories of the wood piles, axes, whisky jug, &c., go to make up a scene that cannot be mistaken by any one who has travelled on the Western Waters.[342]

"A Boatman" (A163), a small picture, was also an American Art-Union purchase; it was submitted by the artist for consideration on August 1, 1849,[343] and bought the following day for $50.[344] It was awarded in December

334. *Bull.* AAU, II (Oct., 1849), #218.
335. *Record*, Western Art Union, I (Sept., 1849), #168.
336. *Catalogue of the Thirty-fourth Annual Exhibition*. PAFA, 1857, #167.
337. AAU, minutes of meeting, executive committee, July 2, 1849, coll. NYHS.
338. AAU, Register of Pictures, coll. NYHS.
339. *Transactions of the AAU, for the Year 1849*. #196.
340. *Bull.* AAU II (Oct., 1849), p. 38, #196.
341. *Transactions of the Western Art Union*, 1849, #34.
342. *Record*, Western Art Union, I (Oct., 1849), #150.
343. Letter, Aug. 1, 1849.
344. AAU, minutes of meeting, committee of management, Aug. 2, 1849.

to "J." of Albany, New York. The Art-Union described it as representing "A figure seated beside a pile of wood, on the banks of the Missouri,"[345] indicating in all probability a woodboatman subject.

"The Stump Orator" (1847) and "Country Politician" (1849), two subjects of the Election series which were repeated by the artist, with some variations, have already been discussed at some length.[346]

Our catalogue also includes a number of "landscapes," "landscapes with cattle," and "cattle pieces"; farmyard scenes such as "Feeding the Cows," "Cock and Hen," and "Flock of Turkeys," as well as the related subjects "Going to Market" and "Pennsylvania Farmer"; and a rare literary theme for Bingham: "Tam O'Shanter." Many of these pictures are discussed elsewhere in this work in other connections.

345. *Bull.* AAU, II (Oct., 1849), p. 43, #241.
346. See above, pp. 129-139.

VII

LANDSCAPE PAINTING

Fewer than half of Bingham's recorded landscapes have come to light; hence the full extent of his contribution to landscape painting in America has yet to be evaluated. The many gaps that still exist must restrain us from attempting a definitive consideration of this area of his artistic activity. On the basis of some fourteen examples now known, however, it is already possible to surmise that his role in the larger development of American landscape was only an incidental one. The field of pure landscape appears to have held little attraction for him, although he consistently introduced outdoor settings into his figure subjects, undoubtedly realizing that they served to define the locale and to emphasize the special character of his Western compositions. He also included landscape elements in the backgrounds of his portraits as early as 1838/1839.

Little is known of his early landscapes. Our first knowledge of this phase of his work is contained in the letter he wrote from St. Louis in December, 1835, in which he mentions having executed "a couple of landscapes representing the bufaloe [*sic*] hunts of our western prairies."[1] Five years later the artist sent a "Landscape" to the National Academy of Design for its annual exhibition,[2] and in 1845 he submitted another painting under that title to the American Art-Union, as well as one called "Cottage Scenery,"[3] both of which were purchased and awarded by the Art-Union to lucky subscribers in December of that year. In 1846, and from 1849 to 1851, Bingham submitted ten landscapes to the American Art-Union, the Western Art Union, and the Philadelphia Art Union—the majority being entitled "Landscape with Cattle," or simply "Cattle Piece." During recent years the American

1. B. to S. E. H., Dec. 16, 1835, coll. SHSMo.
2. *Catalogue of the Fifteenth Annual Exhibition, 1840,* #249.
3. *Transactions of the AAU, for the year 1845,* #98, 102.

Art-Union's "Cottage Scenery" (A138) has been discovered, and a composition of "Landscape with Cattle" (A148) has been in the collection of the City Art Museum of St. Louis for many years. The provenance of the St. Louis version of the cattle series does not indicate any apparent relationship to the Art-Union pictures, but the painting undoubtedly belongs to the larger group of such subjects which the artist painted within the period. Bingham seems to have painted no further landscapes after 1851 in which the domestic herd form the central attraction. Judging by the number of such subjects he turned out, one can assume that he had thoroughly exhausted the possibilities of this field by that time, despite the fact that there must have been a strong popular demand for the pictures.

The first recorded landscape by Bingham that purported to be also a portrait of a specific place, described as "made from a sketch taken on the spot," was one called "Scene on the Ohio River near Cincinnati" (A223). It was reproduced as a wood-engraving in *The Western Journal* for January, 1852,[4] but the picture has not been located, and should not be confused with another painting of a similar title ("Scene on the Ohio") which is now in the collection of the State Historical Society of Missouri (E458).

Bingham's activity in the field of landscape painting seems to have paralleled the patronage that encouraged such production. After the fall of the Art Unions, we find no indication of a continuing activity on his part. During his stay in Düsseldorf, from 1856 to 1859, he is supposed to have painted several views of the local scene. One of those pictures, "Moonlight Scene: Castle on the Rhine" (A267), now in a private collection, serves to afford us a glimpse of the artist's activity during his European period. It is conceivable that he felt newly inspired to return to landscape through his contact with the German school, noted for its landscape painters, although the work he produced at the time was probably not intended for public exhibition or sale.

After his return to America in 1859, Bingham apparently felt no urge to return to landscape painting, despite his experience abroad. There is certainly no evidence of such activity throughout the 1860's, although landscape elements do begin to play a more consistent role than before in the backgrounds of his portraits of this period.[5] Yet the artist was undoubtedly aware of the increased surge of interest in the West which developed soon after the end of the Civil War, an interest that must have been greatly stimulated by the building of railroads linking the two oceans. Not only were exploring

4. *The Western Journal*, VII (Jan., 1852), 289.
5. The portraits of Mrs. Benoist Troost (Mary Ann Gillis), 1859 (plate 158); Mrs. R. L. Todd (Sallie Hall) and daughter, *ca.* 1860 (plate 152); Miss Sally Cochran McGraw, *ca.* 1860 (plate 154); Mrs. Almerin Hotchkiss (Martha Ann Moore), *ca.* 1860 (plate 153).

172

expeditions penetrating to the Far West accompanied by artists who brought back pictorial records of the country, but established painters like Bierstadt[6] and Church[7] were also quick to become aware of the new excitement about distant places, and to respond to it. The results were spread before the public in terms of enormous canvases which appeared to answer every demand of the armchair traveler, rendering the grandiose panorama in faithful detail. Church himself went farther than any other painter of his generation in striving to satisfy the demand for the spectacular, by traveling far beyond the confines of the United States to depict other wonders of the western hemisphere—from the jungles of Central and South America to the icebergs of Labrador. Bingham's own awareness of the development of landscape painting of his time, and particularly of the work of Church, is significantly reflected in some of his thoughts on the subject contained in a letter to Rollins, written in June, 1871:

The productions of our Landscape painters will not suffer in a comparison with any that the pencil of Claude or Turner has left to the world. You can indeed almost safely assert that in our Church we have the *greatest* of Landscape painter[s] whether of the old or modern masters. His "Heart of the Andes" and "Falls of Neagara" [*sic*] seem literal presentations of Nature as she appears in all her transcendant beauty and sublimity. They are scarcely pictures, but rather Nature herself as seen through the eyes of her most devoted worshiper [*sic*].[8]

Perhaps encouraged by the growing interest in pictorial transcriptions of western scenery, and possibly seeing in it as well an opportunity to put in his own bid for a new patronage in a popular and lucrative field, Bingham shortly afterward began to paint landscapes again, after a lapse of many years. On traveling to Colorado for his health during the summer of 1872, he took advantage of the situation to paint a number of studies of the scenic beauties he saw about him, evidently with a view to developing them into final pictures. He concentrated his attention on the area's chief attraction, Pike's Peak, and by late October he had already completed a large composition of the subject (A353). At that time an admirer in Denver addressed a letter to the *Missouri Republican*, giving an elaborate description of "Bingham's Latest Picture":

It may interest your readers and the many friends of Geo. C. Bingham to know that he has finished a view of Pike's Peak which may be seen ere long in your city. This artist has achieved a wide reputation by his successful delineation of American life.

6. Albert Bierstadt (1830-1902). Honorary Member, Professional, National Academy, 1859-1860: Member, Academy, 1860-1902.
7. Frederic Edwin Church (1826-1900). Associate Member, National Academy, 1849; Member, Academy, 1850-1900.
8. B. to R., letter, Kansas City, Mo., June 19, 1871, coll. SHSMo (*MHR*, XXXIII [1938], 72-73).

engravings from which have been extensively published both in this country and in Europe; but we doubt if any of his works of this class, pre-eminent as they may be in originality and fidelity to their subject, are equal in artistic merit to this production, of his skill in a different field. It is, in fact, a realization such as we had scarce believed to be within the power of the pencil. The heavy monarch of the mountains, towering far above surrounding elevations, is revealed to the spectator in all its grandeur, just as he appears in the clear atmosphere of our mountain region. A few clouds that seem actually in motion, reveal the deep azure of the sky, one of which separated from his companions yields homage to the mount as passing beneath his summit, it casts its shadow far down upon the rugged sides. The subordinate mountains to the right and left with their outcroppings of primeval rocks tossed up by the feat that caused the "sea and the dry land" to appear, are presented with equal fidelity.

The artist avails himself of no mist or licensed generalization to escape the labor due to the details of his subject, but like a true lover of nature puts in its proper place and holds in proper keeping all that meets the eye as it scans the magnificent landscape from the immediate foreground to the far distant peaks which fade away in the deep blue of our Colorado sky. The simple majesty of the lofty peak, holding in his storm-riven clefts the snows of unnumbered winters, together with the minor and varied beauties of the scene, in form and color, light and shadow, are given with fidelity to nature which almost reaches the point of illusion. . . .[9]

The correspondent went on to say: "We have been informed that Mr. Bingham intends to devote a large portion of his time in the future to landscape art, and to make this western region, in which nature is exhibited [in] her sublimist aspects, the field of his studies."[10]

Several paintings identified as Colorado landscapes remained in the artist's family, but the large "Pike's Peak" was probably one of the few finished landscapes of these years. The painter was taken up with many portrait commissions, as well as with his various civic and state commitments, and so presumably had little time to devote to "landscape art," despite his reported intentions. However, during his wedding trip to Colorado in late June, 1878, Bingham appears to have made some additional studies of the landscape, at least one of which was later incorporated in a finished work. He referred to the painting in a letter to Rollins on October 4, 1878: "I have sold a Mountain landscape which I painted since our return from Colorado, for 160 acres land in Linn county near Brooklin and near the Hanibal [sic] and St. Joe Rail Road. It cost the gentleman from [whom] I obtained it $2000.00."[11]

On the basis of the few extant examples of Bingham's landscapes dating from his earlier period, together with a study of the landscape elements he

9. *Missouri Statesman,* Nov. 22, 1872, 1-6 (from letter to *Missouri Republican,* Oct. 26, 1872, signed M. G. H.).
10. *Ibid.*
11. B. to R., letter [Kansas City], Oct. 4, 1878, coll. SHSMo (*MHR* XXXIII [1939], 517).

174

used as settings for his genre compositions, it is possible to form a fairly comprehensive judgment of the structure of his landscape style. His approach to landscape painting, like his approach to his figure subjects, evidently involved a precise organization and a considered preparation. From the earliest pictorial evidence available, one senses at once an investigation of some one underlying source or possibly of several published sources such as those which served to form the backbone of his figure compositions. For instance, he may very well have followed the advice given by Francis Nicholson in *The Practice of Drawing and Painting Landscape From Nature*:

The foundation of drawing and painting from nature should be laid by studying and copying the works of the best masters, in order to ascertain the methods of practice, and principles of construction. With such assistance, the learner will acquire the power of seeing what is most perfect in nature. . . . When he is become familiar with the works of those masters, he will readily perceive in nature what would otherwise have been unnoticed: the mind so prepared, on the sight of what is grand and beautiful, feels this to be like Wilson or Poussin, or that like Salvator Rosa, and by finding what the choice of those and other great artists has been, learns to prefer similar forms or combination of objects wherever they present themselves; the principal and most important part of painting being to know what is most beautiful in nature, and most proper for imitation. . . .[12]

All of Bingham's known landscapes are as consciously composed as his better-known genre subjects. Like many other landscape painters of his time, he apparently followed the advice of the instruction-book masters, using prescribed formulas for his compositions. His landscapes are usually composed without any indication of a particular locale, although he undoubtedly on occasion painted scenes of actual places, and certainly those landscape elements that occur in the backgrounds of so many of his figure subjects depict topographical features common to the western scene.

Apart from these considerations, it can be assumed that as early as 1838 Bingham came into contact with landscapes exhibited by Thomas Cole[13] and Asher Brown Durand,[14] perhaps the best-known painters in the field at the time. These two men were leaders of two opposing tendencies in landscape painting: on the one side, the conservative preferences of Durand, with his faithfulness to an observed nature; on the other, the dynamic, grandiose

12. F. Nicholson, *The Practice of Drawing and Painting Landscape From Nature* . . . (2nd ed.: London: John Murray, 1823), p. 18.
13. Thomas Cole (1801-1848). Member, National Academy, 1826-1848. Exhibited five landscapes at the annual exhibition, NAD, in 1838.
14. Asher Brown Durand (1796-1886). Member, National Academy, 1826-1886: President, Academy, 1846-1861. Exhibited nine landscapes at annual exhibition, NAD, 1838.

175

tendency of Cole, who attempted to interpret nature along more idealistic lines. Yet both adapted their interpretations of nature to recognized formulas, and Bingham, in his turn, probably borrowed from each in terms of his own formulated approach, a method of working that the instruction-book masters would have certainly applauded.

The prescription that Bingham and the majority of his contemporaries followed as recognized working procedure included a general arrangement of carefully plotted receding planes, with a stagelike foreground made up of standard equipment such as trees, foliage, and large rocks; a middle distance composed of heavy masses of foliage, often with the inclusion of a small figure or figures to afford an impression of scale; and a farther distance with mountains and additional foliage silhouetted against the sky. It was, in fact, the kind of scheme that had been recommended long since by published manuals of instruction on landscape, which, in their turn, perpetuated the spirit of an earlier classical tradition. A plate in Nicholson's manual (plate 105) included all the desired points, and further indicated the various possible ways of achieving proper balance and desirable effects of light and shade. As in the case of composition, the proper distribution of light and shade in landscape was evaluated and reduced to formula, and rarely was the arbitrary judgment of the painter taken into account. He was warned about the pitfalls of approaching nature directly "without previous practice," and advised instead about the advantages to be gained from, "a careful study of prints, after those masters whose works have been recommended as guides to the acquirement of knowledge requisite to discover in nature what is proper for selection . . . prints may be preferred to pictures; as they exhibit form, light and shade, independent of colour."[15]

Some of Bingham's preliminary studies for landscape compositions — sketches on the verso of sheets of figures for known genre subjects of the 1845/1846 period — afford us a significant glimpse of the artist's basic method in pure landscape at the time. The sketches undoubtedly date from the same period as the well-documented subjects on the obverse of the sheets. The two examples illustrated (plate 106), both from a single sheet, serve to demonstrate his already established compositional formula. In a manner very much like that employed for the demonstration plate in Nicholson's manual, the artist prepared a system of receding planes in which the spectator is led gradually into the distance through an opening in the right foreground which has been built up, in a stagelike fashion, by rocks and enframing trees. In the background, distant hills are visible which may or

15. F. Nicholson, *The Practice of Drawing and Painting Landscape From Nature . . .*, pp. 39-40.

may not necessarily relate to elements of a known region. The play of darks against lights in a carefully organized pattern of receding planes is effectively demonstrated in the lower sketch, which indicates a light mass in the foreground balanced by a shaded middle distance, carried finally to another light area in the background.

The landscape studies date from the same period as the recently discovered "Cottage Scenery" (plate 107), which had been lost to sight since it was awarded by the American Art-Union to James D. Carhart of Macon, Georgia, on the evening of December 19, 1845.[16] The Art-Union had purchased it for $35 when it was submitted to them earlier in the month.[17] We know now that the painting had actually descended in the Carhart family until it appeared on the New York art market in 1960. The specific documentation of the picture establishes its importance as Bingham's earliest signed landscape. But as a pictorial document it is even more significant in that it reveals so much about Bingham and his aesthetic attitudes in a field other than portraiture during a still formative stage of his career.

From a compositional standpoint, the picture indicates a direction similar to that shown in the related studies, with an already well-developed formal sense of spatial values combined with an ability to develop an impression of atmosphere and breadth. As in the studies, darks and lights are carefully organized to effect a distinct impression of receding planes, varying only the areas of emphasis, in a manner suggested by Nicholson and other instruction-book masters. Technical details, such as the foliage, are handled precisely and with painstaking care.

The subject, "Cottage Scenery," is remarkable itself, once we realize that it was in all probability painted within months of "Fur Traders Descending the Missouri," certainly one of the most important of the artist's early paintings of Western genre, by virtue both of its figures and of its setting. "Cottage Scenery," however, does not show any particular regionally descriptive characteristics. Instead, Bingham's intent appears to have been to capture a landscape mood by bringing together all the various ingredients that the observer would ordinarily associate with a sense of rustic flavor. Such a "fancy" landscape, in which an ideal scene was represented, but with no specific regional description intended, had a considerable historical precedent in Dutch landscape painting of the seventeenth century. But Bingham would have been more familiar with the numerous "cottage views" of the English master George Morland, after whose works hundreds of prints had been produced since the latter part of the eighteenth century to satisfy a popular

16. AAU, minutes of meeting, Dec. 8, 1845, coll. NYHS.
17. *Transactions of the American Art-Union, for the Year 1845*, #98.

demand for such sentimental subjects.[18] Thatched-roof cottages framed by trees, with genre-like groupings of figures added for incidental interest, much in the manner of "Cottage Scenery," occur frequently in Morland's work (plate 108).[19] Rustic motifs, including figures, details of houses, and other accessories, were easily available in Bingham's time in the drawing-books of Samuel Prout and William Henry Pyne as well as in publications based on Morland's sketches, and may very well have served as source material for the artist.

If Morland's subject matter had indeed attracted and inspired Bingham during this period, it is also more than likely that he was equally aware of other artists among his fellow Americans who also reflected the English school in their work. In this connection, the work of the Philadelphia painter Joshua Shaw comes particularly to mind, and probably not altogether by chance. Shaw was a mature painter by the time he came to America from England, in 1817.[20] His landscapes, mirroring a prevailing English taste and style strongly reminiscent of Morland and his circle, were exhibited regularly at exhibitions in New York and Philadelphia from 1818 to 1862. Bingham, while he was studying in Philadelphia in 1838, or during his reported visit to that city again in June, 1843, would certainly have had some opportunity of seeing Shaw's work.[21] Typical examples of Shaw's landscape style painted during the period in which he might first have come to Bingham's notice reveal a compositional structure and mood that parallels the Missourian's approach to a similar pictorial problem. A comparison of "Cottage Scenery" with a Shaw landscape painted, by coincidence, in 1838 (plate 109) reveals

18. During Morland's lifetime over 250 prints were produced after his works. Some 80 printmakers were engaged in this activity, including, among the most prolific of the graphic artists, John Raphael Smith, William Ward, and S. W. Reynolds.

19. Engravings after drawings of rustic figures by Morland were also published in drawing-book form by Edward Orme, J. P. Thompson, and R. Bowyer, from 1793/1794 to 1806/1807. Other drawing books, such as those of the popular Samuel Prout and William Henry Pyne, also concentrated on details of rural and cottage scenery. Some of the details of thatched-roof cottages and fences illustrated in Prout could have served as the more likely sources for Bingham during this period: *Easy Lessons in Landscape Painting* ... (London: Ackerman, 1819) ; *Studies of Cottages and Rural Scenery* ... (London: Ackerman, 1816) ; *A Series of Views of Rural Cottages in the North of England* ... (London: Ackerman, 1821). William Henry Pyne's "rustic figures" were obviously designed as motifs for landscape compositions: *Etchings of Rustic Figures, for the Embellishment of Landscape* (London: M. A. Nattali [1814-1819]).

20. Joshua Shaw (*ca.* 1776/1777-1860) had exhibited at the Royal Academy and elsewhere in London by 1802. Mr. Lee B. Anderson, a long-time collector in the field of nineteenth-century American landscape, was the first to call my attention to the possible Bingham-Shaw relationship.

21. S. E. B. to Mary (Amend) Bingham, letter, Washington, D.C., August 24, 1843, coll. SHSMo: Re visit to Philadelphia in June: "Mr. B and Mrs. Shaw went to Pha; Mr B to attend the exhibition of pictures." Four landscapes by Joshua Shaw were on exhibition at the Artists Fund Society that year. Shaw was residing in Philadelphia in 1838. Along with his paintings Bingham could have also been familiar with the series of aquatints by John Hill after Shaw's *Picturesque Views of American Scenery*, published in Philadelphia by Moses Thomas in 1819 and by M. Carey & Son in 1820.

a similar balance of rich foliage with a gnarled tree, and the resemblance appears to be much more than mere chance. Shaw's handling of the tree, defining its silhouette against the sky, is almost a signature of the artist. Bingham's handling of a similar tree form seems an obvious attempt on his part to emulate the crisp style of the Anglo-American artist who was actually residing in Philadelphia when Bingham was there, during the spring of 1838.

A "Landscape with Cattle" (plate 110) can be considered a representative example of the series of cattle subjects that was produced by Bingham during a five-year period dating from about 1846—when the first painting of that title appeared in the American Art-Union offerings for that year—until 1851. In fact, almost all of these "Cattle Pieces" seem to have been destined for the New York organization, or for such offshoots as the Western Art Union and the Philadelphia Art Union. This picture is presently the sole survivor of the group, and is correctly dated among the earliest of Bingham's work in this area, 1846. The painting, like the others yet unlocated, was in all probability conceived as a "fancy picture," intended to evoke a poetic appreciation of the beauties of nature rather than to describe a specific place. Such compositions were usually planned along prescribed lines in which domestic animals in landscape settings form the central subject, and in which spatial divisions, light and shade, and details are balanced in an orderly fashion to form a pleasing and decorative effect.

Yet, it was this painting that was described by one contemporary critic as "a scene on the Mississippi . . . of quiet beauty, representing the majestic old woods rising on the rich bottom; the herd reclining beneath their shade; the river winding its way in the distance, and in the background a bold bluff rearing its high summit, in wild grandeur, beside the Father of waters."[22] This rather inspired description is of more than passing interest because the writer felt compelled to ascribe the scene to a specific place, although those areas upon which he bases its indentity, such as "the river winding its way in the distance" and the "bold bluff rearing its high summit, in wild grandeur," are actually given minor places in the composition. The title of the picture, like that of others of the series, certainly avoided any reference to region. Although some of the pictures obviously included details that were vaguely suggestive of some known area, as evidenced by our critic's reaction, it still must be considered most unlikely that Bingham made any consistent effort to produce descriptive landscapes.

The importance of the cattle motif in developing the mood of a rural landscape had been realized and made popular by Dutch landscapists of the seventeenth century, and in the next century the vogue crossed the Channel.

22. *Weekly Reveille*, (St. Louis), Sept. 28, 1846, 1012-2.

179

Its popularity also continued well into the nineteenth century. Bingham's obvious appreciation of the subject probably came through his contact with English examples or with the work of their adherents in America. For his studies of the cattle, however, Bingham did not necessarily have to go to nature, since such models as he desired were again readily accessible for just that purpose in the various drawing books of the period. In this instance, at least one of Thomas Sidney Cooper's plates (plate 111) could have served him well.

In the early 1850's Bingham continued to produce landscapes that, like the cattle subjects, may be described as "fancy pictures" consisting of arrangements of rocks, trees, and foliage into orderly concoctions which were pleasing to the eye. All of the examples now known include the incidental figure of a fisherman, or a lone deer. As in other instances already mentioned, a distant mountain may have invited a relationship to some recognizable western landmark, but such was probably not the artist's intention in producing the pair of landscapes now in the collections of the Missouri Historical Society (A207, A208; plates 112, 113), and a very similar picture now in the Newark Museum (A209). Subjects of this kind generally appeared in contemporary exhibitions labeled merely as "Landscape."

A "Landscape: Mountain View" (A224; plate 117) can also be dated within this period. All of the usual elements are again present, including the lone fisherman, but the arrangement is shifted so that the lake and distant mountain assume importance. The entire composition strongly suggests the panoramic manner that was already becoming so fashionable in the hands of Bingham's younger contemporaries. It resembles the Missouri Historical Society's "Landscape with a Fisherman" in a general way, but actually achieves far greater breadth in the final solution. This has been achieved largely by the elimination of concentration on foreground enframing features, which are reduced in scale and shifted to the middle ground of the composition. The broadly painted "Landscape with an Indian Encampment" (A225; plate 115) was probably intended as a study for a larger work. Its very obvious relationships to "Landscape: Mountain View," in both composition and intention, suggests a dating within the same period.

The Bingham painting that was described by a contemporary writer as representing a "Scene on the Ohio River near Cincinnati" (plate 114) is known to us only through a wood-engraving based upon the original composition. Familiar features include enframing foreground foliage and a lone figure from which vantage point the observer views the winding river and distant hills in the distance. Like the "Mountain View," this work concentrates attention on the broad sweep of landscape in the panoramic sense. But in the

180

continuing use of the earlier window-frame formula, Bingham reveals himself at a transitional phase of his development toward a landscape style which is already demonstrated in the "Mountain View," despite the impression that the distance in time of execution between the two pictures cannot be great.

Although Bingham, by preference, normally pursued the peaceful aspects of nature in his landscapes, somewhat reminiscent of his English sources and of the American school led by artists such as Thomas Doughty and Asher Brown Durand, he was evidently by no means unaware of the more dramatic possibilities inherent in the subject matter. It can be assumed that Bingham had come into contact with the works of Thomas Cole as early as 1838, when he could have seen his pictures on exhibition at the National Academy of Design, as well as those of Durand's and other members of the conservative school. The dynamic, grandiose tendency of Cole, so directly opposed to Durand, could not have failed to attract his attention. That awareness is best demonstrated in a landscape like "The Storm" (A205; plate 118), in which the familiar motifs of the gnarled tree and the lone deer now appear in an atmosphere richly charged with drama. The sense of drama is largely affected by the thunderous sky, movemented foliage, and the greatly accented use of lights and darks. One is strongly reminded of Cole's own representations of a dynamic and untamed nature, and even the blasted tree motif, used so frequently by Bingham in his pictures, can be ultimately traced to Cole.

Bingham's activity as a landscape painter apparently declined by the mid-1850's, paralleling the greatly reduced production of his figure pictures in which landscape elements invariably played a part. Landscapes appear again briefly during his stay in Düsseldorf, but these paintings were reportedly executed for his own pleasure. One of the known Düsseldorf landscapes, "Moonlight Scene: Castle on the Rhine" (plate 116), is of some interest in that it reflects a continuation of Bingham's experimentation with night scenes. By comparison with the broadly painted night scenes of 1854, the artist has obviously sacrificed the earlier hard-won accomplishment in favor of a hard, sleek finish, a tribute to the Düsseldorfian spell to which he had evidently succumbed during that period. The organization of the composition reflects earlier lessons still adhered to in terms of foreground arrangements, and in the massing of lights and darks to emphasize the progression of planes into the background, although all has been frozen into a postcard image.

Apart from the few landscapes of the German period, and a developing interest in landscape details in portrait compositions painted immediately after his return, the subject disappears from his production until 1872. At that time, stimulated by the sight of Colorado scenery, and by the rise of a

181

new public interest in the West, Bingham seriously considered giving more attention to landscape painting. His large "View of Pike's Peak" (1) (plate 119) was obviously intended to announce his return to the field and to represent his bid for a place in the sun beside those giants among the heroic landscapists of the day, Albert Bierstadt and Frederic E. Church. Unfortunately, the painting is now lost and only a poor reproduction remains of this ambitious effort. As a document it reveals a more concentrated attempt on Bingham's part to move into the area of the panoramists than he had made during the early 1850's, when he painted his first pictures that could be regarded as preliminary efforts in this direction. The "fancy landscape" was soon to be succeeded by a subject matter in which the wonders of actual places were to be exploited by artists using all the technical possibilities within their reach to create a sense of awe in the spectator. The idea was to afford the armchair traveler an impression of all that was grandiose in nature by means of compositions that not only depicted vast areas but frequently appeared on canvases of equally overpowering dimensions.[23] Bingham obviously attempted to follow the new "conventions" on both counts, and made a special effort with this landscape, although it apparently gained him little beyond local recognition. The composition, while still adapted to the usual landscape formula, also shows some probable inspiration from contemporary works. We know that he was particularly impressed by the work of Church, having claimed, not long before, that one could "almost safely assert" that the artist might be rated among the "greatest" of landscape painters, worthy of comparison with Claude or Turner.[24] He evidently knew Church's "Heart of the Andes," a much publicized and exhibited picture, and it seems not inconceivable that he would seek to emulate that achievement, which he considered a "literal" presentation of nature "as she appears in all her transcendant beauty and sublimity."[25] But, by comparison, Bingham's own accomplishment, despite some obvious relationships in composition, seems tight and self-conscious, lacking that impression of breadth and technical skill that had brought such great fame to his younger contemporary.

Another "View of Pike's Peak (2) (A354; plate 120), in all probability dating from the same period as the much publicized lost version, is now in a private collection. Compositionally, the two paintings have a common relation-

23. Baron Alexander von Humboldt, the great naturalist, whose portrait Bingham had been commissioned to paint in 1859, had written extensively on landscape painting and its relationship to the study of nature in his *Kosmos: Entwurf einer Physischen Weltbeschreibung,* published 1845-1862 (English eds., London, 1849-1858; New York, 1850-1859). He recommended that artists paint pictures of great natural scenery on a large scale, taking their example from the painters of panoramas, a means "calculated to raise the feeling for nature" (*Cosmos,* II, 98).
24. B. to R., letter, Kansas City, Mo., June 19, 1871 (*MHR.* XXXII [1938], 72).
25. *Ibid.*

LANDSCAPE PAINTING

ship in the very similar grouping of trees in the left foreground, as well as in the formal organization of receding planes and the carefully placed distribution of lights and darks. The small figures of the hunter and his dog replace the lone figure, but both serve the same purpose in giving the spectator an impression of the awesome scale of the surrounding scene. The picture is rich in description, each part being handled with painstaking care and showing a dedication to the Düsseldorfian code of the smooth finish. The more personal mood of the earlier landscapes has been sacrificed in favor of sleekness of effect and that demonstration of technical proficiency that he so evidently sought to emulate from the German school he had come to admire.

A small "Colorado Mountain Landscape" (A383; plate 121) appears to date from Bingham's second Colorado trip in the summer of 1878. Although a more intimate study than the vast panoramic pictures of 1872, it still reveals the artist's now familiar pattern of foreground arrangements of rocks and stream, with the mountain looming up in the distance—a formal design that can be traced back to lessons learned and assimilated to his style more than thirty years before.

Among the artist's late works, " 'Forest Hill,' The Nelson Homestead" (A377; plate 122) was painted in 1877 while he was in residence there, executing portraits of the family. It is an unusual type of landscape for Bingham, although views of country seats were typical of an older English tradition, and at an early period in America artists such as Thomas Beck and Francis Guy painted views of gentlemen's seats in the English manner for wealthy patrons in Philadelphia and Baltimore. Bingham may have been aware of engravings of the kind and there may have been a more immediate precedence for this fashion of painting in his own time. Here, he seems actually to have gone further than the traditional portrait of an estate, however, by introducing figures that bring the composition into the realm of the storytelling picture. According to family tradition, the figures on horseback, and those in the foreground, represent the Nelson grandchildren, and the horse and buggy drawn up before the house is supposed to be that of the family doctor who has come to deliver an addition to the family.

On a technical side, Bingham's approach to the problem here is much the same as that of his other compositions related to scenes of particular places: a painstakingly organized arrangement in terms of light and shade, receding planes, foreground enframing elements, and a central subject adapted to the formal setting.

Despite the fact that the complete story of Bingham's work as a landscapist is yet to be told—and this cannot be accomplished until more of the pictorial evidence is available—we can still form a fairly conclusive estimate of his

183

place in the field. Pure landscape was not his special forte, although he was concerned with the problems of a landscape painter in establishing the settings for most of his genre pictures. When he did concern himself with pure landscape, however, he tried his hand at everything from fancy landscapes to heroic representations of actual places. His excursion into the field covered the entire gamut of style in American landscape. His paintings of the 1840's and early 1850's are still close to the conventional English taste of the early nineteenth century, reflecting more the influence of Morland than the advanced style of Turner; hence closer to conservative American counterparts like Shaw, Doughty, and Durand. For a brief span in the early 1850's, his work took on the more dramatic direction of Thomas Cole. The latter 1850's were taken up with Düsseldorfian inspirations in both subject and technique. When Bingham resumed his interest in landscape in the early 1870's, after a lapse of ten years—this time with a sincere intention of bringing this area into the mainstream of his activity—he adopted a means of expression that may be considered a cross between a Bierstadt and a Church—heroic in conception and rich in descriptive detail. French influence, already strong in the 1870's, was not to affect him. He remained a conservative to the end.

184

VIII

LATER WORK IN MISSOURI: PORTRAIT PAINTING (1844-1855)

Although the period marking Bingham's return to his home in Saline County in the fall of 1844, following the prolonged sojourn in Washington, also denotes the beginning of his serious career as a genre painter, it by no means was paralleled by a decrease in his activity as a portrait painter. In fact, he would continue to paint portraits "to make the pot boil" until the end of his days, and there is ample evidence, too, to show that he was proud of his local standing in this branch and constantly strove to improve his style in competition with the best painters of his time. He apparently sought to gain a national reputation as a portrait painter by going to Washington, and undoubtedly the fact that such distinguished personages as John Quincy Adams and Daniel Webster sat for him did much toward advancing his professional standing at home. It is probably no mere coincidence therefore that the portraits of several prominent Missourians painted by him can be dated between 1844 and 1845, soon after his return from the East.

By late December, 1844, Bingham had taken a studio in Jefferson City, where a reporter noted "portraits of some of our most distinguished men" and indicated pleasure with their "beauty and accuracy."[1] The portraits observed were those of "some of the members of the present General Assembly," with specific mention being given to two of them: "that of Mr. Hughes[2] of Platte, which is a very excellent likeness, and does honor to Mr. B. as an artist. The portrait of Governor Edwards[3] is very perfect indeed."

1. *Jefferson City Inquirer*, Dec. 26, 1844, 3-5.
2. Probably General Bela M. Hughes of Plattsburg, Mo. The subject, evidently a friend of the artist, mentioned him in a letter written to Col. Andrew Warner, corresponding secretary of the AAU, Aug. 20, 1849 (coll. NYHS).
3. John Cummings Edwards (1806-1888). Governor of Missouri, 1844-1848. He served as U.S. Representative while the artist was in Washington, and occasionally permitted him to mail his personal letters home under his free-franking privilege.

One can readily understand why the portrait of Governor Edwards (A121; plate 123) attracted the particular attention of the reporter, since the painting is an extremely important example of Bingham's growing strength and individuality as a portraitist. The portrait represents the Governor as a full-length figure, striding toward the spectator within a broadly conceived landscape which extends behind him into the distance, with the State Capitol at Jefferson City, symbol of the subject's high office, looming up in the background at the left. Although a relatively small picture, it has a striking monumentality that the artist rarely seems to have achieved during his later years when his full-length portrait commissions were of large dimensions. Of course, it is conceivable that the small picture was actually a preliminary study for a much larger version, a method usually employed by Bingham.

The figure is treated as a bold silhouette, with the cape that encloses it being used to emphasize to the full the dramatic presence of the subject. The atmospheric sky behind the figure serves further to afford the spectator an impression bordering on the theatrical. The subject handling is not entirely original with Bingham. It can be considered a direct descendant of the many full-length figure portraits stemming from the English school of the eighteenth and early nineteenth century. But the manner in which the figure looms up and moves toward the observer, as well as the manipulation of drapery and background, suggests that Bingham could have been familiar with one of the few American paintings of any distinction in this category, the then already well-known portrait of the Marquis de Lafayette, painted by Samuel F. B. Morse for the City of New York in 1825 (plate 124).

It is also entirely possible that Bingham's highly effective portrait of James Lawrence Minor (A135; plate 126) was painted at this time and may have been among those likenesses of "some of our most distinguished men" which were to be seen in the Jefferson City studio.

In Saline County Bingham painted a second pair of portraits of Arrow Rock's most prominent citizens, Dr. John Sappington and his wife Jane (A128, A129), as well as those of two of the doctor's sons, Erasmus Darwin and William Breathitt Sappington (A124, A126), and their respective spouses (A125, A127). In Boonville he executed, among others, portraits of Thomas Withers Nelson and his wife (A132, A133), and of Mrs. Jacob Fortney Wyan (Nancy Shanks) (A142), mother of Mrs. Nelson. In Columbia he probably painted a second portrait of his close friend Major Rollins (A134).

All of these portraits reveal a decided advance over those the artist produced before he went to Washington. Those developments we noted in the few paintings now extant which can be definitely placed within the

186

Washington years become established characteristics of his style during this succeeding period. The portraits are less conventional in the arrangement of the subjects, the painter no longer being limited by the one-pose composition he had adopted from his earliest years. There is also a greater breadth in his treatment of light and shade. Although the figures are still firmly modeled, and the heads frequently betray the starkness that links them with the early examples, there is a decided maturity in the artist's approach to the problem. The figures now take their places within the settings and there is a developed painterly quality in the handling of textures.

The portraits of Dr. John Sappington (plate 130) and his wife (plate 131) are among the more elaborate compositions that can be placed within this period. The subjects face the observer in the now familiar pattern long adopted by the artist, although the positions are reversed. Particularly notable, however, is the special consideration given to the arrangement of the hands and the important role that they assume in the organization of the pictures. In both instances they give an added characterization to the figures which Bingham rarely achieves in his portraits, although such features are certainly found in several of his earlier known works. In the dignified portrait of the doctor the bold handling of lights and shadows seems to lay particular stress on the importance of the hand resting on the manuscript just as much as it serves to afford a rich three-dimensional quality to the entire composition. The sense of confidence in his ability to handle a variety of pictorial problems appears very evident here, as if the artist were making a strenuous effort to indicate how far he had progressed from the first portrait he had painted of the same subject during his early years as a painter.

The portrait of Jane Breathitt Sappington is an especially interesting one, especially when one compares it with Bingham's portrayal of the same sitter executed in 1834 (plate 2), at the beginning of his career. The likeness is immediately recognizable, as is the same determined expression, but the brittle modeling of the head against a flat, lifeless background is now replaced by a figure that takes its place within a setting that has both dimension and atmosphere. There is a greater variety in the modeling of the head, as there is in the textures of the skin against the lace cap. The pose of the crossed hands, the right one holding the spectacles, lends variety and interest to the lower part of the composition, despite the faulty drawing of these details.

The portraits of the younger male members of the Sappington family and of Thomas Withers Nelson (plate 125) adhere to the artist's old mode of representation, despite an increased control of pictorial values. The portrait of Eramus Darwin Sappington actually interests us more because of the subject's near future role as a bitter opponent of Bingham in the 1846 contest

187

for the Saline County seat in the Missouri State House of Representatives.

The portraits of William Breathitt Sappington and his wife (plates 128, 129) are typical examples of the group. The man's portrait is uninspired, but that of Mary Mildred Sappington offers variety and interest in the general arrangement of the figure, and is particularly notable for its sensitive handling of details and varied textures.

The portrait of Nancy Shanks Wyan (plate 132) is one of the finest portraits of women by Bingham that can be assigned to this active period. The artist's still obvious attraction to Thomas Sully's portrait style is visible in his treatment of such features as the eyes, and in the modeling of the head, with its heightened flesh tones. From a compositional standpoint, the concentration is on the subject, all details being deliberately reduced so as not to detract from the strong and lively face which is turned toward the spectator. Details such as the frilled cap and widespread collar are actually used to enframe and accent the importance of the head—a means the artist uses ever more frequently during the following decade. The only exception is the inclusion of the pair of spectacles atop the subject's headdress, presumably a detail that must have had some special association with Mrs. Wyan. Bingham apparently made at least two copies of the portrait.

The artist's increased political activity between 1846 and 1850, as well as the encouragement and patronage he received for his genre subjects during this period, may have contributed to a relaxation of his attention to portraiture. It is only to the latter part of the period that we can assign a number of portraits with any certainty. The tendency toward an ever-developing atmospheric quality, which characterizes Bingham's genre compositions from about 1849 onward, is reflected in the portraits he produced during the same years. A softening of contours and a richer modeling in terms of light and shade typify these portraits, although the tendency also renders the painter's style somewhat less individualistic, bringing him ever closer into the ranks of the capable but frequently undistinguished portraitists of the middle of the nineteenth century.

The portrait of Oscar F. Potter (A155; plate 133) as a youth, reliably dated within this period, is an especially fresh and lively characterization. The simple and unaffected air of the figure is achieved largely by the painter's arrangement of form and light and shade.

An interesting comparison can be made between the portrait of Colonel Granville Craddock Medley (A156; plate 127) and that of General James Lawrence Minor (plate 126) produced a few years earlier. Both are almost identical in pose, but the softening of contours and modeling of the Medley figure marks the most noticeable change in the artist's style.

188

During the fall of 1849 Bingham was once more busily engaged in portrait painting in Columbia. The most important commission was a full-length, life-size portrait of Dr. William Jewell (A170), which was evidently intended for presentation to the college at Liberty of which the subject was the founder.[4] He may have painted the smaller portrait of Dr. Jewell (A169) at this time as well.[5] It is also possible that a portrait of the John H. Lathrop (A176) was executed during this stay in Columbia.[6]

Among the personages the artist probably painted at Columbia were Colonel William Franklin Switzler (A172; plate 134), editor of the town's most important newspaper, *The Missouri Statesman*, where Bingham's activities always received favorable attention, and his wife (A173; plate 135). Both pictures are dignified and skillfully executed likenesses. We can also assign to this time the portraits of Bingham's new in-laws, the Reverend Dr. Robert Stewart Thomas and his wife (A178, A179), as well as those of their children, Dr. William P. Thomas (A180) and Sallie Thomas Moore (or More) (A181). The vital portrait of the ruddy-faced Captain William Johnston (A177), father of Mrs. Thomas, seems to have been painted at this time, too. All of this activity in connection with the Thomas family can probably be accounted for by the fact that the artist married Eliza, another daughter of the Reverend Dr. Robert S. Thomas, at Columbia, on December 2, 1849.[7]

Two portraits of the artist's second wife can be dated within this period. One of these pictures (A183; plate 136) conceivably painted to commemorate her recent marriage, is among Bingham's more inspired portrait compositions. The figure is presented in an oval, shown three-quarter length, with accessories arranged to form a most sensitive and appealing design. The motif of the hand holding the handkerchief recalls the large, equally elaborate portrait the artist painted of his first wife in Washington in 1842 (plate 40), although the later portrait is certainly different in every other respect.

A similar delicacy of treatment is particularly characteristic of the portraits of young women painted by Bingham just before 1850, such as that of his wife's sister, Sallie (Thomas) Moore (plate 140), and the sensitive likeness of Mary Elizabeth Rollins (A174; plate 139), three-year-old

---

4. *Missouri Statesman*, Sept. 28, 1849, 2-2; *Liberty Weekly Tribune*, Oct. 5, 1849, 1-2, 2-2. The portrait was bequeathed to William Jewell College, Liberty, Mo., under the terms of Dr. Jewell's will, in 1852 (*Missouri Statesman*, Aug. 20, 1852; Rusk, *George Caleb Bingham* ... , p. 48).
5. *Missouri Statesman*, Aug. 20, 1852; Rusk, *op. cit.*
6. Bingham presented the portrait to "the ladies of Columbia" in December, 1850, who in turn gave it to the University (*Missouri Statesman*, Dec. 27, 1850, 2-1; *Jefferson City Inquirer*, Dec. 28, 1850, 2-2).
7. *Missouri Statesman*, Dec. 7, 1849, 3-4. Bingham's first wife, Sarah Elizabeth (Hutchison) Bingham, died in Arrow Rock, Nov. 29, 1848 (*Missouri Statesman*, Dec. 29, 1848, 3-2).

daughter of Major Rollins. In all of these pictures a reminiscence of the Sully influence of earlier years seems now to have become more thoroughly assimilated with Bingham's always more decisive and insistent realism, without losing the Sullyesque sense of delicacy and of the decorative values of heightened color. That he was able to introduce a similar quality into his portraits of older subjects is equally well demonstrated in his fine painting of Mrs. James H. McGee (Eleanor Evelyn Fry) (A186; plate 137).

A miniature self-portrait of the artist (A184; plate 138) can also be assigned to the period 1849/1850. Despite its present poor state, the small picture displays much of the freshness and vitality that can be said to be a typical characteristic of the majority of portraits executed by Bingham at this time.

Two oval portraits of Mrs. James H. Bennett (Eliza Rollins) (A175; plate 141) and Vestine Porter (A189; plate 142) reflect a greater emphasis on realism, despite the presence of decorative elements. Both portraits show a more positive and heavier modeling of form than is usual during this period. By contrast with his typical portraits of the time, light and shade is used in a bold fashion, with one side of the head cased in deep shadow relieved only by reflected lights. The balance of Bingham's implicit realism with Sully's idealized manner is superseded, at least for the moment, by a photograph-like focus in which virtually all traces of the Sully inspiration disappear. The treatment of backgrounds in these portraits deserves particular notice. The conventionally neutral backgrounds are given new significance by the artist, in the Bennett portrait by the use of drapery, and in the Porter portrait by the inclusion of landscape elements. The use of landscape is unusual for the period, although Bingham had occasionally introduced such details into a few pictures of his early years, of which the Edwards portrait of 1844 (plate 123) is probably the most outstanding example. But the specific use, in this instance, of landscape and foliage to enhance the decorative quality of a portrait composition prefigures a pattern that the artist does not appear to have adopted in any consistent manner until the late 1850's.

A third portrait of Mrs. Anthony Wayne Rollins (A215; plate 143), the matriarch of the Rollins family, shows the familiar features of the subject in the final years of her life. As in the portraits of her daughter Mrs. Bennett and Vestine Porter, the sitter faces the observer directly. The picture takes its place stylistically with the others, not only from a technical standpoint, but more specifically in the dominant concentration on description. A comparison of this portrait with those Bingham painted of the subject in 1834 and 1837 points up its direct line of descent in terms of that pervading dedication to fact that was the artist's primary inheritance from a native

190

American tradition. The same impression of forthright portraiture, in which all detail is abolished in favor of a positive characterization of the subject, is also clearly demonstrated in the portrait of Washington McLean (A217; plate 144), in all probability dating from this time.

During the greater part of the following two years Bingham devoted most of his attention to genre and landscape subjects, chiefly with the intention of selling them to the Art Unions, although he was also busy with the Goupil commissions and had begun work on his large "County Election." He evidently had little time for portraiture until January, 1852, when a St. Louis reporter announced:

Mr. B. is now engaged principally in portrait painting. In this branch of art he has but few equals, and no superior. We saw the unfinished portraits of several ladies and gentlemen, residents of St. Louis, which could not be surpassed for fidelity of features, and expression. That of a distinguished State Judicial Officer is remarkable for conveying an impression of *identity* rather than that of mere resemblance. The old Judge himself is there, with his benevolent and intellectual face, looking as much at home in a gilt frame as if he had never been any where else.[8]

I have not yet been able to identify the "distinguished State Judicial Officer" among those portraits now known, nor those of the other St. Louis residents referred to in the account, although the fine, vigorous portrait of Thomas Hart Benton (A218; plate 145), the statesman and long-time Missouri Senator, can very probably be dated within this period. As in the portraits of the women, the style is characterized by an emphatic realism which is enforced by the use of studio lighting, a tighter modeling, and a sharp focus.

Bingham's work on the Election series during the two ensuing years, combined with the great amount of time he considered necessary to spend in Philadelphia to superintend Sartain's engraving of "The County Election," as well as his considerable traveling to raise subscriptions for the print, conceivably restricted his activity as a portrait painter. By mid-June of 1855 he had returned to Independence,[9] where he apparently took on any portrait commissions that came his way. He was again in Columbia in September where he opened a studio in the Grand Jury Room of the courthouse, certainly with a view toward soliciting further portrait commissions.[10] By the latter part of November he had evidently exhausted his possibilities there and had already moved on to Jefferson City, where he was reportedly engaged in similar work.[11] A number of portraits still remain to permit us a useful

8. *Jefferson City Inquirer*, Jan. 17, 1852, 1-6 (from *St. Louis Intelligencer*).
9. B. to R., letter, Independence, Mo., June 15, 1855, coll. SHSMo (*MHR*, XXXII [1938], 188).
10. *Missouri Statesman*, Sept. 14, 1855.
11. *Ibid.*, Nov. 23, 1855.

glimpse of the artist's activity in Columbia and elsewhere at this time.

As in the past, his subjects maintain a direct contact with the spectator. The portraits are painted broadly—the artist still evidencing his interest in the presentation of the literal and solid facts that describe the individuality of his sitters. An even greater emphasis than before on a vivid and softer modeling of the heads marks perhaps the chief difference between these portraits and those he painted between 1850 and 1852.

The portrait of Mrs. David McClanahan Hickman (Cornelia Ann Bryan) (A250; plate 147) has a cameo-like quality in which the indication of such details as the lace cap and collar only serve to enforce that effect. A lighter and more delicate approach, recalling the portraits of 1849, is also character-istic of the likenesses of Elijah S. Stephens (A238; plate 146) and his wife (A239). The casting of one side of the face into deep shadow betrays the later tendency, but now without the heavier modeling and harder surfaces that describe the manner he adopted during the earlier 1850's.

IX

VISIT TO PARIS AND DUSSELDORF (1856-1859)

~

Bingham had originally planned to travel abroad during the fall of 1855.[1] His main object was to go to Paris and remain there until the engravings of "Stump Speaking" and the projected "Verdict of the People" were completed,[2] probably intending to supervise the work much as he had previously done in Philadelphia during the engraving of "The County Election." He probably believed he could thus avoid any chance of a repetition of the misunderstanding encountered in the publication of the "Emigration of Daniel Boone," when he had not had any personal contact with the printmaker during its preparation. However, he was unable to follow through with his European plans until the following year. In the meantime he was honored with a commission from the State for full-length portraits of Washington and Jefferson,[3] a patronage he had sought for a long time. Preparations necessary in connection with the portraits may thus have played some part in delaying his departure until August 14, 1856,[4] when he sailed for Le Havre on the steamship *Vigo* with his wife and daughter Clara.[5] His son Horace joined the family later.[6]

1. Letter, Independence, Mo., June 21, 1855 (*MHR*, XXXII [1938], 191).
2. *Ibid.*
3. Contracted for by House Committee by June 1, 1856, to be delivered by Dec. 1, 1858 (*Journal of the House of Representatives*, Feb. 14, 1857). Mentioned by B. in letter to R., Louisville, Ky., June 2, 1856 (*MHR*, XXXII [1938], 191). See also Rusk, *George Caleb Bingham . . .*, pp. 66-67.
4. Bingham had actually "completed all arrangements" prior to sailing by late in July, but a further delay was caused by "the unfortunate mistake" made by the man who was to secure passage for him in New York. (B. to R., letter, Boston, July 29, 1856, coll. SHSMo [*MHR*, XXXII (1938), 197].)
5. B. to R., letter, Philadelphia, Aug. 10, 1856, coll. SHSMo (*MHR*, XXXII [1938], 200). Although his wife and daughter are not specifically mentioned in this reference, they had already arrived in the East, preparatory to sailing. He had included them in his plans as early as June, 1855 (see letter, June 21, 1855).
6. Bingham asked Horace to come abroad to join the family by October, 1857; letter, Düsseldorf, Oct. 12, 1857 (*MHR*, XXXII [1938], 358). He was already in school there by early March, 1858 (B. to R., letter, Düsseldorf, March 8, 1858, *MHR*, XXXII [1938], 359).

Arriving in Paris on September 2, Bingham immediately set about finding suitable living quarters for his family, as well as a studio room capacious enough to accommodate the large State portraits.[7]

He was greatly impressed with his first glimpse of the city: "All that we hear of the splendour of the gay and luxurious city, is fully realized when we enter it."[8] A letter written to Rollins a week after his arrival affords us a valuable insight of his impressions during his first visit to the Louvre, when he was first brought face to face with a vast number of original works of the great masters:

As you may suppose I employed my earliest leisure in a visit to the galery [sic] of the Louvre. The great collection of works of Art there from all nations and schools, perhaps afford a student advantages which he could not obtain elsewhere. But unless he possessed the power to retain a clear perception of nature through the various guises in which she is here portrayed, like a juror bewildered by a mass of conflicting testimony, he might find himself staggering in doubt, scarcely knowing whether he inclined to truth or falsehood. Yet amidst the many conflicting statements presented by the masters of the various schools, there are numerous facts to be found, most forcibly and clearly expressed, which may be laid hold of by a matured judgment—and used to great advantage. I shall be compelled to visit the great gallery often before I can be able properly to appreciate the treasures which it contains.[9]

Bingham's constant studies of the methods of the old masters, largely acquired through the instruction books and engravings after their compositions, undoubtedly prepared him for the bewildering "mass of conflicting testimony" contained in the great collections of the Louvre. He had long ago realized that in "the various guises" used by artists through the ages to represent nature, there was much to be learned; and his own experience had confirmed his belief that a certain amount of guidance was necessary to prepare the student for a better understanding of those facts "most forcibly and clearly expressed," and especially to enable him to translate those facts to his own use. Perhaps the impression of another American, young Alexander Rutherford,[10] who had studied in Paris a few years earlier, underlines Bingham's opinion to a certain extent:

One sees so much here in Art, different and in many respects better than he does at home, that it is hardly to be wondered at if he should be for a time confused and unsettled in his own ideas. . . . I have been in Paris all the time since I left New York, and I find such excellent facilities for study that I think I shall remain here some months yet. I should *like* to stay some *years*. . . . I often hear it said by competent

7. B. to R., letter, Paris, Sept. 7, 1856, coll. SHSMo (*MHR.* XXXII [1938], 340-341).
8. *Ibid.*, 341.
9. *Ibid.*, 341-342.
10. Alexander W. Rutherford (1826-1851). A pupil of Daniel Huntington, exhibited at the National Academy in 1849 and 1850. The AAU purchased and distributed his paintings from 1848 to 1850.

judges that there is no better place in Europe for a young Painter to study than Paris at the present time.[11]

Like Rutherford, Bingham had also intended at the outset to remain in Paris, agreeing with him that "every thing essential to my professional objects could be found there in greater profusion and excellence than elsewhere."[12] However, although Paris was already beginning to take its place as an art center for American students—supplanting London, Rome, and Düsseldorf —he soon found the city "such a wilderness to a stranger"[13] not familar with its orientation and language that he decided finally to seek a more congenial area. Even his arrangements for a suitable studio had met with discouraging results, and he doubtless felt that he could no longer delay his work on the State portraits while he sought other quarters. And since he had made no commitment in Paris regarding the engraving of the "Verdict of the People" —the most competent printmakers there being unable to do the work in less than three years[14]—his original purpose in coming to Paris was somewhat frustrated. There is nothing in any of Bingham's correspondence so far uncovered to account for the sudden move to Germany, nor is there any indication from which direction, if any, the idea first suggested itself. It would certainly appear that the artist hoped to work in an art center, and Paris was his first choice for professional reasons, apart from any immediate impetus that gave shape to the plan. It was also entirely logical, in the 1850's, to think immediately of Düsseldorf as another important working community of artists.

He arrived in Düsseldorf about November 1,[15] and in a letter to Rollins a few days afterward, expressed his instant delight with the change he had made: "Dusseldorf is but a village compared with Paris, or with our large American cities, yet I question much if there can be found a city in the world where an artist, who sincerely worships Truth and nature, can find a more congenial atmosphere, or obtain more ready facilities in the prosecution of his studies."[16] He apparently met with none of the problems of accommodation that had harassed him so much in Paris. He reported that "immediately upon our arrival in Dusseldorf I called upon Leutze, the famous painter, who received me as cordially as if I had been a brother, and without a moment's delay assisted me in finding a Studio, and introduced me to one of his

11. A. W. Rutherford to AAU, letter, Paris, March 1, 1851, coll. NYHS.
12. Letter, Düsseldorf, Nov. 4, 1856, coll. SHSMo (*MHR*, XXXII [1938], 343).
13. *Ibid.*
14. Letter, Düsseldorf, June 3, 1857 (*MHR*. XXXII [1938], 352).
15. Letter, Nov. 4, 1856 (*MHR*, XXXII [1938], 343): "We reached our destination several days since."
16. *Ibid.*

195

American pupils through whose guidance I shortly obtained accommodations of the best kind, and upon the most reasonable terms."[17] Now comfortably settled and expecting "no drawback in the prosecution of my labors," Bingham ordered the large canvas for the State portrait of Washington.[18] He had also discussed with Leutze his plan to engrave the "Verdict of the People," and indicated his special admiration for the work of a Berlin engraver then expected to come to Düsseldorf.[19]

The painter's next letter, written slightly more than a month later, emphasized his "satisfaction" with the town and "more especially in regard to the superior facilities which it affords to artists," stating that "although the city does not contain more than thirty or forty thousand inhabitants, we of the brush burin and chisel muster about five hundred strong. They are from all countries, though, as a matter of course, chiefly from Germany. There are at present but six, including myself, from the United States."[20]

Bingham could add little to what had already been expressed by numerous American artists who had gone to Düsseldorf before him. Almost all agreed that the art center offered much to make the artist's life one "peculiarly devoid of care."[21] The easier living conditions and the liberal attitude of the government enabled him "to prosecute his studies in the most advantageous manner," and professional contacts tended "to improve and instruct him in his favorite profession."[22] With reference to the school itself, Bingham was evidently greatly impressed from the first by the free and congenial atmosphere that greeted the artist "who sincerely worships Truth and nature."[23] He enlarged considerably on the idea during his subsequent correspondence with Rollins:

The striking peculiarity of the school which flourishes here by its own inherent vitality, is a total disregard of the 'old' masters and a direct resort to nature for the truths which it employs. As might be expected, works springing from a principle of execution so simple and so rational are characterized by a freshness and vigor and truth, which captivates those of common understanding and is none the less agreeable to minds of the highest cultivation.[24]

The work of the Düsseldorf painters could not have come to Bingham as something new. The "Düsseldorf School" was extremely well-known in the United States, chiefly through the exhibition held in New York of a large

17. *Ibid.*, 344.
18. *Ibid.*
19. *Ibid.*, 345.
20. B. to R., letter, Düsseldorf, Dec. 14, 1856, coll. SHSMo (*MHR.* XXXII [1938], 347).
21. *Bull.*, AAU, Ser. for 1850, April 1, 1850, p. 7.
22. *Ibid.*
23. Letter, Nov. 4, 1856 (*MHR.* XXXII [1938], 343).
24. Letter, Dec. 14, 1856 (*MHR.* XXXII [1938], 347).

collection of paintings by the best of the German masters then residing in the center. The collection had been formed by John G. Boker and was shown in New York almost continuously from 1849 until after 1861.[25] It was widely publicized by the press from the beginning, and was at the time regarded as one of the most important exhibitions of contemporary European painting ever to come to this country. Bingham could scarcely have overlooked an opportunity to see it, especially in view of its predominantly genre character.

In 1853 New York's great exhibition of the "Industry of All Nations" included sixty-seven paintings by the best of the Düsseldorf artists.[26] Bingham went to the Crystal Palace to see the show, but afterward reported simply: "I saw a few good pictures and several fine products of the chisel."[27] At no time before his arrival in Düsseldorf do we discover any indication in his writings as to any impressions he may have gained from the productions of the Düsseldorf painters. As a matter of fact, by the time Bingham went abroad, the reputation of Düsseldorf as an art center had already fallen into disrepute among younger painters, particularly Americans. Worthington Whittredge, who had been a student at Düsseldorf, afterward related that the great New York exhibition of the German artists did not long remain in favor, adding his own criticism of the school: "Many of these works were in the hardest German style, colorless and with nothing to recommend them except their design. This was to be sure often a compensation for the lack of color and the charm of handling but it was not enough and never will be enough to satisfy us in the realm of art."[28] Eastman Johnson, who was at first devoted to Düsseldorf, spending considerable time in study there, and who later went to Holland where he studied the works of Rembrandt and the other old Dutch masters, wrote from The Hague in 1851: "I must say that I regret having spent so long a time in Düsseldorf where there is nothing to see but the present artists, who, whatever their merits may be, are very different in some of the chief requisites, as in Color, in which they are certainly scarsely [sic] tolerable."[29] And George Henry Hall addressed a letter to the American Art-Union which was intended, to a certain extent, as a rebuke to the organ-

---

25. *Cosmopolitan Art Journal*, I (June 1857), 135. The Cosmopolitan Art Association purchased the collection in the fall of 1857, and continued its exhibition in New York. It was on exhibition at the Institute of Fine Arts, 625 Broadway, in 1861 (*Descriptive Catalogue of the Paintings Now on Exhibition at the Institute of Fine Arts ... Comprising the Celebrated Pictures of the Well-known Dusseldorf Gallery. . . .* New-York: G. Russell, Printer, 1861).

26. Of the 651 pictures on exhibition, 67 were by Düsseldorf resident artists; 75 by painters of other German cities (Munich, Heidelberg, Berlin, etc.). See *Official Catalogue of the Pictures Contributed to the Exhibition of the Industry of All Nations . . .* (New York: Putnam, 1853).

27. Letter, Philadelphia, Oct. 3, 1853 (*MHR*, XXXII [1938], 164).

28. "The Autobiography of Worthington Whittredge 1820-1910," ed. by J. I. H. Baur, *Brooklyn Museum Journal* (1942), p. 24.

29. E. Johnson to AAU, letter, The Hague, Nov. 20, 1851, coll. NYHS.

ization for its apparent inclination toward the ideals and methods of the
German school, sensing in the Union's influence in that direction a danger
that he felt could retard the growth of American artists:

Let me tell you in a few words what I think are the characteristics of that school. Good
composition, accurate drawing, and faithful and elaborate finish; but a lack of invention,
and an entire want of originality,—the subject is illustration, clearly and forcibly, but
the work is very matter of fact, there is nothing left for the imagination, nothing suggestive in it, the mind is wearied with the tedious exactness of the picture. In color they
are *dry, painty* and opaque, the flesh has the same texture as the ground and rocks—they
paint with clay and brick dust. More than one half are landscape painters, and none of
them are good colorists. In the grand compositions of Kaulbach, Cornelius and Overbeck
we pardon the deficiency of color, though they would be improved were they colored in
the same spirit with which they are composed; but a *genre* school of Art, which that
of Dusseldorf is, whose prominent features are execrable color and a lack of spirit and
originality is no model for Genre Painters, particularly for Americans, who have an
extraordinary talent for color.... How unreasonable to attempt to engraft this
Dusseldorf Art on our young American school.[30]

Those characteristics that Bingham and the Düsseldorf painters had in common—the emphasis on carefully constructed composition and accurate
drawing—undoubtedly brought the Missouri Artist into surroundings in
which he might easily have felt a sense of belonging. The illustrative aspect
of the genre works of the Germans and the adherence to descriptive detail
would naturally have special meaning to the American. He could not help
but subscribe immediately to the reported principles of the school—"so
simple and so rational"—based on "truth and nature," to the exclusion of
everything that had gone before, although the "striking peculiarity" of his
own style, rooted in an almost constant observation of the ways and means
of expression conceived by the old masters, was actually contrary to the
Düsseldorf system he had described.

It remains for us to judge how far Bingham's first enthusiastic appraisal
of the Düsseldorf school went in its eventual effect on his own work, realizing
as we must that he did not come to the center as a student, or even with the
student's open-minded outlook. He was actually a mature painter by the
time he went abroad, and he was already forty-five years of age. His most
important genre works, the Election series, were already behind him and his
reputation as a portrait painter was assured by the State commissions. Only
the possibility of a national commission remained as a goal, and he obviously
did not come to Düsseldorf with the expectancy of receiving or preparing
himself for one.

30. G. H. Hall to AAU, letter, Paris, Oct. 28, 1850, coll. NYHS.

198

The large portrait of Washington was well advanced by June 3, 1857, when Bingham wrote to Rollins that he had just taken a new studio, which he felt would afford him the increased space needed to carry the work forward comfortably.[31] At the same time, he announced his intention of completing both the State pictures during the summer and fall, as well as giving details of his arrangement with a German printmaker to have the "Verdict of the People" published as a lithograph instead of engraved as originally planned.[32] In the letter he also mentioned working on another composition of "life on the Mississippi"—without doubt his "Jolly Flatboatmen in Port"—describing it as being "far ahead of any work in that class which I have yet undertaken."[33] He also indicated that his hope to interest Congress in a large scale "Emigration of Boone" was being given some thought.[34] And there is a strong impression that he had entertained hope of obtaining a government appointment abroad, but that the course of political events had crushed that hope, at least for the time being.[35]

By October 12 the full-length portrait of Washington was evidently completed and receiving "high praise from all who see it." Bingham indicated his personal satisfaction with his work by saying that by it he would "prove that our State is none the loser by employing its own painter."[36] Studies for the companion portrait of Jefferson were already in hand, although the artist had not yet decided on the final pose for the figure.[37] The large Flatboatmen subject was almost finished.[38]

The portrait of Jefferson was "pretty well advanced" by early March of the following year and its completion expected within a month.[39] Bingham stated with confidence: "I intend it to quite equal the Washington as a work of art, and will also be disappointed if both shall not be found to surpass any similar representations of the same personages in any of the States of the Union."[40] He hoped to exhibit the portraits in the permanent gallery at Düsseldorf before forwarding them to their final destination.

In order to ensure that the portraits, once they arrived in Jefferson City, would be "properly attended to," Bingham decided to return to the States to personally superintend the unrolling, restretching, and revarnishing of the

31. Letter, June 3, 1857 (*MHR*, XXXII [1938], 351).
32. *Ibid.*
33. *Ibid.*, 353.
34. *Ibid.*
35. *Ibid.*
36. Letter, Oct. 12, 1857 (*MHR*, XXXII [1938], 357).
37. *Ibid.*
38. *Ibid.*
39. B. to R., letter, Düsseldorf, March 8, 1858, coll. SHSMo (*MHR*, XXXII [1938], 359).
40. *Ibid.*, 360.

canvases, as well as the final hanging of the pictures in the Capitol.[41] Once in Jefferson City, however, he even considered prolonging his stay through the Legislative session in the hope that his presence might be "likely to increase the chances of obtaining a commission for portraits of Jackson and Clay."[42] It had also occurred to him to go to Washington with some of his paintings to compete for a national picture commission, especially since he knew that Leutze intended coming to the United States in the near future "with *such an object in view*."[43]

Upon his return in January, 1859, Bingham apparently went directly to Washington, although it is not known whether he was able to carry through his announced intention with regard to the national picture competition. His main activity in Washington actually may have been confined to his service as a member of the second convention of the National Art Association, held there during January 12-14.[44] In view of his interest in making a strong bid for a federal commission, and his prior knowledge that Leutze had already been more or less assured one through his personal contacts in political circles, it is perhaps significant that among the resolutions Bingham presented on the second day's session was one supporting the idea that

. . . an art commission, appointed under the authority of the government of the United States, to be the channel for the distribution of the appropriations to be made by Congress for art purposes, should be so constituted as to represent, as fairly and equit-ably as possible, the art interests of the entire Union, thereby securing to artists, wherever residing within the limits of our national domain, an unbiased adjudication upon the designs they may present for the embellishment of the national buildings.[45]

The painter was in Jefferson City by late January when it was reported that the two State portraits of Washington and Jefferson had been delivered.[46]

41. *Ibid.*
42. Letter, Düsseldorf, July 18, 1858 (*MHR.* XXXII [1938], 364).
43. *Ibid.* Bingham apparently returned to America from Düsseldorf at about the same time as Leutze, although Bingham evidently arrived in Washington before him.
44. *Proceedings of the Second Convention of the National Art Association, Held at the Smithsonian Institute, January 12, 13, 14, 1859* . . . (Washington [D.C.]: W. H. Moore, Printer, 1860).
45. *Ibid.*, p. 7-8. An art commission was provided for by Congress (Acts, June 12, 1858; March 3, 1859); and three distinguished artists — Henry K. Brown, James R. Lambdin, and John F. Kensett — nominated by the National Art Association were appointed by President Buchanan on May 18, 1859. But the commission — "composed of those designated by the united voice of American artists as competent to the office, who shall be accepted as the exponents of the authority and influence of American art, who shall be the channels for the distribution of all appropriations to be made by Congress for art purposes, and who shall secure to artists an intelligent and unbiased adjudication upon the designs they may present for the embellishment of the national buildings" — was actually never enabled to carry out those high purposes with any authority. It was abolished in 1860 after having submitted only one report of its findings. Bingham was one of the members of a committee of conference of the House who dissented from the abolition of the art commission. (35th Congress, 2d Session, House of Representatives, Report no. 198, p. 7; Fairman, *Art and Artists of the Capitol*, pp. 188-189.)
46. *Weekly Missouri Statesman*, Jan. 28, 1859, 3-3.

They were immediately described as "perhaps two of the finest paintings of the kind in the Union."[47] The pictures evidently pleased the legislators, too, for on February 14 a bill was duly passed by the Senate, appropriating $3,500 for two large portraits of Andrew Jackson and Henry Clay, to be painted by Bingham.[48] The artist wrote to Rollins a few days afterward with reference to the new commission: "I feel highly honored by the action of the Legislature upon the reception of the pictures, and in authorizing me, as you have by this time learned, to paint the additional portraits of Jackson & Clay. The bill, for these last works, employs me directly, without the intervention of a Committee."[49]

Bingham also visited Columbia, Brunswick, St. Louis, and Kansas City, and painted portraits along the way before going to the East again on his return to Germany.[50] In St. Louis, early in May, he was commissioned by the St. Louis Mercantile Library Association to execute a full-length portrait of Baron von Humboldt,[51] the great German naturalist who was then living in Berlin. The artist was back in Düsseldorf by June 1, and soon afterward planned to go to the German capital to make some preliminary studies for the portrait, although by coincidence his subject had died on May 6, the day on which Bingham had been awarded the commission in St. Louis.[52] He was to make sketches of Humboldt's study as it appeared in his lifetime, and to seek extant likenesses for the head and figure.[53]

Bingham also intended to travel with his family to Italy and Switzerland, as well as to Paris and London, during the summer,[54] but the sudden death of his wife's father on June 12 probably caused a cancellation of the plan and hastened the family's return to the States. They arrived in New York during the first week in September, and immediately departed for Missouri.[55]

Apart from the two State portraits, landscapes of German scenery, and the "Jolly Flatboatmen in Port," we know relatively little about any other work produced by Bingham in Paris and Düsseldorf. During the short Paris sojourn, within the limits of his working facilities, he seems to have executed

47. *Ibid.*, Feb. 25, 1859, 2-5.
48. *Ibid.*; *Liberty Weekly Tribune*, March 18, 1859, 1-5 (from *Missouri Statesman*).
49. B. to R., letter, St. Louis, Mo., Feb. 19, 1859, coll. SHSMo (*MHR*. XXXII [1938], 368).
50. The artist was "very buisy [*sic*] finishing portraits," when he wrote to Rollins from Jefferson City, March 13, 1859. He had missed seeing his friend when he arrived in Columbia, but left a letter for him there, March 21, stating that he was to leave for Kansas City that day (*MHR*, XXXII [1938], 372-373). He was later in Brunswick, Mo. (*Weekly Missouri Statesman*, April 22, 1859, 3-2), and mentioned his stay there in a letter to Rollins, St. Louis, May 8, 1859, coll. SHSMo (*MHR*, XXXII [1938], 376).
51. Letter, May 8, 1859 (*MHR*, XXXII [1938], 375-376).
52. B. to R., letter, Düsseldorf, June 6, 1859, coll. SHSMo (*MHR*. XXXII [1938], 485).
53. *Ibid.*
54. B. to R., letter, Columbia, Mo., March 21, 1859, coll. SHSMo (*MHR*. XXXII [1938], 375).
55. *Weekly Missouri Statesman*, Sept. 9, 1859, 3-1.

only a preparatory study for the Washington portrait.[56] In Düsseldorf his time was almost completely occupied with the two commissions that had to be finished within a contracted period. The "Jolly Flatboatmen" was in progress at the same time as the Washington portrait.[57] His plans for a large version of the "Emigration of Boone," with a view toward a national commission, and for a composition depicting the "border ruffians"[58] apparently came to nothing. The few landscapes that have been assigned to this period appear to have been painted for the artist's pleasure.

Both of the full-length Washington and Jefferson portraits were destroyed when the State Capitol burned in 1911. We know less about the Washington composition than that of Jefferson, our knowledge about the former being based only on the comparatively scant documentary information now extant. The head was based on Gilbert Stuart's well-known Athenaeum portrait which Bingham traveled to Boston to copy in July, 1856.[59] It is of interest to note that Bingham chose this portrait, taken from life, rather than one of the several other versions by Stuart then available which were painted from it.

The actual execution of the large (12 x 8 feet) canvas was not undertaken until the artist arrived in Düsseldorf at the beginning of November, 1856. On December 14 he advised Rollins: "I have the full length of 'The Father of his Country' standing up six feet and a half in my studio . . . the arrangement and general effect of the picture as well as the likeness is highly approved by my fellow-Americans."[60] The portrait, completed during the fall of 1857, was in all probability a formal representation, according to the style of the day. We can perhaps ascertain some impression of its appearance by a consideration of its companion portrait of Jefferson, about which we know somewhat more. As with the Washington portrait, the artist selected a portrait by Stuart as his model for the head, also one executed from life. He discovered such a portrait in the collection of Edward Coles of Philadelphia and copied it in July, 1856.[61] This copy can, with little doubt, be identified with the portrait now in the collection of the State Historical Society of Missouri (A255; plate 149).

56. Letter, Düsseldorf, Nov. 4, 1856 (*MHR*, XXXII [1938], 344).
57. Letter, June 3, 1857 (*MHR*, XXXII [1938], 353): "I have on hand a large picture of 'life on the Mississippi' which will not require a great while to complete, and which promises to be far ahead of any work of that class which I have yet undertaken."
58. *Ibid.*
59. This copy is now in the collection of the St. Louis Mercantile Library Association, to which it was presented by the artist by late February, 1859, together with its companion, the Athenaeum portrait of Martha Washington. (B. to R., letter, Jefferson City, Mo., Feb. 25, 1859, coll. SHSMo [*MHR*, XXXII (1938), 370]; *Fourteenth Annual Report of the Board of Directors of the St. Louis Mercantile Library Association, January 10, 1860,* p. 24).
60. Letter, Düsseldorf, Dec. 14, 1856 (*MHR*. XXXII [1938], 358).
61. Letter, Boston, July 29, 1856 (*MHR*, XXXII [1938], 197-198): "I found an excellent portrait

Bingham's first notion about the composition of this picture is contained in a letter he wrote to Rollins from Düsseldorf on November 4, 1856: "I have some idea of painting Jefferson in a sitting posture surrounded by his library and other accessories, indicating his character both as Statesman and Philosopher."[62] But this idea was later discarded. In a letter dated March 8, 1858, when the painting was "pretty well advanced," he described its final composition in considerable detail:

.The attitude in which I have placed him, though erect, is quite different from that given to the portrait of Washington. He stands in a legislative hall with a roll of paper in his left, and a pen in his right hand, and with one foot elevated upon a step of the small platform immediately in front of the speakers desk. His well known singularity in regard to costume has given me some little advantage in aid of the picturesque. In conversation with his old intimate friend Gov. Coles, I learned that when he did not wear the scarlet vest he sometimes draped himself in a long light reddish brown frock coat reaching almost to his ancles [sic], and instead of the then common shoe with the silver buckle he wore an invention of his own which he styled the *Jefferson* shoe, and which resembled very closely the present gaiters worn by ladies.

His object in useing [sic] so much red in his apparel appears to have been to counteract the effect of a similar hue in his hair. Availing myself of these facts of dress, I am enabled to make his portrait, in some respects, a complete contrast to that of Washington and to avoid the repetition in it of any thing contained in the latter.[63]

The painting was probably finished during April, 1858.[64] At least one critic hailed it "one of the finest paintings we have ever seen, and will be a lasting monument to the genius and skill of Missouri's Artist Bingham."[65] Fortunately, we have a photograph of the portrait as it appeared *in situ* in the Capitol at Jefferson City before it was destroyed (plate 148).

Although much of the detail of the composition is lost in the reproduction, enough is visible to enable us to form an impression of its general appearance. The subject is shown in the picture as described by the artist. The figure is turned toward the left, with his head turned sharply back over his left shoulder looking out toward the right, affording a greater sense of vitality.

of Jefferson by Stuart in the possession of Ex Gov Coles of Philadelphia, who had purchased it at Mrs. Madison's sale to whose order it was originally [sic] painted from life.... He was the private Sec. of Mr Madison.... It appeared to give him great pleasure to meet my wishes in regard to the portrait of his old Friend (he was intimate with Jefferson also) to whose *political principles* he yet faithfully adheres while those who profess to be his disciples have forgotten them. He insisted upon my ocupying [sic] a room in his house while executing the copy...."

62. Letter, Nov. 4, 1856 (*MHR*, XXXII [1938], 344).
63. Düsseldorf, Mar. 8, 1858 (*MHR*, XXXII [1938], 359-360). The full-length portrait of Jefferson painted by Thomas Sully in 1822, now in the collection of the United States Military Academy at West Point, represents the subject in a costume similar to that adopted by Bingham.
64. *Ibid.*, p. 359: "I have the portrait of Jefferson now pretty well advanced, and expect to complete it about the first of April."
65. *Weekly Jefferson Inquirer*, Feb. 5, 1859, 3-1 (dated Jan. 28).

The head, in three-quarter view, shows its derivation from the Stuart version, although reversed. The composition is an extensive one, the figure being placed within a setting that probably included more details of association interest than can be seen, indicating the painter's growing concern with the pictorial possibilities of portraiture. The light is skillfully adjusted, the strongest concentration being on the head, while the rest of the picture is subordinated to it.

A formal, official portrait in accordance with the requirements of the time, it was nevertheless a picture that could hold its own with the best productions of its class. The companion portrait of Washington was probably identical in size and similar in over-all effect, although Bingham himself had pointed out that he was able to render variety and "in some respects, a complete contrast" between the two through the differences possible in costume. However, these two portraits cannot be said to reveal any specific characteristics that would tend to indicate an influence derived from the region in which they were executed. From what one can observe in the Jefferson portrait, at least on the basis of the handling of light and shade, it appears to belong within the pattern of the artist's stylistic development noted in other portraits painted in Missouri during the period immediately preceding the European trip.

On the other hand, the "Jolly Flatboatmen in Port" (plate 61) could have been more easily exposed to the new surroundings and new contacts. After all, Bingham's reputation as a painter of genre could well have reached his European contemporaries, and he could scarcely have kept himself isolated in a center where its chief masters were known for their genre compositions, nor is it likely that he would have desired to do so.

We have already discussed the Flatboatmen composition in detail, noting that it, too, belonged within the logical development of the artist and its roots readily discoverable in his earlier work with the same theme. Even his organization in terms of light and shade appears based on his more advanced studies during the period prior to the European sojourn. The most significant change in Bingham's style lies in a purely technical aspect, that outstanding characteristic of the Düsseldorf school as a whole which George Henry Hall had described as its "faithful and elaborate finish."[66] It was that "finish"— which was so exacting in its concentration on descriptive detail, and which developed a hard polished surface in the final effect—that was said to leave "the mind . . . wearied with the tedious exactness of the picture"[67] and to

66. G. H. Hall to AAU, letter, Paris, Oct. 28, 1850, coll. NYHS.
67. *Ibid.*

204

result in a sameness of texture that was equally oppressive. The hard outlines in Bingham's "Jolly Flatboatmen in Port"—seen particularly in the lights on the foreground figures and in the brittle modeling of details, as well as in the uniform hardness of textures in the rendering of such details as the bucket, basket, pottery jug, and sacks of grain—reveal the artist's most tangible contact with the Düsseldorfians. In this connection we can recall that an analysis of Bingham's genre subjects of the three years before his departure for Europe actually showed a growing tendency toward greater breadth of technique and a gradual subordination of detail in favor of atmospheric effects. The hard outlines that had described his first efforts, and which had called forth some of his severest criticism, were being progressively toned down during the succeeding years in a deliberate effort to achieve a total pictorial effectiveness. In fact, the Düsseldorf influence, if only from the single standpoint of "finish," was a retrogression for the painter. Indeed, the beginning of a steady decline in quality and merit as well as in the individuality of Bingham's work can be said to date from this time.

Among the private portrait commissions undertaken by the artist during the brief interim period between the two European trips were probably those of Dr. Benoist Troost (A269; plate 157) and his wife (A270; plate 158), of Kansas City. Both portraits are among the most elaborate executed by the painter up to this time. In none of his previous known work had he explored the over-all pictorial possibilities of portraiture; almost all of his earlier work showed a strict adherence to a neutral background, and only in a few pictures was landscape or a drapery motif introduced as accessories. Now for the first time the background assumes a more lively role in adding further interest and dimension to the composition. This rather abrupt change of interest may be partially accounted for in Bingham's more active concentration on portrait ideas, particularly the State portraits of Washington and Jefferson, in which background elements apparently assumed important roles. We also must not discount the notion that during his almost three-year stay in Germany Bingham undoubtedly had ample opportunity to observe the mode of the German painters who frequently conceived their portraits in pictorial terms, employing an elaborate vocabulary which at times approached genre.

The painting of Dr. Troost has rightly been the more highly regarded of the two pictures, for the strong, lively head fixes the attention of the observer. The portrait is painted broadly and modeled in strong lights and darks, achieving a richly atmospheric effect, although it still follows in the first, main line of the artist's development. It is related, along general stylistic lines, to the large portrait of Dr. John Sappington (plate 130) painted about 1844/45, but it reveals a more developed understanding of tactile values and the use of detail. The portrait of Mary Gillis Troost, however, lacks much of the spontaneity of its companion, showing a tightening-up of the modeling, particularly in the head, and an accompanying reduction of contrasts of lights and darks which bespeak an outlook entirely opposed to the approach seen in the portrait of the man. Here, the artist has concentrated his attention on details of costume and accessories.

Portraits of Judge James Turner Vance Thompson (A276; plate 155) and his wife (A277; plate 156), Joseph Baldwin Howard (A271), and the double portrait of Mrs. Isaac Hockaday (Susan C. Howard) and her daughter (A273)[68] also date from this period. The forthright portrayal of Judge Thompson, with its controlled use of detail and well-modulated use of rich color, is related in style to the portrait of Dr. Troost. The double portrait of Mrs. Hockaday and her daughter, probably painted during the spring of 1859, when Bingham returned to America for a brief time during his Düsseldorf years, reveals a grasp of organization and scale which was certainly not in evidence in his earlier group subjects. The design is well-composed within its oval frame, and richly decorative in pattern and in the skillful manipulation of high-keyed colors. The painting prepares the way for a series of similar portrait compositions painted during the years immediately afterward.

68. McDermott, *George Caleb Bingham* . . . , pl. 59.

X

LAST YEARS IN MISSOURI (1860-1879)

~

PORTRAITS (1860-1865)

Bingham's return to Missouri from Germany marks not only a continuation of his portrait-painting activities but actually a far greater concentration on the pictorial possibilities of this particular phase of his work. His career as illustrator of the western scene was almost at an end, and his future livelihood as a painter had to depend chiefly on portraiture. The historical pictures, and the few attempts at genre and landscape subjects during the period after 1860, cannot be considered to be in any way related to his growth during the years preceding his European sojourn, although it is not my intention to imply that the drying-up of this phase of the artist's work had its basis in his European experience. On the contrary, he continued to plan ahead for new pictures and even painted the most elaborate of his "Jolly Flatboatmen" subjects in Düsseldorf. His main incentive in this direction, however—the patronage of the Art Unions—was lost when those organizations passed out of existence after 1852. Apart from the two Goupil commissions, there was apparently little encouragement from other sources. Despite the enthusiasm that greeted his Election pictures and the immediate purchase by a private collector of one of the subjects, Bingham was unable to sell the series for ten years, and his large "Jolly Flatboatmen" remained in his hands for some eight years. The failure to interest the government in his work, followed by his inability to obtain a large national commission, must also have played a decisive part in halting his activity in the genre field and in turning his attention almost entirely to the more lucrative field of portrait painting—an area in which, at that moment, his services were in especially important demand.

Bingham was probably in Washington by the first week of January, 1860, attending to a number of art matters. Seeking a good likeness of Andrew

207

Jackson to be used in connection with his State portrait, he was introduced by General Francis Preston Blair to his brother-in-law Captain Samuel Phillips Lee, who had in his collection a portrait of the hero painted by Thomas Sully.[1] As Bingham reported following his visit to Captain Lee: "I think it suits my design admirably, and as it is kindly placed at my service, I will make a careful copy of it, as soon as I can find a suitable place to work in."[2]

On January 10, 12, and 13, the artist again served as a member of the National Art Association, which was then having its third annual session in Washington.[3] It is interesting to observe that in addition to having three of its group appointed members of a national art commission, the Association's constitution, placed before President James Buchanan, provided for the establishment under its auspices, "of a national gallery at the city of Washington, with departments of Gallery, Museum, Library, and Art Instruction."[4]

It was also during this visit to the capital that Bingham evidently carried through his intention of submitting his Election pictures to the Library Committee of Congress in the hope of selling them to the government.[5] And it may have been at this time that he executed, as a private commission, the portrait of Miss Sally Cochran McGraw (A282), then residing in nearby Baltimore.

Upon his return to Missouri early in March, he probably painted, among others, the portraits of Mrs. Robert Levi Todd and her daughter (A285), of Columbia, and that of Mrs. Almerin Hotchkiss (A283) of St. Louis. But apart from private commissions, the artist was chiefly engaged during the following months on the State portrait of Jackson and the Mercantile Library's large portrait of Humboldt. By April 27 the Humboldt portrait was reported as finished and, "by this time is perhaps in its place in the Library, there to remain as an enduring evidence of the unrivaled genius of Bingham, for this is certainly one of his finest pictures."[6]

The portrait of Jackson was completed by September 15. It was designed as an equestrian composition, and Bingham described it as "the most difficult

1. In all probability the portrait now in the National Gallery of Art, Washington, D.C. Given by the Andrew W. Mellon Educational Trust, it was purchased from M. Knoedler & Co., New York, who acquired it from the collection of E. Brooke Lee, Silver Springs, Md., *ca.* 1938.
2. B. to R., letter, Washington, D.C., Jan. 9, 1860, coll. SHSMo (*MHR*, XXXII [1938], 494).
3. *Proceedings of the National Art Association (Third Session) Held at the Rooms of the Washington Art Association, Jan. 10, 12, 13, 1860*, pp. [12]-19, in *Proceedings of the Second Convention of the National Art Association.*
4. *Ibid.*, p. 17.
5. Letter, Jan. 9, 1860 (*MHR*, XXXII [1938], 494).
6. *Missouri Statesman*, April 27, 1860, 3-3.

work" of the two commissions he then had under contract, and one that he predicted, "will be pronounced by connoisseurs and the public, immeasurably superior to any similar work in the United States, the great Statue at Washington, by Clark Mills, not excepted."[7]

Soon afterward, he began work on the second composition, a full-length portrait of Henry Clay (A280). This was still in progress by late November when the artist was able to profess still greater pride in the latest pair of State pictures:

I feel very confident that neither of the portraits will fall behind the expectations of my most sanguine friends. I think they will perhaps surpass both the Washington and Jefferson, as far as they surpass similar works to be found elsewhere in our Country. These large works I find better adapted to my powers than the small cabinet pictures upon which I had been previously employed. Should I be so fortunate as to get a commission from Congress I have no fear that I will be unable to rival any work which they are likely to obtain from other quarters.[8]

The second portrait was probably finished shortly after the middle of December, 1860.[9] Bingham accompanied the two pictures to their destination, Jefferson City, and evidently did carry through his announced plan to exhibit them in Lexington and Boonville, as well as possibly elsewhere in the state on the way.[10] The two portraits were placed in the House of Representatives on January 7, 1861, in time for the Jackson Day celebration on the following night. As the artist put it, "from all who loved their country" the paintings "elicited spontaneous tokens of admiration."[11] Referring to the Jackson portrait, the press reported that it was "with feelings of unfeigned admiration and pleasure that the audience contemplated the noble picture," adding that the artist "did it justice."[12] The companion portrait of Henry Clay was judged "a fine effort, and well sustains the reputation which the artist has already gained."[13]

Yet on the night of the celebration itself, Bingham was prevailed upon to make a speech, which, owing to its pro-Union theme, apparently offended

7. B. to R., letter, Independence, Mo., Sept. 15, 1860, coll. SHSMo (*MHR*, XXXII [1938], 495). Bingham was referring to a recent work by Clark Mills (1816-1883). An appropriation by Congress for an equestrian statue of Washington, to be executed by Mills, was made no January 25, 1853. It was probably not completed before 1859/1860. An act approving the transporting and setting up of the statue was passed on February 24, 1860 (C. E. Fairman, *Art and Artists of the Capitol . . .*, pp. 175, 204).
8. B. to R., letter, Kansas City, Mo., Nov. 27, 1860, coll. SHSMo (*MHR*, XXXII [1938], 497-498).
9. B. to R., letter, Kansas City, Dec. 9, 1860, coll. SHSMo (*MHR*, XXXII [1938], 504): "The portrait of 'Old Hal' is nearly completed. In eight or ten days more at farthest it will have received [*sic*] all that I can bestow upon it."
10. *Ibid.*, p. 505.
11. B. to R., letter, Jefferson City, Jan. 12, 1861, coll. SHSMo (*MHR*, XXXII [1938], 505).
12. *Jefferson City Inquirer*, Jan. 12, 1861, 4-6.
13. *Ibid.*

certain secessionist elements then in power in the state.[14] Approval of his portraits was afterward delayed, perhaps in retaliation to his remarks, as the artist himself firmly believed.[15] This attitude caused him to think seriously of taking the pictures on tour as a means of reimbursing himself for the work involved in their execution. He wrote to Rollins along this line: "I seriously think there is a fine prospect for a speculation in the matter. I have become so inspired, or excited, if you so prefer to regard it, that I can make a tolerably good Speech to accompany them, and think I can draw a crowd where there are people enough to make one."[16] He had even thought of taking the portraits to Springfield, Illinois, so that he might come "in direct and favorable contact with Lincoln, and if I chose to part with them I would have no difficulty . . . under present circumstances in selling them to the Legislature of his State."[17]

The paintings were eventually accepted and the artist was granted legislative permission to take them to St. Louis, there to arrange for their proper framing, and to exhibit them to his own advantage, although, as the painter reported, this was not accomplished "without considerable opposition in the Senate,"[18] chiefly in the person of Senator Thompson of Clay County.[19] The Senator's opposition was ostensibly based on Bingham's plan to exhibit the pictures for profit in St. Louis, as he had done before he delivered the paintings to the Legislature, but it is more than likely that the venemous attack was based on the painter's remarks in his Jackson Day speech. After some delay in St. Louis, due to the difficulty in finding proper exhibition space and to the general political excitement of the time which was naturally

14. Letter, Jan. 12, 1861 (*MHR*, XXXII [1938], 505-506): "I was called upon without a moment's preparation to make a speech, and prompted by the surroundings of the occasion, made the Union and the *Star Spangled Banner* my theme. I was greeted, as it appeared to me, with general applause throughout, but the Lieut. Gov. [Thomas C. Reynolds] hearing of my speech (he was not present) came in afterwards and ventured to give myself, Judge Birch and Judge Orr a lecture. He received a good deal more in return than he bargained for in each case. . . . A gross misrepresentation of what took place was telegraphed to the Republican; and also appeared next morning in the Secessionist organ here. . . . I have infuriated all the traitors by boldly avowing my love for my Government which they are conspiring to destroy." And with reference to the same speech, B. to R., letter, St. Louis, Jan. 29, 1861, coll. SHSMo (*MHR*, XXXII [1938], 507): "Without intending it I happened to spit in the face of Treason on the 8th inst. and its abettors being thrown offguard by the unexpected insult exhibited their features so as to subject them to unmistakable recognition."
15. Letter, Jan. 12, 1861 (*MHR*, XXXII [1938], 506).
16. *Ibid.*, pp. 506-507.
17. *Ibid.*, p. 506.
18. Letter, Jan. 29, 1861 (*MHR*, XXXII [1938], 507).
19. *Ibid.*: "Thompson of Clay made an exposition of his ignorance, stupidity, vulgarity and malignancy, which will receive its proper attention as soon as I shall be further provoked to stoop low enough to inflict punishment such as he is capable of feeling." Thompson of Clay was undoubtedly the same Judge James Turner Vance Thompson of Clay County, whose portrait Bingham had painted not long before. Thompson's criticism of the portraits of Jackson and Clay appeared in the *Liberty Sentinel*, Feb. 1, 1861, 1-3.

attracting the public's attention elsewhere, the portraits were finally set up in the gallery of the St. Louis Mercantile Library.[20] Arrangements had been made to open on the evening of February 22, 1861, in connection with the celebration honoring Washington's birthday.[21] However, Bingham's earlier expectations of turning the exhibition to profit were apparently no longer so optimistic: "Every thing appears to be in such a depressed condition that I cannot expect to clear much beyond the expenses of the exhibition."[22] He was nevertheless determined to give the St. Louis public a chance to see the pictures and to judge for themselves of their merit, rankling as he still was under the stinging remarks made by Senator Thompson of Clay County.[23]

The State portraits of Jackson and Clay were also among those works by Bingham that were destroyed during the Capitol fire of 1911. However, an old photograph of the Clay portrait (plate 150) gives us some impression of the composition. The erect figure of the statesman, represented in the pose of an orator, extends his left arm toward an open archway in the background through which an architectural vista is seen. As in the earlier portrait of Jefferson, the figure is portrayed in an interior setting surrounded by numerous accessories. Skillfully composed, the central figure effectively dominates the scene, despite the elaboration of detail and finish.

The full-length portrait of Humboldt was in large part destroyed when it fell from its frame some years ago.[24] Only a fragment containing the head remains today of the monumental painting (plate 151), but an old photograph affords us a valuable further impression of its original appearance.[25] The portrait represented the naturalist standing in his study, holding a large open book in his hand. The head and the book obviously received the greatest amount of emphasis in terms of light, while the rest of the figure and the surrounding details of background were submerged in deep shadow. It appears to have been the artist's deliberate intention to direct the spectator's attention to the massive head of his subject and to the open book as symbols of his intellectual powers, subordinating all other detail in order to introduce a note of drama that was usually missing in the typically descriptive official portraiture of the period.

Three of Bingham's most decorative paintings of women, all closely related

20. B. to R., letter, St. Louis, Feb. 17, 1861, coll. SHSMo, (MHR, XXXII [1938], 511).
21. Ibid.
22. B. to R., letter, St. Louis, Feb. 2, 1861, coll. SHSMo (MHR, XXXII [1938], 509).
23. Ibid. Referring to Senator Thompson of Clay County again, stating among other things: "I regard him as the mere instrument of others—of traitors who are plotting the overthrow both of our State and Federal government."
24. Christ-Janer, George Caleb Bingham . . . . p. 97.
25. McDermott, George Caleb Bingham . . . , plate 58. Our knowledge of the picture is amplified by Rusk's full description based on a first-hand observation before its destruction (Rusk, George Caleb Bingham . . . , p. 72).

211

in style, can be assigned with some certainty to the period immediately following his return from Europe. The subjects, all designed as oval compositions, portray Mrs. Robert Levi Todd (Sallie Hall) and her daughter (plate 152), Miss Sally Cochran McGraw (plate 154), Mrs. Almerin Hotchkiss (Martha Ann Moore) (plate 153). The portraits are particularly fine examples of the artist's more highly developed concern with the rendering of accessories and the extension of background to include landscape elements.[26] The double portrait of Mrs. Todd and her daughter is probably the most interesting composition of the group, from a more special point of view. For this picture the painter seems once again to have turned for inspiration to Raphael's "Madonna della Sedia," or to a later derivative of the composition. We recall that he had very probably referred to the same sources for his portrait of Mrs. David Steele Lamme (Sophia Woodson Hickman) and her son (plate 20), painted some twenty-three years earlier.[27] But armed now with a greater technical facility and experience, he attempts to overcome some of the problems he had encountered earlier. The resultant fluidity and ease of the new conception reveals the long way the artist has come from his first experience. His enlarged vocabulary enables him to handle with greater confidence the complicated structure of a composition that had obviously intrigued him through the years. The oval enframement suggests that Bingham was now probably more aware of Raphael's compositional innovations than he had been earlier, and the pose of the child is certainly Raphaelesque in derivation, despite the fact that the impression of energetic movement is still translated ineffectually. The influence of Lawrence continues in the head of the child, recalling such types as those of "The Calmady Children,"[28] and the landscape background is in an English tradition that Bingham could have remembered particularly from the portrait of "Lady Dover and child" (plate 21). The painting is a curious admixture of the artist's ever-increasing inclination toward decorative design in portraiture, combined with the positive character of representation that we have come to associate with the first line of his work.

To the same period belong a group of other pictures, all following a compositional pattern similar to that developed in the Troost portraits of 1859,

26. At least five known portraits attributed to Bingham, dating from an earlier period, include landscape backgrounds: Miss Sallie Ann Camden (plate 33), Col. Samuel B. Churchill (A60), and Leonidas Wetmore (plate 30)—said to have been painted in St. Louis in the 1838-1840 period; John Cummings Edwards (plate 123), painted in Jefferson City in 1844; Miss Vestine Porter (plate 142), painted in Independence, *ca.* 1849/1850.
27. See above, p. 32.
28. "The Calmady Children" (Metropolitan Museum of Art, New York) was painted by Sir Thomas Lawrence in 1823. It was engraved by G. T. Doo in 1829, and by Samuel Cousins in 1835. Perhaps more important in connection with Bingham is the fact that an engraving after the picture, entitled "Infancy," was executed by Thomas Kelly for *The Atlantic Souvenir for 1831* (Philadelphia: Carey & Lea, 1831), opp. p. 44.

212

forming a scheme that Bingham was to continue for some of his important commissions into the 1870's. The portraits of Judge Samuel Locke Sawyer (A286) and of James M. Piper (A304) and his wife (A305), another sister of Eliza Thomas Bingham, all three-quarter length, include hands and background elements such as the column and landscape opening. All of these portraits already reflect a dryness and tightness of handling and a certain rigidity of posing which was to mark a majority of the artist's late works in the field. The portrait of Mary Thomas Piper (plate 159) actually has a far greater warmth and charm than the somewhat uninspired likeness of Mary Gillis Troost (plate 158), but that of her husband has none of the spontaneity and impact of personality that characterizes the portrait of Dr. Troost.

The outbreak of the Civil War and the accompanying problems that confronted people everywhere as a consequence was naturally felt in Bingham's profession, and he soon found himself in a delicate financial position. He described his plight in a letter written to Rollins on June 5, 1861: "We are all out of employment, and Art is far below every thing in such times as these, I am ready to turn my attention, for the time being, to any thing by which I can keep from sinking into debt, and secure the bare necessities of life for those who have a right to look to me for support."[29] Nevertheless, desiring to serve the Union cause to the best of his ability, he accepted an appointment as Captain in the United States Volunteer Reserve Corps during the summer of 1861, serving in Van Horn's Battalion in Kansas City, a company that had been organized to preserve law and order in the city.[30]

Bingham resigned his commission to take over an appointment as State Treasurer on January 4, 1862,[31] a position he was to hold until 1865. Considering the fact that he would have accepted a position as humble as that of "assistant doorkeeper" in the Senate or House,[32] this was a post that paid special honor to the artist-politician, and it was certainly one that also adequately filled his financial need. He would have much preferred to be occupied in his own professional line, however, and still expressed the hope that a national commission could somehow be obtained for him, "to paint a better picture, than that by Leuitze [sic]."[33] From late January, 1862, until the expiration of his term three years later, the artist and his family took up residence in Jefferson City.[34]

29. B. to R., letter, Kansas City, June 5, 1861, coll. SHSMo (MHR, XXXII [1938], 517).

30. B. to R., letter, Kansas City, June 29, 1861, coll. SHSMo (MHR, XXXII [1938], 520, and editor's note 57).

31. Rusk, George Caleb Bingham . . . , pp. 78-79.

32. Letter, June 5, 1861 (MHR, XXXII [1938], 517-518).

33. B. to R., letter, Jefferson City, Dec. 21, 1863, coll. SHSMo (MHR, XXXIII [1938], 63).

34. Bingham took up residence in Jefferson City immediately after taking office. His family joined him there in the spring of 1862: B. to R., letter, Jefferson City, Feb. 12, 1862, coll. SHSMo (MHR, XXXIII [1938], 49); Rusk, George Caleb Bingham . . . , p. 79.

213

A certain amount of artistic activity can be assigned to this period. On August 1, 1863,[35] Bingham was awarded a new State commission, this time for a large portrait of General Nathaniel Lyon, who was killed at Wilson's Creek in August, 1861, while fighting to hold Missouri for the Union.

Among other works that can be ascribed to the period 1862-1865 is a historical subject: the equestrian double-portrait of Generals Lyon and Blair portrayed against a background depicting a then recent event in Missouri history — the departure from the Arsenal in St. Louis to capture Camp Jackson in May, 1861 (A312; plate 160). A composition of similar dimensions and also with the unusual arched top, representing Colonel Franz Sigel, General John C. Frémont, and Captain Blandowski, was painted in 1861 by Charles Wimar, one of the more important of Bingham's Missouri contemporaries (plate 161).[36] The figures of Sigel and Frémont on horseback are posed almost identically with Lyon and Blair on contrasting black and white horses, although faced in the opposing direction. Wimar's composition, painted in grisaille, may have been prepared for engraving. One can only surmise whether Bingham intended his painting for similar purposes, or as a preliminary detailed study for a larger commission. The basic relationship to the Wimar composition suggests some contact between the two artists, and indeed the matter of artistic relationship between the Düsseldorfian-trained Wimar and the Düsseldorf-inspired Bingham merits further investigation. In this instance, it would certainly seem conceivable that Bingham's painting could have been executed with the Wimar composition in mind — perhaps even intended to serve as a pendant to it.

Bingham's private commissions usually assigned to this time include portraits of Robert Beverly Price (A308) of Columbia, and his second wife, Evaline Hockaday (A310), both dated about 1862. The portraits are typical examples of Bingham's later style, displaying a tighter, smoother modeling, and a concentration on textures and decorative accessories.

A more unusual composition by Bingham, called the "Thread of Life" (A307; plate 162), has been placed within this period as well, chiefly on

---

35. Rusk, *op. cit.*, p. 81.

36. For brief biographical details, see chap vi, n. 56. Wimar was one of the founders of the Western Academy of Art in St. Louis, which in 1860 exhibited Bingham's Election pictures and his "Jolly Flatboatmen in Port." He had nineteen paintings in the same show, including his own impressions of life on the Missouri and Mississippi, as well as several Indian subjects. Wimar was obviously a competitor on Bingham's home ground but, apart from the pictorial relationships noted in connection with this painting and "Jolly Flatboatmen by Moonlight" (p. 92), there seems to be no further evidence now available that reveals any personal contact between the two artists. Whether the coincidence of Wimar's residence in Düsseldorf in 1856, the same year in which Bingham went abroad, has any significance with respect to his own eventual decision to settle in the German city has yet to be explored.

the basis of the subject.[37] Stylistically, it could not have been painted before the Düsseldorf sojourn. Its light, decorative quality seems to relate it more to the oval portraits painted about 1860. The subject, suggesting an obscure allegorical theme, represents the draped figure of a woman seated on a cloud which is guided on its way by an angel. She supports a nude child who stands on her lap and draws the thread from a staff behind him. The figures of the woman and child reflect Raphaelesque types of the Madonna and Child as translated into Düsseldorfian terms. Indeed, the downcast eyes and the sentiment are not unlike the Madonna types developed by Carl Muller,[38] a prominent artist of the school. The curious motif of seated figure, cloud, and supporting angel may have been inspired, however, by a similar association contained in a frontispiece vignette (plate 163) designed by Peter F. Rothermel for a gift annual, and engraved by John Sartain.[39]

ORDER No. 11

On August 25, 1863, during the period of Bingham's state treasurership, a military order was issued in Kansas City which was to play an important part in his life, involving him finally in a controversy that was to pursue him until his last days. In actual practice, for perhaps the first time in his career, he was to utilize clearly his illustrative powers to register his strong personal reaction to a contemporary historical event. Up to this time we have noted only the inferences made by some of the artist's acquaintances that he sought to lampoon local politics and personalities in his Election scenes—intimations that seem not necessarily borne out in practice, or through any available documentary evidence. In this instance, however, there can be no doubt that it was a compulsive and deliberate act on his part, intended as a weapon against wrongdoing and the evildoer, as he envisaged it.

The military order, known as "Order No. 11," actually marked the final act in a series of events that reveal a period of exceptional bitterness and violence in the history of Missouri which began during the years before the outbreak of the Civil War itself. The warfare along the Missouri and Kansas borders, growing as it did out of the deep resentments felt on both sides

37. Rusk, *George Caleb Bingham . . .*, p. 75.
38. Similar in type to the "Madonna and Child" by Muller included in the Boker collection of the Düsseldorf Gallery, exhibited in New York as early as 1849: *Catalogue of a Private Collection of Paintings and Original Drawings by Artists of the Düsseldorf Academy of Fine Arts* (New-York: Wm. C. Bryant & Co., Printers, 1851), #124. The picture was in all the later exhibitions, and was illustrated in *Gems from the Düsseldorf Gallery . . .* (New York: Appleton, 1863).
39. "The Angel of the Opal," in *The Opal, A Pure Gift for All Seasons* (New-York: J. C. Riker, 1849). Peter Frederick Rothermel (1817-1895), Honorary Member, Professional, National Academy, 1848-1860.

following the passage of the Kansas–Nebraska Act and the repeal of the Missouri Compromise, consisted mainly of raids by such men as Lane and Jennison, who, with their bands of "Red Legs" and "Jayhawkers," consistently plundered and committed violent aggressions on Missouri border towns. Factional differences of longer standing between the two states had aggravated the affair, but the military order issued by Major General Thomas Ewing, Jr., was a retaliatory measure taken after a bloody raid made from the Missouri side by the guerilla Quantrill and his band on the town of Lawrence, Kansas, on August 19, 1863. Ewing maintained that the guerillas responsible were being harbored in the border counties, and his order requiring evacuation of those areas was intended as a war measure to prevent a further recurrence of such raids. But the order, which commanded the entire population to leave their homes within fifteen days of its issuance, and was thereafter enforced rigidly, brought with it much additional misery and hardship to large numbers of innocent people. Bingham strenuously resented the order and appealed to Ewing's superior officer, General John M. Schofield, to have it rescinded, but to no avail. When he was told that the order would have to stand, Bingham is reported to have advised Schofield: "If God spares my life, with pen and pencil I will make this order infamous in history."[40] His large composition, "Martial Law," better known as "Order No. 11," was the result.[41]

On at least two earlier occasions Bingham had been inspired to consider painting subjects depicting events of his own time which he sensed were of potential historical importance. Writing to Rollins late in 1853, he foresaw the possibilities of a composition in which Thomas Hart Benton ("Old Bullion") would play a leading role:

I have quite a serious notion to follow your suggestion, and make old *Bullion appealing to the people of Missouri* the subject of a future picture. That passage in the commencement of his speech at Fayette, in which he designates the friends whom he came to address, as those only who had *heads to perceive and hearts to feel the truth*, would

40. *The Daily Tribune*, Feb. 27, 1877. 2-1. Rusk, *op. cit.*, p. 82: attributes the statement to Bingham as one made during an interview with General Ewing. The source is not given, although the information may have come verbally from Mr. C. B. Rollins who published it in later years in "Some Recollections of George Caleb Bingham," *MHR*, XX (1926), 480; and again in *MHR*. XXXII (1938), p. 65, note 23. Christ-Janer, *op. cit.*, p. 102, quoted from Rollins' account of 1926. The contemporary report appears to present an accurate account of the incident and of the characters actually involved.

41. The painting became more popularly known in the Missouri press as "Order No. 11." Bingham called his picture "Civil War" when he copyrighted it in December, 1868, and continued to do so in references to the painting as late as March, 1870 (letter, B. to R., Independence, Mo., March 8, 1870 [*MHR*. XXXIII (1938), 65]). He referred to it as "The War of Desolation" in 1871 (*An Address to the Public*... [Kansas City, 1871], p. 4), and the engraving published after the painting (P12) was titled "Martial Law." In 1873 the second version of the painting was on exhibition in Louisville, Ky., as "Order No. 11–Martial Law," indicating a combination of the popular and formal titles presumably adopted by the artist himself by that time.

afford, I think, the best point of time for pictorial representation, as the action which accompanied it, and gave it such emphasis, would display his fine portly figure to the very best advantage, and also tell with most happy effect in the faces of the audience. The subject possesses an additional recommendation for me, from the fact, that I could introduce into it the portraits of many of my old friends who were present upon the occasion, and by a license, which painters, as well as poets can take, I could make others present in the pictures, who were not present in fact. I think an engraving from such a work would sell, and if painted on a large scale it would be well suited for a place either in the Capitol or University of our State.[42]

The passage of the Kansas–Nebraska Bill in 1854, which allowed "Squatter Sovereignty" to decide the touchy slavery question in the national territory north of 36° 30′ N., aroused the artist to call the bill "infamous" and to prophesy that it would "cause partially smothered fires to break out with greater violence than ever."[43] As a result of the bill, "border ruffian" warfare, marked by forays into Kansas by proslavery sympathizers among Missourians trying to turn Kansas into a slave state, brought much violence and bloodshed to the territory. Bingham fully intended to perpetuate these events on canvas, and discussed his plans at some length with Rollins in a letter written from Philadelphia in August, 1856, just prior to his departure for Europe:

After I complete the portraits of our State Capitol, I have it in contemplation to paint a new series of pictures illustrative of "Squatter Soverignty" [sic] as practically exhibited under the workings of the Kansas Nebraska bill. I shall commence with the *March of the "Border Ruffians,"* and will take pains to give those infamous expeditions of organized rowdyism all those odious features which truth and justice shall warrant.

I will want a portrait of Col Samuel Young, of the big negro that played the violin, and of a certain Methodist parson. As I design to give this trio the most conspicuous position upon the canvass, cannot you manage to forward them to me. Musgrove of Lexington I think would assist in procuring them. I wish you also to forward to me all the documents in relation to these affairs in Kansas, the evidence taken by the congressional committee &c.[44]

A year later the artist had not yet given up the idea of painting a subject depicting the "border ruffians,"[45] although nothing apparently ever came of the idea. In our consideration of Bingham's "Martial Law" it is significant to note that the basis of its content was, in fact, somewhat related to the

42. B. to R., letter, Philadelphia, Nov. 7, 1853, coll. SHSMo *(MHR,* XXXII [1938], 167).
43. B. to R., letter, Philadelphia, Feb. 1, 1854, coll. SHSMo *(MHR,* XXXII [1938], 177).
44. Letter, Aug. 10, 1856 *(MHR,* XXXII [1938], 201). A composition depicting the "Border Ruffians Invading Kansas," drawn by F. O. C. Darley (1822-1888), is in the collection of the Yale University Art Gallery, New Haven, Conn. (M. B. Garvan Coll.), illustrated in M. G. Davidson, *Life in America* (Boston: Houghton Mifflin, 1951), II, 382.
45. Letter, Düsseldorf, Oct. 12, 1857 *(MHR,* XXXII [1938], 357): "I have not yet abandoned my purpose of doing justice in the way of Art, to our *far famed* 'border ruffians,' and would like you to send me, enclosed in a letter, the most graphic account extant of one of their most conspicuous forays."

217

composition that he had been considering some seven years earlier.

Although we have referred to the painting depicting "General Nathaniel Lyon and General Francis Preston Blair, Jr., Starting from the Arsenal Gate in St. Louis to Capture Camp Jackson" (plate 160) as chiefly a double-portrait, the background, which serves to enlarge the picture into a scene depicting contemporary history, seems to place it also within that special category of historical illustration that attracted the artist's attention. Bingham's realization of the pictorial possibilities of contemporary historical events is also significant in placing him on a somewhat different level from most painters of American history, who usually followed the accepted trend in painting subjects far removed from their own time. It is true that many artists after the Civil War became more aware of the importance of the panorama of history then passing before them and took up the challenge, but before that time comparatively few artists presented such an awareness—Trumbull's series of paintings commemorating events of the American Revolution being probably the earliest examples seen in this country.[46]

When his term of office as State Treasurer expired, Bingham returned to his home in Independence and by November, 1865, was hard at work on his painting of "Martial Law."[47] It was near completion toward the end of 1868.[48] In all probability this is the version executed on a surface made up of several sections of canvas mounted against a backing of wood planking. Tradition has it that the drying action of the unseasoned wood which occurred soon after the painting was under way caused the canvas to buckle, and the artist temporarily abandoned it to begin a second picture, painted on two linen tablecloths sewed together.[49] Although it is more than conceivable that technical problems with the first canvas (A316) may have occasioned the execution of the second version (A326), the deterioration of the original may not actually have appeared prominently until after the work was com-

46. John Trumbull (1756-1843). Authorized by Congress in 1817 to paint four pictures "commemorative of the most important events in the American Revolution, to be placed when finished in the Capitol of the United States." The compositions were "The Signing of the Declaration of Independence." "The Surrender of General Burgoyne," "The Surrender of Lord Cornwallis at Yorktown," and "George Washington Resigning his Commission as Commander in Chief of the Army." Although the official pictures were executed between 1819 and 1825 (C. E. Fairman, *Art and Artists of the Capitol*..., pp. 34, 35, 44, 46), preliminary oil studies for all the compositions, as well as of some eight others relating to the American Revolution series conceived by Trumbull, were produced between 1785 and 1788, in some instances scarcely more than a decade after the actual events.

47. *Missouri Statesman*, Nov. 24, 1865 (from *Kansas City Journal*).

48. The painting was the subject of the Rev. R. S. Johnson's Thanksgiving Discourse in 1868, and the *Missouri Statesman*, Jan. 1, 1869, 3-2, stated: "This painting, almost before it has received the finishing stroke of the artist's pencil, is achieving a celebrity which significantly foreshadows the high name it will in the future take as a work of genius."

49. Rusk, *George Caleb Bingham* ..., p. 84.

pleted.[50] Contemporary critics make no mention of the unhappy circumstance in referring to what must have been the first picture. There is some evidence to indicate that the second painting was completed between March and April, 1870,[51] and there is no reason to suppose that the artist devoted more than a few months to the second effort, if any conclusion can be drawn from his procedure in former years.

The panel version (A316) remained in the artist's hands at the time of his death in 1879, and was later included in the Administrator's Sale of his estate at Kansas City in March, 1893, when it was sold to Joseph Wayne Mercer of Independence. It was afterward inherited by the latter's family and was on deposit in the William Rockhill Nelson Gallery of Art at Kansas City for several years, where I examined it in 1944. At that time the action of the crude wood backing had caused the canvas to buckle badly. The painting was sold to a picture dealer in 1947 who shortly afterward had it removed from the old support, relined, and restored to a state that probably closely approximated its original appearance.

The second version of "Martial Law" (A326; plate 164), the so-called "tablecloth" picture, was exhibited by the artist to raise subscriptions for the engraving then being produced from the original by John Sartain.[52] Bingham afterward turned the painting over to Major Rollins and Colonel R. B. Price of Columbia to satisfy the loan made by the two men to finance the cost of the engraving. Major Rollins later bought up Price's share. After Rollins' death it was inherited by his son George Bingham Rollins, namesake of the painter, and passed in turn into the hands of his heirs,[53] who in recent years sold it to the present owner.

Bingham himself referred to the second picture as a "duplicate,"[54] and such is evidently what he intended it to be, although at the same time he mentioned "revised studies"[55] which he had sent on to Sartain in connection with the engraving then in progress. Those revisions, minor though they may have appeared to the artist, are significant enough to distinguish the first and second compositions as distinct versions of the subject. The changes consist of slight alterations in the style of the dresses of three of the foreground women; in the pose of the head of the woman bending over the prostrate man; in the costume, treatment of details, in the background groups; and in the

50. It was apparently the first version (A316) that was reportedly on exhibition at Pettes & Leathe's gallery, on Fourth Street, St. Louis, in June 1869 (St. Louis *Daily Missouri Democrat*, June 6, 1869, 1).
51. B. to R., Letter, Independence, Mo., March 8, 1870, coll. SHSMo (*MHR*, XXXIII [1938], 65-66)
52. *Ibid.*
53. Rusk, *op. cit.*, p. 84; C. B. Rollins, *MHR*, XXXIII (1939), p. 205, note 4.
54. Letter, Independence, Mo., March 8, 1870 (*MHR*, XXXIII [1938], 65).
55. *Ibid.*, p. 66.

general distribution of light and shade. The over-all aspect of the composition, particularly in the organization of its chief areas, remained the same in both versions, although the adherence to the minor changes mentioned indicates that it was the second version that served as the basis for Sartain's engraving; hence for the present discussion we shall also refer to this as the final version.

The composition reflects the considered planning so typical of all of Bingham's figure subjects already discussed: the large central mass of figures placed at one side, the smaller group at the opposite side serving to balance it, and the spectator's eye then carried through a "corridor" to distant figures and landscape. The main group, taking the usual pyramidal form, is in turn made up of many smaller pyramidal sections. The strongest light is cast on the foreground group of heroic settlers with the elderly patriarch appearing at the apex. In the shadows behind him, silhouetted against the sky, appears an equestrian figure which actually fills out the form of the larger pyramid and appears at its summit. This is usually an important area in a Bingham composition, reserved for the key figure. The mounted figure has traditionally— and significantly, too—been said to be General Ewing himself, the man the artist despised as the one who issued and enforced the hated order, and whose name he had threatened to make "infamous in history" with his "pen and pencil." The strong contrast in light and shadow at the two focal points, in close proximity, marked by the two figures—one depicting the "honest man" (virtue), the other the "scoundrel" (vice)—would appear to have been a matter of deliberate planning on the artist's part, to which his own statement seems to attest:

He [referring to a critic of the picture] is right in saying that "the mission of true art is to exalt emotions, kindle pure purposes, and inspire to nobleness," but it will never be able to do this by making crime respectable, or by giving to scoundrels the rank due only to honest men. The great Leonardi diVinci [sic], in his immortal painting of the "Last Supper" placed the repulsive face of Judas in close proximity to the benign countenance of the Prince of Peace.

It is thus that I present virtue and vice in my picture, the brightness and divinity of the former appearing only the more conspicuous as relieved by the dark and Satanic features of the latter.[56]

Apart from the recollection of certain well-assimilated methods of concentration which the artist once again employs, the resemblance of this composition to his earlier figure subjects ceases. The slight exaggeration of gestures and the painter's keen observation and representation of facts had formerly combined to form an ideal and effective balance in the larger pictures. That

56. *St. Louis Republican*, March 17, 1869, 1-2.

220

spirit and balance is missing in "Martial Law," leaving in its stead a dreary, third-rate melodrama which tries overhard to tell its story, but, as with most overacted parts, loses all of its force and purpose. Despite the seriousness of the artist's message and the presence of stark tragedy, the spectator becomes so overwhelmed by the exaggerated, stilted behavior of the actors, all of whom seem to be trying to "steal the scene," that the total effect actually borders on the ludicrous. This first large subject undertaken since the Düsseldorf sojourn bears the stamp of that special brand of melodramatic representation that the German school seemed to approve in connection with scenes depicting painful suffering, and thus appears to reflect the artist's more than casual contact with his German colleagues. In the attention given to detail, the high finish of surfaces, and the hard, dry quality of the general effect, we are even more reminded of the productions of this school, as we are convinced of the painter's new allegiance to its ideals. However, strangely enough, although adopting the Düsseldorfian spirit and technique, Bingham still adhered to the usual methods of compositional organization which he had developed during his earlier years. "Martial Law," or "Order No. 11," forms a particularly interesting link with the past; it is a veritable mélange of motifs apparently derived from engravings after the old masters, although now curiously infused with a spirit quite foreign to the originals. The central group containing the old man, the young girl, and the small child seems to have been taken from the central group of Greuze's "The Father's Curse" (plate 167), with two of the figures reversed, although the figure of the old man more closely resembles the pose of the Apollo Belvedere (plate 165). The fainting figure supported by a negro servant, as well as the woman bending over her fallen husband, may have been inspired by Fra Bartolommeo's "Pietà" (plate 168). And the weeping negro walking off at right seems to be a distant relative of Masaccio's Adam from "The Expulsion" (plate 166). Thus it seems that classical antiquity, and the fifteenth, sixteenth, and eighteenth centuries all played a role in a Düsseldorfian drama staged on the Kansas–Missouri border in the mid-1860's!

In view of the unconvincing treatment of the subject, it is difficult to understand, from this vantage point, how the painting could have aroused the strong emotional reactions it did when first brought before the public. In fact, the storm of criticism that greeted the painting from the beginning placed Bingham continually in a defensive position. It rapidly became one of the most publicized paintings of its day, although its fame was necessarily limited to the Missouri scene. The painting was even bitterly attacked from the pulpit itself; it was said to be "a departure from moral law," and that

221

its representation of facts was of such a nature as to be "no better than false-hood."[57] The minister further declared that "as one acquainted with the circumstances looks at that painting, he gathers the impression which the artist meant to convey, that of an unjustifiable outrage by the people of Kansas upon the people of Missouri."[58] To this Bingham replied:

I can be a competent witness, at least, to the fact, that the artist meant to convey no such impression, and I think that any one who looks at the picture with an unclouded vision, will testify that it contains no facts which, fairly interpreted, make such an impression.[59]

And in rebuttal to yet another criticism:

. . . the design of my picture is not "to perpetuate a diseased idea of an historical event," . . . but to present its severe and rugged features in the enduring forms of art, and thus hand over to eternal infamy the perpetrators and defenders of outrages which scarcely find a parallel in the annals of the most barbarous ages. . . .

The writer of the criticism endeavors to make it appear that the central figure in my foreground is intended to represent the "rebels of that region," but there is nothing in the figure or its surroundings that warrants his assumption. To those whose visions are unclouded by prejudice, it represents that large class of law-abiding men who are known as honest and thrifty cultivators of the soil, standing where they had a right to stand, at their own homes, and where the Government was bound, in honor and justice, to protect them in all their rights of person and property. Instead of this, their thrift was reckoned as rebellion, and without being charged with, or convicted of crime, were robbed or murdered as the whim of their persecutors might dictate.

The scene in the picture is but one of hundreds of a similar character, and the charred remains of broken walls and solitary chimneys yet to be seen all over that fearfully desolated region, attest the truth of my delineations, and would cause any other than the art critic of the Democrat to blush at attempting to discredit them.[60]

Bingham eventually found it necessary to publish an even more expansive "vindication" of the painting, *An Address to the Public*, in which he saw fit to express his own philosophy of art with relationship to this particular work:

Art being the most efficient hand-maid of history, in its power to perpetuate the record of events with a clearness second only to that which springs from actual observation. I sometime since became impressed with the conviction, that, as one of its professors, I could not find a nobler employment for my pencil, than in giving to the future, through its delineations, truthful representations of extraordinary transactions indicative of the character of the military rule which oppressed and impoverished large numbers of the best citizens of our State during the late sectional war.

57. Referring to the discourse of the Rev. R. S. Johnson delivered on Thanksgiving Day, 1868, quoted by the artist in his reply, which was published in the form of a letter in *Jefferson City People's Tribune*, Dec. 23, 1868, 1-4 (from the *Independence Sentinel*).
58. *Ibid.*
59. *Ibid.*
60. *St. Louis Republican*, March 17, 1869, 1-2.

222

By such and similar means can only our bitter and tragical experience give due warning to posterity. It is not Christian charity, but rather sympathy with crime and its perpetrators, that would consign to oblivion those excesses of lawless and arbitrary power which have marked with ruin and devastation some of the fairest portions of our land. . . .[61]

During the period the artist spent in Independence occupied with painting the first "Order No. 11," he was also hard at work on the large State portrait of General Nathaniel Lyon (A324). The execution of the State commission would account, to a large extent, for the relatively long period that elapsed between the start and final work on "Order No. 11." The portrait of the General was commissioned in August, 1863,[62] but was not delivered until March, 1867.[63] A Kansas City reporter described the final appearance of the painting:

The immortal hero is represented as mounted upon his beautiful and well remembered dappled gray steed, which appears suddenly reigned [sic] up as the well poised rider turns to his followers, and waves his hat in the direction of the rebel hosts, who are dimly seen through the smoke of battle. As we view the fixed determination and resolute purpose which exhibit themselves in every lineament of his countenance, we are at no loss as to the source of their aspiration, which so suddenly endowed the "plow boys" of Missouri and Kansas with the qualities of veterans. To behold such a man necessarily begets trust and confidence. Whatever man can dare or do may be dared and done with such a leader.[64]

The same critic reported his first impressions of the portrait as a work of art:

We feel confident that all who see this portrait of the lamented Lyon will regard it as a most successful representation, creditable alike to the artist and the State.

61. G. C. Bingham, *An Address to the Public, Vindicating a Work of Art, Illustrative of the Federal Military Policy in Missouri During the Late Civil War* . . . (Kansas City, Mo., 1871).
62. Contracted for on August 1, 1863; Rusk, *op. cit.*, pp. 81, 89.
63. The portrait was delivered and placed in the Senate chamber of the State Capitol during the first week of March, 1867 *(The Liberty Tribune, March 8, 1867, 2-1)*. The bill appropriating $3,000 in payment for the work was passed by mid-March *(The Liberty Tribune, March 15, 1867, 2-4)*. It has been stated that "the contract was made in pursuance of a resolution of the House of Representatives which appropriated nothing from the treasury for the purpose, but designated that the Secretary of State should solicit subscriptions and engage a competent artist." (Rusk, *op. cit.*, p. 89). No time limit had been set under the terms of the contract, and a study for the picture was not submitted for official approval until November, 1865. At that time Bingham advised: "In the large picture I can make any improvements which may suggest themselves to my judgment." He expected to complete the work during the summer of 1866 (Rusk, *op. cit.*, pp. 89-90, from *Journal of the Adjourned Session of the 23rd General Assembly of Missouri,* app. pp. 855 ff.). Almost four years elapsed from the time the contract was made to the date of delivery of the picture. Work on the full-length painting was probably not begun until after November, 1865, and carried out, along with other works in progress, from that time until March, 1867. It is difficult to accept the statement made by Mrs. Abram Neff, the artist's niece, to the effect that Bingham "finished it in a much shorter time than he was wont to do when fulfilling such large commissions—that he painted the picture in five weeks" (Rusk, *op. cit.*, p. 90).
64. *Missouri Statesman*, March 22, 1867, 2-4.

When viewed from a proper distance all idea of paint and canvas entirely disappears, and the whole is presented with the strength and force of a living and breathing reality. In looking at it, we very readily fancy that we are not contemplating a picture, but the noble hero himself, setting firmly and self-collected in the saddle, while every muscle of his firy [sic] and impatient steed seems to quiver with a repressed energy, which at the first slacking of the firmly held rein, will bear him onward with the impetuosity of a tornado.

All the accessories are in most admirable keeping with the principal. The saddle, bridle, holsters, sword, etc. all seem actual and all contributed to the leading idea without in the slightest degree detracting therefrom.

This painting can not fail to receive a cordial and appreciative reception from the members of our present Legislature. A work which so fully meets the commemorative purpose for which it was intended, can not be otherwise than duly prized by those in whose breasts the memory of its great subject is enshrined.[65]

Bingham had earlier painted a small historical portrait composition in which the General had appeared as a central figure: "General Nathaniel Lyon and General Francis Preston Blair, Jr., Starting from the Arsenal Gate in St. Louis to Capture Camp Jackson" (plate 160).

The large equestrian portrait of Lyon was destroyed during the Capitol fire of 1911, but fortunately an old photograph of the picture is preserved for us (plate 169). Together with the elaborate description and criticism by the Kansas City reporter, this photograph affords us a fair impression of the appearance of the original. Much of the detail and background is lost in the poor reproduction, but its monumental quality is still clearly visible. Diagonal lines and angular forms are boldly utilized to achieve a movemented effect, as well as to develop a more effective impression, tending away from the more formal representation. The turn of the General's head and the introduction of dramatic background elements reveal the artist's attempt to achieve a greater pictorial emphasis—actually more in the direction of historical genre. This tendency again recalls the double equestrian portrait of Generals Lyon and Blair, although that composition still adhered to the more formal idea of equestrian representations in the principal subjects.

It was also at this time that Bingham painted another portrait that approaches historical genre in its portrayal of the central figure in a setting reflecting an important incident in his career. The picture, known as "Major Dean in Jail" (A319; plate 170), painted by July, 1866,[66] in a sense reflects a similar motivation to "Order No. 11," and reveals the artist again making use of his brush to record a contemporary event for posterity. Major Dean, a Baptist minister and Union soldier, had been imprisoned at Independence for preaching without first having taken a loyalty oath. Possibly planned in

65. *Ibid.*
66. *Ibid.*, July 6, 1866 (from *St. Louis Dispatch*).

224

connection with a larger effort, or with a view toward an engraving, the composition shows Major Dean seated slightly to the left of center, with the light from the cell window concentrated on him. Unlike "Order No. 11," this painting does not show any attempt at dramatization or sentiment of any kind. It is a story simply told, with only a mattress, a crumpled blanket, and a newspaper included as accessories to further describe the scene. As a composition it recalls an engraving after E. M. Ward's "Napoleon in the Prison at Nice" (plate 171), even to the use of the crumpled blanket motif, although Bingham eliminates the secondary figures in his effort to concentrate attention on the figure of the imprisoned preacher. The photographic insistence on details af costume, walls, and flooring, accompanied by the hard outlining of the figure, indicates the change in direction that distinguishes so much of the artist's work after 1860, underlying chiefly the greater stylistic allegiance to Düsseldorfian precepts.

Bingham was again active on the Missouri political scene in 1866 and again in 1868. In June, 1866, his name was submitted as a candidate for Congress from his district,[67] but he was not appointed by the nominating convention. Two years later he was chosen to represent his district as an Elector to the Democratic State Convention.[68] Despite these activities, however, his painting efforts continued unabated. In addition to the larger works then under way, he also necessarily devoted more and more attention to portraiture during the closing years of the decade.

Among his subjects were three children: his son James Rollins Bingham (A332; plate 172), Hugh Campbell Ward (A327, plate 173), and the latter's infant sister Mary Frances, all probably painted about 1870. The portraits of the boys are typical of the more restrained manner of painting affected by the artist following his return from Düsseldorf. The modeling is smoother and subdued, with an emphasis on decorative and descriptive detail. Both are portraits of considerable charm, despite the formal and quiet mood, and can be considered among the most successful of Bingham's portrayals of children. The painting of Mary Frances Ward is a somewhat less effective design, despite the similarity in the subdued modeling.

Portraits of James Thomas Birch (A329) and his wife (A330; plate 180) were also painted during the same period. Mrs. Birch (Margaret Elizabeth Nelson) was a most attractive woman and one of the artist's favorite subjects. It was she who was later to serve as the model for one of the best known of his later pictures, "The Palm Leaf Shade." The high finish of this portrait of Mrs. Birch and the modeling in delicate contrasts, combined with the interest

67. *Ibid.*, June 1, 1866.
68. *Ibid.*, June 5, 1868.

in the rendering of decorative accessories, bring it within the new line of the artist's development. The Birch pictures are also of particular interest in that they are two of the very few portraits signed by Bingham (see p. 19, n. 23).

In May, 1870, Bingham moved from Independence to Kansas City,[69] where he maintained a permanent residence for the remaining years of his life. The artist enjoyed a considerable patronage during these years, and also became prominently associated with the town's civic affairs. He had also been active at Independence, where in 1869 he had been elected a school director.

THE FINAL DECADE (1870-1879)

At the time of his removal to Kansas City, Bingham was commissioned to execute a full-length portrait of General Francis Preston Blair, Jr. This was to be his first large official portrait commission involving a celebrated living personage. What probably was a bust portrait made from life, to be used in connection with the painting, was completed by January, 1871, and was on view in the artist's studio in Jefferson City when it was observed by a local reporter:

Mr. Bingham.

This distinguished artist is now spending a few days in town. His studio is at Miss Lusk's, where may be seen portraits of Gen. Blair and some of our own citizens. The portrait of Blair is to be full-length when completed, and even in its present incomplete condition is pronounced by many to be superior to the portrait painted some years ago by Boyle. . . . [70]

The reporter also noted other portraits in the studio, adding that he had been "authorized by Mr. Bingham's friends to say that he will paint the portraits of all who may desire it."[71]

By March 6 the artist had prepared a small study for the full-length portrait of Blair and had sent a photograph of it to his friend Rollins, requesting his opinion of the "attitude expression and composition," although warning him of the false impression he might get from the reproduction. He described his own attitude toward the representation: "As the work which is expected from Blair is of a beligerent [sic] nature I think it best to give his face the expression which accords therewith."[72] The portrait was well advanced when he again wrote to Rollins, on May 21:

69. *Ibid.*, May 6, 1870, 4-1 (from *Independence Sentinel*).
70. *The People's Tribune*, Jan. 25, 1871, 3-1. "Boyle" was Ferdinand Thomas Lee Boyle (1820-1906), an associate member, National Academy, 1850-60; b. England; came to St. Louis from New Rochelle, N.Y., 1855; one of founders of the Western Academy of Art; after 1866 resided in New York City, (G. C. Groce and D. H. Wallace, *Dictionary of Artists in America . . .*, p. 73).
71. *Ibid.*
72. B. to R., letter, Kansas City, Mar. 6, 1871, coll. SHSMo (*MHR*, XXXIII [1938], 67).

I think it is by far the most striking full length portrait that I have painted. I have endeavored to give the head all the rugged force which nature has bestowed upon the original, and I have also given the figure the bearing and attitude which would mark it as Blair's even if the head were out of sight. . . . At the request of Blair I sent one of the photographs to his father, and have received a letter from Montgomery Blair stating that the old folks were much pleased with it. When you see the large picture you will regard it, in every respect, in advance of the photograph.[73]

The painting was probably completed during the first week of June, at which time Bingham enthusiastically advised his friend: "*It is my best picture of the kind*, and you will hardly dislike even the pantaloons which by letting out a few stitches in some places and taking in a few in others, I place my tailorship on a par with my art."[74]

The picture was commissioned by a number of Blair's friends, including Major Rollins, each contributing to the total of $800 which the artist received for it.[75] The destination of the picture, however, was evidently not decided upon by July 1, 1871.[76] The original plan was to present the painting to the State Legislature for its approval,[77] undoubtedly with a view toward its permanent placement in the Capitol. But, for some reason as yet undetermined, the portrait found its way to the St. Louis Mercantile Library, where it was on exhibition for many years.[78] In more recent times it was turned over to the Missouri Historical Society, where it was apparently lost from sight until recently when I identified a bust-length portrait in the Society's storage as being the upper portion of the long missing picture.

The small full-length study (A343; plate 174) for the portrait reveals Blair in his role as senator, standing beside his desk in his legislative office, facing left almost in profile. As the artist himself described it, the head has a "rugged force" which is further emphasized in the aggressive pose of the figure—an attitude Bingham felt marked the subject's individuality "even if the head were out of sight." The strong vertical figure is echoed in the lines of the pilaster behind it, but other accessories are limited to essentials, at least in this small version. The study reveals a view at left into what was probably an anteroom, but how much of the appearance of the small study was carried over into the final picture is open to question, especially in view of the painter's own advice that "in painting the large picture every part shall be

73. B. to R., letter, Kansas City, May 21, 1871, coll. SHSMo (*MHR*, XXXIII [1938], 68).
74. B. to R., letter, Kansas City, June 4, 1871, coll. SHSMo (*MHR*, XXXIII [1938], 70).
75. B. to R., letter, Kansas City, July 1, 1871, coll. SHSMo (*MHR*, XXXIII [1938], 75).
76. *Ibid.*
77. Letter, Kansas City, May 21, 1871 (*MHR*, XXXIII [1938], 68).
78. The only other contemporary report of the picture indicated that the painting, "lately framed," was placed on exhibition at the gallery of Pettes & Leathe, on Fourth Street, St. Louis, during the summer of 1874 (*Missouri Republican*, July 19, 1874, 4; *St. Louis Democrat*, Aug. 9, 1874, 1).

227

carefully revised." In too many instances of a similar kind, the general breadth and vitality that was achieved in the small-scale study was lost in the enlargement, largely as a result of the accompanying concentration on abundant detail and high finish.

In at least one known example—a portrait of Major James Sidney Rollins —Bingham brought even the small preparatory study to a relatively complete state (A346), indicating in a rather convincing way how far the artist was expected to demonstrate the final design, and revealing how much of the original force was actually dissipated in the process. The full-length portrait of Rollins was probably commissioned by the Major's friends and associates in Columbia, at about the time Bingham was completing his portrait of General Blair. To the artist, this portrayal of his closest friend of almost forty years standing was a labor of love and devotion. His letter to the subject on June 4, 1871, reveals something of his emotional reaction in connection with the proposed portrait:

As to your own chances for immortality they certainly are good, whether realized in full length upon canvass or not. For that rare honor many of our friends will be indebted entirely to my pencil but you are not of the number that will be forgotten unless they are painted or chiseled. Your name is identified with too much that is to be permanent in our state to render doubtful the certainty of its reaching posterity, and when you leave it, as I hope and believe, for the better land, you will not be "unwept unhonored and unsung." Still, I intend to work for the full length portrait, but with a view quite as much to my own immortality as yours.[79]

During the succeeding months Bingham came to Columbia and, as was his custom in executing these larger works, painted a bust-length portrait of the subject (A345; plate 176). It is not known whether Rollins actually posed for a full-length figure study, but by early November the artist was able to submit photographs of his design for the final composition. He informed Rollins: "The head and figure is very perfect, the accessories, being in colors, take a little uneavenly [sic] as is allways [sic] the case, but it makes a striking and effective little picture and will please your friends."[80]

Unforeseen delays, the chief of which must have been due to his protracted stay in Philadelphia during the winter of 1871 superintending the engraving of "Order No. 11,"[81] followed by a decline in his health, undoubtedly halted the progress of the work. Bingham did not order a canvas for the picture until late in November, 1872,[82] planning to execute the work during the

79. Kansas City, June 4, 1871 (*MHR*, XXXIII [1938], 70).
80. B. to R., letter, Kansas City, Nov. 5, 1871, coll. SHSMo (*MHR*, XXXIII [1938], 76).
81. See p. 232 for further discussion.
82. B. to R., letter, Kansas City, Nov. 20, 1872, coll. SHSMo (*MHR*, XXXIII [1939], 218).

winter months to have it ready by the spring of 1872 for presentation to the University. It was completed late in March, 1873. As soon as the picture was finished he advised Rollins: "I have felt a deep personal interest in the work and have spared no effort to make it such as will give to the future youth of our State a correct idea of the man to whom they will be so much indebted.[83]

The portrait was on view in Columbia in April, 1873,[84] and was submitted for acceptance to the Board of Curators of the University on June 24; it was described by the presentation committee as "a faithful likeness of the original, and a most excellent work of art."[85] It was formally presented, with appropriate ceremony, on June 26. The remarks of Colonel Switzler[86] were directed toward the subject of the portrait, while those of Alban J. Conant,[87] a fellow-artist, emphasized the personal relationship between the painter and his subject in this case, undoubtedly occasioning Bingham's statement afterward: "They send us to immortality together. . . ."[88]

Conant had said:

As I look at that full-length portrait of the esteemed President of this Board, painted by one whom I am proud to call my personal friend and professional brother, Geo. C. Bingham, I am reminded of a fact which may not be generally known, outside of the circle of personal friends; the fact that both the subject of this picture and the artist have been from early youth to manhood's ripened years, the warmest personal friends, and next to their own kith and kin, each by the other has been the best beloved.

Together they have traveled life's pathway; side by side have they labored; contributing in the legislature and out it as best they might, all the power of their united personal influence to promote the best interests of this great commonwealth.

In political life—in patriotic action, they have been one, and in sentiment and affection, like David and Jonathan, they have been united by ties most intimate and tender.

The portrait of the founder of this University, painted by the father of Missouri art, and the crowning work of his life in the line of portraiture—whose fame rests not alone upon this branch of art, for he has given to posterity those inimitable delineations of human character as presented in the history of the early political life of Missouri in those well known election scenes—this portrait, I say, to us who are gathered here to-day, has not alone the interest of being a worthy tribute to a worthy man, but around

83. B. to R., letter, Kansas City, Mar. 24, 1873, coll. SHSMo (*MHR* XXXIII [1939], 220).
84. *Missouri Statesman*, April 11, 1873, 3-2: "The whole portrait is excellently executed and adds another wreath to the brow of the distinguished artist."
85. "Letter of Presentation," from the Hon. Elijah Perry, Vice-President of the Board of Curators, University of Missouri, Columbia, June 24, 1873, in *Presentation of a Life-size Portrait of Hon. James S. Rollins to the Board of Curators of the University of the State of Missouri, by the Citizens of Boone County, Mo. . . .* (Columbia, Mo.: Statesman Book and Job Office, 1873), p. [3].
86. Col. William Franklin Switzler (1819-1906), editor of *Missouri Statesman*.
87. Alban Jasper Conant (1821-1915) was a painter of portraits and historical subjects; moved to St. Louis from Troy, N.Y., in 1857; one of the founders of the Western Academy of Art; Curator of the University of Missouri, 1868-1875; after 1885 resided in New York City (G. C. Groce and D. H. Wallace, *Dictionary of Artists in America . . .*, p. 143).
88. B. to R., letter, Kansas City, Aug. 3, 1873, coll. SHSMo (*MHR*, XXXIII [1939], 225).

it cluster the memories of hard-fought battles of civil and political conflict, and the tender associations of undying friendship.[89]

Bingham regarded Conant's remarks as being "such as became a true artist, devoted to Art and generous to its professors."[90]

The large full-length portrait was destroyed during the University fire of 1892, but the small study extant (plate 175) gives us an adequate impression of the final version. As noted earlier, Bingham went somewhat further in the study than was his custom, providing it with all of the detail he intended for the final picture. Since the small painting found its way into the subject's collection, probably through the artist himself, it is conceivable that much of the finish ordinarily reserved only for the final effort was also afforded the small study as a special compliment to his friend.

As in the portrait of Blair, the Major is shown standing, looking out to one side, his head almost in profile. In a similar fashion, too, the column in the background serves to accent the figure. The accessories of table and chair also recall the earlier composition. A view through a draped opening in the right distance reveals the main University building, symbolizing the subject's role as Father of the University, while other details and the pose seem to suggest his position as a figure in national and state affairs.

The final effect, which obviously demanded an even greater insistence on the high finish of such details as the elaborately embroidered and fringed table covering and the floor pattern, must have tended to detract from the central subject. It is surmised that much of the expressive quality of the head, such as is displayed in the bust-length portrait, must have been lost in the translation. This bust-length portrait, which can be considered among the best of Bingham's accomplishments in the 1870's, belongs, in terms of its inherent vitality and breadth of handling, in the direct line of stylistic development with the 1859 portrait of Dr. Troost.

Among the more important private portrait commissions undertaken by Bingham were those of Thomas Hoyle Mastin (A349) and his young son John Jerome (A350), both painted about 1871. The portrait of the elder Mastin (plate 177), a three-quarter length composition, including hands and background accessories, forms a link with the series of portrait designs developed by Bingham more than a decade earlier. The pose is particularly reminiscent of the portraits of James M. Piper and Dr. Benoist Troost. What sources Bingham may have based his earlier portraits upon have yet to be recognized, but one can assume that the artist still looked to the works of older masters for inspiration. For this portrait, however, a comparison of the design

89. *Presentation of a Life-size Portrait of Hon. James S. Rollins . . .* , p. 13.
90. Letter, Aug. 3, 1873 (*MHR*, XXXIII [1939], 225).

with an engraving after the portrait of Frans Snyders by Van Dyck which Burnet reproduced in an instruction book he might well have known,[91] reveals some rather specific relationships, although Bingham freely alters the general placement of the figure, the pose of the right hand, and the background to suit his own established notions and those ideas of formal portraiture that were more in keeping with his own time.

By comparison with the portrait of Dr. Troost, which it resembles in general arrangement, the painting, like so many others of this period, is much more subdued in mood. The strong contrasts of light and shade that afford the Troost portrait so much of its vital force, despite the equally formal pose, have been replaced by a subtler, smoother modeling of closely related tones. The freer, atmospheric handling of the earlier work has been replaced by a dry and crisp manner defined by tight outlines.

The full-length portrait of John Jerome Mastin (plate 178) affords us an even more complete impression of Bingham's more ambitious efforts in portraiture at that time. The boy is shown in a formal garden setting, seated on a low stone wall, his right arm resting on the head of an enormous dog. Decidedly a "fancy" composition, the entire effect is based on the details and accessories, with the result that the textural quality of the velvet dress and the pelt of the sad-eyed dog attract the observer far more than does the subject himself. The insistence on a sleekness in the rendering of the child's head actually robs the portrait of any vitality. The usual difficulty the artist encountered in the handling of a small figure is again obvious here, despite the over-all "veneer." The portrait of the artist's son Horace (plate 39), painted some twenty-five years before that of the Mastin child, forms an interesting comparison. Both children are about the same age, and the pose of the legs is almost identical. Yet much of the natural ease and charm that characterized the earlier portrait has been lost in the more sophisticated effort.

A second portrait of Mrs. James Sidney Rollins (Mary Elizabeth Hickman) (A351; plate 179) was executed between 1871 and 1872, during the period in which the artist was at work on the full-length portrait of her husband. Bingham had painted her many years earlier, a fact he recalled in a letter to the Major on June 4, 1871: "As I painted her when she was a bride I would like to prove to her that the real and deathless beauty which beams from the

91. Burnet, *Practical Hints on Light and Shade . . . ,* pl. 4, fig. 5. Burnet's etched reproduction is in reverse of the painting (Frick Collection, New York), a situation that is not unusual in the reproduction of designs by graphic means. Furthermore, the print actually translates the pose of the figure rather ineffectually, seeming to represent him seated, with his right hand resting across his lap, whereas in the painting the figure is standing, with his hands resting upon drapery thrown over the back of a chair. The design adopted by Bingham, indicating a very possible contact with the Burnet illustration, could have understandably misinterpreted the amorphous form of the lower section of the picture as representing a seated figure.

231

face of the grandmother can triumph in the comparison with that of the girl as she was led to the altar.[92] The resultant portrayal, painted in his more academic style, lacks the liveliness of the first portrait, despite Bingham's more developed technical skill. It serves, too, as a strong contrast to the rather vital portrait of the Major painted at the same time.

The publication of the engraving of "Order No. 11" also took up much of the artist's attention during the greater part of 1871. Undertaken by Bingham in partnership with Rollins and Price,[93] the work was again entrusted to John Sartain in Philadelphia. Work on the plate evidently dragged on over a long period. Bingham attempted to maintain contact with Sartain via correspondence, but long periods elapsed during which he received no word from the East as to the progress of the work.[94] His impatience grew as the months slipped by, and the contracted period came near its end. At length, in a letter to Rollins early in December, 1871, he began to indicate his growing suspicion of Sartain's possible motive behind the delay: "Can it be possible that he is tampered with? I know nothing of his politics and as Ewing has learned through his friends, that the work is being executed by Sartain, it is just beginning to be a slight suspicion in my mind that he may have stronger inducements to destroy the plate than to complete it."[95]

Soon afterward the painter went to Philadelphia to look into the matter himself.[96] It was then he realized that his momentary suspicions were actually groundless, and that the engraver was, in fact, "a thorough gentleman, but one of those who have not the fortitude to say no to friends who continually call upon him for services, which when yielded render it impossible for him to comply with his engagements to those at a distance who cannot stimulate him by their personal presence."[97] Bingham therefore decided to remain in Philadelphia until the plate was completed.[98]

It was apparently during this time that the artist finally brought his large composition of "Washington Crossing the Delaware" (A261; plate 181) to completion, and it may well be that the work was accomplished in Philadelphia as one means of filling in his time while keeping an eye on Sartain's progress. He had begun work on the painting in Columbia some fifteen years

92. Letter, June 4, 1871, coll. SHSMo (*MHR*, XXXIII [1938], 71).
93. Robert Beverly Price (1832-1924), banker of Columbia, Mo.
94. B. to R., letters, Kansas City, June 19 and Dec. 9, 1871, coll. SHSMo (*MHR*. XXXIII [1938-1939]. 74, 203).
95. Letter, Dec. 9, 1871 (*MHR*, XXXIII [1939], 203).
96. Bingham arrived in Philadelphia, Dec. 22, 1871: B. to R., letter, Philadelphia, Dec. 24, 1871. coll. SHSMo (*MHR*, XXXIII [1939], 204).
97. B. to R., letter, Philadelphia, Jan. 17, 1872, coll. SHSMo (*MHR*, XXXIII [1939], 209-210).
98. B. to R., letter, Philadelphia, Jan. 7, 1872, coll. SHSMo (*MHR*, XXXIII [1939], 206): "I will remain with him [Sartain] until the work is done as, should I leave, I can have no assurance that it would not be further postponed."

232

earlier.[99] This subject had first attracted him after he had observed Leutze's impressive version, possibly when it was on exhibition at the New York "Industry of All Nations" in 1853.[100] He referred to the composition when he announced to Rollins in January, 1855: "I should like to present the 'Father of his Country,' connected with some historical incident, in a manner that would rival the far famed picture by Leutze."[101] This idea was first projected by him in connection with a hoped-for State commission, and he may have been encouraged to go ahead with it in the event the Legislature suddenly felt the urge for a "pictorial embelishment [sic] of the Capitol," whose "bare walls" Bingham obviously longed to fill.[102] But the State never seems to have encouraged his talents beyond the range of portraiture, which may very well account for the long-deferred completion of his own version of "Washington Crossing the Delaware."

The artist announced his final work on the painting in a letter to Rollins written from Philadelphia on January 7, 1872, at the same time indicating Sartain's interest in the picture:

He [Sartain] seems quite anxious to engrave my picture of "Washington Crossing the Delaware" which is now finished and of which I gave him a photograph. He thinks it would find a large sale here and in New York, and is disposed to engrave it as a partnership or a half interest in the copyright. He thinks it is far superior to Leuitzes [sic] picture of the same subject.[103]

There are no further indications that anything ever developed of the plan to engrave the composition. During the fall of the following year the picture was on exhibition at the Louisville Exposition. It was evidently still in the artist's studio in 1879 and was included in the Adminstrator's Sale of the Bingham estate in March, 1893, when it was purchased by Thomas Hoyle Mastin of Kansas City. The painting is still in the possession of the Mastin heirs.

Although, by his own admission, Bingham sought to "rival" Leutze's well-known interpretation of the subject, his own composition bears a strong resemblance to it in the organization of the theme and its central motif. In both versions Washington assumes the dominant role at the apex of a pyramidal arrangement of figures, but Leutze's relatively fluid construction is supplanted by Bingham's heavily crowded and tightly enclosed form, in line with the

99. *Weekly Missouri Statesman*, March 14, 1856, 3-4: "Mr. Geo. C. Bingham, the distinguished Missouri Artist, is engaged in this place on a historical painting—*Washington Crossing the Deleware*."
100. *Official Catalogue of the Pictures Contributed to the Exhibition of the Industry of All Nations* ..., #616.
101. Letter, Philadelphia, Jan. 12, 1855 (*MHR*. XXXII [1938], 187).
102. *Ibid.*
103. Letter, Jan. 7, 1872 (*MHR*. XXXIII [1939], 206).

formula he had followed so prominently in his Election series. He takes over Leutze's figure of the oarsman at left, so that the strongly oblique line formed by the boathook establishes a side of the pyramid in both examples. The principal differences between the two pictures lie along more descriptive lines. Varying the somewhat inconceivable idea of Washington standing upright in a rowboat on an ice-choked river, Bingham substitutes the more practical flat-bottomed raftboat and is thereby able to give the hero a plausible monumentality through an equestrian representation. It is entirely possible that the idea for the more practical raft was suggested by William Ranney's composition of "Marion Crossing the Pedee"[104] (plate 182), in which equestrian figures also appear.

The atmospheric treatment of lights and darks, throwing the central figure into strong relief against a dramatic sky, while subordinate figures fall into half-lights and deep shadows, reflects the tendency that describes the artist's stylistic development about 1855. In this aspect the painting is closely related to the second version of the "Verdict of the People," dating from that period, thus suggesting that the complete plan of the composition, including the patterning of lights and darks, was probably well advanced in 1856, and executed in later years according to the original idea. Despite the obvious inspiration from Leutze's composition, it is also significant to note that at the time Bingham developed the design of his picture, the theatrical emotionalism of the Düsseldorfian interpretation had as yet made no impression on him, and he still used the stolid types and even manipulated his presentation of the raftboat in a manner reminiscent of the early "Jolly Flatboatmen."

Bingham seriously considered opening a studio in New York during the winter of 1873-74. The depressed condition of business in Kansas City at the time undoubtedly contributed to this wish to move, coupled with the encouragement he had received from his first wife's brother, Dr. Joseph B. Hutchison, then living in New York. It also revived the idea of trying his luck once again for a new eastern patronage. With this in mind, he wrote to Rollins from Kansas City on September 28, 1873:

I might go and try the experiment this winter, leaving my family here. I think his [Dr. Hutchison's] general acquaintance there would be of great service to me, both in

104. "Marion Crossing the Pedee," painted by William Ranney in 1850 (ca. 50 x 74½), was exhibited by the American Art-Union in 1851 (#348) and sold at the sale of the Art-Union's holdings in 1852. Grubar records that the painting was purchased at that time by W. H. Webb who, by coincidence, also acquired Leutze's "Washington Crossing the Delaware," and also notes a parallel between the two pictures. (Grubar, *William Ranney* . . . , pp. 38-39, #56). The engraving executed by Charles Burt after the painting was intended for distribution to the Art-Union membership of 1851, although the prints seem not to have been actually received by the members until 1852/1853. We have already noted (p. 120) that another well-known painting by Ranney, "Daniel Boone's First View of Kentucky," also an Art-Union picture which had been published in engraved form, had in all probability attracted Bingham's attention.

having my works brought into notice, and in securing me business as a portrait painter. New York is a great Democratic City, and consequently the mass of its population would sympathize with such a work as my "Martial Law."[105]

Perhaps less openly, Bingham also hoped to "try the experiment" with the notion of attempting to regain once more his standing as an illustrator of the western scene, a reputation that had been established in the East in former years through his patronage by the old American Art-Union. He evidently had more definite ideas along this line when he advised his friend on October 26: ". . . I employ all my leizure [sic] in making drawings to be elaborated into pictures which I intend as my winter work in New York. While there I will try to make arrangements with Harpers and others to supply them with illustrations of western life and manners, as exemplified upon our rivers, plains and mountains."[106]

Bingham was enthusiastic and obviously looking forward to the New York stay. His health was better than it had been, and he felt he could "flatter myself that I will yet be able to make many pictures which will afford pleasure to others after I am called hence."[107] His plans called for his departure from Kansas City by the middle of November, but several unexpected requests for portraits came along which he could not afford to turn away, thus delaying him.

As matters turned out, he was evidently delayed so long by these commissions, or else compelled by other additional circumstances, that he canceled the trip altogether. Perhaps the necessity of concentrating his attention on his financial interests kept him in Kansas City. Bingham had complained to Rollins about the "miserable City administration"[108] which was supported by gamblers and others who had located themselves in that part of the city in which the artist owned some property. This caused such a depression of real-estate values in that area that Bingham's income from the property was "reduced to a bare sufficiency to pay taxes and insurance, if indeed they shall prove sufficient for that."[109] In fact, to support his family, he was "compelled" to paint portraits all winter, and for an indefinite period thereafter.[110] In any event, all further thought of his plans to reëstablish himself as a painter of the western scene was set aside, and as late as June, 1874, he could only refer to his then current portrait activity as "pot-boiling."[111]

105. B. to R., letter, Kansas City, Sept. 28, 1873, coll. SHSMo (*MHR*, XXXIII [1939], 229).
106. B. to R., letter, Kansas City, Oct. 26, 1873, coll. SHSMo (*MHR*, XXXIII [1939], 349).
107. *Ibid.*
108. B. to R., letter, Kansas City, Dec. 14, 1873, coll. SHSMo (*MHR*, XXXIII [1939], 350).
109. *Ibid.*, p. 351.
110. B. to R., letter, Kansas City, May 26, 1874, coll. SHSMo (*MHR*, XXXIII [1939], 353-354).
111. "To make the pot boil"—an expression used by Bingham in connection with his portrait-painting activities (B. to R., letter, Kansas City, June 7, 1874, coll. SHSMo [*MHR*, XXXIII (1939), 355]).

It was in pursuit of such activity that Bingham found himself in Boonville that year at the home of Captain Joseph Kinney, who resided in nearby New Franklin. The fine portraits of the Captain and his wife, and the double portrait of the younger Kinneys, were undoubtedly painted at this time. In the double portrait of Mrs. B. W. Clarke (Mary Jane Kinney) and her brother (A366; plate 183), Bingham was confronted with the problem of posing two adult figures in a single portrait composition, a situation that obviously was an unusual one for him. Indeed, it is a unique instance in his known works. The unconvincing spatial relationship of the figures can be considered indication enough of Bingham's inability to cope with what must have been for him an unaccustomed problem. Yet, aside from the general criticism, the more favorable characteristics in terms of the expressiveness of the portraits themselves, the strong color and smooth modeling, and evident attention lavished on decorative detail place this portrait among the artist's more ambitious productions of the period.

Bingham's civic, as well as his personal interest in the unfortunate administration of the city was brought into even sharper focus when he was appointed president of the Kansas City Board of Police Commissioners by the Governor in May, 1874.[112] The artist believed that the appointment was "a mere accident" on the part of the Governor, who had acted, as he stated shortly afterward, without the advice of the group of politicians for whose "selfish ends" a Metropolitan Police bill for Kansas City had been passed by the Legislature during the previous winter.[113] Taking full advantage of his new powers, however, Bingham later informed Rollins: ". . . the first evening after we were installed in power, I had, in the course of one hour, from two to three hundred gamblers turned out on the streets, and every gambling house in the city suppressed and that without the slightest disturbance of the peace."[114] Within two weeks he could report with some finality: "The gamblers are driven beyond our limits. The saloons are all closed on Sunday, no blood has been shed, and *'peace reigns all along the line.'* "[115]

During the next few months, Bingham's name was submitted as a candidate for Congress before the state nominating convention, but by late August it was announced that he had withdrawn his candidacy "rather than take the oath to support the nominee, because he considered one of his competitors a man unworthy of his support."[116]

112. May 11, 1874 (*MHR*, XXXIII [1939], p. 354, note 5).
113. Letter, Kansas City, May 26, 1874 (*MHR*, XXXIII [1939], 354).
114. *Ibid.*
115. Letter, Kansas City, June 7, 1874 (*MHR*, XXXIII [1939], 355).
116. Rusk, *op. cit.*, p. 88 (from the Missouri Statesman, Aug. 28, 1874). Also *Missouri Republican*, Sept. 2, 1874, 5; *Jefferson City People's Tribune*, Sept. 16, 1874, 2-4; *ibid.*, Sept. 30, 1874, 1-6.

Early in January, 1875, the artist was appointed Adjutant-General by the new governor,[117] and shortly afterward he took up residence in Jefferson City. Later that month, Governor Hardin instructed Bingham to investigate an unfortunate incident in Clay County which had grown out of the various attempts then being made to apprehend the notorious James brothers.[118] On another occasion the governor sent him to Ripley County to handle a troublesome situation being caused there by a band of desperadoes.[119] As part of his duties he also investigated war claims, during the course of which he discovered that many were actually fraudulent. As one newspaper of the time put it: "If Geo. C. Bingham, Adjutant-General, is not 'the head center' of Hardin's administration, it cannot be questioned that he is 'the head scenter' of the fraudulent military claims."[120]

Early in 1876 he was sent to Washington to urge through Congress a bill adjusting Missouri's war claims. He drew up the bill himself, stating that it

... consists of the claims of citizens for supplies furnished Federal Troops and state militia ... and a separate claim of the State for additional reimbursement for moneys expended in the payment of her Militia for services rendered during the War, said moneys being expended since the settlement of her account for like expenditures, in 1866, and consequently not included in said amount.[121]

Bingham spent about four months in Washington on the matter, returning to Jefferson City on May 1.[122]

117. *MHR*, XXXIII (1939), p. 356, note 6.
118. Refers to attack on home of Reuben Samuels, stepfather of the James boys, Jan. 26, 1875, during which a young stepbrother was killed and the mother severely injured. The Governor was requested by the State legislature to look into the matter. Bingham was sent to report on the affair, and was in Liberty on his way to the scene, Jan. 31 *(Liberty Tribune,* Feb. 5, 1875, 2-1, 2-3). He made his report immediately afterward *(ibid.,* Feb. 12, 1875, 1-4, 2-1).
119. Rusk, *op. cit.,* pp. 100-101 (from the *Daily Tribune,* Aug. 30, 1876). According to this account "a ku-klux organization" made up of about thirty members "was doing much damage and creating great excitement" in the area, and "while Bingham was there, nine members of the band were arrested and the names of the remainder were ascertained."
120. *Missouri Statesman,* Nov. 12, 1875, 2-1. Bingham's report in *Missouri Republican,* Oct. 28, 1875, 5. Rusk, *op. cit.,* pp. 98-99 (from *Missouri Adjutant General's Report, 1875-76,* submitted Dec. 31, 1876). It was probably in connection with his disclosure of these frauds, committed during his predecessor's administration, that Bingham was described by one newspaper as having been "malignantly denounced as an enemy to the Democratic party, and an intermeddler in business that did not concern him." The newspaper account maintained that "undeterred by these unfriendly indications, he prosecuted his work without fear or favor till the completed exposure showed that there was, probably, a combination engaged in the fraud, and that it had official assistance in the work" *(Liberty Tribune,* Jan. 7, 1876, 2-4, from *St. Louis Republican).* Indictments were made against the perpetrators, but Bingham estimated that they would likely escape punishment through political manipulation, but added, in a letter to Rollins, Dec. 3, 1876: "If others permit them to escape it will be nothing to me. Having done my duty I can rest easy on the subject." *(MHR,* XXXIII [1939], 376).
121. B. to R., letter, Washington, D.C., March 9, 1876, coll. SHSMo *(MHR,* XXXIII [1939], 357).
122. *The Daily Tribune,* May 2, 1876, 1-2.

At this time there also was some mention being made of Bingham's possible candidacy for the governor's seat.[123] His own view of the idea was contained in a letter he wrote to Rollins from Washington:

As to my candidacy for Governor, I hold it, for the present, among the scarcely probable things of the future. The little money in the position has caused it, in these sordid times, to be underrated, but I regard it as second only to that of president of the U. S. States. yet my modesty need not prevent me from saying that my ability to fill it is equal to that of some who have ocupied [sic] it, and if you can succeed in arousing a hopeful public sentiment in my favor I may venture to make the race.

If I should do so, and succeed, after the treachery which defeated you, it will be but another exemplification of the fact, that, in a republic like ours, secondary ability often grasps the prize which is due only to the first.[124]

Upon his return to Missouri, evidently with some preliminary effort on Rollins' part, his name was seriously put forth in connection with the high post. As the date for the meeting of the state convention drew closer, Bingham advised his friend of his stand: "If I conclude to become a candidate for the nomination for Gov. I will immediately make public my position in regard to important matters which concern our state. I will denounce rings clicks [sic] and political combinations of every kind for selfish purposes, and declare war against corruption whether Democratic or Republican."[125] Not long afterward, however, he announced his decision to abandon any idea of competing for the Governorship, in view of the "political condition to which our state is tending." He told of his future plans in a letter to Rollins: "I expect as soon as my present duties are ended to return to my profession and devote myself thereto during the few years that life and sufficient health may be granted me. I have lost all party feeling. . . ."[126]

Shortly after his return to Missouri in May, 1876, tragedy struck the artist's household. His wife suffered a severe mental aberration, and he was finally compelled to place her in the state asylum at Fulton, where she died on November 3.[127] (A number of unpublished letters [restricted, coll. SHSMo] written by Bingham to his friend Rollins refer to his great distress during this period.) Bingham was badly shaken by the event, but determined to stay in his post at Jefferson City until the work of his office was completed, or for as long as the governor desired him to remain, despite the fact that he no longer felt any enthusiasm for public service and now preferred to devote

123. *Missouri Republican*, Feb. 21, 1876, 5; March 24, 1876, 3.
124. Letter, March 9, 1876 (*MHR*, XXXIII [1939], 357-358).
125. B. to R., letter, Jefferson City, May 26, 1876, coll. SHSMo (*MHR*, XXXIII [1939], 367).
126. B. to R., letter, Jefferson City, June 29, 1876, coll. SHSMo (*MHR* XXXIII [1939], 370).
127. *Missouri Republican*, Oct. 29, 1876, 3; *Jefferson City People's Tribune*, Nov. 8, 1876, 3-5; *Missouri Statesman*, Nov. 10, 1876, 3-5.

himself to his art.[128] As he confessed in a note to Rollins on December 14:

By pursuing my art profession as in the more happy period of my past life I think I will find much greater comfort than attends the discharge of the thankless duties of public office. I now covet freedom and cheerful society. The latter especially is invaluable to me under by great bereavement, and as an artist I am more likely to have its benefit than when shut up as now in the narrow confines of an office.[129]

When Bingham occupied his position on the Board of Police Commissioners in Kansas City, and especially later as Adjutant-General, he had necessarily to devote a large part of his time to his official duties. As an artist his efforts were now evidently given over almost completely to portrait painting in the "pot-boiling" sense. He had obviously looked forward to an opportunity to spend a winter in New York in 1873, painting once more as the artist of the western scene, and he must have bemoaned the loss of that chance as time went on. And the "thankless duties of a public office" only increased the sense of frustration he had begun to feel during these declining years.

His single figure composition of these years, "The Puzzled Witness" (A363; plate 184), was executed during his term on the Board of Police Commissioners, and its unusual subject matter suggests a direct inspiration from his experience in that office. The painting was not quite finished when it was placed on exhibition in St. Louis late in November, 1874.[130] While there it was described at some length by a visiting art critic:

We dropped in at Harding's on Olive street a few days since to find a picture of Capt. Geo. C. Bingham's on exhibition. We are all familiar with the "County Election," "The Flatboatmen," and similar works of this artist, which in their way are equal in their wonderful exactness of character and surroundings to any that have appeared from the pencils of Wilkie, to whom in his remarkable power to transfer peculiarities of familiar action, Capt. Bingham bears a striking resemblance. "Puzzling a Witness" is one of these pictures of western life, recognizable at once as faithful to the circumstances as art could make it. We are in the office of a country justice of the peace. There is the "court," the opposing lawyer, the defendant, the jury and the witness on the stand, all taken from the streets of a country town, as familiar as the post office itself, and in the homespun which we all know so well in the land of the granger. The artist has seized upon the strong moment. The witness for the prosecution is up, and the attorney for the defense has just put a puzzler to him. It is a stunner. The witness is, in point of fact, stumped. He scratches his head for the answer, but it don't seem to be there, or perhaps it is a neat bit of acting. There is a dog belonging to the witness. That dog looks as if he would be gratified in going for a pound or two of that prosecuting attorney

128. B. to R., letter, Jefferson City, Dec. 3, 1876, coll. SHSMo (*MHR*, XXXIII [1939], 377).
129. B. to R., letter, Jefferson City, Dec. 14, 1876, coll. SHSMo (*MHR*, XXXIII [1939], 378).
130. The picture was on exhibition at Harding's Store on Olive Street, St. Louis (*Missouri Republican*, Nov. 29, 1874, 8). George M. Harding was a dealer in "looking glasses and picture frames."

who has stumped his master. Then there is the lawyer on the other side. He is satisfied with his witness, and smiles as if to say, "well, when you have made anything of that witness, just call around and tell me, will you." The story is capitally told, and will add greatly to the reputation of Capt. Bingham, who, as it is, stands unequivocably at the head of his profession in this country as what may be called a character artist. The picture required a few finishing touches, and has been taken to Kansas City, but will be returned in about a week to Harding's for exhibition.[131]

In his recognition of Bingham's "striking resemblance" to Wilkie in his "remarkable power to transfer peculiarities of familiar action," the critic was making an observation that appears to have been missed by his peers, who had often enough compared Bingham to his American contemporary William Sidney Mount (himself at times referred to as the "American Wilkie"). It was actually a very astute observation, since we have been already able to show that Bingham had very probably turned to the Scottish master from the outset of his career as a painter of genre.

"The Puzzled Witness" was still in the artist's possession in 1879 and was included in the Administrator's Sale of 1893, when it was sold to Judge James E. Gibson of Kansas City.

The composition has already been discussed in another connection.[132] Stylistically, the painting lacks the spirit and vitality of the earlier genre subjects. The stilted appearance of the figures and the dryness of the handling recall "Order No. 11," although the painter obviously attempts to recapture some of the atmospheric organization of the pictures he produced before 1856.

Several brief sketches, contained on small sheets of paper formerly mounted in a scrapbook kept by Major Rollins (S116, S120; plates 185, 186) and now in the collection of the State Historical Society of Missouri, seem related to the composition. They were probably made during the time the artist was developing the picture. Although not to be considered as preparatory drawings for "Puzzling the Witness," they nevertheless reveal his obvious concentration on the painting then in hand. Long considered as idle scribbles created merely for the entertainment of the Rollins children, the sketches are actually far more significant; they show the continuing characteristic strength of line of the graphic style of the artist, and, in some examples, reveal his respect for the works of the old masters in brief notations of such compositions as Titian's "Lavinia" and "Danae."

While Bingham was in Washington in the early months of 1876, awaiting the settlement of state military claims, he occupied part of his time in painting.

131. *Missouri Statesman*, Dec. 11, 1874, 1-5 (from *St. Louis Republican*).
132. See above, p. 117.

240

He had been requested by a group of ladies from Missouri to lend some of his work to the forthcoming Centennial Exposition at Philadelphia.[133] It is important to observe that he decided to submit portraits, choosing as his subjects Miss Vinnie Ream, the sculptress, and Miss Florence Crittenden Coleman, granddaughter of John J. Crittenden of Kentucky. Bingham wrote at some length to Rollins about the portrait of Vinnie Ream:

As to your dear little friend Vinnie my wife had been in advance of you in the request that I would avail myself of the leizure [sic] forced upon me here, to paint her portrait. As she has in her possession a portrait of herself painted by the distinguished artist Healy which I am forced to regard as a failure, I hesitated to comply with my wifes request fearing that where such generally recognized ability had failed I might fail also. As the dear little woman, however, expressed her willing[ness] to risk the result, I commenced the work in her own studio. It is now nearly completed, and I am gratified in knowing that it gives satisfaction to herself family and those who rank as her best friends. Voorhees of Indianna [sic] appears chief of these last. He is delighted with the portrait and claims the honor of contributing to it an appropriate frame. I represent her in her simple working costume, as engaged in modeling the bust of President Lincoln.[134]

This undoubtedly refers to the portrait (A372; plate 187) that remained in the possession of the subject and was presented to the State Historical Society of Missouri by her husband, General Robert L. Hoxie. In this three-quarter length portrait, Vinnie Ream appears as described by the artist in his letter. She stands beside her bust of Lincoln, looking out toward the spectator, as if interrupted during the course of her work. The composition was not an original conception of the painter, however. He appears to have used a photograph (plate 188), probably taken some years earlier, showing the young sculptress in the same pose and with the same accessories. Bingham simply reversed the composition, reduced its size, and rearranged some of the details to form a more interesting picture. 'It seems probable, however, that the subject posed for the head. The general weakness of the conception of the form beneath the drapery, particularly the left arm, may possibly be accounted for by the lack of contact with the model during that phase of the work, and a resultant dependence on the photograph. However, the over-all result is a smooth, decorative painting in keeping with the style of the artist at the time.

Bingham actually executed two portraits of Vinnie Ream, probably within the same period. The second portrait (A373), representing the subject playing her favorite instrument, the harp, was also once owned by Miss Ream, and later given to the State Historical Society of Wisconsin by General Hoxie.

133. *The Daily Tribune*, April 30, 1876, 2-1.
134. B. to R., letter, Washington, D.C., April 13, 1876, coll. SHSMo (*MHR*. XXXIII [1939], 363-364).

Apart from the fact that the harp could be directly associated with the sitter, it was also a motif popularly used by fashionable English portrait painters of the eighteenth and nineteenth centuries. Stylistically, the second portrait is closely related to its better-known companion, although it is the more elaborate of the two in terms of accessories and details.

The portrait of Miss Coleman has not been located and the subject's descendants are not aware of the existence of this painting.[135]

Bingham's long sojourn in Washington came under some scrutiny at home. One critic wondered why the state should support the artist's residence in the East, "when the law requires, and his business is, to live at Jefferson City at his own expense."[136] Direct reference was also made to his portrait painting activity in the capital. Bingham felt outraged and made a forceful reply to the editor of the newspaper in which the criticism appeared, springing to the defense of the young women he had painted and whose names he believed had been maliciously introduced into the matter.[137] The editor's rebuttal gave Bingham little satisfaction; it referred to him as "that chronic and sputtering old railer" and to his "chivalry" with regard to the ladies as "ridiculous and unnecessary."[138]

A portrait of Dr. Alexander M. Davison (A370; plate 189) has been dated 1876,[139] probably painted shortly after Bingham's return to Jefferson City from Washington. A strong, forceful portrait treated in simple, direct terms, it belongs to the first line of Bingham's style, and is closely related to such earlier portraits as that of Dr. Sappington of about 1844/1845 (plate 130). The sculptural modeling of the head and the reduction of detail is quite removed from the smoother, more elaborate portrait style he affected during the years immediately following his European experience.

The artist's self-portrait (A378; plate 190), said to have been painted about 1877,[140] is a slightly milder portrayal, the planes of the head being handled in a more fluid manner, while retaining much of the character and simplicity that place the Davison portrait among the best produced by the artist at the time. It actually falls beween the two stylistic lines adopted by Bingham, although leaning heavily in the direction of his earlier achievements.

135. Verbally, Mrs. Florence Crittenden Booth Wigglesworth, Washington, D.C., Dec., 1955, a direct descendant of the subject.
136. *The Daily Tribune*, May 4, 1876, 2-1.
137. *Missouri Statesman*, May 10, 1876, 1-4 (letter dated May 8); also in *Missouri Republican*, May 10, 1876, 4.
138. *The Daily Tribune*, May 16, 1876, 2-2 (letter dated May 11); also in *Missouri Republican*, May 13, 1876, 5.
139. Rusk, *op. cit.*, p. 125.
140. *Ibid.*, p. 126.

242

Although self-portraits of the artist at work before his easel or at his drawing board can be found in prototypes of the seventeenth century, it seems more than possible that Bingham derived his own immediate inspiration from a more contemporary source, the then well-known self-portrait of the popular Sir Edwin Landseer (plate 191). Despite the shift in the placement of the figure and the obvious elimination of the canine spectators, there are decided points of resemblance between the two pictures, particularly in the arrangement of the hands.

Bingham's awareness of Landseer at this time, an awareness that must have bordered on admiration, can be considered as probably more than mere conjecture. Recently a hitherto unknown Bingham painting of two dogs, titled by its owner "Guarding Their Master's Hat" (A381) turned up during the preparation of a Bingham exhibition at Kansas City's Nelson Gallery.[141] Without question a close copy after Landseer's "Spaniels of King Charles' Breed,"[142] the picture probably dates from the same period as the self-portrait. Perhaps it would not be too far-fetched a notion to consider the self-portrait a further tribute on Bingham's part of his enthusiasm for yet another master of the English school.

Although Bingham had long since learned the value of the use of various reproductive sources for his own pictures, the actual copying of the work of another artist must be considered a much rarer occurrence. The copies he made after engravings of Sully's "Fanny Kemble" and Vanderlyn's "Ariadne," both executed by him more than three decades earlier, seem to have been painted as evidences of his growing prowess as a painter, and all contemporary documentation indicates that there was certainly no attempt on his part to conceal his sources. Certainly one cannot assume a similar demonstration to be at the basis of the Landseer copy. Any possible Landseer inspiration must be regarded as a late one and of no importance in the evolution of Bingham's style. In this instance, the copy of what was undoubtedly a very

141. *George Caleb Bingham, Sesquicentennial Exhibition*... [held at] William Rockhill Nelson Gallery of Art, Kansas City, Mo., March 16-April 30, 1961; City Art Museum, St. Louis, Mo., May 16-June 30, 1961; #43, illus. *(The Nelson Gallery and Atkins Museum Bulletin*, Vol. III, no. 3). The painting, in the collection of Dr. Joseph B. Williams, Los Angeles, Calif., is signed "Geo. Bingham," a version of his signature which the artist adopted in only three other instances now known: "Colorado Mountain Landscape," which originally belonged to the same owner as the Landseer copy (both pictures reportedly the artist's gift to a favored student); and "The Belated Wayfarers" and "Captured by Indians," a pair of genre subjects originally in the collection of Charles Derby of St. Louis.
142. The painting was also known as "The Cavalier's Pets." Bingham very probably based his copy upon an engraving, possibly the one that appeared in *The Vernon Gallery of British Art. Engravings from the Works of British Artists in the National Gallery, Presented to the Nation by the Late Robert Vernon, Esq*... [London]: published for the Proprietors [1849-1854]). The subject was evidently very popular, for it was widely copied by artists as well as reproduced for commercial purposes.

popular subject by Landseer seems to have been destined for presentation purposes, further evidenced by the use of the less formal signature ("Geo. Bingham").

That the idea of securing a national commission still occupied Bingham's thoughts is evidenced by the correspondence he exchanged with Rollins while he was in Washington in March, 1876. Rollins had evidently suggested that the artist seek out Missouri's Representatives in Congress and attempt to persuade them to put through a bill in the House granting him a national picture commission. If he could succeed in that, Rollins had promised to come to the Capitol "at any sacrifice and aid in putting it through the Senate."[143] But the artist felt that the Missouri Representatives would not see matters in the same way, and so informed his friend:

You know that very few of our delegation have any taste for, or knowledge of Art, and I have therefore said nothing to them upon the subject of an Art commission for my benefit. Your proposed letter to them, may perhaps interest them in the matter, but in the fierce struggle now pending for party ascendancy I have but a feeble hope, that if disposed to do so, they would be able to effect the passage of such a bill, unless the subject, for the picture, which you may suggest, shall commend itself to a common sentiment entertained by both political parties, in such a manner as to excite the predjudices [sic] of neither.[144]

Bingham finally advised Rollins that he thought it best to plan to come to Washington during the following winter, open a studio near the Capitol, bringing along his paintings and the engravings made after other of his compositions, and thus "attract the notice of Congress and give evidence of my ability to execute a work quite equal to any which now adorns the Capitol."[145] The plan was never carried out.

The artist was apparently relieved of his duties as Adjutant-General early in 1877. At about that time he announced, in a dispatch from Boonville, that he planned to retire from public life in order to devote himself to painting, indicating a desire to settle in Boonville.[146] On June 5, however, a School of Art was established at the University of Missouri, in Columbia, and Bingham was immediately elected to the post of professor of art.[147] From then on he did indeed concern himself almost entirely with art matters, as he had promised—although the old fire still continued to blaze fiercely every time he sensed what he firmly believed to be a breach of truth and justice, particularly

143. Letter, March 9, 1876 (*MHR*, XXXIII [1939], 356). Evidently a direct quotation from Rollins' letter.
144. *Ibid.*
145. B. to R., letter, Washington, D.C., March 25, 1876, coll. SHSMo (*MHR*, XXXIII [1939], 362).
146. *Missouri Republican*, Jan. 20, 1877, 2.
147. *Boonville Weekly Eagle*, June 22, 1877, 2-5. At the annual meeting of the Curators of the University, June 5-7, 1877, the artist was elected Professor of Art; the School of Art itself was established at this meeting.

244

the various continuing attempts to whitewash General Ewing and "Order No. 11" during these years.[148]

While he was still in office, and thinking of the hoped-for days ahead which he could devote completely to painting, Bingham discussed with Rollins a subject for a new historical picture. It referred to an episode taken from the career of Andrew Jackson—representing his submission to the judgment of a Civil Court at New Orleans.[149] The proposal was eventually brought before the Legislature, and by late March, 1877, the artist was authorized to execute the picture,[150] although the terms of the commission provided no assurance of payment to the artist and gave the State the privilege of rejecting it upon completion. Bingham was greatly displeased with the terms of the commission, and had already decided against accepting it, when he explained his stand in a letter addressed from Jefferson City on April 18:

I did not consider it any compliment to be commissioned to devote two or three years of my life in painting a picture for my State, with the understanding that the State was not to be bound to pay for it. If my life and health shall be spared so as to enable me to execute the picture, it will more likely become the property of my native State of Virginia than of my adopted State of Missouri, as I will naturally feel no disposition to subject it to the refusal of our State Legislature. In my present condition however it suits me best to paint portraits chiefly as in doing so I am more constantly brought into agreeable association with appreciative friends.[151]

Early in July the artist was in Boonville, where he was indeed able to spend considerable time in "agreeable association with appreciative friends," at the home of Thomas Withers Nelson and his family.[152] He had painted portraits of various members of the family in years past, and was now engaged to execute a number of new commissions which were to fully occupy his time until early in the fall. He was still at the Nelson homestead when he wrote to Rollins

148. Ewing revived the issue himself on January 1, 1877, when he addressed his former superior officer, General Schofield, requesting a statement on the still controversial matter of the infamous Order. The Schofield reply, clearing Ewing of any blame, duly appeared in the press. Bingham lost no time in returning to the fray, answering Schofield in an article which appeared under the published heading "A Scorcher." In fact, he relentlessly pursued Ewing to end of his days. Two weeks before his death, the artist revived the matter in a letter "making a bitter attack upon the kind of Democracy which permitted the nomination of Order No. 11 Ewing for the gubernatorial honors" (Ewing was then running for Governor of Ohio). The published letter appeared in at least one Ohio newspaper, as well as the various Missouri papers. Former Missouri Governor B. Gratz Brown then replied to Bingham, and the artist's final words on the subject, in preparation at the time of his death—his reply to Brown—were published shortly afterward under the heading "A Voice from the Grave." (*Missouri Republican*, Feb. 21, Feb. 26, 1877; *The Daily Tribune*, Feb. 27, March 1, March 7, 1877; *Cincinnati Commercial*, June 17, 1879; *Missouri Statesman*, June 20, 1879; *St. Louis Post-Dispatch*, July 23, 1879).
149. Letter, Jefferson City, Mo., Dec. 14, 1876 (*MHR*, XXXIII [1939], 378-379).
150. *Jefferson City People's Tribune*, March 22, 1877, 1-4.
151. B. to R., letter, Jefferson City, Mo., April 18, 1877, coll. SHSMo (*MHR*, XXXIII [1939], 380).
152. *Missouri Statesman*, July 6, 1877, 2-1.

245

from Boonville on September 9: "Two portraits which I have painted here of my friend Mrs Nelson and her daughter Mrs Birch of St. Louis, are kindly loaned to me for the present, and will be sent to me from St. Louis as soon as they can be framed. They are, I think, the best female portraits that I have ever painted, and may show that my skill rather increases than diminishes with increasing years."[153] Bingham was referring to the two three-quarter length portraits he had just completed of Mrs. Thomas Withers Nelson (Mary Gay Wyan) and Mrs. James Thomas Birch (Margaret Elizabeth Nelson)[154] (A375, A376), both of whom had sat for him in earlier years. The portraits represent the sitters in outdoor settings, an idea the artist had adopted on other occasions. Landscape elements, introduced as window arrangements in other-wise interior settings, first appeared in the portraits he executed shortly after his return from Europe. Mrs. Nelson's portrait, now in the Boonville Public Library, shows the subject dressed in a riding habit against a landscape back-drop. Her daughter's portrait (plate 192) reveals her in a garden setting, holding a bouquet of flowers in her hand. It is a well-composed, richly decora-tive painting on which the artist obviously lavished much attention insofar as detail and finish is concerned; it is also one of the few portraits he deemed important enough to sign and date.

If Bingham's long established *modus operandi* can be applied in this in-stance, it would appear to be no mere coincidence that the portrait of Mrs. Birch bears more than a passing relationship with the well-known etching of "Spring" (Parthey 610) (plate 193) from the series of "Seasons" by Wenzel Hollar. The composition of Hollar's figure, shown in three-quarter view look-ing out toward the spectator, could scarcely have failed to attract Bingham's attention, since it had long been a pose he had favored for his portraits. In Mrs. Birch's portrait the pose has been retained almost without change, the only alterations being in the arrangement of the hands. The left hand has been slightly raised, perhaps to display the jewelry better, while the flowers have been shifted to the right hand, with some modification. The column in the background of the Birch portrait had become by this time a characteristic feature of Bingham's more important portraits, but, as in the Hollar design, the enframement of the left side of the design serves to afford the composition greater stability and spatial importance, as well as allowing for the introduc-tion of the landscape and atmospheric sky at right which acts as an enriching backdrop for the figure.

153. B. to R., letter, Boonville, Mo., Sept. 9, 1877, coll. SHSMo (*MHR*, XXXIII [1939], 382).
154. Very probably the "handsome portrait" of Mrs. Birch which was announced as "among other works" he had accomplished during his stay at the Nelson home (Boonville *Weekly Topic*, Aug. 18, 1877).

The only known landscape by Bingham that is actually a "portrait" of a gentleman's estate, as well as a kind of "conversation piece," was also executed during the Boonville stay. It is the composition depicting "Forest Hill," the Nelson homestead (plate 122), which has already been discussed in another section.[155]

Leaving Boonville during the latter part of September, Bingham came to Columbia to superintend his studio arrangements, then located in the English and Art School building on the University campus. He was especially anxious to have the studio "somewhat tastefully fitted up and furnished in harmony with the purpose for which it is intended," knowing as he did that many strangers would be attracted to the place. He wished to include a number of casts after the antique in the furnishings, feeling that these were "indispensable" for study purposes. He planned also to have several of his own paintings sent down from Kansas City. The artist was permitted to use the studio provided by the University for his professional purposes, as well as for teaching, and he was not required to be in constant attendance, even during the school year. His arrangement was, in a large sense, not dissimilar to that of present-day artists in residence provisions adopted by a number of universities and colleges.

We know relatively little of Bingham's actual teaching activities during his tenure as a professor of art at the University. He never developed a school or a following, although he was evidently sought after for instruction at various times during his career. A few years before the University appointment, another Missouri painter, Charles P. Stewart, was reported to have left Columbia for Kansas City, "to study his profession and practice it beneath the eye" of Bingham, but within two months he had returned to his Columbia studio, with no further mention being made about any benefits he may have gained from the experience.[156] And a Virginia portrait painter, Henry James Brown, was said to have studied with Bingham in Missouri at a somewhat earlier period.[157] It was certainly not unusual for an artist of prominence to take on private pupils, but Bingham does not seem to have indulged in that activity in any consistent way.

In November, 1877, having learned that Congress had made a large appropriation to have the United States favorably represented at the forthcoming Paris Exposition, Bingham expressed a wish to be appointed a delegate from Missouri. He sought his friend's assistance in that direction:

155. See above, p. 183.
156. *Missouri Statesman*, July 15, 1870, 3-1; Sept. 9, 1870, 3-2.
157. Henry James Brown was b. Woodlawn Plantation, Cumberland County, Va., 1811; d. Buckingham Female Seminary, Va., 1855. Besides Bingham, the artist studied under Thomas Sully in Philadelphia, 1845. (G. C. Groce and D. H. Wallace, *Dictionary of Artists in America ...*, p. 86.)

I beleive [*sic*] by writing to your friend Schurtz [*sic*] and others who may have influence with the President, you can likely secure my appointment as delegate. My being an artist of long standing reputation and now professor of Art in the University of Missouri ought to give strength to my claims. I suppose you can have me recommended by Doct Laws and professors of our University and also by your friend Doct. Reed [*sic*].[158]

Rollins evidently did what he could to effect an appointment for Bingham, and after two honorary commissioners from Missouri were named in January of the following year, he encouraged him to consider his chances still good for an assistant commissionership.[159] But the desired appointment did not materialize.

Although his health had improved, Bingham had planned to go to Texas during the winter months, but he deferred the trip pending the possible appointment to Paris. When he was relatively certain that he would not receive one, he decided to go to Washington in an attempt to settle an old claim for the Thomas estate still pending before the Senate Committee, and also make the stay "both pleasant and profitable by painting portraits."[160] He arrived in the capital about the middle of February. With him he had brought several unfinished portraits, including the full-length painting of little Eulalie Hockaday, granddaughter of Major Rollins, the "Palm Leaf Shade," and a new version of "The Jolly Flatboatmen."[161] Of these pictures, the "Palm Leaf Shade" and the portrait of Eulalie Hockaday, better known as "Red Riding Hood," remain as typical examples of the final phase of Bingham's work.

The "Palm Leaf Shade" (A380; plate 194), said to be a portrait of Margaret Elizabeth Nelson Birch, is one of the painter's most attractive efforts in his decorative style. The background is opened up completely to landscape elements, and the entire picture takes on the sunny aspect of the outdoors, in terms of light and shade and color. It is probably the first portrait in which Bingham was able to capture successfully a unified atmospheric effect of this kind. In the portrait of Mrs. Birch, painted in Boonville in 1877, and the earlier portrayal of John J. Mastin, the landscape settings seem to act merely as backdrops, while the figures are handled in terms of indoor lighting, despite the artist's effort to relate figure and background through association motifs.

Although the actual resemblance to Mrs. Birch is unmistakable, the portrait

158. B. to R., letter, Kansas City, Nov. 4, 1877, coll. SHSMo (*MHR*. XXXIII [1939], 383). Refers to Carl Schurz (1829-1906), statesman: Minister to Spain, 1861, U.S. Senator from Missouri, 1869-1875, Secretary of Interior under Hayes, 1877; Samuel Spahr Laws (1824-1921), seventh President of the University of Missouri; Daniel Read, President of the University of Missouri, 1866-1876.
159. B. to R., letter, Kansas City, Jan. 20, 1878, coll. SHSMo (*MHR*. XXXIII [1939], 502).
160. B. to R., letter, Kansas City, Jan. 31, 1878, coll. SHSMo (*MHR*. XXXIII [1939], 505-506).
161. Letter, Feb. 22, 1878 (*MHR*. XXXIII [1939], 511).

is still an idealized one, the painter being obviously more interested in creating a specific mood and pictorial effect. The motif of the fan may have been inspired by a vignette engraving by John Cheney after a painting by Thomas Sully, the "Lady with Fan" (plate 195), which appeared in a gift annual in 1839.[162]

The portrait of Eulalie Hockaday as "Little Red Riding Hood" (A390; plate 196) was not completed until early in 1879.[163] It was commissioned by the subject's grandfather, Major Rollins, and was intended for presentation to her when she came of age.[164] When seen in the artist's studio in Columbia in March, 1879, it was described as the "most beautiful and attractive"[165] picture there. The full-length figure of the child is presented life-size within a woodland landscape setting. She moves toward the spectator, wearing a scarlet cape and hood over a cerulean blue dress. Her dark hair contrasts strongly with the bright colors of her garments, and the red-striped stockings below the peeping pantaloon form an additional coloristic note. As "Red Riding Hood," she carries the familiar basket to her grandmother, and the artist has introduced even the traditional wolf in the background. Unfortunately, the landscape appears to have no real relationship to the figure. The hard studio look and finish of the portrait contrast sharply with the light, atmospheric effect he achieved in the "Palm Leaf Shade."

Bingham always had difficulty with his portraits of the very young, and this is no exception. The body is stumpy and formless, and the head seems overlarge for the figure that supports it. It is strictly a tour de force, and as such a somewhat sad note on which to conclude our consideration of the artist's work. On the other hand, the picture is an extremely interesting one, revealing as it does the painter's continuing preoccupation throughout his career with ideas borrowed from older sources. It is obvious that Bingham derived this composition, with little alteration, from the portrait of Emily Anderson as "Little Red Riding Hood" (plate 197) by Sir Thomas Lawrence, which had been engraved by John Sartain for a gift book in 1852.[166] The artist undoubtedly knew this engraving or another made after the well-known picture. The motif was a popular one in this country, too; at least thirteen paintings of that title appeared between 1838 and 1866 in exhibitions of the National

162. *The Gift, a Christmas and New Years Present for 1839* ... (Philadelphia: E. L. Carey & A. Hart, [1838]).
163. The painting was described as "one of the artist's greatest efforts" while it was on exhibition in Bingham's studio in the Normal Building of the University in February, 1879 *(Missouri Republican,* Feb. 9, 1879, from *Columbia Herald-Statesman)*.
164. *Missouri Statesman,* March 7, 1879, 2-4.
165. *Ibid.*
166. *The Wild Flower, a Gift Book for the Holydays, for 1852* ... (Philadelphia: J. & J. L. Gibson, 1852), opp. p. 103. Since Bingham apparently referred to an engraving after the Lawrence portrait as early as 1837, he undoubtedly knew other sources of reproduction (see p. 33, note 59).

Academy of Design and the American Art-Union in New York, and of the Pennsylvania Academy and the Artists Fund Society in Philadelphia.

Bingham's correspondence during the early months of 1878 also revealed a growing affection for an "old and dear friend" in Kansas City, Martha A. Livingston Lykins, the widow of Dr. Johnston Lykins. He probably discussed marriage with the lady before he left for the East. Mrs. Lykins named the date of their wedding in a letter received by the artist in Washington late in February.[167]

Bingham left Washington in the spring and traveled to Texas, primarily to visit with his daughter Clara and her family.[168] One can presume that he wished especially to inform her personally of his forthcoming marriage. He returned to Kansas City by the latter part of May and the wedding took place on June 18 at the Lykins Institute, a Home for Widows and Orphans of Confederate Veterans, of which Mrs. Lykins was the principal. The couple left immediately afterward for Colorado.[169]

On his return to Missouri Bingham planned to exhibit some of his latest pictures at the Kansas City Exposition, "with a view to taking the premiums offered."[170] These included the "Palm Leaf Shade" and the "Jolly Flatboatmen,"[171] both of which he had only recently completed in Washington. He soon changed his mind about entering his pictures in the competition, however:

... as I saw indications which lead me to beleive [sic] that the premiums would be awarded without the slightest regard to the merit of the works. I withheld mine from the competition therefor. I did the same two years ago, and I cannot possibly account for the awards made then and last year, and also some that were made yesterday, upon any supposition, other than they are secured by some influence entirely outside of any real or pretended merit of the productions upon which they were bestowed. When I go to Columbia I will send down my collection to be deposited in my studio. As it no[w] hangs in the exposition gallery, it forms the chief and almost the only Art attraction there.[172]

167. Letter, Feb. 22, 1878 (*MHR*, XXXIII [1939], 512).
168. B. to R., letter, Kansas City, May 24, 1878, coll. SHSMo (*MHR*, XXXIII [1939], 512-513).
169. *Jefferson City Daily Tribune*, June 20, 1878, 1-4; *Jefferson City People's Tribune*, June 26, 1878, 4-5; *Boonville Weekly Advertiser*, June 21, 1878, 4-2; *Missouri Statesman*, June 21, 1878, 2-1.
170. Letter, Kansas City, Aug. 25, 1878, coll. SHSMo (*MHR*, XXXIII [1939], 513). The exposition probably was the Kansas City Industrial Exposition and Agricultural Fair, generally held annually in Mid-September. An examination of the "Premium List" for the 1875 Fair reveals that it was backed by an association "organized on a permanent basis," with fair grounds located within the Kansas City limits. Its buildings included a Fine Art Hall, "built with special reference to displaying most favorably Pictures, Statuary, and all other classes of this Department." There were three classes for cash premiums in the Division of Painting in Oil and Water colors: 1. Best portrait painting in oil, original—Diploma and $15; 2. Best landscape painting in oil, original—Diploma and $15; 3. Best collection of oil paintings—not less than six—first premium, $125, second premium, $75. Bingham was probably hoping to compete successfully for the large cash prize being offered for a collection of paintings.
171. See above, pp. 96-97.
172. B. to R., letter, Kansas City, Sept. 19, 1878, coll. SHSMo (*MHR*. XXXIII [1939], 516).

At about this time Bingham made some outspoken, strongly critical statements about the condition of Missouri politics. He was bitterly opposed to
what he described as "our rotten convention system,"[173] and also was in favor
of impeachment for several of the state's chief officers, including the governor.[174] But Rollins advised him against any involvement.[175]

In the late fall Bingham received word from the governor's office inviting
him to accept an appointment as one of the commissioners of the Lee Monument Association which was to meet in Richmond, Virginia, to select a design
for a monument to General Robert E. Lee. Obviously, the appointment did
not come directly from Governor Phelps, who must have had some inkling
of the artist's criticism of his administration. Bingham's letter to Rollins on
November 3, referring to the circumstances surrounding his appointment,
seems meaningful in that respect:

A few days ago I received a letter from the private secretary of the Governor stating
that his Excellency had been requested by the managers of the Lee Monument Association to appoint me as one of the Commissioners, on the part of our state, who are to
select a design for the monument, and who are to meet in Richmond on the 27th of this
month. The Gov. wishes to know if I will accept such appointment. As the appointmen[t]
will come to me in such a complimentary manner at the special request of the managers
of the Association after our Governor had appointed other parties, I have concluded to
accept it, and will so inform the Secretary in a few days. . . .[176]

Speaking of the appointment, his friends on the *Missouri Statesman* could
only say: "No more honest, capable, or distinguished citizen could have been
chosen, for the performance of so delicate a task, than Missouri's great artist,
Gen'l George C. Bingham."[177] Indeed, Bingham took his responsibility to the
Association, and to the competing artists, very seriously. In order to avoid
the possibility of any political influence being brought to bear on the selection of any one design, he hoped to persuade the commissioners to judge the
models without revealing the names of the artists by whom they were executed.[178] He knew that the competition would be keen and was determined
to judge the designs solely on their merit: "As it will be a matter of considerable importance I will take care to express no judgment which I cannot
defend upon recognized principles of Art."[179]

The artist stopped off in Columbia on the way to Richmond, and again on

173. *Ibid.*
174. Letter, Aug. 25, 1878 (*MHR*, XXXIII [1939], 514).
175. Letter, Sept. 19, 1878 (*MHR*, XXXIII [1939], 516).
176. B. to R., Kansas City, Nov. 3, 1878, coll. SHSMo (*MHR*, XXXIII [1939], 518).
177. *Missouri Statesman*, Nov. 8, 1878, 2-2.
178. B. to R., letter, Columbia, Nov. 12, 1878, coll. SHSMo (*MHR*, XXXIII [1939], 519).
179. *Ibid.*

his return, on November 29.[180] Because of his university commitment and his private commissions, Bingham apparently divided his time between Columbia and Kansas City during this period. He became seriously ill with pneumonia, probably in Columbia, in February, 1879, and spent the following months at his home in Kansas City, recuperating and painting portraits.[181] He was not well enough to give his prepared address on "Art, the Ideal of Art, and the Utility of Art" at the University on March 1, so Major Rollins delivered it in his place.

By mid-May Bingham was able to return to Columbia to complete some unfinished work, remaining there until July 5. Of his activity during this brief period we know relatively little, although Judge North Todd Gentry clearly recalled an event that apparently occurred at the time:

In the spring of 1879 General Bingham gave an exhibit of his pictures in his studio, then in the two-story frame building situated in the Northwest corner of the University of Missouri campus, known as the "English & Art Building." He made a most interesting and instructive talk on how he happened to paint many of his pictures: and he said he had in mind to paint three historical pictures, one to represent a Camp meeting in Missouri, one a County fair in Missouri and one a Circus day in Missouri....[182]

It is perhaps significant to note that even at this late date Bingham still had some ambitious plans in mind for figure pictures of a decidedly western character. Certainly "The Jolly Flatboatmen," which he completed in 1878, is indication enough of his determination to return once more to the field that marked his earlier triumphs and gave him national fame as an artist.

Bingham left Columbia for Kansas City on July 5, seemingly in good health, but on the following day he was suddenly stricken with an attack of what was reported as "cholera morbus," from which he did not recover. He died on the morning of July 7. The many tributes that appeared in the press immediately afterward reveal the esteem in which he was held in the state, both as an artist and as a public figure, despite the often bitter antipathies he incurred through his outspoken public pronouncements. One such pronouncement, a reply to former Governor B. Gratz Brown, relating to General Ewing, was prepared just prior to his death and was published afterward under the heading "A Voice from the Grave."[183] But a more appropriate memorial appeared in a Kansas City paper on the day of his death:

General Bingham was in his 68th year, and no man was better known in Missouri either as an artist, as a powerful writer, or a patriot of incorruptible integrity, always fearless

180. *Missouri Statesman*, Dec. 6, 1878, 3-1.
181. B. to R., letter, Kansas City, May 5, 1879, coll. SHSMo (*MHR*, XXXIII [1939], 520).
182. Statement prepared for the author by Judge N. T. Gentry, Columbia, Mo., 1944 (typescript).
183. *St. Louis Post-Dispatch*, July 23, 1879.

252

and untiring in combating whatever he considered wrong. He had been respected in the councils of Missouri's foremost men for a generation past. His artistic labors have reflected lustre upon the taste and culture of the State. His record both as a citizen and as a public officer employed in trusts that test the purity of men, is one that the whole people may be proud of. His knightly spirit, always ready for the fray in the course of justice, and public morals, was unsubdued, and his brilliant mind was unclouded to the last. Dying at home in the bosom of the community he has served so long and so well, his old neighbors and friends will have the melancholy satisfaction of seeing that he is buried with the honors due to a citizen whose career has been so stainless and so eminent.[184]

184. *Kansas City Mail*, July 7, 1879. Copied in *Jefferson City People's Tribune*, July 16, 1879, 2-2.

XI

BINGHAM'S ACHIEVEMENT

The pattern of Bingham's development as a painter is not an unfamiliar one in the annals of American art during the first half of the nineteenth century. Like many another aspiring artist brought up on the frontier, he was mainly self-trained, his first contacts with art being those pictures he could see produced by some itinerant who happened to be in the neighborhood. Older contemporaries such as Thomas Cole and Chester Harding related to Dunlap that they had gained their own first impressions from itinerants and were inspired to higher efforts by them. Instruction books, the equivalents of today's "do-it-yourself" books, dealing with the theory and practice of painting in its every phase, served to answer some of the questions, and engraved reproductions of the paintings of old and contemporary masters gave some further insight into ideas of design and composition.

Since portrait painting was the one sure means of making a livelihood, especially in those centers away from the eastern seaboard, a young painter wisely chose this field for his first attempts. And Bingham was no exception. A number of the portraits he executed during his earliest years while traveling from town to town in Missouri as an itinerant already show the elements of a style which were to remain characteristic of his portraits during the years to follow. The extant portraits of his first period, dating from about 1834 to 1838, reveal in the primary phase the adoption of a single formula, with the model always maintaining a direct contact with the observer, the rendering hard and brittle though solidly modeled, and but little tactile sense. Already present, however, is that over-all quality which marks the individuality of Bingham's portraits of this period and which continues to characterize his best efforts in his first line, namely, his preoccupation with the literal and his respect for character (e.g., Mrs. Meredith Miles Marmaduke [plate 4], Major

254

James Sidney Rollins [plate 7], Dr. and Mrs. Anthony Wayne Rollins [plates 5, 6], Colonel John Thornton [plate 9]). In the later phase, although he retains the formula, there is a tendency toward a softening of contours, and an obvious attempt to cope with problems of textures as well as to develop some variety in design and composition (e.g., Mrs. David Steele Lamme and her son [plate 20], Mrs. James Sidney Rollins [plate 18]). The trip to St. Louis in 1835 had undoubtedly opened Bingham's eyes to the work of other painters, and for the first time he was able to observe paintings by older masters, or at least tolerably good copies made after them.

The relatively brief visit to the East during the spring of 1838 marks a turning point in Bingham's career. In Philadelphia he could see a number of pictures other than portraits by contemporary Americans, and if he also went to New York, as he must have, he could have benefited by the sight of an even greater variety of pictures by living painters as well as by old masters. He was also to discover a new field of painting for himself there and to return to Missouri with an urge to become an illustrator of the western scene, possibly in emulation of William Sidney Mount who had already earned a reputation in the East for his portrayals of farm life on Long Island. The result was his first subject of genre connotation, "Western Boatmen Ashore," which was exhibited at the Apollo Gallery in New York in the fall of 1838. But a lack of encouragement, which can be considered due at least partly to his technical deficiency, coupled with the necessity of turning again to portrait painting as a means of livelihood, made him put aside at least temporarily any ideas of becoming a genre painter.

Meanwhile the portaits he painted on his return to Missouri, and those executed during the subsequent Washington years, 1840-1844, exhibit an ever-developing painterly breadth. His greater facility now enabled him to cast aside the unvarying, limiting formula that characterized his earlier portraits for so many years, and a variety of highly competent portraits date from this later period (Mrs. Thomas Shackelford [plate 23], Leonidas Wetmore [plate 30], Sallie Ann Camden [plate 33], John Quincy Adams [plate 34], Elizabeth Hutchison Bingham [plate 40]). A decorative quality, acquired through a happier use and variety of textures, particularly in the portraits of women, marks a further development in his style during these and the next few years (Mrs. John Sappington [plate 131], Mrs. William Breathitt Sappington [plate 129], Mrs. James H. Bennett [plate 141]). The influence of Sully is at times visible, although it is not an enduring one—its traces in portraiture being superimposed over the lines formed by Bingham's own style, marked by his insistence on literal and solid characterization ("The Dull Story" [plate 43], Mrs. Jacob Fortney Wyan [plate 132]).

Bingham's serious career as a painter of western genre also gains appreciable momentum at this period. Encouraged now by the patronage of the American Art-Union, which purchased four of his paintings in 1845, including "Fur Traders Descending the Missouri" (plate 50) and "The Concealed Enemy" (plate 75), he felt for the first time in a position to concentrate his attention on a field that was to bring him fame as "The Missouri Artist." From the beginning his compositions reveal a considered and organized plan of approach reflecting a long, careful preparation, each step seemingly planned with the precision of an architect. Taking to heart the lessons taught him by the instruction books, he planned his compositions along lines developed by the old masters, adopting principally the classical pyramidal form as a basic and effective means of figure organization—used at first in the rigid and obvious fashion displayed in "The Jolly Flatboatmen" (1) (plate 53) and later in terms of a more complex and fluid scheme, as in "The Jolly Flatboatmen in Port" (plate 61), "The County Election" (1) (plate 94), and "The Verdict of the People" (1) (plate 104). The formal approach to form and composition that dominated all of Bingham's major efforts as a figure painter have time and again compelled modern critics to sense a classical spirit in his work which suggests a link with the Renaissance-Baroque tradition, and Poussin's name in particular has most frequently been invoked in that connection. Although one can be certain that Bingham never conceived of himself as an "American Poussin," he was naturally drawn into the orbit of the old classical tradition by his search for what was still recognized as proper form and structure in picturemaking. That he was able to develop such extraordinary skill in the construction of the many-figured composition—a challenge to even the most sophisticated of artists—alone deserves Bingham a place among the outstanding painters in American art history.

Certain parallels can be drawn between Bingham and Mount which indicate his close observation of the work of the eastern painter, but the inspiration is actually mainly of a general nature, reflecting similar influences on both men, such as the instruction books and a common admiration for the Scottish painter David Wilkie. A more direct influence, both in form and in specific motif, can be discovered in the works of older masters of all periods which were readily available through the engraved reproduction. Bingham had evidently collected prints after paintings covering a wide range anywhere from Masaccio to Wilkie, and did not appear to hesitate to draw on their forms and ideas for his own use—a means that had actually been used by artists from the moment a method had been found of multiple reproduction of design on paper.

His experience in drawing from the antique was a lesson alike remembered, and thus figures based on well-known classical sculpture turn up in western garb continually throughout his career—"Order No. 11" (plate 164) being perhaps the artist's largest single repository of elements taken from classical antiquity to the eighteenth century. This analysis and digestion of master-pieces in which, according to the "rules," it was possible to mix the Apollo Belvedere with designs derived from Raphael and other masters of the Renaissance and Post-Renaissance places Bingham close to the practice formulated by the classicists more than a hundred years earlier, although the methodology had its roots in an even earlier tradition.

A further lesson that Bingham learned early was the importance of good draughtmanship as a preliminary to painting. Although none of his extant drawings can be dated with any certainty before the mid-1840's—already a period of maturity in the style of the artist—there can be little doubt that his studies in Philadelphia in 1838 and the lessons taught by the drawing books had prepared the way for an understanding of the value of drawing as an essential prerequisite for all his future efforts. The drawings that have come down to us, chiefly from the 1840's and 1850's, reveal a vigorous style, gen-erally broad in handling despite the insistence at all times on precise and descriptive detail which seems to have been based on a penetrating observation of actual models.

By far the finest group of figure drawings by Bingham now known are those in the St. Louis Mercantile Library which appear to have formed a kind of model-book for the artist during his career as a genre painter. They afford us an important clue to the types preferred by the artist during that period: fishermen, boatmen, citizens, politicians, and just plain spectators who watch and listen at those events that Bingham himself must have observed and par-ticipated in. The more we examine these drawings, the more we come to realize that Bingham as an illustrator of the western scene was always highly con-scious of the importance of the observer and of the need to establish for him a feeling of direct contact with his pictorial counterparts.

All of the figures suggest, by their easy manner and gesture, the component parts that make up a familiar Bingham composition. Seen as a whole, they form a fascinating pattern for more complete understanding of the artist's position as a painter of the frontier life he saw and wished others to see. Cer-tainly, like all the painters of realism before him, he instinctively sought out those hardy types that so strongly characterized his place and time—indeed, so familiar and so typical are they that even in Bingham's time his contem-poraries felt sure they could identify the figures with well-known personalities.

257

But this could not have been the artist's intention. He was never a satirist and none of his compositions contain even the mildest suggestion of a Hogarth, despite the fact that he undoubtedly came to know the English master's pictures and was even inspired by at least one of them.

With the downfall of the American Art-Union and its sister organizations in the early 1850's, Bingham lost a necessary patronage which must account to a very large extent for the decline in his productiveness as a genre painter during the succeeding years. There was no similar patronage to fill the breach, either public or private. Thus, with few isolated exceptions, following the completion of his Election series in 1855, Bingham's career as a painter of genre can be said to have ended.

His trip to Europe in 1856, with its prolonged sojourn in Düsseldorf, though not undertaken as a student, nevertheless had its influence on his style. Bingham admired the method of the Düsseldorf School, and in an attempt to acquire some of the technical finish for which the school was noted, his own work lost much of its earlier freshness and spontaneity. Hard, dry outlines and a sameness of textures—characteristics he had sought so long to overcome in his struggle to attain breadth and atmosphere in his pictures—became again the dominant qualities of most of his work after 1860. The period following the return from Germany was one marking a steady decline in the individuality of his production; it was a period of retrogression from which he did not recover.

Also attributable to his stay in Düsseldorf, however, must be the artist's new attraction to the larger pictorial possibilities of portraiture, in which background elements such as landscape form a prominent part of the design. This new attitude is reflected in the second line of his development, which can be traced from the 1859 portrait of Dr. Benoist Troost (plate 157) to the "Little Red Riding Hood" (plate 196) of his last days (1878/1879). But in general the portraits of the later period are dull and dry and lack the attractive positive qualities of many of the earlier paintings. The artist was seemingly more concerned in this period with finish and detail than with the characterization of the sitter. Only occasionally during the years that follow do we discover a portrayal that is reminiscent of his earlier style. Nevertheless, Bingham's local fame as a portrait-painter grew during these years to a point where he could be described as Missouri's first painter in the field. Most of the large public commissions for portraits for the State Capitol and elsewhere came his way. Those western subjects which had formerly gained him national recognition as "The Missouri Artist" no longer figured prominently in his production, although Bingham longed to retain a foothold in the field. But this was not to come to pass, and the artist's name was almost forgotten in the East by the last decade of his life.

Bingham's few excursions in historical painting did not gain him the reward he had thought within his grasp—a national commission. His "Order No. 11," because of its local subject interest, did not add to his reputation beyond the Kansas–Missouri borders, and the excitement it developed at home was actually concerned far more with the political implications of the theme and the man who had conceived it than with any artistic value of the painting itself.

As a landscape painter, Bingham reveals less of himself than in any other phase of his work, although the results are frequently competent. Despite our growing knowledge of this area of his efforts, gained through the relatively recent recovery of a body of pictorial evidence, landscape cannot be considered a significant aspect of his total artistic accomplishment. Perhaps the most significant impression that can be drawn from his extant landscape work relates to the artist's ever-present concern with the problem of structure in composition. His preoccupation with formal composition in the classical sense, so strongly evident in his figure pictures, was equally adopted as an ideal throughout his work as a landscapist. It can indeed be said to be as notable a characteristic of his preliminary studies for imaginary landscapes dating from his first years (plate 106) as of his Colorado subjects from the close of his career in this special field (plate 121).

Although it is more than conceivable that Bingham considered himself a many-sided artist, opportunism and expediency also played important roles in directing his hand at various stages of his career. I should like to think that he valued his work in the field of genre painting above any other, despite the lack of any personal testimony by the artist to that effect. Certainly in our consideration of his total contribution there can be no doubt that his reputation will always be based on his figure compositions. Indeed, even in his own time, Bingham's fame as "The Missouri Artist" was earned through those pictures which reflect the happiest note of his art and which also place him high among the forebears of a true regionalist movement in American painting.

Both in his role of painter and in his role of politician, Bingham was unfailingly observant and perceptive. His voluminous correspondence with Rollins reveals an extremely sensitive personality, as quick to grasp and enjoy the humor of a situation as he was to recognize and decry another that might imply man's inhumanity to man in any shape or form. In his letters he reveals himself as an important commentator on his own time. His discerning, lively observations on national and local politics deserve separate consideration. He had an equally acute insight, of course, into the difficulties and temptations

259

of his own situation as an artist, which was not an atypical one for an ambitious mid-nineteenth-century American painter. In fact, the general cultural atmosphere of those times, the specific conditions in the artistic sphere, the means adopted by the aspiring artists to compensate for their lack of formal training during the formative years, the struggle for recognition—indeed, the entire panorama that defines the background for those generations of painters rising up in America from the third to the seventh decades of the nineteenth century—can be no more graphically described and illustrated than by the experiences of this one man, George Caleb Bingham of Missouri.

BIBLIOGRAPHY

The bibliography is arranged under the headings of Manuscript Sources, Books, Periodicals, Exhibition Catalogues, Auction and Booksellers' Catalogues, and Newspapers.

MANUSCRIPT SOURCES

Historical Society of Pennsylvania, Philadelphia:
Contract for engraving "The County Election." Bingham–Sartain, Aug. 24, 1852.

Kansas City Public Library, Kansas City, Missouri:
Bingham file: letter, Bryan Obear to Jesse P. Crump, St. Louis, Mo., Oct. 23, 1918.

Kansas City Museum, Kansas City, Missouri:
Bingham documents: Copyright, registered in Western District of Missouri (no. 52), Dec. 22, 1868, titled "Civil War; As realized in the Desolation of Border Counties of Missouri during the operation of 'General Order No. 11,' issued by Brigadier General Ewing, from his Head Quarters, Kansas City, August 25, 1863"; Passport issued 1856; Appointment as State Treasurer of Missouri, 1862; Appointment as Police Commissioner, Kansas City, 1874; Appointment as commissioner, Lee Monument Association of Virginia, 1878.

M. Knoedler & Co., New York:
Goupil & Co. papers: Letter, Bingham to Goupil, Jan. 31, 1852.

Massachusetts Historical Society, Boston:
Adams Manuscript Trust: John Quincy Adams diary, references to painting of portrait of Adams by Bingham, 1844.

Missouri Historical Society, St. Louis, Missouri:
Bingham–Sartain correspondence, 1852-1853: nine letters by Bingham to John Sartain, relative to engraving of "The County Election"; one letter, James S. Rollins to Sartain.

Native Sons of Kansas City, Kansas City, Missouri:
Bingham file: Bingham holograph will, Aug. 9, 1871, reaffirmed Nov. 28, 1873.

New-York Historical Society, New York:
American Art-Union papers: 8 letters by Bingham to the organization and its secretary, Col. Andrew Warner, 1848-1852; copies of replies; letters relating to Bingham and his work by Edward C. Bruce, Thomas Doney, William J. Hoppin, Maj. James S. Rollins; minutes of meetings, committee of management; register of pictures; memoranda. My text includes references to letters of other artists to AAU: George Henry Hall, Eastman Johnson, Alexander W. Rutherford. Six letters by Bingham and one by Andrew Warner to the artist were published by J. F. McDermott. "George Caleb Bingham and the American Art-Union," *New-York Historical Society Quarterly*, XLII (Jan., 1958), 60-69. My research on the Art-Union was referred to in M. B. Cowdrey, *American Academy of Fine Arts and American Art-Union* (New York: New-York Historical Society, 1953), Vol. 1, p. 232, and published in article. "The American Art-Union's Downfall." *New-York Historical Society Quarterly*. XXXVII (Oct., 1953), 331-359.

Probate Court of Jackson County, Missouri:
Appraisal of Bingham estate, Sept. 1, 1879 (estate no. 534).

State Historical Society of Missouri, Columbia:
Rollins papers: Bingham–Rollins correspondence, 1837-1879. 123 letters, edited by Curtis Burnam Rollins, were published in *MHR*, XXXII (Oct., 1937) to XXXIII

(July, 1939). An additional group of letters, of highly personal content, was not published.

Letter, Washington Adams to Rollins, Boonville, Mo., March 20, 1882.

Bingham papers: Bingham family correspondence, 1835-1873. 18 letters by Bingham to Elizabeth Hutchison Bingham, Mary Amend Bingham, Amanda Bingham Barnes; letters by Elizabeth Hutchison Bingham, George Bingham; letters by W. B. Hood. Jane Shaw, John Shaw, Dr. Nathaniel Hutchison. Largely unpublished. Account of family background, by George C. Bingham. Bingham family ancestry, by James Rollins Bingham (Appendix A).

Note: My personal files contain letters and other documentation referring to Bingham paintings, 1944-1963; typescripts of Bingham letters and other family correspondence, edited by Mrs. W. P. Bowdry; Bingham family reminiscences; Missouri family genealogies and records. Specific references to much of this material are made in my companion catalogue of pictures.

BOOKS

Adams, Charles Francis, ed., *Memoirs of John Quincy Adams. Comprising Portions of His Diary from 1795 to 1848.* . . . Philadelphia: J. B. Lippincott & Co., 1874-1877. 12 vols.

[American Art-Union, New York]. *Charter and Constitution of the American Art-Union; and By-Laws of the Committee of Management.* New York: George F. Nesbitt, Stationer and Printer, 1848.

American Newspapers, 1821-1936; a Union List of Files Available in the United States and Canada. Ed. by Winifred Gregory. Under the Auspices of the Bibliographical Society of America. . . . New York: H. W. Wilson, 1937.

Ashton, John, *Historic Ravenswood; Its Founders and Its Cattle.* . . . Columbia, Mo.: Printed by E. W. Stephens Co., 1926.

The Atlantic Souvenir; A Christmas and New Year's Offering, 1828. Philadelphia: Carey, Lea & Carey . . . [*ca.* 1827].

———.; *A Christmas and New Year's Offering, 1829.* Philadelphia: Carey, Lea & Carey . . . [*ca.* 1828].

Aubrat, Odette, *La Peinture de Genre en Angleterre de la Mort de Hogarth (1764) au Préraphaelisme (1850).* . . . Paris; En Dépôt à la Maison du Livre Français [1935].

Audubon, John James, *Delineations of American Scenery and Character.* . . . New York: G. A. Baker & Co., 1926.

Barker, Virgil, *American Painting: History and Interpretation,* New York: MacMillan, 1950.

Barns, Chancy Rufus, ed., *The Commonwealth of Missouri; A Centennial Record.* . . . St. Louis: Bryan, Brand & Co., 1877.

Bay, W. V. N., *Reminiscences of the Bench and Bar of Missouri, with an Appendix Containing Biographical Sketches.* St. Louis: F. H. Thomas & Co., 1878.

Bell, Sir Charles, *Essays on the Anatomy of Expression in Painting.* London: Printed for Longmans, Hurst, Rees, & Orme, 1806.

Benjamin, Samuel Greene Wheeler, *Art in America; A Critical and Historical Sketch.* . . . New York: Harper & Brothers, 1880.

Béraldi, Henri, *Les Graveurs du XIXe Siècle; Guide de l'Amateur d'Estampes Modernes.* Paris: L. Conquet, 1885-1892. 12 vols.

Biddle, Edward, and Mantle Fielding, *The Life and Works of Thomas Sully (1783-1872).* . . . Philadelphia: Wickersham Press, 1921.

Bingham, George Caleb, *An Address to the Public, Vindicating a Work of Art Illustrative of the Federal Military Policy in Missouri During the Late Civil War. By the Artist.* . . . Kansas City, Mo., 1871.

――――, "Art, the Ideal of Art and the Utility of Art." *Public Lectures Delivered in the Chapel of the University of the State of Missouri, Columbia, Missouri, by Members of the Faculty, 1878-79.* Course II, Vol. 1. Columbia, Mo.: Statesman Book & Job Print, 1879, pp. [311]-324.

[Bingham, George Caleb], *Who Is Colonel Jennison? Jennison—His Raids in Missouri —His Murders, Robberies, and House Burnings.* [Jefferson City, Mo., 1862].

Bingham, Theodore Alfred, *The Bingham Family in the United States, Especially of the State of Connecticut.* . . . Ea[s]ton, Pa.: the Bingham Association, 1927-1930. 3 vols.

Boas, George, ed., *Romanticism in America. Papers Contributed to a Symposium Held at the Baltimore Museum of Art, May 13, 14, 15, 1940.* . . . Baltimore, Md.: Johns Hopkins Press, 1940.

Bolton, Theodore, *Early American Portrait Painters in Miniature.* . . . New York: F. F. Sherman, 1921.

[Boone, Daniel], *Life and Adventures of Colonel Daniel Boon[e], the First White Settler in the State of Kentucky. Comprising an Account of His First Excursion to Kentucky in 1769, Then a Wild Wilderness, Inhabited by No Other Human Beings but Savages—His Remove There with His Family in 1773—and of His Various Encounters with the Indians, from the Year 1769 to 1782. Written by Himself.* . . . Brooklyn (N.Y.): Printed by C. Wilder, 1823.

Born, Wolfgang, *American Landscape Painting; An Interpretation.* New Haven, Conn.: Yale University Press, 1948.

[Boston, Museum of Fine Arts], *M. & M. Karolik Collection of American Watercolors & Drawings, 1800-1875.* Boston, Mass.: Museum of Fine Arts, 1962. 2 vols.

[Boston, Museum of Fine Arts], *M. and M. Karolik Collection of American Paintings, 1815 to 1865.* Published for the Museum of Fine Arts, Boston, Mass. Cambridge, Mass.: Harvard University Press, 1949.

Breckinridge, James Malcolm, *William Clark Breckinridge, Historical Research Writer and Bibliographer of Missouriana; His Life Lineage, and Writings.* . . . St. Louis, Mo., 1932.

Brieger, Lothar, *Das Genrebild, die Entwicklung der Bürgerlichen Malerei.* . . . München: Delphin-verlag [1922].

Brimo, René, *Art et goût, l'Evolution du Goût aux Etats-Unis.* Paris: J. Fortune [1938].

British Museum, Department of Greek and Roman Art. *Description of the Collection of Ancient Marbles in the British Museum; with Engravings.* . . . London: Printed by W. Bulmer & Co., 1812-1861. 11 vols. in 7.

Brooks, Van Wyck, *The World of Washington Irving*. New York: Dutton, 1944.

Bryan, William Smith and Robert Rose, *A History of the Pioneer Families of Missouri, with Numerous Sketches, Anecdotes, Adventures, etc., Relating to the Early Days of Missouri*. . . . St. Louis, Mo.: Bryan, Brand & Co., 1876.

Burnet, John, *An Essay on Education of the Eye with Reference to Painting*. . . . 2d ed.; London: J. Carpenter, 1837.

———, *Practical Hints on Portrait Painting; Illustrated by Examples from the Works of Vandyke and Other Masters*. . . . London: D. Bogue, 1850.

———, *A Practical Treatise on Painting. In Three Parts. Consisting of Hints on Composition, Chiaroscuro, and Colouring. The Whole Illustrated by Examples from the Italian, Venetian, Flemish, and Dutch Schools*. . . . London: Printed for the Proprietor, and Sold by James Carpenter & Son . . . , 1828. 3 vols. in 1. (Burnet's *Practical Hints on Light and Shade* forms a part of this treatise.)

Burroughs, Alan, *Limners and Likenesses: Three Centuries of American Painting*. Cambridge, Mass.: Harvard University Press, 1936.

Butts, Porter, *Art in Wisconsin*. [Madison, Wis.: Madison Art Association, 1936.]

Case, Theodore S., *History of Kansas City, Missouri*. . . . Syracuse, N.Y.: D. Mason & Co., 1888.

Christ-Janer, Albert, *George Caleb Bingham of Missouri; The Story of an Artist*. . . . New York: Dodd, Mead, 1940.

The Cincinnati Miscellany, or Antiquities of the West: and Pioneer History and General and Local Statistics. Compiled from the Western General Advertiser, from April 1st, 1845, to April 1st, 1846. . . . Cincinnati, O.: Robinson & Jones, 1846. 2 vols.

Cist, Charles, *Sketches and Statistics of Cincinnati in 1851*. . . . Cincinnati, O.: W. H. Moore & Co., 1851.

Clement, Clara Erskine, and Laurence Hutton, *Artists of the Nineteenth Century and their Works*. . . . Revised ed.; Boston, Houghton, Mifflin [1884]. 2 vols. in 1.

Collins, Earl Augustus, and Albert F. Elsea, *Missouri; Its People and Its Progress*. St. Louis, Mo., Dallas, . . . : Webster Publishing Co. [*ca.* 1940].

Conard, Howard L., ed., *Encyclopedia of the History of Missouri*. . . . New York, Louisville, St. Louis: Southern History Co., 1901. 6 vols.

Cook, Clarence Chatham, *Art and Artists of Our Time*. New York: S. Hess, 1888. 3 vols.

Cooper, Thomas Sidney, *Groups of Cattle, Drawn from Nature, by T. S. Cooper*. London: Ackermann & Co. [1839].

Cowdrey, Mary Bartlett, comp., *American Academy of Fine Arts and American Art-Union*. . . . New York: The New-York Historical Society, 1953. 2 vols.

———, comp., *National Academy of Design Exhibition Record, 1826-1860*. . . . New York: Printed for the New-York Historical Society, 1943. 2 vols.

———, and Hermann Warner Williams, Jr., *William Sidney Mount, 1807-1868; An American Painter*. . . . New York: Published for the Metropolitan Museum of Art by Columbia University Press, 1944.

Cumings, Samuel, *The Western pilot; Containing Charts of the Ohio River, and of the Mississippi . . . with Directions for Navigating the Same, and a Description of the Towns on Their Banks* . . . Cincinnati, O.: Morgan, Lodge & Fisher, 1825.

Cummings, Thomas Seir, *Historic Annals of the National Academy of Design, New-York Drawing Association, etc., with Occasional Dottings by the Way-Side, from 1825 to the Present Time* . . . Philadelphia: George W. Childs, 1865.

Cunningham, Allan, *The Life of Sir David Wilkie.* . . . London: J. Murray, 1843. 3 vols.

Darby, John Fletcher, *Personal Recollections of Many Prominent People Whom I Have Known and of Events—Especially Those Relating to the History of St. Louis.* . . . St. Louis, Mo.: G. I. Jones & Co., 1880.

Davis, Walter Bickford, and Daniel Steele Durrie, *An Illustrated History of Missouri; Comprising Its Early Record, and Civil, Political, and Military History, from the First Exploration to the Present Time.* . . . St. Louis, Mo.: A. J. Hall & Co.; Cincinnati, O.: Robert Clarke & Co., 1876.

De Silver's Philadelphia Directory and Stranger's Guide for 1837. . . . Philadelphia.: Published for Robert De Silver . . . , Jan. 1837.

DeVoto, Bernard, *Across the Wide Missouri* . . . *Illustrated with Paintings by Alfred Jacob Miller, Charles Bodmer and George Catlin. With an Account of the Discovery of the Miller Collection by Mae Reed Porter.* Boston: Houghton Mifflin; Cambridge, Mass.: The Riverside Press, 1947.

Dickey, Dallas C., *Seargent S. Prentiss, Whig Orator of the Old South.* . . . Baton Rouge, La.: Louisiana State University Press, 1946.

Dickson, Harold E., *John Wesley Jarvis, American Painter, 1780-1840.* . . . New York: The New-York Historical Society, 1949.

Dictionary of American Biography; Under the Auspices of the American Council of Learned Societies. . . . Ed. by Allen Johnson and Dumas Malone. New York: C. Scribner's Sons, 1928-1944. 21 vols.

Dobson, Austin, *William Hogarth.* . . . New York: The McClure Co., 1907.

Düsseldorf Gallery, New York. *Gems from the Düsseldorf Gallery, Photographed from the Original Pictures.* . . . *Under the Superintendence of B. Frodsham.* New York: D. Appleton, 1863.

Dunlap, William, *History of the Rise and Progress of the Arts of Design in the United States.* . . . New-York: George P. Scott and Co., Printers, 1834. 2 vols.

Encyclopedia Americana. . . . New York, Chicago: Americana Corporation, 1941. 30 vols.

Evans, Rella [Bright], and S. P. A. Thompson, comps., *Marriage Records of Boone County, Missouri, 1821-1870.* . . . Columbia, Mo. [1933]. (Mimeographed)

————, comps., *Tombstone Records of Boone County, Missouri.* . . . Columbia, Mo. [*ca.* 1934]. (Mimeographed)

Fairman, Charles E., *Art and Artists of the Capitol of the United States of America.* . . . Washington, D.C.: Government Printing Office, 1927.

Fanning, W. H. W., *Historical Sketch of the St. Louis University.* . . . St. Louis, Mo.: St. Louis University, 1908. (*St. Louis University Bull.*, vol. 4, no. 4.)

Faxon, Frederick Winthrop, *Literary Annuals and Gift-Books; a Bibliography with a Descriptive Introduction.* Boston: Boston Book Co., 1912.

Fielding, Mantle, *Dictionary of American Painters, Sculptors, and Engravers.* . . . Philadelphia, Printed for Subscribers [1926].

Flagg, Edmund, *The Far West: or, A Tour Beyond the Mountains. Embracing Outlines of Western Life and Scenery; Sketches of the Prairies, Rivers Ancient Mounds, Early Settlements of the French, etc. . . .* New York: Harper & Brothers, 1838. 2 vols.

Flint, Timothy, *The First White Man of the West; or, The Life and Exploits of Col. Dan'l Boone, the First Settler of Kentucky. . . .* Cincinnati, O.: E. Morgan & Co., 1850.

————,*The History and Geography of the Mississippi Valley; to Which is Appended a Condensed Physical Geography of the Atlantic United States, and the Whole American Continent.* Second ed.; Cincinnati, O.: E. H. Flint & L. R. Lincoln, 1832. 2 vols.

————, *Recollections of the Last Ten Years, Passed in Occasional Residence and Journeyings in the Valley of the Mississippi. . . .* Boston: Cummings, Hilliard & Co., 1826.

Ford, James E., *A History of Jefferson City, Missouri's State Capitol and of Cole County. . . .* Jefferson City, Mo.: The New Day Press [*ca.* 1938].

————, and Marvin Crawford, *History of Moniteau County, Mo.* [California, Mo.]: Published by Marvin H. Crawford, 1936.

The Gallery of Modern British Artists; Consisting of a Series of the Most Eminent Artists of the Day. London: Simpkin & Marshall [1834].

Gentry, Richard, *The Gentry Family in America, 1676 to 1909. . . .* New York: The Grafton Press, Printed for the Author, 1909.

The Gift, a Christmas and New Year's Present for 1836. Ed. by Miss Leslie. Philadelphia: E. L. Carey & A. Hart [*ca.* 1835].

————, *a Christmas and New Year's Present for 1839.* Ed. by Miss Leslie. Philadelphia: E. L. Carey & A. Hart [*ca.* 1838].

————, *a Christmas and New Year's Present for 1842.* Ed. by Miss Leslie. Philadelphia: Carey & Hart [*ca.* 1841].

Gilbey, Sir Walter, and E. D. Cuming, *George Morland, His Life and Works. . . .* London: Adam & Charles Black, 1907.

Goldwater, Robert, and Marco Treves, comps. and eds., *Artists on Art from the XIV to the XX Century.* New York: Pantheon Books [1945].

Greve, Charles Theodore, *Centennial History of Cincinnati and Representative Citizens.* Chicago, Ill.: Biographical Publishing Co., 1904. 2 vols.

Groce, George C., and David H. Wallace, *The New-York Historical Society's Dictionary of Artists in America, 1564-1860.* New Haven, Conn., Yale University Press; London: Oxford University Press, 1957.

Grubar, Francis S., *William Ranney, Painter of the Early West.* New York: Clarkson N. Potter [1962].

Hall, Basil, *Forty Etchings, from Sketches Made with the Camera Lucida, in North America in 1827 and 1828. . . .* Edinburgh: Cadell & Co.; London: Simpkin, Marshall, & Moon, Boys, Graves, 1829.

Hall, James, *Sketches of History, Life, and Manners in the West.* St. Louis, Mo.: Meech & Dinnies, 1835. 2 vols.

268

Hall, Samuel Carter, *Gems of European Art: The Best Pictures of the Best Schools.* . . . London: G. Virtue, 1846-[1847]. 2 vols.

Hamilton, Frances Frazee, *Ancestral Lines of the Doniphan, Frazee and Hamilton Families.* . . . Greenfield, Ind.: William Mitchell Publishing Co., 1928.

Hamilton, Thomas, *Men and Manners in America.* . . . Philadelphia: Cary, Lea and Blanchard, 1833.

Harding, Chester, *My Egotistigraphy.* . . . Cambridge, Mass.: John Wilson and Co., 1866.

History of Clay and Platte Counties, Missouri, Written and Compiled from the Most Authentic and Private Sources, Including a History of Their Townships, Towns and Villages, Together with a Condensed History of Missouri; a Reliable and Detailed History of Clay and Platte Counties in Their Pioneer Period, Resources, Biographical Sketches of Prominent Citizens. . . . St. Louis, Mo.: National Historical Co., 1885.

History of Howard and Cooper Counties Missouri. . . . *from the Most Authentic Sources.* . . . *With a Condensed History of Missouri; A . . . Detailed History of Howard and Cooper Counties . . . Biographical Sketches . . . General and Local Statistics.* . . . St. Louis, Mo.: National Historical Co., 1883.

The History of Jackson County, Missouri, Containing a History of the County, Its Cities, Towns, etc., Biographical Sketches of Its Citizens; Jackson County in the Late War, General and Local Statistics, Portraits of Its Early Settlers, and Prominent Men. . . . Kansas City, Mo. Union Historical Co., 1881.

History of Saline County, Missouri, Carefully Written and Compiled From the Most Authentic Official and Private Sources. . . . St. Louis, Mo.: Missouri Historical Co., 1881.

Hough, Franklin Benjamin, ed., *Historical Sketches of the Universities and Colleges of the United States.* . . . Washington, D.C.: Government Printing Office, 1883.

Howard, Frank, *Colour as a Means of Art, Being an Adaptation of the Experience of Professors to the Practice of Amateurs.* . . . London: J. Thomas . . . , 1838.

————, *The Science of Drawing, Being a Progressive Series of the Characteristic Forms of Nature.* . . . London: W. Pickering, 1839.

Howard, Henry, *A Course of Lectures on Painting.* . . . *Edited with a Memoir of the Author, by F. H.* [Frank Howard]. London: H. G. Bohn, 1848.

[Hoxie, Richard Leveridge, comp.], *Vinnie Ream. Printed for Private Distribution Only; and to Preserve a Few Specimens of Artist Life from 1865 to 1878.* Washington, D.C.: Gibson Bros [1908]. [Reprinted, with additions, 1915.]

Huebner, F. M., and V. Pearce Delgado, *Die Maler der Romantik in Amerika.* . . . Bonn: P. Vink [1953].

Humboldt, Baron, Friedrich Alexander von, *Cosmos: A Sketch of a Physical Description of the Universe . . . Translated by E. C. Otté,* London: H. G. Bohn, 1849-1858. 5 vols.

Hyde, William, and Howard L. Conrad, ed., *Encyclopedia of the History of St. Louis.* . . . New York, Louisville, St. Louis; Southern History Co., 1899. 4 vols.

269

Irving, Washington, *Astoria; or Anecdotes of an Enterprise Beyond the Rocky Mountains....* Philadelphia: Carey, Lea, & Blanchard, 1836. 2 vols.

————, *A Tour on the Prairies. By the Arthor of "The Sketchbook."* London: J. Murray, 1835.

Isham, Samuel, *The History of American Painting. New Edition with Supplemental Chapters by Royal Cortissoz.* New York: Macmillan, 1944.

Koetschau, Karl Theodor, *Rheinische Malerei in der Biedermeier-zeit; Zugleich ein Rückblick auf die Jubiläums-Ausstellung Düsseldorf 1925 der Jahrtausendfeier der Rheinlande....* Düsseldorf: Vereins für die Rheinlande und Westfalen, 1926. (Staedtisches Kunstmuseum, Düsseldorf Schriften [Bd. 1].)

Lancour, Harold, *American Art Auction Catalogues, 1785-1942; A Union List....* New York: New York Public Library, 1944.

Larkin, Lew, *Bingham: Fighting Artist. The Story of Missouri's Immortal Painter, Patriot, Soldier and Statesman....* St. Louis, Mo.: State Publishing Co. [1955].

Larkin, Oliver W., *Art and Life in America....* New York: Rinehart [1949].

Lee, Edmund Jennings, ed. and pub., *Lee of Virginia, 1642-1692; Biographical and Genealogical Sketches of the Descendants of Col. Richard Lee. With Brief Notices of the Related Families....* Philadelphia [Franklin Printing Co.], 1895.

Lester, Charles Edwards, *The Artists of America; A Series of Biographical Sketches of American Artists; with Portraits and Designs on Steel.* New York: Baker & Scribner. 1846.

Levens, Henry C., and Nathaniel M. Drake, *A History of Cooper County, Missouri. from the First Visit by White Men, in February 1804, to the 5th Day of July, 1876.* ...St. Louis, Mo.: Perrin & Smith, Stearn book and job printers, 1876.

Lionberger, Isaac Henry, *The Annals of St. Louis and a Brief Account of Its Foundation and Progress, 1764-1928....* [St. Louis], 1929.

McDermott, John Francis, *George Caleb Bingham, River Portraitist.* Norman, Okla.: University of Oklahoma Press [1959].

M'Elroy's Philadelphia Directory for the Year 1837.... Philadelphia: E. C. Biddle .... 1837.

Maple, J. C., and R. P. Rider, *Missouri Baptist Biography....* Kansas City, Mo.: Western Baptist Publishing Co. [*ca.* 1914]. 4 vols.

Marryat, Frederick, *A Diary in America; with Remarks on Its Institutions....* Philadelphia: Carey & Hart, 1839. 2 vols.

Marshall, Humphrey, *The History of Kentucky. Exhibiting an Account of the Modern Discovery; Settlement; Progressive Improvement; Civil and Military Transactions; and the Present State of the Country....* Frankfort, Ky.: G. S. Robinson, printer. 1824. 2 vols.

Martineau, Harriet, *Retrospect of Western Travel....* London: Saunders and Otley; New York: Sold by Harper & Brothers, 1838. 2 vols.

Matthiessen, Francis Otto, *American Renaissance; Art and Expression...the Age of Emerson and Whitman....* London, New York; Oxford University Press [*ca.* 1941].

270

Melton, Elston Joseph, *History of Cooper County, Missouri, an Account from Early Times to the Present, Written in Narrative Style, for General Use. . . .* Columbia, Mo.: E. W. Stephens Publishing Co., 1937.

A Memorial and Biographical Record of Kansas City and Jackson County, Missouri. . . . Chicago: Lewis Publishing Co., 1896.

Missouri, General Assembly, *Journal of the Adjourned Session of the 23rd General Assembly. . . . 1865.* Jefferson City, Mo., 1866.

Missouri, General Assembly, House of Representatives, *Journal of the House of Representatives. . . . 1859.* Jefferson City, Mo., 1860.

Missouri, General Assembly, Senate, *Journal of the Senate . . . 1859.* Jefferson City, Mo., 1860.

Missouri University, Columbia, Mo., *Catalogue of the Missouri State University at Columbia, Missouri, 1876-1877. . . .* Jefferson City, Mo.: Regan & Carter, 1877.

————, *The Rollins Portrait; Presentation of a Life-Size Portrait of Hon. James S. Rollins, to the Board of Curators of the University of the State of Missouri, by the Citizens of Boone County, Mo., June 24, 1873.* Columbia, Mo.: Statesman Book and Job Office, 1873.

The Modern Gallery of British Artists; Consisting of a Series of Engravings of Their Most Admired Works. London: C. Tilt, 1836.

Mott, Frank Luther, *A History of American Magazines, 1741-1850. . . .* New York, London: D. Appleton, 1930.

Murray, Sir Charles Augustus, *Travels in North America During . . . 1834, 1835, and 1836. Including a Summer Residence with the Pawnee Tribe of Indians and a Visit to Cuba and the Azore Islands. . . .* London: R. Bentley, 1839. 2 vols.

Napton, William Barclay, *Past and Present of Saline County, Missouri. . . .* Indianapolis & Chicago: B. F. Bowen & Co., 1910.

National Academy of Design, New York. *Catalogue of Statues, Busts, Studies, etc., Forming the Collection of the Antique School of the National Academy of Design.* New York: Israel Sackett, 1846.

National Art Association, Washington, D.C. *Proceedings of Annual Conventions of the National Art Association, Held at Washington City, from 1858 to 1860, Inclusive.* Washington, D.C.: William H. Moore, Printer, 1860.

The National Cyclopaedia of American Biography. New York: J. T. White & Co., 1893————.

Neuhaus, Eugen, *The History and Ideals of American Art. . . .* Stanford University, Calif.: Stanford University Press, 1931.

Nicholson, Francis, *The Practice of Drawing and Painting Landscape from Nature in Watercolours; Exemplified in a Series of Instructors Calculated to Facilitate the Progress of the Learner . . . with Observations on the Study of Nature. . . .* 2d ed.; London: John Murray, 1823.

The Opal; A Pure Gift for All Seasons. Edited by Mrs. Sarah Josepha Hale. New-York: J. C. Riker, 1849.

Park, Laurence, *Gilbert Stuart; An Illustrated Descriptive List of His Works, Com-*

piled by Laurence Park, with an Account of His Life by John Hill Morgan, and an Appreciation by Royal Cortissoz. New York: W. E. Rudge, 1926. 4 vols.

Parrington, Vernon Louis, *Main Currents in American Thought; An Interpretation of American Literature from the Beginnings to 1920....* [New York: Harcourt, Brace, 1927-1931]. 3 vols.

Pennsylvania Academy of the Fine Arts, Philadelphia. *Catalogue of the Permanent Collection (14th ed.). With an Appendix of Works on Deposit.* [Philadelphia], 1888.

Peters, Harry T., *America on Stone; The Other Printmakers to the American People. A Chronicle of American Lithography Other Than That of Currier & Ives, from Its Beginning, Shortly Before 1820, to the Years When the Commercial Single-Stone Hand-Colored Lithograph Disappeared from the American Scene....* New York: Doubleday, Doran, [1931].

Powell, Lyman Pierson, *Historic Towns of the Western States....* New York & London: G. P. Putnam's Sons (The Knickerbocker Press), 1901.

Prout, Samuel, *Easy Lessons in Landscape Drawing, Contained in Forty Plates, Arranged Progressively, from the First Principles in the Chalk Manner, to the Finished Landscape Colours....* [London: R. Ackermann, 1819]

————, *Hints on Light and Shadow, Composition, etc. As Applicable to Landscape Painting; Illustrated by Examples....* London: M. A. Nattali, 1848.

————, *A Series of Views of Rural Cottages in the North of England, Drawn and Etched in Imitation of Chalk....* [London: R. Ackermann, 1821]

————, *Sketches at Home and Abroad. Hints on the Acquirement of Freedom of Execution and Breadth of Effect in Landscape Painting; to Which Are Added, Simple Instructions, in the Proper Uses and Application of Colour....* London: M. A. Nattali, 1844.

————, *Studies of Cottages and Rural Scenery, Drawn and Etched in Imitation of Chalk.* [London, R. Ackermann, 1816]

Pyne, William Henry, *Etchings of Rustic Figures, for the Embellishment of Landscape.* ... London: M. A. Nattali [1814-1819].

Richardson, Edgar Preston, *American Romantic Painting.... Ed. by Robert Freund.* New York: E. Weyhe [1944].

————, *The Way of Western Art (1776-1914)....* Cambridge, Mass.: Harvard University Press, 1939.

Riegel, Robert E., *Young America, 1830-1840....* Norman, Okla.: University of Oklahoma Press [1949].

Rusk, Fern Helen, *George Caleb Bingham: The Missouri Artist....* Jefferson City, Mo.: The Hugh Stephens Co., 1917.

Rutledge, Anna Wells, comp. and ed., *Cumulative Record of Exhibition Catalogues; The Pennsylvania Academy of the Fine Arts, 1807-1870; The Society of Artists, 1800-1814; The Artists Fund Society, 1835-1845.* Philadelphia: The American Philosophical Society.... 1955.

St. Louis Mercantile Library Association, St. Louis, Mo. *Catalogue of Books Belonging* to the St. Louis Mercantile Library Association. January 1850. . . . St. Louis, Mo.: The Association, 1850.

Sartain, John, *Reminiscences of a Very Old Man, 1808-1897.* . . . New York: D. Appleton & Co., 1899.

Scharf, John Thomas, *History of Saint Louis City and County, from the Earliest Periods to the Present Day.* . . . Philadelphia: L. H. Everts & Co., 1883. 2 vols.

Schmidt, Paul Ferdinand, *Biedermeier-malerei; zur Geschichte und Geistigkeit der Deutschen Malerei in der Ersten Hälfte des Neunzehnten Jahrhunderts.* . . . München: Delphin-verlag [1922].

Schofield, John M., *Forty-Six Years in the Army.* . . . New York: The Century Co., 1897.

Sheldon, George William, *American Painters; With Eighty-Three Examples of Their Work Engraved on Wood.* New York: D. Appleton & Co., 1879.

Shoemaker, Floyd Calvin, *Missouri and Missourians; Land of Contrasts and People of Achievement.* . . . Chicago: Lewis Publishing Co., 1943. 5 vols.

————, *Missouri — Day by Day.* . . . Jefferson City, Mo.: State Historical Society, 1942.

————, *Missouri's Hall of Fame; Lives of Eminent Missourians.* . . . Columbia, Mo.: Missouri Book Co., 1923.

Smith, Ralph Clifton, *A Biographical Index of American Artists.* . . . Baltimore, Md.: Williams & Wilkins Co., 1930.

Smith, William Benjamin, *James Sidney Rollins; Memoir.* New York: De Vinne Press, 1891.

Spencer, Thomas E., *A Missourian Worth Remembering* (George Caleb Bingham). St. Louis, Mo., 1930.

Stauffer, David McNeely, *American Engravers Upon Copper and Steel.* . . . New York: The Grolier Club of the City of New York, 1907. 2 vols.

Stevens, Walter Barlow, *Centennial History of Missouri.* . . . St. Louis, Chicago: S. J. Clarke Publishing Co., 1921. 6 vols.

————, *Missouri the Center State, 1821-1915.* . . . Chicago & St. Louis: S. J. Clarke Publishing Co., 1915. 4 vols.

Stewart, A. J. D., ed., *The History of the Bench and Bar of Missouri; With Reminiscences of the Prominent Lawyers of the Past, and a Record of the Law's Leaders of the Present . . . ; Containing Also Personal Recollections of the Most Eminent Jurists, Able Lawyers and Learned Authorities of the State.* . . . St. Louis, Mo.: The Legal Publishing Co., 1898.

Sully, Thomas, *Hints to Young Painters; the Process of Portrait-Painting as Practiced by the Late Thomas Sully.* . . . Philadelphia: J. M. Stoddart & Co., 1873.

Swann, Mabel Munson, *The Athenaeum Gallery, 1827-1873; The Boston Athenaeum as an Early Patron of Art.* . . . [Boston]: The Boston Athenaeum, 1940.

Switzler, William Franklin, comp., *History of Boone County, Missouri; Written and Compiled from the Most Authentic Official and Private Sources; with a History of Townships, Towns, and Villages.* . . . St. Louis, Mo.: Western Historical Co., 1882.

273

Taylor and Crooks, *Sketchbook of St. Louis*. . . . St. Louis, Mo.: G. Knapp & Co., 1858.

Thompson, Ralph, *American Literary Annuals and Gift Books, 1825-1865*. New York: H. W. Wilson Co., 1936.

Thwaites, Reuben Gold, ed., *Early Western Travels, 1748-1846; a Series of Annotated Reprints of Some of the Best and Rarest Contemporary Volumes of Travel, Descriptive of the Aborigines and Social and Economic Conditions in the Middle and Far West, During the Period of Early American Settlement, ed. with notes, introduction, index, etc.* . . . Cleveland, O.: A. H. Clarke Co., 1904-1907. 32 vols.

Tuckerman, Henry Theodore, *Book of the Artists; American Artist Life, Comprising Biographical and Critical Sketches; Preceded by an Historical Account of the Rise and Progress of Art in America.* . . . New York: G. P. Putnam & Son; London: Sampson Low & Co., 1867.

The United States Biographical Dictionary and Portrait Gallery of Eminent and Self-Made Men; Missouri Volume. New York, Chicago, St. Louis, and Kansas City: U.S. Biographical Publishing Co., 1878.

The Vernon Gallery of British Art. Engravings from the Works of British Artists in the National Gallery, Presented to the Nation by the Late Robert Vernon, Esq. . . . London: Published for the Proprietors [1849-1854]. 2 vols.

The Washington Directory; and Government Register for 1843. . . . Washington, D.C.: Comp. and Pub. by Anthony Reintzel [1843].

Wauchope, George Armstrong, *Burning of the University of Missouri, Jan. 9, 1892; Descriptive Sketch . . . Published by Board of Curators*. Columbia, Mo.: E. W. Stephens, 1895.

Wetmore, Alphonso, *Gazeteer of the State of Missouri; to Which is Added an Appendix, Containing Frontier Sketches, and Illustrations of Indian Character.* . . . St. Louis, Mo.: C. Keemle, 1837.

White, Margaret E., ed., *A Sketch of Chester Harding, Artist; Drawn by His Own Hand.* . . . New ed. with Annotations by His Grandson W. P. G. Harding. Boston & New York: Houghton Mifflin, 1929.

Whitley, Edna Talbott, *Kentucky Ante-Bellum Portraiture*. Lexington, Ky.: National Society of The Colonial Dames of America in the Commonwealth of Kentucky, 1956.

Whitley, William T., *Art in England, 1800-1837.* . . . Cambridge, England: Cambridge University Press, 1928-1930. 2 vols.

Whitney, Carrie Westlake, *Kansas City, Missouri; Its History and Its People, 1800-1908.* . . . Chicago: S. J. Clarke Publishing Co., 1908. 3 vols.

Wiegmann R., *Die Königliche Kunst-Akademie zu Düsseldorf. Ihre Geschichte, Einrichtung und Wirksamkeit und die Düsseldorfer Künstler*. Düsseldorf: Buddens'schen Buch-und Kunsthandlung (E. Schulte), 1856.

The Wild Flower; A Gift Book for the Holydays, for 1852. Edited by Grace Maylove. Philadelphia; J. & J.L. Gihon, 1852.

[Wilkie, Sir David], *The Wilkie Gallery; A Selection of the Best Pictures of the Late Sir David Wilkie.* . . . London & New York: G. Virtue [1848-1850].

Williams, Walter, *The State of Missouri, an Autobiography.* . . . Columbia, Mo.: E. W. Stephens, 1904.

————, and Floyd C. Shoemaker, *Missouri, Mother of the West.* . . . Chicago, New York: American Historical Society, 1930. 5 vols.

Williamson, George C., *George Morland, His Life and Works.* George Bell & Sons, 1904.

Winthrop, Theodore, *A Companion to the Heart of the Andes.* . . . New York: D. Appleton & Co., 1859. (The painting by Frederic E. Church.)

Woodson, Henry M., *Historical Genealogy of the Woodsons and Their Connections.* . . . [Columbia, Mo.]: Published by the Author, 1915.

PERIODICALS

(Arranged in chronological order)

National Academy of Design, reviews of annual exhibitions: *The New-York Mirror,* VII (May 15, 1830), 359; VIII (May 7, 1831), 350; IX (June 9, 1832), 391; XV (May 26, 1838), 382; XV (June 2, 1838), 390-391; XVI (July 7, 1838), 15.

Fraser, Charles, "An Essay on the Condition and Prospects of the Art of Painting in the United States of America," *American Monthly Magazine,* VI (Nov., 1835), 213-220; VI (Dec., 1835) 240-247.

"Private Collections," *The New-York Mirror,* XVII (March 7, 1840), 294.

"John Banvard's Great Picture, Life on the Mississippi," *Howitt's Journal of Literature and Popular Progress,* II (Sept. 4, 1847), 145-148.

National Academy of Design, reviews of annual exhibitions: *The Literary World,* I (July 3, 1847), 517-518; II (Oct. 23, 1847), 377-378; III (June 3, 1848), 350-351.

American Art-Union, "The Art-Union Gallery," *Bulletin,* I (Nov. 25, 1848), 29. (From *The Evening Post.*)

————, "The Art-Union Prizes For the Present Year," *Bulletin,* I (Nov. 25, 1848), 31. (From *The New-York Courier & Enquirer.*)

————, "The Gallery—No. 4," *Bulletin,* II (Aug., 1849), 10-12.

————, "What Has the American Art-Union Accomplished?" *Bulletin,* II (Oct., 1849), 12.

Western Art Union, *Record,* I-II (1849-1850).

American Art-Union, "New Work by Bingham," *Bulletin,* Series for 1850 (July, 1850), 64-65.

————, "Mr. Bingham the Western Artist," *Bulletin,* Series for 1850 (Dec., 1850), 157.

————, "Development of Nationality in American Art," *Bulletin,* New Series (Dec. 1, 1851), 139.

————, "New Works by Bingham," *Bulletin,* New Series (Dec. 1, 1851), 151.

"Bingham," *Western Journal,* VII (1851), 45.

Philadelphia Art Union, *Reporter,* I (1851-1852).

"The American School of Art," *American Whig Review,* XVI (Aug. 1852), 138-148.

Cosmopolitan Art Association, *Cosmopolitan Art Journal,* I-II (1856-1857).

275

————, "The Dusseldorf Gallery," *Cosmopolitan Art Journal*, I (June, 1857), 135.

"Foreign Correspondence—Dusseldorf, August 1858" (Notice), *The Crayon*, V (Oct., 1858), 292.

Tuckerman, Henry T., "Art in America; Its History, Condition, and Prospects," *Cosmopolitan Art Journal*, III (Dec., 1858), [1]-8.

St. Louis Mercantile Library Association, *Annual Reports*, 1860, 1861, 1863, 1867, 1879.

Benjamin, Samuel G. W., "Fifty Years of American Art, 1828-78," *Harper's Magazine*, LIX (1879), 241-257.

[Parsons, Helen R.], "Missouri's Greatest Painter, George C. Bingham (1811-1879)," *Kansas City Public Library Quarterly* I (July, 1901), 65-68.

Simonds, May, "A Pioneer Painter," *American Illustrated Methodist Magazine*, VIII (Oct., 1902), 71-78.

————, "Missouri History as Illustrated by George C. Bingham," *Missouri Historical Review*, I (April, 1907), [181]-190.

Broadhead, Garland C., "A Few of the Leading People and Events of Early Missouri History," *Missouri Historical Review*, I (July, 1907), 287-288.

"George Caleb Bingham, an Early Painter of Missouri," *Art World*, III (Nov., 1917), 94-98.

Viles, Jonas, "Old Franklin: a Frontier Town of the Twenties," *The Mississippi Valley Historical Review*, IX (March, 1923), 269-282.

Herklotz, Hildegarde Rose, "Jayhawkers in Missouri, 1858-1863," *Missouri Historical Review*, XVII (April, July, 1923), 266-284, 505-513; XVIII (Oct., 1923), 64-101.

Rogers, Jane Harris, "The Model Farm of Missouri and Its Owner," *Missouri Historical Review*, XVIII (Jan., 1924), 146-157.

Powell, Mary M., "George Caleb Bingham," *Bulletin of the City Art Museum of St. Louis*, IX (Oct., 1924), 57-62.

Rollins, Curtis Burnam, "Some Recollections of George Caleb Bingham," *Missouri Historical Review*, XX (July, 1926), 463-484.

Grissom, D. M., "Personal Recollections of Distinguished Missourians," (Claiborne Fox Jackson), *Missouri Historical Review*, XX (Oct., 1926), 504-508.

Gentry, North Todd, "David Todd," *Missouri Historical Review*, XXI (July, 1927), 527-537.

————, "General Odon Guitar," *Missouri Historical Review*, XXII (July, 1928), 419-445.

————, "William F. Switzler," *Missouri Historical Review*, XXIV (Jan., 1930), 161-176.

Hall, Thomas B., "John Sappington," *Missouri Historical Review*, XXIV (Jan., 1930), 177-199.

"Bingham's Portrait of Vinnie Ream," *Missouri Historical Review*, XXIV (Jan., 1930), 288-289.

Rollins, Curtis Burnam, "Some Impressions of Frank P. Blair," *Missouri Historical Review*, XXIV (April, 1930), 352-358.

276

Atchison, Theodore C., "David R. Atchison: A Study in American Politics," *Missouri Historical Review*, XXV (July, 1930), 502-515.

Wehle, Harry B., "An American Frontier Scene by George Caleb Bingham," *Bulletin of the Metropolitan Museum of Art*, XXVIII (July, 1933), 120-122.

Bender, J. H. "George C. Bingham," *Fine Prints*, II (1933), 164-171.

Childs, Marquis W., "George Caleb Bingham," *American Magazine of Art*, XXVII (Nov., 1934), 594-599.

"John Hardeman's Garden," *Missouri Historical Review*, XXVII (Jan., 1934), 130-133.

Rogers, Meyric R., "An Exhibition of the Work of George Caleb Bingham, 1811-1879, 'The Missouri Artist,'" *Bulletin of the City Art Museum of St. Louis*, XIX (April, 1934), 14-24.

"Bingham, First Missouri Artist Painted American Scene Vividly. Exhibit at Museum of Modern Art, New York, Shows His Skill as Portrait and Genre Painter," *American Collector* III (Feb. 7, 1935), 1, 6.

Rollins, C. B., ed., "Letters of George Caleb Bingham to James S. Rollins," *Missouri Historical Review*, XXXII (Oct., 1937-July, 1938), 3-34, 164-202, 340-377, 484-522; XXXIII (Oct., 1938-July, 1939), 45-78, 203-229, 349-384, 499-526.

Anderson, Hattie M., "The Evolution of a Frontier Society in Missouri, 1815-1828," *Missouri Historical Review*, XXXII (April, July, 1938), 298-326, 458-483; XXXIII (Oct., 1938), 23-44.

King, Roy T., "Portraits of Daniel Boone," *Missouri Historical Review*, XXXIII (Jan., 1939), 171-183.

[Newman, Harry Shaw], "Accident or Design? Bingham's County Election and Hogarth's Canvassing for Votes," *Antiques*, XXXVII (Feb., 1940), 92-93.

Hall, Virginius C., "George Caleb Bingham, the Missouri Artist," *The Print Collector's Quarterly*, XXVII (Feb., 1940), 9-25.

Bender, J. H., "Catalogue of Engravings and Lithographs After George C. Bingham," *The Print Collector's Quarterly*, XXVII (Feb., 1940), 106-108.

"Acquisition of 'Major Dean in Jail' by William Jewell College," *Missouri Historical Review*, XXXV (July, 1941), 306.

"Acquisition by Boatmen's Bank, St. Louis of the 'County Election,'" *Missouri Historical Review*, XXXV (July, 1941), 644.

"Portraits of William Parkinson and his Wife of Potosi, Mo.; Possibly the Work of G. C. Bingham," *Antiques*, XLI (May, 1942), 320.

"The Autobiography of Worthington Whittredge 1820-1910," Edited by John I. H. Baur, *Brooklyn Museum Journal* (1942), 5-68.

"A Bingham Portrait in Kansas City," *Antiques*, XLIII (Feb., 1943), 54.

Musick, James B., "Praise the Lord and Pass the Ammunition: Drawings of Missouri Life," *Antiques*, XLIII (Feb., 1943), 60-63.

Kimball, Fiske, "The Stuart Portraits of Jefferson," *Gazette des Beaux Arts*, XXIII (1943), 329-344.

"St. Louis Acquires County Election and Jolly Flatboatmen," *Art Digest*, XIX (Dec. 15, 1944), 11.

Musick, James B., "County Election Purchased by St. Louis," *Pictures*, VI (Dec., 1944), 36.

"St. Louis Acquires County Election and Jolly Flatboatmen," *Antiques*, XLVII (Jan., 1945), 48.

"The Road West in 1818, the Diary of Henry Vest Bingham," Edited by Marie George Windell, *Missouri Historical Review*, XL (Oct., 1945-Jan., 1946), 21-54, 174-204.

Bloch, E. Maurice, "Art in Politics," *Art in America*, XXXIII (April, 1945), 93-100.

Born, Wolfgang, "Sources of American Romanticism," *Antiques*, XLVIII (Nov., 1945), 274-277.

Penn, Dorothy, "George Caleb Bingham's 'Order No. 11,'" *Missouri Historical Review*, XL (April, 1946), 349-357.

"Society Purchases Bingham Landscape 'Scene on the Ohio,'" *Missouri Historical Review*, XL (April, 1946), 436-438.

McDermott, John Francis, "Leon Pomarede, 'Our Parisian Knight of the Easel,'" *Bulletin of the City Art Museum of St. Louis*, XXXIV (Winter, 1949), 8-18.

"Special Acquisition of the Society, George Caleb Bingham's Thomas Jefferson," *Missouri Historical Review*, XLIV (Jan., 1950), 105-109, 185-186.

Richardson, Edgar P., "Trapper's Return," *Detroit Institute Bulletin*, XXX (1950-51), 81-84; *Art Quarterly*, XIV (1951), 78-79.

"Bingham's Woodboat Acquired by St. Louis," *The Art Digest*, XXV (Aug., 1951), 12.

Ravenswaay, Charles van, "Judge Matthias McGirk," *Missouri Historical Society Bulletin*, VIII (April, 1952), 244-248.

Richardson, Edgar P., "Checker Players by George Caleb Bingham," *Detroit Institute Bulletin*, XXXII (1952-53), 14-17; *Art Quarterly*, XV (Autumn, 1952), 251-256.

"Society Receives Another Portrait by Bingham" [Humboldt], *Missouri Historical Review*, XLVII (Oct., 1952), 69-70.

Arrington, Joseph Earl, "Leon D. Pomarede's Original Panorama of the Mississippi River," *Missouri Historical Society Bulletin*, IX (April, 1953), 261-273.

Shoemaker, Floyd C., "Remarks on Senator Allen McReynolds and the Bingham Portrait of Thomas Jefferson," *Missouri Historical Review*, XLVIII (Oct., 1953), 42-45.

Bloch, E. Maurice, "The American Art-Union's Downfall," *New-York Historical Society Quarterly*, XXXVII (Oct., 1953), 331-359.

Taylor, James L., Jr., "Shubael Allen, Native of Orange County, New York, and Pioneer in Western Missouri," *The New York Genealogical and Biographical Record*, LXXXV (July, 1954), 133-139.

Shapley, Fern Helen (Rusk), "Bingham's 'Jolly Flatboatmen,'" *The Art Quarterly*, XVII (Winter, 1954), 352-356.

"A New Bingham Painting in Kansas City," *Antiques*, LXVII (March, 1955), 248.

Taggart, Ross E., "'Canvassing for a Vote' and Some Unpublished Portraits by Bingham," *The Art Quarterly*, XVIII (Autumn, 1955), 229-240.

Parrish, William E., "David Rice Atchison, Frontier Politician," *Missouri Historical Review*, L (July, 1956), 339-354.

278

McDermott, John Francis, "Another Bingham Found: The Squatters," *The Art Quarterly*, XIX (Spring, 1956), 68-71.

————, "Bingham's Portrait of John Quincy Adams Dated," *The Art Quarterly*, XIX (Winter, 1956), 412-414.

————, "George Caleb Bingham's 'Stump Orator,'" *The Art Quarterly*, XX (Winter, 1957), 388-399.

————, "The Quandary About Bingham's 'In a Quandary' and 'Raftmen Playing Cards,'" *Bulletin of the City Art Museum of St. Louis*, XLII (1957), 6-9.

————, "George Caleb Bingham and The American Art-Union," *New-York Historical Society Quarterly*, VLII (Jan., 1958), 60-69.

————, "Jolly Flatboatmen: Bingham and His Imitators," *Antiques*, LXXIII (March, 1958), 266-269.

————, "Some Unpublished Sketches by George Caleb Bingham," *Missouri Historical Review*, LIV (Oct., 1959), 46-51.

Westfall, Ruth Rollins, "Thomas Miller," *Missouri Historical Review*, LVI (Jan., 1962), 136-145.

Bloch, E. Maurice, "George Caleb Bingham and His Landscape 'Method,'" *Corcoran Bulletin*, XIII (Oct., 1963), 3-9.

EXHIBITION CATALOGUES

(Arranged in chronological order. Asterisks indicate publications in which pictures by George Caleb Bingham are included.)

American Academy of the Fine Arts, New York, *Catalogue of Paintings, Statues, Busts, Drawings, Models, and Engravings, Exhibited by the American Academy of the Fine Arts, 1817. . . . The Second Exhibition.* New-York: Printed by T. & W. Mercein [1817].

The Pennsylvania Academy of the Fine Arts, Philadelphia, *A Catalogue of the Paintings, Statues, Prints, etc., Exhibiting at the Pennsylvania Academy of the Fine Arts, July, 1818.* Philadelphia: Printed by John Bioren, 1818.

American Academy of the Fine Arts, New York, *A Catalogue of Italian, Flemish, Spanish . . . and English Pictures; Which Have Been Collected in Europe, and, Brought to This Country by R. Abraham, and Are Now Exhibiting at the American Academy of Fine Arts*, New-York: C. Brown, 1830.

————, *A Descriptive Catalogue of the Paintings, by the Ancient Masters, Including Specimens of the First Class . . . Open at the American Academy. . . .* New-York: W. Mitchell, 1832.

[Hayward, William], *Catalogue of W. Hayward's Collection of Pictures, Now Exhibiting, at the Gallery, Cor. of Broadway and Chambers-St. . . .* New-York: Printed by Charles Vinten, 1837.

The Pennsylvania Academy of Fine Arts, Philadelphia, *Exhibition of the Pennsylvania Academy of the Fine Arts. Chestnut, Above Tenth Street. 1838.* Philadelphia: William S. Martien, Printer . . . , 1838.

Artists Fund Society of Philadelphia, *Catalogue of the Fourth Annual Exhibition. 1838.* Philadelphia: C. Sherman & Co., Printers, 1838.

National Academy of Design, New York, *Catalogue of the Thirteenth Annual Exhibition. 1838.* New-York: Printed by E. A. Clayton, 1838.

*Apollo Gallery, New York, *Catalogue of the First Fall Exhibition of the Works of Modern Artists, at the Apollo Gallery, no. 410 Broadway, New-York, 1838....* New-York: J. M. Marsh, Printer [1838].

Stuyvesant Institute, New York, *Catalogue; Descriptive, Biographical and Historical, of the Exhibition of Select Paintings, by Modern Artists, Principally American ... at the Stuyvesant Institute ... November 19, 1838 (For the Benefit of Mr. Dunlap).* New-York: G. D. Scott, 1838.

American Academy of the Fine Arts, New York, *Catalogue of a Collection of Paintings, Exhibiting at the American Academy of the Fine Arts on Barclay Street.* New-York: C. Vinten, 1840.

*National Academy of Design, New York, *Catalogue of the Fifteenth Annual Exhibition. 1840....* New-York: E. A. Clayton, Printer, 1840.

*————, *Catalogue of the Seventeenth Annual Exhibition. 1842....* New York: E. A. Clayton, Printer, 1842.

Artists Fund Society of Philadelphia, *Catalogue of the Eighth Annual Exhibition ... 1843.* Philadelphia: C. Sherman, Printer, 1843.

*American Art-Union, New York, *Transactions of the American Art-Union, for the Year 1845.* New-York: Printed at the Office of the Evening Post [1846].

*————, *Transactions of the American Art-Union, for the Year 1846.* New-York: G. F. Nesbitt, Stationer and Printer ... , 1847.

*————, *Transactions of the American Art-Union, for the Year 1847.* New-York: George F. Nesbitt, Printer, 1848.

*————, *Transactions of the American Art-Union, for the Year 1848.* New-York: George F. Nesbitt, Printer, 1849.

*National Academy of Design, New York, *Catalogue of the Twenty-Third Annual Exhibition....* New York: Israel Sackett, Printer, 1848.

*Western Art Union, Cincinnati, *Transactions of the Western Art Union, for the Year 1849.* Cincinnati, O.: Printed at the Daily Times Printing Office, 1849.

*American Art-Union, New York, *Transactions of the American Art-Union, for the Year 1849,* New-York: George F. Nesbitt, Printer, 1850.

*Western Art Union, Cincinnati, *Transactions of the Western Art Union, for the Year 1850.* Cincinnati, O.: Printed at Daily Times Job Office, 1850.

Düsseldorf Gallery, New York, *Catalogue of a Private Collection of Paintings and Original Drawings by Artists of the Düsseldorf Academy of Fine Arts.* New York: Wm. C. Bryant & Co., Printers, 1851.

Exhibition of the Industry of All Nations, New York, *Official Catalogue of Pictures Contributed to the Exhibition of the Industry of All Nations in the Picture Gallery of the Crystal Palace.* New York: G. P. Putnam & Co., 1853.

*The Pennsylvania Academy of the Fine Arts, Philadelphia, *Catalogue of the Thirty-*

Fourth Annual Exhibition of the Pennsylvania Academy of the Fine Arts. 1857.... Philadelphia: T. K. & P. G. Collins, Printers, 1857.

*St. Louis Agricultural and Mechanical Association, St. Louis, *Report of the Fourth Annual Fair of the St. Louis Agricultural and Mechanical Association, 1859.* St. Louis: George Knapp & Co., Book & Job Printers, 1860.

*Washington Art Association, Washington, D.C., *Fourth Annual Exhibition of the Washington Art Association.* Washington, D.C.: Henry Polkinghorn, Printer, 1860.

*The Pennsylvania Academy of the Fine Arts, Philadelphia, *Catalogue of the Thirty-Seventh Annual Exhibition of the Pennsylvania Academy of the Fine Arts. 1860....* Philadelphia: Collins, Printer, 1860.

*Western Academy of Art, St. Louis, *Catalogue of the First Annual Exhibition of the Western Academy of Art....* St. Louis, Mo., 1860.

*Mississippi Valley Sanitary Fair, St. Louis, *Catalogue of the Art Gallery of the Mississippi Valley Sanitary Fair, 1864.* St. Louis, Mo.: R. P. Studley & Co., Printers and Lithographers, 1864.

*Industrial Exposition, Louisville, *Catalogue of Paintings and Sculpture; With a Classification of the Natural History Department, 1873.* Louisville, Ky.: J. P. Morton & Co. [1873].

Centennial Exhibition, Philadelphia, *International Exhibition, 1876, Official Catalogue. Part II, Art gallery, Annexes, and Outdoor Works of Art....* Philadelphia: John R. Nagle and Co...., 1876.

*St. Louis, Mo., *Loan Exhibition in Aid of the St. Louis School of Design.* St. Louis, Mo.: Woodward, Tiernan & Hale, Printers, 1879.

*World's Columbian Exposition, Chicago, *Official Catalogue. Part X, Art Galleries and Annexes, Department K, Fine Arts.... Edited by M. P. Handy.* Chicago: W. B. Conkey Co., 1893.

*Missouri, University, Columbia, Mo., *Special Exhibition of the Paintings of George Caleb Bingham "The Missouri Artist," April nine to twenty-four, Nineteen hundred ten. In the Museum of Classical Archaeology of the University of Missouri.* [Columbia, Mo.: E. W. Stephens Publishing Co., 1910].

*City Art Museum of St. Louis, St. Louis, *An Exhibition of the Work of George Caleb Bingham, 1811-79, "The Missouri Artist," April 1934.* St. Louis, Mo.: City Art Museum [1934]. (*Bulletin of the City Art Museum of St. Louis,* XIX.)

*The Museum of Modern Art, New York, *George Caleb Bingham, The Missouri Artist, 1811-1879. January 30-March 7, 1935.* New York: The Museum of Modern Art [1935].

*Whitney Museum of American Art, New York, *American Genre; the Social Scene in Paintings & Prints (1800-1935). March 26 to April 29, 1935.* New York: Whitney Museum of American Art [1935].

*M. H. De Young Memorial Museum, San Francisco, Calif., *Exhibition of American painting. June 7-July 7, 1935.* [San Francisco, Calif.: H. S. Crocker Co., printers, 1935].

*Carnegie Institute, Pittsburgh, Pa., *An Exhibition of American Genre Paintings ...*

February 13-March 26, 1936. [Pittsburgh, Pa.]: Department of Fine Arts, Carnegie Institute [1936].

*Whitney Museum of American Art, New York, *A Century of American Landscape Painting, 1800 to 1900. January 19 to February 25, 1938.* New York: Whitney Museum of American Art [1938].

*Musée du Jeu de Paume, Paris, *Trois Siècles d'Art aux Etats-Unis. Exposition Organisée en Collaboration avec le Museum of Modern Art, New York. Musée du Jeu de Paume, Paris. Mai-Juillett 1938.* [Paris]: Editions des Musées Nationaux [1938].

*The Metropolitan Museum of Art, New York, *Life in America; a Special Loan Exhibition of Paintings Held During the Period of the New York World's Fair. April 24-October 29* [1939], *New York.* [The Metropolitan Museum of Art], 1939.

*Carnegie Institute, Pittsburgh, Pa., *Survey of American Painting. October twenty-fourth-December fifteenth, 1940.* [Pittsburgh, Pa.]: Department of Fine Arts, Carnegie Institute [1940].

*Santa Barbara Museum of Art, Santa Barbara, Calif. . . . *Painting Today and Yesterday in the United States . . ., June fifth-September first, 1941.* Santa Barbara, Calif. [1941].

*The Detroit Institute of Arts, Detroit, Mich., *Five Centuries of Marine Painting; Twenty-Third Loan Exhibition of Old Masters. Catalogue, The Detroit Institute of Arts. March 6 through April 5, 1942.* [Detroit, 1942].

*The Museum of Modern Art, New York, *American Realists and Magic Realists. . . .* [New York]: The Museum of Modern Art [1943].

*————, *Romantic Painting in America, by James Thrall Soby and Dorothy C. Miller.* New York: The Museum of Modern Art [1943].

*National Gallery of Art, Washington, D.C., *American Battle Painting 1776-1918.* [The exhibition . . . held at the National Gallery of Art, Washington, from July 4 to September 4, and at the Museum of Modern Art, New York, from October 5 to November 18, 1944.] Washington, D.C., National Gallery of Art, Smithsonian Institution; New York: The Museum of Modern Art [1944].

*Museum of Fine Arts, Boston, *Sport in American Art. October 10 through December 10, 1944.* Boston, Mass: Museum of Fine Arts [1944].

*Knoedler Galleries, New York, *American Painting; Landscape, Genre, and Still Life of the 19th and 20th Century. November 20-December 9, 1944.* [At Knoedler Galleries, New York.] [New York, 1944].

*The Detroit Institute of Arts, Detroit, Mich., *The World of the Romantic Artist; A Survey of American Culture from 1800 to 1875. Catalogue by E. P. Richardson. Twenty-Sixth Loan Exhibition. December 28, 1944-January 28, 1945.* [Detroit, 1944]

*The Art Institute of Chicago, Chicago, *The Hudson River School and the Early American Landscape Tradition, by Frederick A. Sweet, The Art Institute of Chicago. February 15 to March 25, 1945; Whitney Museum of American Art, New York, April 17 to May 18, 1945.* [Chicago: The Art Institute of Chicago, 1945]

*Brooks Memorial Art Gallery, Memphis, Tenn., *A Loan Exhibition of American

282

Paintings; Portraits, Landscapes and Genre of the 18th and 19th Century. October 5 to 29, 1945. [Memphis, Tenn., 1945]

National Gallery [The Tate Gallery], London, American Painting from the Eighteenth Century to the Present Day. June-July, 1946. [London, The Tate Gallery, 1946]

Dallas Museum of Fine Arts, Dallas, Texas, 200 Years of American Painting. October 5 to November 4, 1946. Assembled for the State Fair of Texas. [Dallas, Texas, 1946]

M. Knoedler and Co., New York, Washington Irving and His Circle; A Loan Exhibition Observing the Restoration of "Sunnyside." October 8 through October 26, 1946. At M. Knoedler & Co., New York. [New York: The Gallery Press, 1946]

City Art Museum of St. Louis, *Charles Wimar, 1828-1862, Painter of the Indian Frontier. [Exhibition at] City Art Museum of St. Louis, 13 October to 18 November 1946.* St. Louis, Mo.: City Art Museum, 1946.

The Washington County Museum of Fine Arts, Hagerstown, Md., American Romantic; A Loan Exhibition—Oil Paintings of That Phase of Romantic American Art Popularly Known as the Hudson River School. March 30, 1947 through April 27, 1947. Hagerstown, Md., [1947].

The Corcoran Gallery of Art, Washington, D.C., De Gustibus; An Exhibition of American Paintings Illustrating a Century of Taste and Criticism. January 9 Through February 20, 1949. Washington, D.C.: The Corcoran Gallery of Art [1949].

The Brooklyn Museum, New York, Westward Ho, by Herbert J. Spinden . . . a Handbook for the Exhibition of the Same Name on the Romantic History of Westward Expansion in the United States. Exhibition Dates; February 9-April 10, 1949. [New York]: The Brooklyn Museum, [1949].

City Art Museum of St. Louis, St. Louis, Mississippi Panorama; Being an Exhibition of the Life and Landscape of the Father of Waters and Its Great Tributary, the Missouri . . . at the City Art Museum of St. Louis, in the Fall of 1949. [St. Louis, Mo.: City Art Museum of St. Louis, 1949]

The Corcoran Gallery of Art, Washington, D.C., American Processional, 1492-1900. A Special Exhibition Held at the Corcoran Gallery of Art from July 8 through December 17, 1950, to Commemorate the Establishment of the Parmanent Seat of the Federal Government in Washington in the Year 1800. [Washington, D.C.]: The Corcoran Gallery of Art [1950].

National Academy of Design, New York, The American Tradition, 1800-1900; Dec. 3-23 1951. [New York, 1951]

Wildenstein & Co., New York, A Loan Exhibition of Great American Paintings. Landmarks in American Art, 1670-1950. . . . February 26 to March 28th 1953. At Wildenstein. . . . [New York, 1953]

Whitney Museum of American Art, New York, American Painting of the Nineteenth Century. Organized by the American Federation of Arts and Exhibited Under the Sponsorship of the United States Information Agency by Seven Museums in Germany and Italy, 1953-1954. . . . [At the Whitney Museum of American Art, New York.] *April 22-May 23, 1954.* [New York, 1954]

283

*The Joslyn Art Museum, Omaha, Neb., *Life on the Prairie; The Artist's Record, May 12-July 4, 1954. An Omaha Centennial Exhibition at The Joslyn Art Museum.* [Omaha, Neb., 1954]

*City Art Museum of St. Louis, St. Louis, *Westward the Way; The Character and Development of the Louisiana Territory as Seen by Artists and Writers of the Nineteenth Century. Edited by Perry T. Rathbone, City Art Museum of St. Louis in Collaboration with the Walker Art Center, Minneapolis.* [St. Louis, Mo.: City Art Museum of St. Louis, 1954]

*The American Academy of Arts and Letters; the National Institute of Arts and Letters, New York, *The Great Decade in American Writing, 1850-1860 . . . Books and Manuscripts: With Paintings and Friends and Contemporaries of the Authors. December 3-30, 1954.* . . . [New York, 1954]

*The Pennsylvania Academy of the Fine Arts, Philadelphia, *The One Hundred and Fiftieth Anniversary Exhibition, January 15 Through March 13, 1955.* Philadelphia: The Pennsylvania Academy of the Fine Arts [1955].

*The Cincinnati Art Museum, Cincinnati, Ohio, *Rediscoveries in American Painting, Oct. 3-Nov. 6, 1955.* [Cincinnati, O., 1955]

*Des Moines Art Center, Des Moines, Iowa, *Communicating Art From Midwest Collections, October 13 Through November 6, 1955.* [Des Moines, Iowa: Des Moines Art Center, 1955]

*The Carnegie Institute, Pittsburgh, Pa., *American Classics of the Nineteenth Century.* [Pittsburgh, Pa.: The Carnegie Institute, 1957]

*William Rockhill Nelson Gallery of Art, Kansas City, Mo., *The Last Frontier, An Exhibition of the Art of the Old West, October 5 to November 17, 1957,* [Kansas City, Mo.: William Rockhill Nelson Gallery of Art, 1957]

*Wildenstein & Co., New York, *The American Vision: Paintings of Three Centuries . . . October 23 to November 16, 1957.* New York: Wildenstein [1957].

*The Brooklyn Museum, New York, *Face of America: The History of Portraiture in the United States. . . . November 14, 1957-January 26, 1958.* [New York: The Brooklyn Museum, 1957]

*Dallas Museum of Fine Arts, Dallas, Texas, *Famous Paintings and Famous Painters, October 4 Through November 2, 1958.* [Dallas, Texas: Dallas Museum of Fine Arts, 1958]

*The Cincinnati Art Museum, Cincinnati, Ohio, *Two Centuries of American Painting, October 4 to November 4, 1958.* [Cincinnati, O., 1958]

*The Corcoran Gallery of Art, Washington, D.C., *The American Muse: Parallel Trends in Literature and Art . . . , April 4-May 17, 1959.* [Washington, D.C.: The Corcoran Gallery of Art, 1959]

*————, *American Painters of The South, April 23-June 5, 1960.* [Washington, D.C.: The Corcoran Gallery of Art, 1960]

*John Herron Art Museum, Indianapolis, Ind., *Romantic America, January 8-February 5, 1961.* [Indianapolis, Ind.: John Herron Art Museum, 1961]

*Bowdoin College Museum of Fine Arts, Brunswick, Maine, *American Paintings of the*

284

*19th and 20th Centuries, from the Collection of Mr. and Mrs. Norman B. Woolworth
... January 29 to February 28, 1961.* [Brunswick, Maine: Bowdoin College Museum
of Fine Arts, 1961]

*William Rockhill Nelson Gallery of Art, Kansas City, Mo., *George Caleb Bingham,
Sesquicentennial Exhibition, 1811/1961.* [Exhibition] *March 16 - April 30, 1961*
[and] *at City Art Museum of St. Louis May 16-June 30, 1961.* Kansas City, Mo.:
William Rockhill Nelson Gallery of Art, 1961. *(The Nelson Gallery and Atkins
Museum Bulletin, III.)*

AUCTION AND BOOKSELLERS' CATALOGUES

*(Arranged in chronological order. Asterisks indicate publications in which pictures by
or attributed to George Caleb Bingham are included.)*

M. Thomas & Son, Philadelphia, *Fine Arts. M. Thomas & Son, Will Sell at Auction.
At Their Auction Rooms ... The Elegant Paintings, Drawings, Etchings & Engrav-
ings of William Carey, London, lately in the Rembrandt Exhibition at Its Close.*
[Sale, May 2, 1838.] [Philadelphia, 1838]

Carey & Hart, Philadelphia, *Carey & Hart's Catalogue of Choice, Rare, and Valuable
Books, Forming the Most Complete ollection of English Editions Ever Imported ...
Are for Sale ...* Philadelphia [1839].

————, *Carey & Hart's Catalogue of a Valuable Collection of Books, in the Various
Branches of Architecture, Engineering, and Science ... Most of Which Have Been
Recently Imported ...* Philadelphia [1839].

*American Art-Union, New York, *Catalogue of Pictures and Other Works of Art, the
Property of the American Art-Union. To be Sold at Auction by David Austen, Jr....
the 15th ... 16th, and ... 17, December, 1852....* [New York, 1852]

*————, *Artists' Sale ... Catalogue of Very Valuable and Choice Paintings Recently
Selected from the Studios of the Most Distinguished and Resident Artists, to be Sold
... at Auction ... Thursday, Dec. 30, 1852.* [New York, 1852.]

*Thomas Dowling, Washington, D.C., *Catalogue of the Collection Paintings, Statuary,
Bronzes, & c. Belonging to the Estate of the Late J. C. McGuire, to be Sold by Order
of His Executors on December 10th* [1888], *& Following Days ... at Salesrooms of
Thomas Dowling....* [Washington, D.C., 1888]

*Administrator's Sale, Kansas City, Mo., Notice, dated March 9, 1893, announcing
"Administrator's Sale of Original Paintings of the Late Gen. Bingham," to be sold
"at Public Auction, at Findlay's Art Store ... Kansas City, Mo." on "the 25th ...
of March, 1893." (Broadside)

*Rains Galleries, New York, *Important Collection of Paintings of Scenic and Historical
Americana from the Estate of the Late W. F. Hammond, Esq. of Brooklyn, N.Y., with
Additions ... May 23, 1935....* [New York, 1935]

*Ben J. Selkirk & Sons, St. Louis, *Traditional Americana ... Removed from Promi-
nent Civil War Residence Belonging to the Estate of the Late Hugh Campbell ...
Together with Selections from Private Consignors ... Public Sale ... Beginning ...*

February 24th ... Continuing ... February 25th and 26th [1941]. St. Louis, Mo., 1941.

Parke-Bernet Galleries, Inc., New York, Paintings of Various Schools ... Property of Mrs. Dwight F. Davis ... Paintings Collected by the Late John P. Porter ... and from Other Owners. Public Sale ... March 20 [1941]. New York [1941].

Kende Galleries, Inc., New York, Property of Mrs. Charles Waldo Stickle, New York ... Paintings from the Collection of the Late J. H. Braun, Philadelphia, and from Other Sources ... Public Sale ... April 17th and 18th [1941]. New York [1941].

Parke-Bernet Galleries, Inc., New York, Art of Four Centuries ... A Distinguished Inventory, Property of Arnold Seligmann, Rey & Co., Inc., New York ... Public Auction Sale, January 23 ... January 24 and 25 [1947].... New York, 1947.

NEWSPAPERS

(This is a selective listing only. In a few instances important articles have been repeated in the listing of those papers that reprinted the original report. The references are arranged alphabetically by town, and chronologically by paper and date. Many newspapers changed their mastheads from time to time, as well as their places of publication. Such changes are indicated, based on information provided by American Newspapers, 1821-1936; A Union List ... [New York, 1937]. *Abbreviations used here are: Ad. [Advertisement]; B. or G.C.B. [George Caleb Bingham]; Ed. [Editorial]; H.V.B. [Henry Vest Bingham, Sr.]; Not. [Notice].)*

I. Boonville, Mo.:

1. Boonville *Observer* (1840-ca. 1846); Boonville *Weekly Observer* (ca. 1846-1862); *Central Missouri Advertiser* (1862-1873); Boonville *Missouri Advertiser* (1873-1875); Boonville *Weekly Advertiser* (1876-1921)

"The Convention," Oct. 15, 1844, 2-1.

Ed., Candidacy of B. for State Legislature, June 24, 1846, 2-1.

Text of B. speech before House of Representatives of State Legislature, concerning contested election, March 11, 1847, 1-6.

"George C. Bingham, the Artist," Sept. 30, 1854, 1-7 (from the Philadelphia *Register*, Sept. 7).

Re B.'s portrait of Thomas Jefferson; resolution of Mr. King concerning placement in House of Representatives at Jefferson City, Feb. 26, 1859.

B. a spiritualist, Jan. 25, 1878, 2-5.

Marriage, B. to Mrs. Lykins, June 21, 1878, 4-2.

B. visits Boonville, Oct. 11, 1878, 8-1.

B. visits Boonville on way to Virginia, Nov. 15, 1878, 4-1.

Life sketch of B., July 11, 1879, 4-3.

Not., death of B., Dec. 12, 1879.

"Characterization of Kansas Citian, Formerly of Boonville," Jan. 2, 1885. 1-5.

Biographical Sketch of Missouri's Greatest Painter" (Louella Styles Vincent), Feb. 25, 1898, 2-1 (from St. Louis *Globe-Democrat*, Feb. 20).

"Bingham's Famous Painting" ("Order No. 11") (W. L. Webb), June 14, 1901, 2-1.

2. Boonville *Tri-Weekly Topic* (1877-1890[?]); *Topic* (1877-1888)

B. visiting Boonville, at Nelson home, painting portrait of Mrs. J. T. Birch, Aug. 18, 1877.

3. Boonville *Weekly Eagle* (1865-1878)

School of Art established at University; B. made Instructor, June 22, 1877, 2-5.

B. an instructor in School of Art at University, Oct. 12, 1877, 2-2.

4. *Missouri Register* (1839-1854[?])

"Multilation of Banners," Oct. 15, 1844, 2-2.

II. Columbia, Mo.:

1. Columbia *Herald-Statesman*: Missouri *Intelligencer* and *Boon's Lick Advertiser* (1819); Missouri *Intelligencer* (1819-1835); Columbia *Patriot* (1835-1842); Missouri *Statesman* (1843-1851[?]); Weekly Missouri *Statesman* (1851-1860[?]); Columbia Missouri *Statesman* (1861[?]-1905[?]); Columbia *Statesman* (1905[?]-1913). Published in Franklin, April, 1819-June 1826; in Fayette, 1826-April, 1830; afterward in Columbia.

Ad., H.V.B. opens tavern at Franklin, May 6, 1820, 2-4.

H.V.B. appointed judge, County Court, Howard Co., Jan. 1, 1821, 3-1.

Not., H.V.B., death of daughter Eliza Bingham, March 5, 1821, 3-3.

H.V.B. chairman of assembly preparing petition to general assembly, May 7, 1821.

H.V.B. named justice of peace, Howard Co., June 25, 1821.

H.V.B. opens tobacco factory at Franklin, Nov. 13, 1821.

Ad., H.V.B. and William Lamme, Tobacco Factory: Nov. 13, 1821; Nov. 27, 1821; Jan 22, 1822, 4-4; Feb. 12, 1822, 4-4; Oct. 7, 1823.

H.V.B. builds tobacco storage warehouse, Franklin, Nov. 19, 1822.

H.V.B. charter member, treas., on constitutional committee, local Masonic Lodge, Union #7, May 14, 1822.

H.V.B. judge of circuit court, Howard Co.: July 9, 1822; July 16, 1822; Aug. 20, 1822, 3-5; May 27, 1823, 2-5; Aug. 12, 1823, 3-4; Dec. 30, 1823, 3-4.

H.V.B. unable to hold court, May 20, 1823.

Not., Death of H.V.B. (Dec. 26), Dec. 27, 1823.

Not., Funeral of H.V.B., Dec. 30, 1823.

H.V.B. (Estate), Not., Property to be sold, Jan. 15, 1824, 3-2.

Not., Public sale of H.V.B. household property in Franklin, Jan. 22, 1824, 4-2.

Visit to Columbia studio of G.C.B., March 14, 1835, 3-1.

B. as politician, June 19, 1846.

Contested Election, B. and Sappington letters, Oct. 2, 1846, 3-1.

B. in State Legislature, Nov. 27, 1846.

287

Contested election, Sappington awarded seat, Dec. 25, 1846, 1-4, 1-3.

Contested election, Reports of committee on elections, Jan. 22, 1847.

Letter from Marshall (June 29) mentioning B.'s candidacy for Legislature, July 7, 1848, 2-5.

B. elected over Sappington, Aug. 11, 1848, 2-1.

Not., Death of Sarah Elizabeth Bingham at Arrow Rock (Nov. 29), Dec. 29, 1848, 3-2.

American Art-Union, engraving of "The Jolly Flatboatmen," July 6, 1849, 2-2.

Sketch of life and work of B., Aug. 31, 1849, 1-5.

B. in Columbia, at work on portraits, Sept. 28, 1849, 2-2.

Not., Marriage of B. to Eliza Thomas (Dec. 2), Dec. 7, 1849, 3-4.

"The Lathrop Portrait," Dec. 27, 1850, 2-1.

B. in Columbia from New York, May 23, 1851, 3-1
    (from St. Louis *Republican*, May 13).

"New Works of Art by Bingham," Oct. 31, 1851, 2-4.

"The Missouri Artist," Jan. 9, 1852, 3-2
    (from St. Louis *Intelligencer*).

"The County Election" ready for engraver, March 19, 1852.

B. Delegate to Whig National Convention, Baltimore, June 4, 1852.

B.'s portrait of Dr. William Jewell in subject's will, Aug. 20, 1852.

"New Pictures by Bingham," Sept. 10, 1852, 1-7
    (from the New York *Mirror*).

"Bingham's Splendid Pictures," Oct. 29, 1852, 2-5.

Re "The County Election," April 22, 1853.

Re "The County Election," June 10, 1853.

Re "The County Election," June 17, 1853.

"The Fine Arts.—George C. Bingham, Esq.," Nov. 18, 1853, 2-1.

Sartain at work on engraving of "The County Election," Feb. 3, 1854.

Engraving of "The County Election," June 30, 1854
    (from St. Louis *Pilot*).

Engraving of "The County Election," Sept. 15, 1854.

Re engraving of "The County Election," Sept. 22, 1854, 3-3, 4-1.

B. in Columbia, painting portraits, Sept. 14, 1855.

B. in Jefferson City, painting portraits, Nov. 23, 1855.

B. speaks at Whig meeting in Jefferson City (Dec. 1), Dec. 14, 1855, 1-6.

B. in Columbia, at work on "Washington Crossing Delaware," March 14, 1856, 3-4.

B. leaves for Europe, May 16, 1856, 1-5
    (from St. Louis *Republican*).

B. in Düsseldorf, painting State portraits and "Jolly Flatboatmen," Dec. 18, 1857, 3-3
    (from Fulton *Telegraph*).

B. returns to Jefferson City from Düsseldorf, Jan. 28, 1859, 3-3.

B. in Columbia, Feb. 4, 1859, 3-2.

B. commissioned to paint portraits of Jackson, Clay for State, Feb. 25, 1859, 2-5.

B. in Brunswick (Mo.), April 22, 1859, 3-2.

B. returns from Germany; in Columbia, Sept. 9, 1859, 3-1.

Re Commission for portrait of Humboldt, April 27, 1860.

Re Commission for portrait of Humboldt, June 29, 1860.

Painting of "Order No. 11" in progress, Nov. 24, 1865
    (from Kansas City *Journal*).

B. submits name to Congressional Nominating Committee as candidate from Sixth District, June 1, 1866.

B. at work on painting of Major Dean, July 6, 1866
    (from St. Louis *Dispatch*).

B. defeated by nominating convention, Oct. 5, 1866.

"Portrait of Lyon by Bingham," March 22, 1867, 2-4.

B. appointed Elector for Sixth District by Democratic State Convention, June 5, 1868.

"Bingham's Picture, 'Order No. 11,'" Jan. 1, 1869, 3-2.

B. on School Board at Independence, Oct. 1, 1869.

B. sells residence in Independence to move to Kansas City, May 6, 1870, 4-1
    (from Independence *Sentinel*).

Artist Charles P. Stewart in Kansas City to study with B., July 15, 1870, 3-1.

B. in Columbia, at work on portrait of Rollins, Oct. 13, 1871, 3-3.

"Bingham's Latest Picture" ("Pike's Peak"), Nov. 22, 1872, 1-6.

B.'s portrait of Rollins completed, on view, April 11, 1873, 3-2.

B.'s law suit against Michael Dively, Jan. 23, 1874, 2-2.

B. withdraws candidacy for Congress, Aug. 28, 1874.

Re "The Puzzled Witness," Dec. 11, 1874, 1-5
    (from St. Louis *Republican*).

B. as Adjutant-General, Nov. 12, 1875, 2-1.

"The Adjutant-General," May 4, 1876, 2-1.

B. letter to Dr. Mumford (May 8), May 10, 1876, 1-4.

Not., Death of Eliza Thomas Bingham at Fulton (Nov. 3), Nov. 10, 1876, 2-5, 3-5.

B. in Boonville at Nelson residence, portrait painting, July 6, 1877, 2-1.

B. in Columbia superintending studio arrangements at University, Sept. 28, 1877, 3-2.

B. in St. Louis, Jan. 4, 1878, 3-1.

B. in Kansas City, Jan. 18, 1878, 3-2.

"Order No. 11," Edwards defends Ewing against attack by B., March 29, 1878, 4-3 (from Sedalia *Democrat*).

Not., Marriage of B. to Mrs. Lykins, June 21, 1878, 2-1.

Re Marriage of B. to Mrs. Lykins, July 5, 1878, 3-2.

B. appointed member of Commission on Lee Monument, Nov. 8, 1878, 2-2.

B. in Columbia from Richmond, Va., Dec. 6, 1878, 3-1.

Visit to B's studio in Columbia, March 7, 1879, 2-4.

"Gen. Bingham's Lecture," March 7, 1879, 2-3.

B.'s letter on Ewing referred to, June 20, 1879, 1-2.

B.'s studio in Franklin, Aug. 15, 1879.

"Portrait of Judge Todd," Jan. 16, 1880, 1-2.

2. *State Argus* (1852-1860) ; Weekly Missouri *Sentinel* (1852-1853) ; Dollar Missouri *Journal* (1853-1855) ; Weekly Missouri State *Journal* (1856) ; Union *Democrat* (1856-1857). Suspended Dec. 13, 1855-Jan. 17, 1856; Oct. 25, 1858-April 7, 1859.

Re "The County Election," Oct. 28, 1852.

3. *University Missourian*, later Columbia *Missourian*. Published by School of Journalism, University of Missouri, Columbia. A laboratory daily town newspaper, not in *Union List*. *(Note:* M refers to articles in *The Missourian Magazine*, Sat. Section.)

Portrait of Washington by Clara Bingham, Sept. 17, 1908.

Sketch of life of B., list of portraits and owners, July 31, 1917, 2-3.

Sketch of B., portraits of Columbians, April 21, 1922, 3-4.

Re Painting "Order No. 11," Oct. 19, 1922, 6-4.

B. home at Arrow Rock, Aug. 27, 1924, 4-3.

"George Bingham, Missouri's First Artist, Portrays Pioneer Life," March 26, 1926, 7-2.

Move to preserve Jackson–Bingham home, March 11, 1927, 4-3.

"G. B. Rollins Recalls Early Missouri Artist," Sept. 28, 1929, 6-1 (M).

"Bingham's Portrait of Adams Owned by Rollins," Sept. 28, 1929, 7-2 (M).

Vinnie Ream portrait by B. given to Society, Oct. 26, 1929 (M).

Life of B., Oct. 11, 1930 (M).

"Historical Library Houses Original Bingham Paintings," Oct. 18, 1930 (M).

B. and his paintings, Feb. 16, 1939.

III. Franklin, Mo.:

Missouri *Intelligencer* and *Boon's Lick Advertiser*, founded in Franklin in 1819, later *Missouri Intelligencer*, was published continuously in Franklin, 1819-1835; afterward in Columbia. See under Columbia, Mo., Columbia *Herald-Statesman* for Franklin listings.

IV. Glasgow, Mo.:

Glasgow *Weekly Times:* Western *Monitor* (1827-1836) ; *Missourian* (1837-1840) ; *Boon's Lick Times* (1840-1848) ; Glasgow *Times* (1848-1861) ; Howard *Union* (1865-1866). Published in Fayette, 1827-Sept., 1848. Suspended 1861-June, 1865.

Re "The County Election" and "Daniel Boone Coming Through Cumberland Gap," Nov. 11, 1852.

"The County Election"; B. in Glasgow on way to Boonville, Sept. 28, 1854, 2-2 (from Missouri *Statesman*).

Re Engraving of "County Election," Nov. 23, 1854, 2-1.

V. Jefferson City, Mo.:

1. Jeffersonian *Republican: Jeffersonian* (1825-1831). Published in St. Charles in 1825.

    Visit to B. studio in St. Louis, Jan. 2, 1836, 4-2 (from St. Louis *Bulletin*).

2. Jefferson City *Metropolitan*

    "The Jolly Raftmen, by G. C. Bingham," Aug. 17, 1847
    (from New-York *Express*).

3. Jefferson City *Weekly Democrat-Tribune:* People's *Tribune* (1865-1885) ; Jefferson City *Tribune* (1885-1899)

    B. speech at State Convention in St. Louis, July 11, 1866, 3-4.

    Letter B. to Johnson re "Order No. 11," Dec. 23, 1868, 1-4 (from Independence *Sentinel*).

    Letter, B. on "Civil War," March 24, 1869, 1-4.

    B. shows pictures in Jefferson City, Jan. 25, 1871, 3-1.

    Letter, B. on "Order No. 11," Sept. 24, 1873, 2-4.

    B. withdraws candidacy for Congress, Sept. 16, 1874, 2-4; Sept. 30, 1874, 1-6.

    B. in Washington, his opinion on chances of obtaining military claims, March 4, 1876, 1-5 (from Saline County *Progress*).

    Sketch of B., March 8, 1876, 4-4.

    B. suggested for governorship of Missouri, March 22, 1876, 2-4.

    "A Startling Rumor," April 21, 1876, 2-1.

    Re portraits of Vinnie Ream and Miss Coleman, April 30, 1876, 2-1.

    B. returns from Washington (May 1), May 2, 1876, 1-2.

    Letter, Mumford's reply to B. (May 11), May 16, 1876, 2-2.

    B.'s investigation in Ripley County disorders, Aug. 30, 1876.

    Not., Death of Eliza Thomas Bingham, Nov. 8, 1876, 3-5.

    Re B.'s reply to Schofield letter on Ewing, Feb. 27, 1877, 2-1; March 1, 1877, 2-4; March 7, 1877, 4-2.

    B. authorized to paint historical picture, March 22, 1877, 1-4; March 28, 1877, 3-3.

    B. marriage to Mrs. Lykins, June 20, 1878, 1-4; June 26, 1878, 4-5.

    Not., Death and life sketch of B., July 9, 1879, 2-1.

    Not., Death and funeral account, July 16, 1879, 1-3, 2-2 (from *Kansas City Mail*, July 7, 1879).

    Sale of B. paintings to be held, Kansas City, March 21, 1893, 2-1.

    "Order No. 11" sold at auction in Kansas City, April 5, 1893, 4-3.

4. Jefferson *Weekly Inquirer:* Jefferson *Inquirer,* 1838 (?)-1854
B. painting portraits in Jefferson City, Dec. 26, 1844, 3-5.
B. in St. Louis, June 26, 1845, 3-1.
B. presents Lathrop portrait to Ladies of Columbia, Dec. 28, 1850, 2-2.
"New Works of Art by Bingham," Nov. 15, 1851, 3-2
(from Missouri *Statesman,* Oct. 31).
"The Missouri Artist," Jan. 17, 1852, 1-6
(from St. Louis *Intelligencer*).
Re engraving of "The County Election," Nov. 6, 1852, 3-1.
B.'s portrait of Jefferson placed in House, Feb. 5, 1859, 3-1.
B.'s portraits of Jackson and Clay in Capitol, Jan. 12, 1861, 4-6.

VI. Kansas City, Mo.:

1. Kansas City *Journal-Post*: Kansas City *Journal* (1854-1927); united with Kansas City *Post* in 1927
"The Bingham Paintings," March 25, 1893, 3-1. "Sold at Auction: The Best of General Bingham's Paintings Went at Low Prices," March 26, 1893, 2-4.
Sketch of life of B., Feb., 22, 1922.
Sketch of life of B., Feb. 27, 1927.
Reminiscences of B's niece, Mrs. F. M. McKinney at memorial dinner, May 31, 1934.

2. Kansas City *Star* (1880—)
"For the Ex-Confederates: Works of the Late G. C. Bingham to be Sold March 25," March 18, 1893, 5-1. "The Bingham Paintings Sold," March 25, 1893, 1-6.
B. studio torn down, Oct. 6, 1901.
Reminiscences of B's son, J. Rollins Bingham, Dec. 5, 1909, 13-1.
"The Immortal Canvas of George Caleb Bingham Preserved the Animosities of Border Strife," Dec. 27, 1925.
"A Bingham Painting at Missouri University" ("Watching the Cargo"), Feb. 22, 1927.
B. as Arrow Rock figure (by Richard B. Fowler), Oct. 12, 1930.
Re "Order No. 11" (by C. B. Rollins), Nov. 13, 1932.

3. Kansas City *Times* (1868—)
Re B.'s paintings of Vinnie Ream and Miss Coleman, April 29, 1876.
Death of B., July 8, 1879.
"In Kansas City Forty Years Ago" (re death of B.), July 8, 1919.
Re "Order No. 11," Aug. 24, 1925, 3-3.
Life sketch of B., Nov. 7, 1929.
Life sketch of B. (by M. K. P.), June 2, 1934.
B. Police Commissioner in 1874, April 25, 1939.
"A Famous Bingham Painting to William Jewell College" ("Major Dean in Jail"), Sept. 13, 1941.

VII. Lexington, Ky.:

The Kentucky Statesman

B. Exhibiting "The County Election" in Lexington, May 24, 1853, 3-2.

"Public Weal," criticism of "The County Election," May 31, 1853.

VIII. Liberty, Mo.:

Liberty *Tribune* (1846-after 1895): Liberty *Weekly Tribune* (1846-ca. 1860)

B. candidate for Legislature, June 13, 1846, 3-1.

B. elected to Legislature, Aug. 15, 1846, 3-1; Oct. 31, 1846, 2-5.

B.'s election contested by Sappington, Oct. 10, 1846, 2-4.

"Representative from Saline County Assails Governor Edwards' Message to General Assembly," Nov. 28, 1846, 2-5.

Ed., B. mentioned, Dec. 19, 1846, 2-1.

"Contested Election Case from Saline County Between Bingham and Sappington Decided in Sappington's Favor," Jan. 2, 1847, 3-3.

B. attends Whig Convention at Boonville, April 14, 1848, 2-4.

Re B. campaign for Representative from Saline, Aug. 18, 1848, 2-2.

B. elected Representative, Sept. 29, 1848, 1-2.

B. member of committee in House, Jan. 5, 1849, 2-5.

B. paints portrait of Dr. William Jewell for William Jewell College, Oct. 5, 1849, 1-2, 2-2.

Not., B. marriage to Eliza K. Thomas, Dec. 14, 1849, 3-1.

B. Delegate from Eighth Electoral District to National Whig Convention, April 30, 1852, 2-2.

B. correspondence with J. Winston re Jackson Resolution, June 18, 1852, 1-6.

B.'s portrait of Jewell mentioned in subject's will, Aug. 27, 1852, 2-4.

B. superintends engraving of "County Election," at work on "County Canvass," in Philadelphia, Nov. 25, 1853, 2-5.

B. paints Washington, Jefferson portraits, "Jolly Flatboatmen" in Düsseldorf, Dec. 18, 1857, 2-1.

Re Portraits of Jackson, Clay for Capitol, Mar. 18, 1859, 1-5 (from Missouri *Statesman*).

B. commissioned to paint portrait of Humboldt, March 9, 1860, 1-4.

"Senator Thompson on The Fine Arts," Feb. 1, 1861, 1-3.

B.'s portrait of General Lyon, March 8, 1867, 2-1.

Re Appropriation for Lyon portrait, March 15, 1867, 2-4.

B. investigates attack on house of Reuben Samuels, Feb. 5, 1875, 2-1.

"The Clay County Tragedy," report by B., Feb. 12, 1875, 1-4, 2-1.

"Indictment of the late Adjutant-General," investigation by B. of frauds during predecessor's administration, Jan. 7, 1876, 2-4.

"The War Claims," B. in connection with, Feb. 4, 1876, 1-4.

Life Sketch of B., July 11, 1879, 2-3 (from Kansas City *Journal*).

IX. Louisville, Ky.:

1. *Daily Louisville Times*
"An Exquisite Painting," re "The County Election," on exhibition in Louisville, April 6, 1853, 2-1.
"That Painting 'The County Election,'" May 14, 1853, 3-3.
"Mr. Bingham's Picture," May 19, 1853, 3-1.

2. Louisville *Daily Courier* (1844-1868); Louisville *Morning Courier* (1844-1850); united with Louisville *Daily Journal* to form Louisville *Courier-Journal*, 1868
Re "The County Election," May 18, 1853.

3. Louisville *Daily Journal* (1830-1868); united with Louisville *Daily Courier* to form Louisville *Courier-Journal*, 1868
Re "The County Election," May 16, 1853.
Re "The County Election," May 19, 1853.

X. Marshall, Mo.:

Saline County Progress (1865-1917)
B. addresses the public, July 31, 1868, 3-2.
B.'s "Order No. 11," March 19, 1869, 1-4.
Letter from B. on "Civil War," March 26, 1869, 1-5.
B. in town to deliver engravings of "Order No. 11," July 9, 1873, 3-1.
"Arrow Rock Items," B. in town, July 16, 1873, 4-4.
Re "Order No. 11," Oct. 1, 1873, 2-2.
"Bingham's Great Picture" ("Order No. 11"), May 1, 1874, 3-6.
"Death of Mr. Bingham," July 17, 1879, 3-6.

XI. New Orleans, La.:

Times-Picayune (1836——); *Daily Picayune* (1836-1914)
"An American Work of Art," re exhibition of "The County Election" at H. D. Hewitt's music store, March 18, 1853, suppl., 1-1.
"A Good Picture Well Sold," re sale of "The County Election": to "a Kentucky gentleman" [Ward], March 24, 1853, 2-1.

XII. New York, N.Y.:

New York *Daily Tribune*
B. in New York; his pictures in American Art-Union, Aug. 13, 1849, 2-3.

XIII. Petersburg, Va.:

American Statesman (1839-1843)
B. has studio in Petersburg, painting portraits, June 18, 1841.

XIV. Philadelphia, Pa.:

Philadelphia *Daily Register* (1847-1854); title varies: *Daily Register*; Philadelphia *Evening Register*
Re Engraving of "The County Election," Sept. 7, 1854.

XV. St. Louis, Mo.:

1. *Daily Commercial Bulletin* (1835——); St. Louis *Commercial Bulletin* and

Missouri *Literary Register* (1835-1836) ; *Daily Commercial Bulletin* and Missouri *Literary Register* (1836-1838)

"Rocheport Convention," June 22, 1840, 2-1.

2. *Daily New Era* (1840——)

Re "The Stump Orator," on exhibition at Mr. Wool's store, in St. Louis, Nov. 29, 1847, 2-4.

3. *Evening Gazette* or *Daily Evening Gazette* (1838——)

Refers to Bingham's work in St. Louis, June 26, 1839, 2-1.

4. *Mill Boy* (1844-1845)

"Boonville Convention" (Oct. 11), Oct. 26, 1844, 3-2.

5. *Missouri Saturday News* (1840——)

Professional card, B. studio at No. 60 Main Street, Jan. 25, 1840.

B. reported in Fayette, painting portraits, Feb. 8 and 15, 1840.

6. *St. Louis Democrat* (1842-1875) ; *Native American Bulletin* (1842-1842[?]) ; *Old School Democrat* and St. Louis *Herald* (1843-1844[?]) ; St. Louis *Democrat* (1844-1851[?]) ; *Daily Missouri Democrat* (1852-1872) ; united with St. Louis *Daily Globe* to form St. Louis *Globe-Democrat* (after 1872)

"George C. Bingham's Great Historical Painting, 'Civil War,'" on exhibition at Pettes & Leathe's Gallery, St. Louis, June 6, 1869, 1.

Portrait of Gen. F. P. Blair by B. on exhibition at Pettes & Leathe's Gallery, St. Louis, Aug. 9, 1874, 1.

"An Artist at Rest, The Rather Unexpected Demise of Ex-Adjutant-General Bingham," July 8, 1879, 2-4, 4-1.

"Missouri's Greatest Painter" (by Louella Styles Vincent), Feb. 20, 1898, 40-1.

"Missouri's great painter of American political campaign scenes. Gen. George C. Bingham . . . (by Shannon Mountjoy), Nov. 6, 1904, 5-3 (mag. section).

7. St. Louis *Republic* (1835-1919) : *Daily Missouri Republican* (1835-1873[?]) ; St. Louis *Republican* (1873-1876[?]) ; *Missouri Republican* (1876-1888) ; merged with St. Louis *Globe-Democrat*

Card announces presence of B. in St. Louis, March 24, 1835, 3-2.

B. and his work noted, Dec. 13, 1836, 2-1.

"Native Talent," May 16, 1839, 2-1.

"Portrait Painting," June 6, 1839, 2-2.

Card announces absence of B. from St. Louis until Sept. 5th, Aug. 19, 1839, 2-4.

B. returned to St. Louis, Sept. 10, 1839, 2-1.

Description of fire that destroyed B. studio in St. Louis, Dec. 12, 1839, 2-1.

"Portrait Painting," referring to B.'s return to St. Louis after his long sojourn in the East, June 4, 1845, 2-2.

Reference to B.'s portraits of J. Q. Adams and D. R. Atchison, June 18, 1845, 3-1.

Refers to two paintings ("Lighter Relieving a Steamboat Aground" and "Raftsmen Playing Cards") on exhibition in St. Louis, April 21, 1847, 2-1.

Majority report of B. and others in state legislature on slavery, March 24, 1849, 2-2.

"The Missouri Artist" (refers to "County Politician," "St. Louis Wharf," and "Wood Yard"), April 17, 1849, 2-1.

"Beautiful Paintings," referring to paintings by B. then on exhibition at Mr. Jones's store, Oct. 11, 1850, 2-2.

Notes arrival of B. in St. Louis for winter; description of "The County Election," still incomplete, Nov. 12, 1851, 2-1.

B. in St. Louis; painting, "Verdict of the People," on exhibition at Spore's, May 6, 1856, 2-2.

" 'Civil War,' A Stinging Letter from the Artist," March 17, 1869, 1-2.

Letter from B. re withdrawal of his candidacy from Congress, Sept. 2, 1874, 5.

B.'s painting, "Puzzling a Witness," on exhibition at Harding's, Nov. 29, 1874.

Report of B. on war claims fraud, Oct. 28, 1875.

B. suggested for governor by Jackson County writer, Feb. 21, 1876.

B. urged for governor in letter from "Central Missouri," March 24, 1876, 3.

B.'s reply to letter published in Kansas City *Times*, May 10, 1876, 4.

Mumford's reply to B., May 13, 1876.

Re insanity of B.'s wife, and her placement in state hospital at Fulton, Oct. 27, 1876, 3.

In despatch from Boonville, B. announces desire to retire from public life, and plan to settle in Boonville, Jan. 20, 1877, 2.

"Gen. Ewing's Missouri Order: Letter from Maj.-Gen. Schofield" (Jan. 25), Feb. 21, 1877, 5-4.

"A Scorcher, Gen. Bingham on Order No. 11" (Feb. 22), Feb. 26, 1877, 5-3.

B. on short visit to St. Louis, left for Columbia, Oct. 8, 1877, 8.

Report of visit to B. studio at University of Missouri; lists pictures on exhibition there, Feb. 9, 1879, 5 (from Columbia *Herald-Statesman*).

Description of painting of Daniel Boone (probably signboard) then in Alsop's Store, New Franklin, which is said to have been painted by B. "while a boy," Feb. 13, 1879, 7.

Not., Death of B., July 8, 1879, 4-1.

Sketch of life of B., July 9, 1879, 4-6.

"Order No. 11" or "Martial Law," Feb. 17, 1901.

8. St. Louis *Post-Dispatch* (1878——)

"A Voice from the Grave"; B.'s reply to Gov. Brown on Order No. 11, July 23, 1879.

9. *Weekly Reveille* (1844-1850[?])

"Very Fine Paintings," referring to B.'s pictures then on exhibition in St. Louis, March 23, 1846, 798-3.

Description of landscape painting by B., Sept. 28, 1846, 1012-2.

Re B. painting "The Stump Speech," Dec. 6, 1847, 1511-3.

XVI. San Francisco, Calif.

San Francisco Chronicle

"A Lost Masterpiece of American Painting" (B.'s "Boatmen on the Missouri") (by Alfred Frankenstein), June 6, 1966, 53.

XVII. Washington, D.C.:

1. *Daily Madisonian* (1841-1845)

"A Capital Likeness," referring to B.'s portrait of C. A. Wickliffe, June 22, 1843, 2-1.

2. *National Intelligencer* (1813-1869); in 1814 *Daily National Express and Washington Intelligencer*, later *Daily National Intelligencer*

Re B.'s copy of Vanderlyn's "Ariadne," based on Durand engraving, Feb. 17, 1841, 3-5.

Re B.'s portrait of C. A. Wicklixe, Postmaster General, June 26, 1843, 3-5.

297

CHRONOLOGY

CHRONOLOGY

1811   Born on plantation, Augusta County, Virginia, March 20.

1819   Family moved to Franklin, Howard County, Missouri.

1820   Father operated tavern in Franklin.

1821-   Father took partnership in tobacco factory in Franklin; was appointed judge
1822   of county court, Howard County, January, 1821, and circuit court judge,
        1822-1823.

1823   Father died, December 26.

1827   Mother and children moved to farm near Arrow Rock, Saline County.

Ca.   In Boonville, ca. 1827/1828, apprenticed to the Reverend Justinian Williams,
1827/   cabinetmaker. Inspired by unknown itinerant portrait-painter; decision to be-
1828-   come painter during this period; sign-painting and probable early attempts at
1832   portraiture. Said to have attempted trip to St. Louis, ca. 1830, but turned back
Ca.   owing to illness.

1833   Began career as portrait painter, probably at Arrow Rock.

1834-   In Columbia, portrait painting, until March, 1835. Friendship with Major Rol-
1835   lins. In St. Louis by mid-March. Afterward to Liberty, Clay County, portrait
        painting, contracted smallpox, remained until early June. Returned to St. Louis
        by late November.

1836   In St. Louis, probably until March. Married Sarah Elizabeth Hutchison, April,
        returned to St. Louis by September. Winter in Natchez, Mississippi, painting
        portraits.

1837   In Natchez until about mid-May. Returned to Missouri, in Boonville; summer
        in Columbia, painting portraits. Son Newton born March 26.

1838   Went to Philadelphia to study, between March and early June; may have also
        visited New York. Afterward paid short visit to Baltimore, probably returned to
        Missouri by early July. Exhibited "Western Boatmen Ashore" at Apollo Gallery,
        New York, fall show. Probably spent winter in Saline County, painting portraits.

1839   Still in Saline County, early in year. Returned to St. Louis by May.

1840   Sent six paintings to National Academy of Design, New York; address given as
        St. Louis. At Rocheport, Missouri, in June, attended convention in connection
        with presidential campaign, made political speech, reportedly painted campaign
        banners. In Washington, D.C., by late December.

1841-   Washington, D.C., portrait painting. In 1842 sent picture to National Academy
1844   exhibition. Visited exhibition in Philadelphia, painted portraits there, mid-June,
        1843.
        Painted portrait of John Quincy Adams in Washington, May, 1844. Spent six
        months in Petersburg, Virginia, during this period (1841). Returned to Boon-

ville by September, 1844, painted banners for national Whig convention. One son, Newton, died in Washington, March 13, 1841; another son, Horace, was born there, March 15, 1841. Late December in Jefferson City, studio in Capitol; painted portraits of governor and others there.

1845   In St. Louis, submitted first pictures to American Art-Union, New York, by late June: "Fur Traders Descending the Missouri," "The Concealed Enemy," and two landscapes. Daughter Clara born March 14.

1846   In Arrow Rock. Candidate for State Legislature from Saline County, nominated June 24; elected by small majority, August 14; election contested by opponent, E. D. Sappington, November 20; case decided in favor of Sappington, December 18. Submitted "The Jolly Flatboatmen" to American Art-Union; purchased October.

1847   Paintings "Lighter Relieving a Steamboat Aground" and "Raftsmen Playing Cards" on exhibition in St. Louis.

1848   In Arrow Rock. Nominated to represent Saline County in State Legislature, July; elected over Sappington, August. Death of Sarah Elizabeth Bingham at Arrow Rock, November 29. In Jefferson City, late December, named to Committee on Federal Relations. "Stump Orator" in National Academy of Design exhibition.

1849   In Jefferson City during January and February. In New York, July and August, submitted "Raftsmen on the Ohio," "Watching the Cargo," "St. Louis Wharf," "Country Politician," and "A Boatman" to American Art-Union. Afterward probably in Philadelphia. Three paintings, including "Feeding Time," purchased by Western Art Union, Cincinnati. In Columbia, painted portraits, late September. Married Eliza K. Thomas (second wife) at Columbia, December 2.

1850   In Columbia, late May; by July in St. Louis, where he painted "Shooting for the Beef." November in New York, submitted "The Squatters" and "The Wood-Boat" to American Art-Union. Probably sent two landscapes to Western Art Union, and two paintings, "Mississippi Boatman" and "Daybreak in a Stable," to Philadelphia Art Union at this time.

1851   Still in New York by late March, painted "Emigration of Daniel Boone" while there, and very probably "In a Quandary" for Goupil & Co. Submitted "Trappers' Return" and "Fishing on the Mississippi" to American Art-Union. In St. Louis in May, on way home. By mid-May in Columbia, evidently remained there until October, at work on "The County Election," "Candidate Electioneering" ("Canvassing for a Vote"), and other pictures. In St. Louis in November to spend winter. Death of mother, Mary Amend Bingham, at Arrow Rock.

1852   Remained in St. Louis probably through March, painted portraits. By April in Columbia. Went to Baltimore in June as delegate for Eighth District to Whig national convention; later in month in Philadelphia and New York, consulted with engravers for "The County Election." By November in Glasgow and St. Louis. Spent winter in St. Louis.

1853 Left St. Louis, March 10, for New Orleans, exhibited "The County Election" there, and sold the picture. In Louisville and Lexington, Kentucky, in May, to raise subscriptions for the engraving. By July had also visited other towns in Kentucky—Danville, Frankfort, Harrodsburg, and intended going to Paris and Richmond. During September in New York, visited exhibition of Industry of All Nations, then to Philadelphia. Began to paint "Stump Speaking" there by early November. Spent winter in Philadelphia, superintending work on engraving by Sartain of "The County Election."

1854 Remained in Philadelphia, probably through mid-July, with at least one short trip to New York. Completed "Stump Speaking" by early February; "The Verdict of the People" begun by late May. Returned to Missouri, probably to St. Louis. In Columbia in September en route to Boonville, where he attended State Fair.

1855 Returned to Philadelphia by January. Late June in Independence, remained there at least until early August. "The Verdict of the People" completed at Philadelphia by late spring. Painted portraits in Columbia by September 14. At work on portraits in Jefferson City by November 14; remained until December, attending Whig meeting and making a speech in Capitol, December 1.

1856 Began painting "Washington Crossing the Delaware" in Columbia by March 14. In St. Louis during May, exhibited "The Verdict of the People." Commissioned by Missouri State Legislature to paint full-length portraits of Washington and Jefferson; June, July in Boston to copy portraits of subjects in connection with work. In Philadelphia in August. Sailed for Europe August 14; in Paris September 2. Arrived in Düsseldorf about November 1. Painting of portrait of Washington in progress during December.

1857 "The First Lesson in Music" in exhibition of Pennsylvania Academy of Fine Arts. At work in Düsseldorf; portrait of Washington completed during fall; afterward began portrait of Jefferson. Began work on "Jolly Flatboatmen in Port" before June, completed by late October.

1858 Completed portrait of Jefferson in Düsseldorf, probably during April.

1859 Returned to United States; in Washington, D.C., served as member of convention of National Art Association meeting there, January 12-14. Later in month in Jefferson City, where he delivered portraits of Washington and Jefferson; afterward in Columbia. In February in St. Louis and again in Jefferson City, where he was commissioned by State Legislature to execute portraits of Clay and Jackson, February 14. Remained in Jefferson City until mid-March, painted portraits; then in Columbia and Kansas City. Went to Brunswick, Missouri, in April. Stopped off at St. Louis early in May on way to Washington and New York; then sailed for Europe. Commissioned to paint portrait of Humboldt for St. Louis Mercantile Library Association in May. Returned to Düsseldorf early in June, planned to go to Berlin to make studies for Humboldt portrait. Back in New York in September; by December in Jefferson City.

1860   First week of January in Washington, D.C., painted portrait of Jackson after Sully in connection with state commission; also served again as member of National Art Association there, January 10, 12-13, as well as on a committee of conference of the House of Representatives. Returned to Missouri, in Columbia, early March. Delivered portrait of Humboldt to Mercantile Library, St. Louis, late April. Exhibited pictures at Pennsylvania Academy of Fine Arts, Philadelphia, and at Western Academy of Art, St. Louis. By mid-September in Independence, painted portraits; had completed portrait of Jackson at Kansas City. Portrait of Clay finished by December, probably at Kansas City.

1861   Portraits of Clay and Jackson set up in House of Representatives at Jefferson City, January 7. Later in month in St. Louis to arrange for frames for portraits, exhibited them there as well, late February. Left March 6 for Houston, Texas, to settle estate of elder brother, Matthias A. Bingham, who had died January 12; returned to Kansas City by mid-May. Appointed captain in U.S. Volunteer Reserve Corps in Kansas City during summer. Son James Rollins born September 21.

1862   Moved to Jefferson City, late January, having been appointed state treasurer, January 4; position held until 1865.

1863   Commissioned by Secretary of State of Missouri to paint a portrait of General Nathaniel Lyon, August 1. "General Order No. 11" issued by General Thomas Ewing in Kansas City, August 25.

1865   Completed term of office as state treasurer. Began to paint "Order No. 11" at Independence by November.

1866   In June a candidate for Congress from Sixth District, made speech at state convention; not appointed by nominating convention, October. July in St. Louis. Painted "Major Dean in Jail."

1867   In Independence, completed portrait of General Lyon, late March.

1868   Chosen elector at Democratic state convention, late May. Completed "Order No. 11" in December.

1869   In Columbia, March. Elected school director at Independence, October. Death of son Horace.

1870   Painted second version of "Order No. 11" at Independence between March and April. Moved from Independence to Kansas City, May.

1871   In Jefferson City in January, exhibited portrait of General F. P. Blair, Jr. In Kansas City, March, at work on full-length portrait of Blair, completed by July. September in Columbia, at work on portrait of Major Rollins, commissioned for the University. November in Kansas City; by late December in Philadelphia in connection with engraving of "Order No. 11" then in progress by Sartain.

1872   Still in Philadelphia, late January; completed "Washington Crossing the Delaware," begun in 1856; plate of "Order No. 11" almost finished. May in Kansas City; July in Baltimore; later in Denver, painted view of "Pike's Peak" by late October. By November had returned to Kansas City, at work on portraits.

304

1873 Completed full-length portrait of Rollins at Kansas City, late March. In Houston and then Austin, Texas, April, settling brother's estate. Returned to Kansas City, May. July in Marshall and Arrow Rock; August in Kansas City. Exhibited "Order No. 11" and "Washington Crossing the Delaware" at Louisville, Kentucky, Industrial Exposition, September; attended exposition and afterward back in Kansas City; at work on portraits by mid-December.

1874 In Kansas City, painted portraits through winter. Appointed president of Kansas City Board of Police Commissioners, May 11. At work on portraits, June. A candidate for Congress from Eighth District, late July, but withdrew from list of candidates for nomination at Democratic convention in Kansas City, September. Almost completed "The Puzzled Witness," exhibited in St. Louis, December.

1875 Appointed adjutant-general of Missouri, January; by January 19 in Jefferson City. Made report on Samuels case in Clay County, February.

1876 In Washington, D.C., March and April, in connection with disposition of war claims for state; painted portraits of Vinnie Ream and Florence Crittenden Coleman there. During May and June in Jefferson City; October in Fulton, where his wife was institutionalized. Death of Eliza Thomas Bingham at Fulton, November 3, after his return to Jefferson City.

1877 Authorized by State Legislature to paint historical picture of Jackson before Civil Court of Louisiana, March. Appointed professor of art of University of Missouri's newly established School of Art, June. From July to September in Boonville, painted portraits, afterward in Columbia. November in Kansas City.

1878 In St. Louis in January, and later in Kansas City. Between February and March in Washington, D.C., completed "The Jolly Flatboatmen" and "Palm Leaf Shade," at work on "Little Red Riding Hood." In Columbia, and returned to Kansas City by late May. Married Mrs. Martha Livingston Lykins (third wife) in Kansas City, June 18; couple afterward in Denver. Appointed one of commissioners of Robert E. Lee Monument Association, November 8; on way to Richmond by mid-November for meeting of commissioners; November 27 stopped off at Columbia; again in Columbia on return, November 29.

1879 In Kansas City. Visited Columbia late May, remained until July 5. Returned to home in Kansas City, died there July 7.

Some Dates After 1879

1890 September 20, death of (third) wife, Mrs. Martha Livingston Bingham, at Kansas City.

1893 March 25, administrator's sale of Bingham estate held at Findlay's Art Store, Kansas City.

1901 May 5. Death of daughter Clara (Mrs. Thomas Benton King) at Stephenville, Erath County, Texas.

1910 December 31, death of son, James Rollins Bingham.

APPENDIXES

PREFATORY NOTE: The following three appendixes, relating to the Bingham family and their origins, were prepared by the artist's son, James Rollins Bingham, and by his granddaughter, Mrs. Clara King Bowdry. All of the documents were in the possession of Mrs. Bowdry in 1945, and were at that time very generously made available to me. They are here reproduced in their entirety, not so much for their immediate relevance to the purposes of the present volume but rather for the value they may have for future historians. Although the genealogical sketch by James Rollins Bingham (Appendix A) includes information that must be regarded as highly improbable, its value as a document by a painter's son is indisputable.

According to Mrs. Bowdry, the document reproduced as Appendix A was prepared by James Rollins Bingham while he was at the home of Dr. Abram Neff and his wife Louisa Bingham Neff, in 1905 or 1906. It seems probable that the essay was prepared in connection with the material then being gathered by Theodore A. Bingham for his *Bingham Family in the United States* (Ea[s]ton, Pa., 1927-1930). Rollins Bingham is given as one of the authorities (vol. 3, p. 787) and many of the statements agree with the data contained in the essay.

Mrs. Bowdry used various sources in connection with her essays, included here as appendixes B and C. Among her references she has cited *Burke's Peerage, Baronetage, and Knightage* (Earls of Lucan–Clanmorris), *Burke's Landed Gentry* (Binghams of Melcombe Bingham), *Chalkeley's Abstract of Augusta County, Va.*, Records of Albemarle County, Va., Watson's *Annals of Philadelphia*, and the New Jersey Archives.

308

APPENDIX A
The Bingham Family
(A genealogical sketch by James Rollins Bingham, the artist's son.]

The first authentic information I have of the ancestors of the Bingham family of Missouri, more particularly of Saline County, Missouri, is of my great-grandfather, George Bingham, or George Washington Bingham, the middle name not being a birth name but adopted as such late in life.

Of the Binghams prior to my great-grandfather the information is vague. An old letter written by an aunt many years ago relates that the Binghams came to America from the north of England. That England however, was not the original home of the family but that the early Binghams came into England from Scotland. There is also a shadowy family tradition that the Binghams who came to America from England were three brothers, one of whom settled in the South and the others in New England. It is inferentially certain that the coming of the first Binghams of our line to America was a considerable time before the Revolutionary war.

With reference to my great-grandfather, George Bingham, information becomes more definite. It is certain that he was born and raised in some one of the New England States, from whence, about the close of the Revolution, he migrated to Virginia and settled on the east side of the Blue Ridge about eighteen miles west of Charlottesville, the seat of the University of Virginia.

He was what is termed a local Methodist preacher and as such ministered to a congregation at a meeting house erected for its accommodation on his own plantation. He cultivated grain and tobacco by the aid of slaves to whom he was exceedingly kind and indulgent, never using the lash nor allowing it to be used on his place. In Virginia he married Louisa Vest and members of her family are represented by descendants in Missouri. Our late U.S. Senator, George G. Vest, was one of them.

I have at hand two letters written by this planter, minister great-grandfather, both being to his nephew and son-in-law, Wyatt Bingham, who had married his cousin Rebecca Bingham. The first bears the date November 18, 1814, and is written from his home in Orange County, a fact which leads to the supposition that the writer had moved from his first settlement, which I take to have been in Rockingham County. Wyatt Bingham was at that time in camp at Richmond as a member of the Albemarle, now Green County, militia. This Wyatt Bingham came to Missouri with his wife Rebecca in the early eighteen-twenties and settled in the southern portion of Saline County, in what is now Blackwater Township. The second letter was written to Wyatt, the son-in-law and nephew, in Missouri on October 19, 1826, and was mailed from Stannardsville, Va.

Of course Wyatt being a nephew shows George Bingham to have had a brother who probably lived in Albemarle, now Green County. Whether this brother emigrated from New England with George I do not know. There is some evidence that this brother's name was Joseph. Wyatt Bingham and his wife settled in Missouri, died leaving but one child, a daughter named Rebecca, who married John M. Trigg and is the ancestress of a numerous family of Triggs in Missouri, who are of the Bingham blood

309

but not of the name. I impose this branch of the family here for convenience sake in order to avoid confusion with the others.

George Bingham, my great-grandfather, was the father of a number of children, to wit: Elizabeth, John, Joseph (Josias), Rhoda, wife of George Douglass, Henry Vest, Sr. (my grandfather), Mary wife of Anthony Harvey, Mildred wife of ————— Rife, Rebecca wife of Wyatt Bingham, Maria wife of ————— Estess. Of these, Henry Vest, Sr., my grandfather, emigrated to Missouri in 1819 and his brother John followed about 1823. From these came all that is remaining of the name of the Missouri Binghams. Of those remaining in Virginia, it seems that no communication was kept up after the deaths of the elder immigrants. I hear occasionally of those of the name in Virginia but am of the opinion that the male line has about become extinct.

All the Missouri Binghams of our family who are of the male line and bear the name are descended from the emigrant brothers, Henry Vest, Sr., and John.

First I will give an account of Henry Vest, Sr., my grandfather, and the line as it descends from him. Henry V. Bingham was the oldest son of George Bingham, the preacher-planter. When he grew to maturity, his father entrusted the entire management of his plantation to him. It happened in a very dry year that Henry Vest, Sr., was obliged to take a load of grain over the mountains to the west side of the ridge to get it ground. The miller over there was a German named Amend who had come to Virginia from Pennsylvania and owned a mill and a considerable farm. The old German was a widower with one daughter about grown, daughter named Mary. My grandfather fell in love with Mary Amend and married her Sept. 8, 1808. My great-grandfather Amend gave with his daughter to his son-in-law all his property, stipulating only that he should have a home with his daughter and her husband during his life. This was faithfully and affectionately carried out. So Henry Vest Bingham, Sr., came to live at the Amend farm and mill in Augusta County, and became the proprietor. On this farm the well known Weyer's cave is situated. In Virginia at the Augusta County home six children were born of this marriage: Matthias Amend Bingham, Nov. 19, 1809, George Caleb (my father), Mar. 20, 1811, Elizabeth, Nov. 18, 1812, Isaac Newton, June 27, 1814, Henry V. Bingham, Jr., Jan. 11, 1817, Frances Louisa, Nov. 4, 1818. In Missouri, after the family emigrated in 1819, another child Amanda was born Sept. 14, 1821. Of these none is now alive and of their descendants there are none of the Bingham name but myself, childless, unmarried, and forty-four years old.

Of the daughters, only my Aunt Amanda lived to maturity and married. She married James Barnes in Saline County, Mo., and died in 1901, and there are living of her children three sons and two daughters.

In 1819 Henry V. Bingham, Sr., with his father-in-law, wife, and children, the Augusta County home place having been sold, emigrated to Missouri. They landed at Franklin, in Howard County. My grandfather entered into the tobacco manufacturing business there with a partner and also purchased land in Saline County, near the present town of Arrow Rock. The family first lived at Franklin and then moved to the Saline County farm, my grandfather going to and from his business at Franklin, some eighteen miles, on horseback. A few years after the arrival of the family in Missouri

310

my great-grandfather Amend was accidentally drowned in the Missouri River. In 1823, my grandfather Henry V. Bingham, Sr., died. From his estate, owing to the rascality of his business partner, my grandmother was able to save only the farm in Saline County. As fast as her sons grew old enough they helped to earn the family support, not only working on the home land but hiring out for wages to neighboring farmers. They received but little schooling, but Grandmother, being a woman of excellent education, managed to add to this by her own instruction. Grandmother Mary Amend Bingham died in 1851.

The oldest son, Matthias Amend Bingham, in 1835, after his mother's position and support were assured, rode overland horseback to Texas, joined Sam Houston's force, engaged in the Revolutionary struggle with Mexico, fought as a first sergeant at the battle of San Jacinto, was soon a captain, and during the few years of the existence of the Texas Republic, was its Quartermaster General. After the troubles were over, he settled on a farm near Houston, Texas, and died there in 1861. He was never married. We have many of his letters written during these years to his mother, his sister Amanda, and his brothers in Missouri.

The second son was my father, George Caleb Bingham. He left the home farm some time about 1830 and went to Boonville, some twenty miles, where he learned the cabinet maker's trade. While there Gilbert Stuart, the painter, came also to Boonville, to paint portraits of some wealthy residents there and discovered that my father had undeveloped talent as an artist. Stuart advised a course of study and that my father adopt that profession. My father studied a term at St. Louis, soon became sufficiently proficient to earn his living by painting, studied later and painted at Philadelphia and Washington, also at Dusseldorf in Germany for two years in 1858 and 1859. He became well known throughout Missouri as an artist and public man. He was originally a Whig, served in the State Legislature as a member of the House from Saline County before the war. Though strongly attached to the South through family and other ties, he was a strenuous opponent of secession and took the side of the Union. He was State Treasurer during the war under the Lincoln administration. Opposed the Reconstruction policy after the war and with Gen. Frank Blair and others joined the Democratic party. He was Adjutant General of the state 1874 to 1876 and at the time of his death, July 7, 1879, was a member of the faculty of the State University, being the head of the Art Department.

My father was married three times. His first wife, Elizabeth Hutchison, died in 1848. Of this union there were four sons, Newton, Horace, Nathaniel, and Joseph, and a daughter Clara. None of these is now living. The sons all died very young, save Horace, who died in 1869. He was unmarried. My sister Clara married Thos. B. King and they went to Erath County, Texas, in 1873. My sister died in 1901 and is survived by eight children, six of them married, and her husband, who lives at Stephenville, Erath County, Texas.

My father's second wife was Eliza K. Thomas, my mother. They were married in 1849. I am their only child and was born Sept. 21, 1861. My mother died in 1876. In 1878 my father married his third wife, Mrs. Martha A. Lykins. She survived him until September, 1900, when she died. There were no children of this third marriage.

The third son of my grandfather, Isaac Newton, was drowned in Saline County in 1831.

The fourth son, Henry V. Bingham, Jr., was an architect and builder. He was twice married. First to Sarah Vaughn, Nov. 17, 1840. Of this marriage there were three daughters, all of whom while still very young died of cholera in 1849 and their mother also. Uncle Henry Bingham Jr., married the second time in 1850 to Lamenda A. McMahan. Of this union there was one daughter, Louisa Jane, born April 11, 1851. My cousin married Dr. Abram Neff in 1873. She and her husband are living and have two children living: Jesse and Nadine, both unmarried. I make my home at my cousin's and more than any one she has preserved old family letters and documents and interested herself in the family history. From her I have obtained the greater part of the information I am able to impart to you. Henry V. Bingham, Jr., died Dec. 26th, 1876.

Of Amanda Bingham, the only daughter of Henry V. Bingham, Sr., and his wife Mary Amend, who married, I have previously given a statement.

So of the direct line of Henry V. Bingham, Sr., who came from Virginia in 1819 there remain the surviving children and their children of my Aunt Amanda Barnes, the children of my half-sister, Mrs. Clara B. King, my cousin Mrs. Louise Neff, her son and daughter, and myself, last of the name.

But a few years after the emigration of Henry V. Bingham, Sr., and family there followed from Virginia his brother John and his cousin and likewise brother-in-law, Wyatt Bingham. Of the latter I have previously given an account.

John Bingham and his wife Polly, maiden name Harshberger, came to Missouri about 1823 and settled in Saline County at what is now the town of Arrow Rock. He was the donor of twenty-five acres, half the original townsite, of that town in 1826. John Bingham and wife, both long since passed away, were the parents of the following children: Melvina wife of John Jones, Jacob, Mary, Margaret, George M., Julia wife of Daniel Watts, William, and Harriet. Of these my second cousin Jacob Bingham is living, an old gentleman about eighty-six years old, on a farm adjacent to Arrow Rock. He is married and has one child living, an unmarried daughter named Mary Pearl. My cousin Mrs. Julia Watts is also living and her husband Daniel Watts, in the town of Arrow Rock. They have several grown sons and daughters and also grandchildren.

Of the others, the only ones living of the Bingham name are the children of Capt. George M. Bingham, who died at his home in Arrow Rock a short time ago. Capt. George M. Bingham married Minerva Valdenar who is still living. They were parents of the following: Mary unmarried, William, Nellie wife of Mr. Standard Shemwell. Frank who died unmarried, Maggie deceased, wife of Clark Swinney, and George. There are children living of Mrs. Shemwell and Mrs. Swinney. William Bingham lives at Arrow Rock and has four children, three sons and a daughter. George Bingham. the Captain's youngest son, lives in northern Arkansas. He is married but has no children.

312

To recapitulate, of the male line descended from the planter-minister George there are of Missouri the descendants of his son John as follows: Jacob Bingham son of John, George a grandson, William a grandson, and the four sons of William, great-grandsons.

Of the male line descended from George Bingham of Virginia through his son Henry V. Bingham, Sr., I am the only representative.

The Binghams of this race possessed marked characteristics. From the number of letters I have looked over, dating back nearly a century, it is plain that they were all the reverse of illiterate. They seem always to have possessed an education higher than common though none of them, I know, could have had much advantage of school. As an example, my grandfather, though commonly supposed to have been a college bred man, never attended school six months all together. His education was the result of constant reading, study, and observation, a life time of acquirement. All the Binghams seem to have had the literary gift, well constructed and easily understood expression.

There is little probability that they spring from any aristocracy of birth or wealth. They have almost without exception preferred the country to the town, and while not prone to acquire wealth, have always lived comfortably and been good providers. They were all honest, whole-souled, good men and women, kind-hearted and, while reserved, really affectionate and deeply loving their kindred and fellow men. Never a Bingham was there who was not absolutely fearless and outspoken in action and words in upholding what he thought was right. There has never been a "trimmer" nor a "straddler" among them. In fact, this tenacity of opinion and firmness in standing by the right of the Binghams is proverbial in Missouri and, truth is, many speak of it as the "Bingham stubbornness." Speaking for myself, I am proud of my homely lineage and were I given the choice, would prefer it to any other. In that feeling we Binghams all share equally.

J. R. B.

APPENDIX B
Paternal Ancestry of George Caleb Bingham
(A genealogical account prepared by Mrs. Clara King Bowdry, granddaughter of the artist.)

Early records in England seem to prove that the Binghams of England were of Saxon origin, settling first in Scotland and then in the north of England, before the Norman invasion. The family name was derived from the place of residence of the first comers to England. Ancient records give many different spellings of the name but the form "BINGHAM" is generally used today. At very early dates branches of the family were found in the English counties of Somerset, Nottingham, Kent, Derby, Dorset, Wilts, Essex, and in London; later a branch in County Down, Ireland. These families were, for the most part, of the landed gentry and nobility of Great Britain. And in the various lines have been many distinguished authors, educators, clergymen, jurists, soldiers and military experts, as well as successful tradesmen.

One of the earliest progenitors of the family in England was Sir John de Bingham, Knight, living at Sutton Bingham in Somersetshire in the time of Henry I, about the middle of the eleventh century. From him descended Sir Ralph Bingham, a Crusader, and his younger brother, Robert Bingham, who in 1229 was consecrated Bishop of Salisbury. This Sir Ralph was ancestor of the Binghams of Melcombe Bingham in Dorset, of the Earls of Lucan and Lords Clanmorris, and of all the families of the Bingham name in America. When Sir Ralph returned from the Crusades he founded the town of Bingham about nine miles from Nottingham and there built a beautiful Norman church. In the church, which is still standing unless destroyed by German bombs in the present World War II, is a recumbent statue of Sir Ralph. The Binghams of London and of Sheffield in Yorkshire were descended from this branch in Nottingham.

In seeking the ancestry of the Virginia family from which George Caleb Bingham descended, several family traditions have led to research along different lines: one tradition that the Virginia Binghams were related to the New England family; another tradition that they were originally Quakers; another that they were of the same line as the Binghams who came to North Carolina and founded the Bingham School at Asheville. Each of these traditions seems to have had its foundation in facts.

As to the relationship to the New England family, older members of the family who had settled in Missouri in 1819 told of a visit to them by Thomas Bingham of Virginia who had stopped in Ohio to visit other relatives there. And the Ohio Binghams were from New England. George Caleb Bingham himself stated that his grandfather, Rev. George Bingham of Albemarle County, Va., had come about the close of the Revolution "from some one of the New England states." Perhaps in George's time Pennsylvania was called a New England state, for it seems conclusive that he was from Pennsylvania. Col. Theodore Bingham, in his very complete and comprehensive history of the New England family, "The Bingham Genealogy," fails to find a direct connection between the New Englanders and the Virginians. However he quotes information from Weaver's Records of Norwich, Connecticut, as having been furnished by the venerable Col. Elijah Bingham of East Haddam, that *two brothers* came from

England to New London, Conn., about 1660, accompanied by their mother, Anne Stenton Bingham, widow of Thomas Bingham, a Master Cutler of Sheffield, Yorkshire, England.

One brother, Thomas Bingham, moved to Windham, where he lived and died leaving seven sons, all over six feet tall, all of whom lived to a great age and died in succession as they were born. These seven sons and their descendants are all accounted for in Col. Bingham's Genealogy. The other brother (given name unknown, either Abel, Stephen, Edward, or Robert) died at New London and his family returned to England. *"A descendant came back afterwards and settled in Philadelphia and became very wealthy."*

It is certain that the settler in Philadelphia was James Bingham who, according to the Annals of Philadelphia, died possessed of a large landed property. His tombstone in the burial ground of Christ Church in Philadelphia gives the date of his death as December 20th, 1714, age forty-six. Therefore he was born in 1668 and could have been a son of the Bingham who died at New London some time after 1660. Early records of New Jersey give much information concerning James. His mother was a *Quaker,* hence the Quaker tradition. She was Bridgett (Scott) Bingham, daughter of Benjamin Scott, an influential member of the Quaker colony who came to New Jersey on the ship "Kent" in 1677. Benjamin Scott was a Proprietor of West Jersey and one of the first magistrates appointed in 1677. Bridgett Bingham was a widow with several children when she came to New Jersey with her parents. She and her children probably were connected in some way with John Bingham, citizen and goldsmith of London, and his wife Mary, who on April 25, 1675, received patent to 1000 acres of land to be surveyed in West Jersey. It is not determined that John and Mary came to America but evidently they had a substantial interest in the colony.

Bridgett Bingham first appeared in the records of New Jersey when she assigned land to her son James Bingham on Nov. 30, 1687. Perhaps that is when James married although he was only nineteen years of age at that time. The land had been deeded to Bridgett by her father, Benjamin Scott. James Bingham married in New Jersey, accumulated property there and in 1705 became a citizen of Philadelphia, being "admitted a freeman" on April 9th of that year. For which privilege he paid 31 pounds, 2 shillings, 6 pence. His wife was Anne (maiden name not known) who died Oct. 11, 1750 and was buried beside her husband in Christ Church burial ground, with others of the family; among them their son James Bingham who died Nov. 9, 1737, and his wife Ann who died July 9, 1759. The wife of this son James was Ann Budd, daughter of William Budd of Northampton, Burlington County, N.J., also a prominent figure in the Quaker colony.

The younger James Bingham purchased land in *Virginia.* A deed dated 1735 in Orange County, Va., shows that *James Bingham of Philadelphia, Sadler,* bought 2000 acres of land on the Shenandoah river. An earlier purchase of land between the Nottoway and Meherrin rivers by James Bingham is mentioned in the will of George Nicholson of Surry County, Va., dated Feb. 3, 1712. This earlier purchase could have been by either father or son, but these records place this family of Binghams very definitely in Virginia. In 1745 Christopher, George, and John Bingham were in Augusta County, which was cut off from Orange. George and John patented their own lands but no record of a patent for Christopher. It is thought that they were sons of James and Ann Budd Bingham. James and Ann Budd Bingham had another son, William Bingham who married in 1745 Mary Stamper, daughter of John Stamper, mayor of Philadelphia. The Stampers were Virginians. William and Mary Stamper Bingham had, with others, a son William born 1752 who married 1780 Ann Willing, daughter of Thomas Willing. This William became U.S. Senator and built the famous Bingham Mansion at Walnut and Spruce Streets, one of the show-places of Philadelphia in that day.

It seems reasonable to conclude that the Rev. George Bingham, grandfather of George Caleb Bingham, must have been a son of William and Mary Stamper Bingham of Philadelphia. Had he been a son of the Augusta County George, John, or Christopher, he would have been in Virginia before the Revolution. The first Census of the United States lists George Bingham as living in Hanover County, Va., in 1782, with two in family, wife and no children. His brothers, Thomas and Josias, in Hanover, and James in Chesterfield, all married and with children. George was probably married in 1782, as his oldest son, Henry Vest Bingham, was born in 1783.

Rev. George Bingham of Hanover, Albemarle, and Orange Counties, Va., married first Louisa Vest, daughter of Charles Vest of Hanover County, and she was the mother of all his children. The exact date of her death is not known. She is not mentioned in the deed records of Albemarle County where George was living in 1788. Later in life, on June 8, 1825, Rev. George Bingham married second Priscilla Ross in Albemarle County. He died in 1829 and the widow Priscilla went to Missouri and lived with her step-daughter Rebecca (Bingham) Bingham who had married her cousin Wyatt Bingham, son of Josias, sometimes called Joseph.

James Rollins Bingham in his manuscript written in 1905 or 1906 gives accounts of Henry Vest Bingham and George Caleb Bingham, son of Henry Vest and father of James Rollins Bingham.

C. K. B.

Fort Worth, Texas
March 5, 1945

316

APPENDIX C
Maternal Ancestry of George Caleb Bingham
(A genealogical account prepared by Mrs. Clara King Bowdry, granddaughter of the artist.)

The maternal grandparents of George Caleb Bingham were Matthias Amend and his wife Elizabeth Bushong, of York County, Pennsylvania. Matthias was the grandson of the original immigrant, Johann George Amend (Amendt), who arrived in America Sept. 11, 1732, on the ship "Pennsylvania," and settled in York County, Penna. George Elias Amend (son of Johann George) and his second wife Eva Maria (maiden name not known) were the parents of Matthias Amend. His birth record is to be found in the records of Christ Lutheran Church, York, Penna. On Feb. 2, 1753, he was born, and baptized Feb. 8, 1753, as Johann Matthias. Witnesses to his baptism were John Matthias Demouth and Mary Magdalena Paul. He enlisted in the Revolutionary Army from York County, married there in 1781 and soon removed to Virginia.

Elizabeth Bushong, wife of Matthias Amend, was a granddaughter of Hans Bushong (Jean Beauchamp) of French Huguenot descent who arrived in America in 1731 on the ship "Brittannia," accompanied by his wife Barbara (maiden name not known) and four children. They settled in Lancaster County, Penna., where two more children were born, one of whom was a son John Bushong born between 1731 and 1736. This son John removed to York County. He was a man of more than average education for that day and time and it is interesting to note that when his father's estate was settled in Lancaster County in 1750, he was the only one of the heirs signing in English. He was one of the first captains in the Revolutionary Army and after the war removed to Virginia. In York County, Penna., he married Elizabeth Sprenckell, daughter of William and Catharine Sprenckell, and they had four sons and three daughters, one of whom was the daughter Elizabeth Bushong who married Matthias Amend. They were the parents of Mary Amend who married Henry Vest Bingham and had son *George Caleb Bingham*. The story of their life in Virginia is told in the memoirs of George Caleb Bingham and by George Caleb Bingham's son, James Rollins Bingham.

C. K. B.

Fort Worth, Texas
March 5, 1945

317

INDEXES

GENERAL INDEX

physiognomy and phrenology, interest in, 61-62, 132-134

Renaissance-Baroque tradition, influence of, 88-89, 135, 148-149, 153, 256, 257

self-instruction, observation as means of, 25, 27, 30, 36, 37, 43, 44, 45-48, 68-69, 194, 255

statements, public, on art: "Art, the Ideal of Art, and the Utility of Art," 14, 252; "An Address to the Public. Vindicating a Work of Art," 222-223

students, and teaching of, 247, 247 n. 157

Bingham, George Caleb, work

drawing: emphasis on, 37-38, 257; as basis for composition, 83, 103, 132, 152-153, 176-177, 235, 240, 257; stylistic characteristics of, 102, 240, 257; expression in, 134; *for known and identifiable subjects*—66 n. 40 (The Bathing Girl [Musidora ?]; 66 n. 40, 240 (copies after Titian); 83 (Fur Traders Descending the Missouri; The Trappers' Return); 84 (Boatmen on the Missouri); 92 (The Jolly Flatboatmen [1]); 96 (The Jolly Flatboatmen in Port); 96, 100 (Raftsmen Playing Cards; In a Quandary); 102 (Lighter) Relieving a Steamboat Aground); 103-104 (Watching the Cargo); 110 (Fishing on the Mississippi; The Squatters; The Woodboat; Watching the Cargo by Night; Western Boatmen Ashore by Night); 120 (Shooting for the Beef); 128 (Emigration of Daniel Boone); 96, 136-137 (The Stump Orator); 137-138 (The Country Politician); 138, 156-157 (Canvassing for a Vote); 152-153 (The County Election); 162 (Stump Speaking); 240 (The Puzzled Witness)

genre and other figure subjects: signboard painting, 16, 16 n. 10, 54, 123 n. 149;

early inclination toward, 26, 48, 61-62, 66; political banners, 61, 73-79; contemporary criticism of, 61, 76-77, 88, 91, 98, 100-101, 118, 131-132, 134, 136, 137, 144, 146, 154, 165, 233, 239; first public exhibition of, 61-62, 64; the nude in, 66, 66 n. 40; stimulus and patronage, 68-69, 71-73; themes of, 69-70, 79-81, 84-85, 85-87, 97, 98, 100-101, 103, 104-106, 110, 113, 115, 117-118, 120, 123, 125-127, 128-129, 137, 144, 146, 158-159, 163, 167-170, 214-215, 216, 217, 222, 233; activity: 79-170, 191, 256; prices and evaluation of, 79, 86, 97, 102, 104, 105, 106, 111, 119, 121, 130, 137, 143, 168, 169, 170; stylistic characteristics of, 81-82, 83-84, 85, 87-89, 93-94, 95-96, 98-99, 101-102, 103, 107-109, 112, 114, 115, 116, 117, 119, 127-128, 134-136, 148-152, 160-162, 165-167, 204-205, 220-221, 224, 233-234, 240, 248-249, 256-258, 259; forms of signature on, 111, 111 n. 110, 243 n. 141, 243-244; night scenes, 113-114; personal attitude toward, 123, 157, 158, 159, 163, 202 n. 57, 209, 213, 220; historical subjects, 125, 199, 202, 215-218, 232-233, 259; Düsseldorf influence on, 198, 204-205, 215, 221, 258

landscape: earliest work in, 26, 171; first public exhibition of, 64, 171; attraction to, 171; work for the Art-Unions, 171-172; in Düsseldorf, 172, 181; "heroic" landscapes, 173, 182, 184; in Colorado, 173-174, 181-183; contemporary criticism of, 173-174; prices and evaluation of, 174, 177; stylistic characteristics of, 175, 179, 180-181, 183, 259; "cottage views," 177-178; "fancy" landscapes, 177, 179, 180, 182, 184; "cattle pieces," 179-180; night scenes, 181; Düsseldorf in-

fluence on, 181, 183, 184; "country seats," 183; range and estimate of activity in, 183-184

portraits: first commissions, 16-17; earliest examples extant, 19-20, 254; signatures on, 19 n. 23, 26-27, 60, 226, 246; stylistic characteristics of, 19-20, 21-22, 30, 31-34, 49-50, 51-52, 52-53, 53-55, 58-61, 62-64, 186-191, 192, 203-204, 205-206, 209, 211-213, 214-215, 224, 225-226, 227-228, 230-232, 241-243, 246, 249, 254-255, 258; prices of, 20, 20 n. 26, 29, 201, 227; first Columbia period, 20-22, 254-255; contemporary criticism of, 21, 27, 52, 66, 67, 185, 191, 199, 203, 209, 223-224, 226, 229-230; itinerant painting in St. Louis and Liberty, Missouri, 22-23, 255; in St. Louis (1835), 23-29; personal attitude toward, 25-26, 185, 199, 209, 227, 228, 235, 241, 246; in Natchez, Mississippi, 29; in Columbia, Missouri (1837), 30-34; in Fayette, Missouri (1839), 49, 50-51; in various Missouri towns (1838-1840), 49-55, 255; as "pot-boiling" activity, 51, 69, 185, 235 n. 111; in Washington, D.C. (1840-1844), 55-61, 255; portraits in guise of genre, 63, 65, 73-74, 248-249; in Petersburg, Virginia (1841), 67; in Missouri (1844-1855), 185-192, 255, 258; official commissions for, 193, 199-201, 202-204, 209-211, 214, 224, 226-230; in Washington, D.C. (1859, 1860, 1876, 1878), 199-201, 205-206, 207-208, 238; possible German influence on, 205; later portraiture in Missouri (1859-1879), 207-213, 214-215

prints: Goupil as publisher of, 99, 121, 122, 154, 155, 159, 164; attitude toward lithography, 122, 164; preference

325

Raimondi, Marcantonio, 81, 81 n. 28

Ranney, William, 117 n. 125, 120, 120 n. 135, 121, 121 n. 137, 234, 234 n. 104; *Daniel Boone's First View of Kentucky*, 120, 121 n. 137, 234 n. 104; *Marion Crossing the Pedee*, 234, 234 n. 104, pl. 182

Raphael, 23, 24, 32, 33, 88-89, 100, 135, 149, 153; *Madonna della Sedia*, 33, 212; *Holy Family* (Canigiani), 100; *Death of Ananias*, 135; *School of Athens*, 153

Read, Daniel, 248, 248 n. 158

Red-Hot Politician, The (De França), 129 n. 175

Red Jacket (Weir), 54, pl. 31

Red Legs, 216

Reed, Luman, New York (collection), 5

Reedy River Massacre (Shaw), 111, pl. 76

Régnier, Claude (lithographer), 155; *In a Quandary* (Bingham), 99; *Emigration of Daniel Boone* (Bingham), 121, 122, 126, pl. 84; *Canvassing for a Vote* (Bingham), 154, 155

Rembrandt, 45

Renaissance and Baroque masters, methods of, 41, 43, 89, 90, 135, 148, 149, 150, 153, 256

Reni, Guido, 24

Rescue, The (Chapman), 112, pl. 77

Reynolds, Miss E. E., Lafayette, Indiana (collection), 169

Reynolds, S. W. (engraver), 178 n. 18

Richmond, Kentucky, 143

Richmond, Virginia, 251, 252

Rindisbacher, Peter, 26, 46

Rocheport, Missouri, 55, 74

Rollins, Curtis Burnam, 142, 161 n. 297

Rollins, George Bingham, Columbia, Missouri (collection), 219

Rollins, Major James Sidney, 14, 29-30, 35, 75, 77, 78, 96, 116, 120, 121, 122, 123, 139, 141, 144-145, 157, 158, 159, 163, 168, 173, 174, 194, 195, 196, 202, 203, 210, 213, 216, 217, 219, 226, 227, 228, 229, 231, 232, 233, 235, 236, 238, 239, 240, 241, 244, 245, 247, 248, 251, 252; marriage of, 30, 31, 32, 33; B. portraits of, 21, 186, 228-230, 232, pls. 7, 175, 176; opinion of B.'s work, 139, 144-145; B. sketches in collection of, 240

Rolph, John A. (engraver), *The Rescue* (Chapman), 112, pl. 77

Rosa, Salvator, 44, 47, 175; B. reference to, 175

Rosierse, J., 114 n. 175

Ross, Priscilla, 316. *See also* Bingham, Rev. George

Rothermel, Peter Frederick, 64, 125 n. 160, 128, 215; *The Pioneers* or *The Western Emigrant*, 128, pl. 85; *Angel of the Opal*, 215, pl. 163

Rubens, Sir Pieter Paul, 24, 25, 45

Rush, William, 41

Rusk, Fern Helen (Mrs. John Shapley), vii, 14, 99, 101, 111, 142

Rutherford, Alexander W., 194, 194 n. 10, 195

St. Louis, Missouri, 22, 23, 24 n. 39, 26, 27, 28, 29, 30, 52, 53, 54, 61, 64, 68, 71 n. 7, 80, 91 n. 54, 92, 92 n. 56, 94, 97, 99, 100, 101, 104, 110, 120 n. 133, 121, 122, 123, 129, 137, 140, 141, 154, 155, 159, 164, 171, 191, 201, 208, 210, 211, 239, 246, 255, 311; early cultural life in, 23

St. Louis, Missouri, Cathedral of St. Louis, 23-24, 24 n. 39; collection of paintings in, 23-24; murals in (Pomarede), 24 n. 39

St. Louis, Missouri: City Art Museum (collection), 94, 142, 172

St. Louis, Missouri: Missouri Historical Society (collection), 180, 227

St. Louis, Missouri: O'Fallon Polytechnic Institute, 94

St. Louis, Missouri: St. Louis Mercantile Library Association (collection), B. paintings, 94, 160, 165, 202 n. 208; B. drawings (John How collection), viii, 83, 84, 92, 96, 100, 102, 103, 110, 120, 128, 136-137, 137-138, 152-153, 156-157, 162, 176-177, 240, 257, 259; B. exhibits at, 211; B. paintings on loan to, 94, 141-142, 160, 165

St. Louis, Missouri: St. Louis University (collection), 24-25

St. Louis, Missouri: Washington University (collection), 123

St. Louis, Missouri: Western Academy of Art, 94, 101, 141, 160, 165, 171, 226 n. 70, 229 n. 87

Saline County, Missouri, 12, 49, 55, 74, 185, 186, 309, 310, 311

Samuels, Reuben, 237 n. 118

Sappington, Erasmus Darwin, 128-129, 147 n. 261, 161 n. 297, 187

Sargent, Henry, 114 n. 115, *The Dinner Party*, 114 n. 115; *The Tea Party*, 114 n. 115

Sartain, John (engraver), 37, 40, 45, 57 n. 21, 123, 128, 140-141, 140-141 n. 224, 143, 143 n. 246, 157, 158, 159, 191, 215, 219, 220, 232, 232 n. 98, 233, 249; *Charles Anderson Wickliffe* (Bingham), 57 n. 21; *The Pioneers* [or *The Western Emigrant*] (Rothermel), 128, pl. 85; *The County Election* (Bingham), 140-141, 141 n. 224, 143, 143 n. 246, 157, 158, 191, 193; *Angel of the Opal* (Rothermel), 215, pl. 163; *Martial Law* or *Order No. 11* (Bingham), 219, 220, 228, 232-233, 232 n. 98; *Little Red Riding Hood* (Lawrence), 249, pl. 197

Schaick, Benjamin van, New York (collection), 87

Schendel, P. van, 114 n. 114

Schofield, General John M., 216, 245 n. 148

School of Athens (Raphael), 153

Schurz, General Carl, 248, 248 n. 158

Sea Captains Carousing at Surinam (Greenwood), 114 n. 115

Shackelford, Thomas, 147 n. 261

331

333

INDEX OF PAINTINGS
BY GEORGE CALEB BINGHAM

(includes only the pictures discussed in this volume)

~

Genre and Other Figure Subjects

335

Landscapes

Portraits

336

Prints after Bingham Paintings

339

PLATES

1. *Dr. John Sappington*, 1834 (A3), oil (27 x 21¾), Missouri State Park Board, Jefferson City, Missouri.

2. *Mrs. John Sappington (Jane Breathitt)*, 1834 (A4), oil (27 x 21¾), Missouri State Park Board, Jefferson City Missouri.

3. *Meredith Miles Marmaduke*, 1834 (A5), oil (28 x 22¾), Missouri Historical Society, St. Louis, Missouri.

4. *Mrs. Meredith Miles Marmaduke (Lavinia Sappington)*, 1834 (A6), oil (27¼ x 21¾), collection Mrs. Grover F. Stephens, Marshall, Missouri.

5. *Dr. Anthony Wayne Rollins*, 1834 (A7), oil (29 x 23), collection Mrs. James S. Lackey and Mrs. Jessie B. Terrill, Richmond, Kentucky.

6. *Mrs. Anthony Wayne Rollins (Sarah [Sallie] Harris Rodes)*, 1834 (A8), oil (28 x 23), collection Mrs. Ellsworth A. MacLeod, Columbia, Missouri.

7. *Major James Sidney Rollins*, 1834 (A9), oil (28 x 23), estate of Curtis Burnam Rollins, Columbia, Missouri.

8. *Josiah Woodson Wilson*, 1834 (A10), oil (27 x 24), collection Mr. J. Dozier Stone, Columbia, Missouri.

9. *Colonel John Thornton*, 1835 (A17), oil
(26½ x 22¼), collection Mr. and Mrs.
Charles P. Hough, Jr., Kansas City, Missouri.

10. *Portrait of a Man*, 1835 (A19), oil (34⅜ x 29⅛), Isaac Delgado Museum of Art, New Orleans, Louisiana.

11. Reverse, *Portrait of a Man*, 1835 (A19), Isaac Delgado Museum of Art, New Orleans, Louisiana.

12. *General Richard Gentry*, 1837 (A33),
oil (27½ x 22½), collection Mr. William
Richard Gentry, Jr., St. Louis, Missouri.

13. *Judge Warren Woodson*, 1837 (A36), oil (26 x 20½), collection Mrs. William Ashley Gray, Clayton, Missouri.

14. *Thomas Miller*, 1837 (A44), oil (3½ x 2½), State Historical Society of Missouri, Columbia.

15. *Priestly Haggin McBride*, 1837 (A42),
oil (28½ x 23), collection Mrs. Howard
Hammond, Fayette, Missouri.

16. *Mrs. William Johnston (Rachel Spears)*, ca. 1837 (A45), oil (24½ x 22), collection Mr. John Lawrence Johnston, New York.

17. *Mrs. Anthony Wayne Rollins (Sarah [Sallie] Harris Rodes)*, 1837 (A38), oil (29 x 24), estate of Curtis Burnam Rollins, Columbia, Missouri.

18. *Mrs. James Sidney Rollins
(Mary Elizabeth Hickman)*,
1837 (A39), oil (29½ x 25¼),
collection Mrs. Curtis Field Burnam, Baltimore, Maryland.

19. Thomas Sully (1783-1872),
*Frances Anne (Fanny) Kemble
as "Beatrice"* (1833), engraving
(vignette: 3⅛ x 3⅜), John
Cheney (1801-1885) after painting. Ill.: *The Gift... for 1836*,
frontis.

20. *Mrs. David Steele Lamme (Sophia Woodson Hickman) and Son*, 1837 (A32), oil (35¼ x 28), estate of Curtis Burnam Rollins, Columbia, Missouri.

21. Sir Thomas Lawrence (1769-1830), *Lady Georgiana Dover and Son* (1830), engraving, James Henry Watt (1799-1867) after painting.

22. *Miss Sarah Helen Rollins*, 1837 (A40),
oil (60 x 32) collection Mr. Rollins Field
Burnam, Shreveport, Louisiana.

23. *Mrs. Thomas Shackelford
(Eliza Chives Pulliam)*, 1838/
1839 (A51), oil (35½ x 29½),
collection Mrs. Harold E. Edwards, Santa Fe, New Mexico,
and Miss Margaret Shackelford,
Brandywine, Maryland.

24. *Mrs. John Fletcher Darby
(Mary M. Wilkinson)*, ca. 1839
(A78), oil (35¾ x 28), Mis-
souri Historical Society, St.
Louis, Missouri.

25. *Judge Henry Lewis*, 1839 (A63), oil (29 x 22), collection Mrs. Richard Hawes, St. Louis, Missouri.

26. *Mrs. Henry Lewis (Elizabeth Morton Woodson)*, 1839 (A64), oil (29 x 22), collection Mrs. Richard Hawes, St. Louis, Missouri.

27. *Jacob Fortney Wyan*, ca. 1838/1839
(A57), oil (26⅛ x 22½), collection Mrs.
Curtis Pigott, Merrick, New York.

28. *Thomas Erskine Birch*, 1839
(A71), oil (30 x 25), collection
Mr. George Harrison Whitney,
Upland, California.

29. *Mrs. Lewis Bumgardner
(Hetty Ann Halstead)*, 1839
(A66), oil (30½ x 21⅝), collection Mr. Rudolph Bumgardner, Jr., Staunton, Viriginia.

30. *Leonidas Wetmore*, 1839/1840 (A86), oil (60 x 48), Market, St. Louis, Missouri.

31. Robert Walter Weir (1803-1889), *Sa-go-ye-wat-ha (Red Jacket)* (1828), engraving (5 x 3⅜), Moseley Isaac Danforth (1800-1862) after painting.

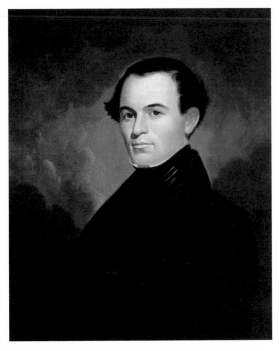

32. *Richard Henry Robinson*, ca. 1838/1839 (A61), oil (32 x 27), collection Mrs. William Patterson, Lexington, Kentucky.

33. *Miss Sallie Ann Camden*, 1839 (A74), oil (36 x 29½), private collection.

34. *John Quincy Adams*, 1844 (A112),
panel (10 x 7¾), collection Mr. James
Sidney Rollins II, Columbia, Missouri.

35. *John Quincy Adams*, ca. 1850 (A211), oil (10 x 7⅞), Detroit Institute of Arts, Detroit, Michigan.

36. *John Quincy Adams*, ca. 1850 (A210), oil (29¼ x 24½), collection Mrs. W. D. A. Westfall, Columbia, Missouri.

37. *Daniel Webster*, 1844 (A113), oil (30 x 25), Thomas Gilcrease Institute of American History and Art, Tulsa, Oklahoma.

38. *Mrs. George Caleb Bingham (Sarah Elizabeth Hutchison) and Son Newton*, 1840/1841 (A97), oil (35 x 29), collection Mrs. W. P. Bowdry, Dallas, Texas.

39. *The Sleeping Child: Horace Bingham*, 1843/1844 (A111), oil (35 x 29), collection Mrs. George Bingham King, Stephenville, Texas.

40. *Mrs. George Caleb Bingham (Sarah Elizabeth Hutchison)*, 1842 (A104), oil (16 x 15; originally approx. 35 x 29), collection Mrs. W. P. Bowdry, Dallas, Texas. (From a daguerreotype.)

41. William Fisher, *Portrait*, engraving (5½ x 4), W. Osborn after painting(?).

42. *Mrs. Hartwell Peebles Heath (Elizabeth Anne Cureton Rives)*, 1841 (A100), oil (30 x 24, approx.), collection Mrs. Randolph Crump Miller, New Haven, Connecticut.

43. *The Dull Story*, 1843/1844 (A110), oil
(50⅜ x 38⅞), collection Mr. Charles van
Ravenswaay, Boonville, Missouri.

44. *Miss Anna Rives Heath*, 1841 (A103),
oil (30 x 24½, approx.), collection Mrs.
Ernest P. Buxton, Jr., Richmond, Virginia.

45. *The Mill Boy: The Boonville Juvenile
Clay Club Banner*, 1844 (A116,) oil (37¼ x
46½), collection Mr. and Mrs. Leslie
Cowan, Columbia, Missouri.

46. Detail, *The Mill Boy: The Boonville Juvenile Clay Club Banner*, 1844 (A116), collection Mr. and Mrs. Leslie Cowan, Columbia, Missouri.

47. Thomas Sully (1783-1872), *The Torn Hat*, 1820, oil (19 x 14½), Museum of Fine Arts, Boston, Massachusetts.

48. *Trappers' Return*, 1851 (A222), oil (26⅛ x 36¼), Detroit Institute of Arts, Detroit, Michigan.

49. William Sidney Mount (1807-1868), *Eel Spearing at Setauket*, 1845, oil (29 x 36), New York Historical Association, Cooperstown, New York.

50. *Fur Traders Descending the Missouri*, 1845 (A136), oil (29¼ x 36¼), Metropolitan Museum of Art, New York (Morris K. Jessup Fund, 1933).

51. *Boatmen on the Missouri*, 1846 (A145), oil (25 x 30), Market, New York.

52. Study of *Boatman* for *Boatmen on the Missouri*, 1846 (S111), pencil, brush and ink (9½ x 8), collection Mr. John S. Kebabian, Scarsdale, New York.

53. *The Jolly Flatboatmen* (1), 1846 (A146), oil (38 x 48½), collection Senator Claiborne Pell, Washington, D.C.

54. Sir David Wilkie (1785-1841), *The Blind Fiddler* (1806), engraving (6½ x 8⅝) , C. W. Sharpe after painting. Ill.: S. C. Hall, *Gems of European Art ...* (1846), Ser. 1, opp. p. 129.

55. William Sidney Mount (1807-1868), *Dance of the Haymakers* or *Music is Contagious* (1845), lithograph, 1849 (14⅝ x 18¾), Alphonse-Léon Noël (1807-1884) after painting. Published by Goupil, Vibert & Co., New York; entered 1849.

56. *The Jolly Flatboatmen* (2), ca. 1848
(A157), oil (25¾ x 36), collection Mr. Mastin
Kratz, Kansas City, Missouri.

57. *Dancing Satyr*, from Casa del Fauno, Pompeii, Museo Nazionale, Naples.

58. Jean-Louis Théodore Géricault (1791-1824), *The Raft of the Medusa*, 1818/1819, oil (16 ft. 1 in. x 23 ft. 5⅞ in.), Louvre, Paris.

59. Sir David Wilkie (1783-
1841), *Card Players* (1808),
engraving (6⅛ x 8⅝), W.
Greatbach after painting. Ill.:
*Royal Gems from the Galleries
of Europe* [1846-1847], vol. 2.

60. Louis-Léopold Boilly (1761-
1845) *Card Players*, lithograph,
1825. Bér. II, 144, 4.

61. *Jolly Flatboatmen in Port*, 1857 (A265), oil (47½ x 69½),
City Art Museum, St. Louis, Missouri.

62. *Raftsmen Playing Cards*, 1847 (A152), oil (28 x 36),
City Art Museum, St. Louis, Missouri.

63. *In a Quandary* or *Mississippi Raftmen at Cards*,
1851 (A220), oil (17¼ x 21), collection the Right
Reverend Paul Moore, Jr., Washington, D.C.

64. Detail, *In a Quandary* or *Mississippi Raftmen at Cards*, 1851 (A220), collection the Right Reverend Paul Moore, Jr., Washington, D.C.

65. *Lighter Relieving a Steamboat Aground,*
1846/1847 (A150), oil (29½ x 35½,
prob.), private collection (?). (From a
daguerreotype.)

66. *The Wood-Boat* 1850 (A191), oil
(24¾ x 29⅝), City Art Museum, St.
Louis, Missouri.

67. *Watching the Cargo*, 1849 (A162), oil (26 x 36), State Historical Society of Missouri, Columbia.

68. *The Squatters*, 1850 (A192), oil
(23 x 28), collection Mr. Henry Lee
Shattuck, Boston, Massachusetts.

69. *Fishing on the Mississippi*, 1851 (A221), oil (28¾ x 35⅞), William Rockhill Nelson Gallery of Art, Kansas City, Missouri.

70. Detail, *Western Boatmen Ashore by Night*, 1854 (A234), Museum of Fine Arts, Boston, Massachusetts (M. and M. Karolik Collection).

71. Sir David Wilkie (1785-1841), *The Jew's Harp* (1809), engraving (9¾ x 7⁹⁄₁₆), E. Smith after painting. Ill.: S. C. Hall, *Gems of European Art* ... (1846), Ser. 1, opp. p. 89.

72. *Watching the Cargo by Night*, 1854
(A235), oil (24 x 30), estate of Norman B.
Woolworth, Winthrop, Maine.

73. *Mississippi Fisherman*, ca. 1850
(A206), oil (29½ x 24½), collection Mr.
Marshall Field, Chicago, Illinois.

74. *Western Boatmen Ashore by Night*, 1854 (A234), oil (29 x 36), Museum of Fine Arts, Boston, Massachusetts (M. and M. Karolik Collection).

75. *The Concealed Enemy*, 1845 (A137), oil
(28½ x 35½), Peabody Museum, Harvard
University, Cambridge, Massachusetts.

76. Joshua Shaw (ca. 1770-1860), *Reedy River Massacre*, ca. 1838, oil (14 x 17½), Brigham Young University, Provo, Utah.

77. John Gadsby Chapman (1808-1889), *The Rescue*, engraving (3¼ x 4⅜), John A. Rolph (1799-1862) after painting.

78. *Captured by Indians* or *The Captive*, 1848 (A154), oil (25 x 30), City Art Museum, St. Louis, Missouri.

79. *Belated Wayfarers* or *In Camp*, 1852
(A231), oil (25 x 30), City Art Museum,
St. Louis, Missouri.

80. *Interior with Figures: Night Scene,*
ca. 1846/1848 (A151), oil (24½ x 29½),
private collection.

81. *Old Field Horse: Stable Scene*, after 1850 (A213), oil (12½ x 15), City Art Museum, St. Louis, Missouri.

82. Charles Deas (1818-1867), *The Turkey Shoot*, ca. 1836, oil (25 x 30), private collection.

83. *The Checker Players* or *Playing Chec-
quers*, 1850 (A193), oil (25 x 30), Detroit
Institute of Arts, Detroit, Michigan.

84. *The Emigration of Daniel Boone* (1851; A219), lithograph, 1852 (P6) (18¼ x 23¾), Claude Régnier (active 1840-1866) after painting by Bingham.

85. Peter Frederick Rothermel (1817-1895), *The Pioneers* or *The Western Emigrant*, engraving (4 x 6), John Sartain (1808-1897) after painting (?). Ill.: *The Opal . . .* (1849), opp. p. 143.

86. *Shooting for the Beef*, 1850 (A195), oil (33½ x 49), Brooklyn Museum, New York.

87. *The Emigration of Daniel Boone or Daniel Boone Escorting a Band of Pioneers into the Western Country*, 1851 (A219), oil (36½ x 50), Washington University, St. Louis, Missouri.

88. *Jason* or *Cincinnatus*,
Louvre, Paris.

89. *Doryphorus*, Museo
Nazionale, Naples.

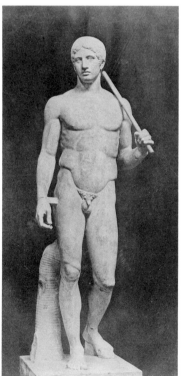

90. *The Stump Orator*, 1847 (A153), oil
(dimensions unrecorded), present location
unknown. (From a daguerreotype.)

91. Study of *Spectator* for *The Stump Orator*, 1847 (S123), pencil, brush and ink (8½ x 4⅛), William Rockhill Nelson Gallery of Art, Kansas City, Missouri.

92. Sir David Wilkie (1785-1841), *The Village Politicians* (1806), engraving (6¾ x 8⅞), C. W. Sharpe after painting. Ill.: S. C. Hall, *Gems of European Art...* (1847), Ser. 2, p. 21.

93. William Sidney Mount (1807-1868), *The Tough Story* or *The Long Story* (1837), engraving (3¼ x 4⅝), Joseph Ives Pease (1809-1883) after painting. Ill.: *The Gift ...for 1842*, opp. p. 99.

94. *The County Election* (1), 1851/1852 (A229), oil (35⁷⁄₁₆ x 48¾),
City Art Museum, St. Louis, Missouri.

95. *The County Election* (2), 1852 (A230), oil (38 x 52), Boatmen's National Bank of St. Louis, St. Louis, Missouri.

96. William Hogarth (1697-1764), *Canvassing for Votes*, engraving, 1757 (15⅞ x 21), C. Grignion after painting. (From edition published by James Heath, London, 1822.)

97. Frans van Mieris, the Elder (1635-1681), *The Man of Letters* or *The Writing Master*, engraving (8⅛ x 6¼), R. Wallis after painting. Ill.: S. C. Hall, *Gems of European Art . . .* (1846), Ser. 1, opp. p. 119.

98. *Seated Female Figure*, engraving. Ill.: *Description of the Collection of Ancient Marbles in the British Museum* (1815), pt. 2, Pl. XXVIII.

100. *The Verdict of the People* (2), after 1855 (A248), oil (22¾ x 30⁵⁄₁₆), collection Mr. Richard W. Norton, Jr., Shreveport, Louisiana.

99. Samuel Prout (1783-1852), *Composition*, lithograph. Ill.: S. Prout, *Hints on Light and Shade* ... (1848), Pl. XV (3).

101. Detail, *The Verdict of the People* (1), 1854/1855 (A237), Boatmen's National Bank of St. Louis, St. Louis, Missouri.

102. *Canvassing for a Vote* or *Candidate
Electioneering*, 1851/1852 (A228), oil
(25⅛ x 30³⁄₁₆), William Rockhill Nelson
Gallery of Art, Kansas City, Missouri (Nelson Fund).

103. *Stump Speaking* or *The County Canvass*, 1853/1854 (A233), oil (42½ x 58), Boatmen's National Bank of St. Louis, St. Louis, Missouri.

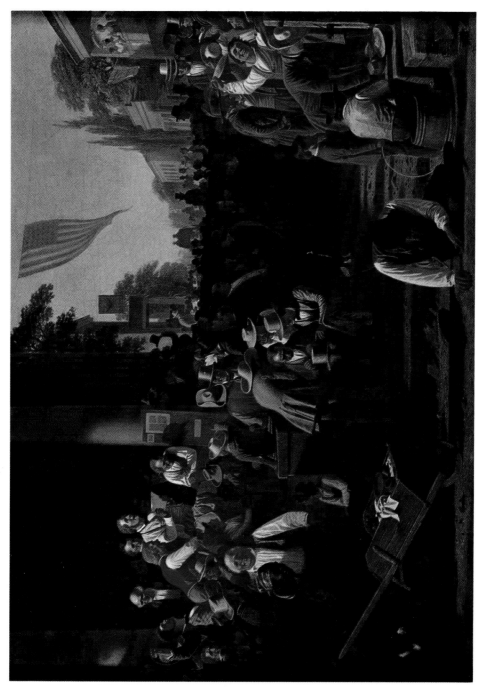

104. *The Verdict of the People* (1) or *Announcement of the Result of the Election*, 1854/1855 (A237), oil (46 x 65), Boatmen's National Bank of St. Louis, St. Louis, Missouri.

105. Francis Nicholson (1753-1844), *Landscape Composition*, lithograph. Ill.: F. Nicholson, *The Practice of Drawing and Painting Landscapes from Nature . . .* (1823).

106. *Studies of Landscapes*, 1845/1846 (S11, *verso*), pencil (10⅛ x 8⅛), St. Louis Mercantile Library Association, St. Louis, Missouri.

107. *Cottage Scenery*, 1845 (A138), oil
(25½ x 30), Corcoran Gallery of Art, Washington, D.C.

108. George Morland (1763-1804), *The Country Inn*, oil (20 x 26½), Newhouse Galleries, New York.

109. Joshua Shaw (ca. 1770-1860), *Landscape*, 1838, oil (20 x 27), Victor Spark, New York.

110. *Landscape with Cattle* (2), 1846
(A148,) oil (38 x 48), City Art Museum,
St. Louis, Missouri.

111. Thomas Sidney Cooper (1803-1902),
Studies of Cattle, lithograph, J. E. Goodall
after drawing (?). Ill.: T. S. Cooper, *Groups
of Cattle, from Nature* ... (1839).

112. *Landscape with Deer*, ca. 1850
(A208), oil (24¾ x 30), Missouri Historical Society, St. Louis, Missouri.

113. *Landscape with Fisherman*, ca. 1850 (A207), oil (24¾ x 30), Missouri Historical Society, St. Louis, Missouri.

114. *Scene on the Ohio River Near Cincinnati* (1851; A223), wood engraving (P5) (3 x 3¾), G. A. Bauer after painting by Bingham. Ill.: *Western Journal*, VII (Jan., 1852), 289.

115. *Landscape with an Indian Encampment*, after 1851 (A225), oil (15 x 19), Thomas Gilcrease Institute of American History and Art, Tulsa, Oklahoma.

116. *Moonlight Scene: Castle on the Rhine*, ca. 1857/1859 (A267), oil (14 x 20), collection Mr. William J. Poplack, Birmingham, Michigan.

117. *Landscape: Mountain View*, after 1851 (A224), oil (21 x 30), Los Angeles County Museum of Art, Los Angeles, California.

118. *The Storm*, ca. 1850 (A205), oil (25⅛ x 30⅟₁₆),
Wadsworth Atheneum, Hartford, Connecticut.

119. *View of Pike's Peak* (1), 1872 (A353),
oil (48 x 60, approx.), destroyed (?).

120. *View of Pike's Peak* (2), 1872 (A354),
oil (30 x 48), collection Mr. William
Howard Adams, Kansas City, Missouri.

121. *Colorado Mountain Landscape*, 1878 (A383), oil (10½ x 14¼), William Rockhill Nelson Gallery of Art, Kansas City, Missouri.

122. *"Forest Hill," The Nelson Homestead, Boonville, Missouri*, 1877 (A377), oil (23 x 29), collection Mr. James E. Birch, St. Louis, Missouri, and Mrs. Fulton Stephens, Esparto, California.

123. *John Cummings Edwards*, 1844 (A121), oil (35½ x 28½), Missouri Historical Society, St. Louis, Missouri.

124. Samuel Finley Breese Morse (1791-1872), *The Marquis de Lafayette*, 1825/1826, oil (95 x 64), Art Commission of the City of New York.

125. *Thomas Withers Nelson*, ca. 1844/1845 (A132), oil (29 x 24), collection Mr. George Bingham Birch, Teaneck, New Jersey.

126. *James Lawrence Minor*, ca. 1844/1846 (A135), oil (29¼ x 24½), collection Mrs. Gilmer Meriwether, Jr., Kansas City, Missouri.

127. *Colonel Granville Craddock Medley*, 1848 (A156), oil (30 x 25), collection Mr. L. W. Donaldson, Kansas City, Missouri.

128. *William Breathitt Sappington*, ca. 1844/1845 (A126), oil (30 x 25), collection Mrs. Charles Wayne Elsea, Marshall, Missouri.

129. *Mrs. William Breathitt Sappington (Mary Mildred Breathitt)*, ca. 1844/1845 (A127), oil (30 x 25), collection Mrs. Charles Wayne Elsea, Marshall, Missouri.

130. *Dr. John Sappington*, ca. 1844/1845
(A128), oil (35½ x 27¾), collection Mrs.
C. Lester Hall, Jr., Kansas City, Missouri.

131. *Mrs. John Sappington (Jane Breath-itt)*, ca. 1844/1845 (A129), oil (35½ x 27¾), collection Mrs. C. Lester Hall, Jr., Kansas City, Missouri.

132. *Mrs. Jacob Fortney Wyan (Nancy Shanks)*, ca. 1845 (A142), oil (25½ x 21½), collection Mrs. Curtis Pigott, Merrick, New York.

133. *Dr. Oscar F. Potter*, 1848 (A155), oil
(25 x 20), City Art Museum, St. Louis,
Missouri.

134. *Colonel William Franklin Switzler*, 1849 (A172), oil (30 x 25), Missouri Historical Society, St. Louis, Missouri.

135. *Mrs. William Franklin Switzler (Mary Jane Royall)*, 1849 (A173), oil (30 x 25), State Historical Society of Missouri, Columbia.

136. *Mrs. George Caleb Bingham (Eliza K. Thomas)*, 1849/1850 (A183), oil (35½ x 27½), estate of Mrs. Arthur Palmer, Independence, Missouri.

137. *Mrs. James H. McGee (Eleanor Evelyn Fry)*, 1849/1850 (A186), oil (29½ x 24½), collection Mrs. Webster W. Townley, Kansas City, Missouri.

138. *Self-Portrait of the Artist*. 1849/1850
(A184), oil (3 x 2½), collection Dr.
Eleanor Cook, Lake Charles, Louisiana.

139. *Miss Mary Elizabeth Rollins*, 1849 (A174), oil (23¼ x 19½), collection Mrs. Sidney Rollins Overall, St. Louis, Missouri.

140. *Mrs. Sallie (Thomas) Moore* or *More*, 1849/1850 (A181), oil (29½ x 23¾), collection Mrs. Thomas B. Hall, Kansas City, Missouri.

141. *Mrs. James H. Bennett (Eliza Rollins)*, 1849 (A175), oil (30 x 24), collection Mrs. Stephen McCready, Ocala, Florida.

142. *Miss Vestine Porter*, ca. 1849/1850 (A189), oil (22¼ x 18¼), William Rockhill Nelson Gallery of Art, Kansas City, Missouri.

143. *Mrs. Anthony Wayne Rollins (Sarah [Sallie] Harris Rodes),* after 1850 (A215), oil (30 x 24), collection Mrs. James S. Lackey and Mrs. Jessie B. Terrill, Richmond, Kentucky.

144. *Washington McLean,* after 1850 (A217), oil (30 x 25), Market, New York.

145. *Thomas Hart Benton*, after 1850
(A218), oil (30 x 25), Missouri Historical
Society, St. Louis, Missouri.

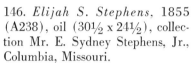

146. *Elijah S. Stephens*, 1855 (A238), oil (30½ x 24½), collection Mr. E. Sydney Stephens, Jr., Columbia, Missouri.

147. *Mrs. David McClanahan Hickman (Cornelia Ann Bryan)*, ca. 1855/1856 (A250), oil (30 x 24¾), collection Mr. Arch Y. Guitar, New Orleans, Louisiana.

148. *Thomas Jefferson*, 1857/1858 (A266), oil (life-size; dimensions unrecorded), destroyed by fire, Capitol, Jefferson City, Missouri, 1911.

149. *Thomas Jefferson* (copy after Gilbert Stuart), 1856 (A255), oil (26 x 22), State Historical Society of Missouri, Columbia.

150. *Henry Clay*, 1860 (A280), oil (life-size; dimensions unrecorded), destroyed by fire, Capitol, Jefferson City, Missouri, 1911.

151. *Baron Friedrich Heinrich Alexander von Humboldt*, 1860 (A281), oil (16 x 12) (present state), State Historical Society of Missouri, Columbia.

152. *Mrs. Robert Levi Todd (Sallie Hall) and Daughter Matilda Tete*, ca. 1860 (A285), oil (35 x 28), collection Mrs. James P. Bennett, Berkeley, California.

153. *Mrs. Almerin Hotchkiss (Martha Ann Moore)*, ca. 1860 (A283), oil (34½ x 27½), collection Mrs. Frank Hotchkiss Jordan, Des Moines, Iowa.

154. *Miss Sally Cochran McGraw*, ca. 1860
(A282), oil (29¼ x 23¾), collection Mrs.
Frederic James, Kansas City, Missouri.

155. *Judge James Turner Vance Thompson*, ca. 1859/1860 (A276), oil (29½ x 24¼), William Rockhill Nelson Gallery of Art, Kansas City, Missouri.

156. *Mrs. James Turner Vance Thompson (Emily Warner Drew)*, ca. 1859/1860 (A277), oil (29½ x 24¼), William Rockhill Nelson Gallery of Art, Kansas City, Missouri.

157. *Dr. Benoist Troost*, 1859 (A269), oil
(40½ x 29⅝), William Rockhill Nelson
Gallery of Art, Kansas City, Missouri (Gift
of the Kansas City Board of Education).

158. *Mrs. Benoist Troost (Mary Ann Gillis)*, 1859 (A270), oil (40⅜ x 29⅞), William Rockhill Nelson Gallery of Art, Kansas City, Missouri.

159. *Mrs. James M. Piper (Mary Thomas)*, ca. 1860/1862 (A305), oil (44 x 36), estate of Mrs. Arthur Palmer, Independence, Missouri.

161. Charles Wimar (1828-1862), *Colonel Franz Sigel, General John Charles Frémont, and Captain Constantin Blandowski,* 1861, oil (29¼ x 24¼), collection Mrs. Edwin H. Conrades, St. Louis, Missouri.

160. *General Nathaniel Lyon and General Francis Preston Blair, Jr., Starting from the Arsenal Gate in St. Louis to Capture Camp Jackson,* ca. 1862/1865 (A312), oil (26 x 23½), collection Mrs. Frank Rollins, Columbia, Missouri.

162. *Thread of Life,* ca. 1862 (A307), oil (27½ x 22½), collection Mr. A. J. Stephens, Kansas City, Missouri.

163. Peter Frederick Rothermel (1817-1895), *The Angel of the Opal,* engraving (vignette: 7 x 5), John Sartain (1808-1897) after drawing (?). Ill.: *The Opal* ... (1849), frontis.

164. *Martial Law* or *Order No. 11* (2), ca. 1869/1870 (A326), oil (56½ x 78), State Historical Society of Missouri, Columbia.

165. *Apollo Belvedere*, Vatican, Rome.

166. Masaccio (1401-1428), *Expulsion*, ca. 1427, fresco (6 ft. 9 in. x 2 ft. 11 in.), Brancacci Chapel, Sta. Maria del Carmine, Florence.

167. Jean-Baptiste Greuze (1725-1805),
The Father's Curse, oil (51¼ x 63⅞),
Louvre, Paris.

168. Fra Bartolommeo (1475-1517), *Pietà*,
panel (59⅞ x 76¹³⁄₁₆), Pitti, Florence.

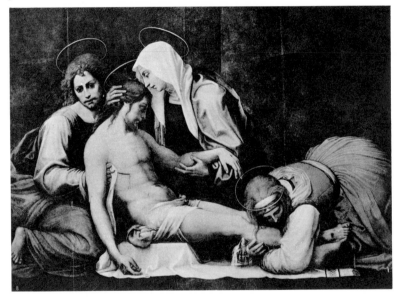

169. *General Nathaniel Lyon*, 1867 (A324),
oil (life-size; dimensions unrecorded),
destroyed by fire, Capitol, Jefferson City,
Missouri, 1911.

170. *Major Dean in Jail*, 1866 (A319), oil on paper (14½ x 14¼), William Jewell College, Liberty, Missouri.

171. Edward Matthew Ward (1816-1879), *Napoleon in the Prison at Nice*, engraving (7⅞ x 6¼), J. Outrim after painting.

172. *James Rollins Bingham*, ca. 1870 (A332), oil (28 x 24), collection Mrs. John B. Hutchison, Independence, Missouri.

173. *Hugh Campbell Ward*, ca. 1869/1870 (A327), oil (23½ x 19½), collection Mr. Hugh C. Ward, Cohasset, Massachusetts.

174. *General Francis Preston Blair, Jr.*, 1871 (A343), oil (34 x 26¼), Market, New York.

175. *Major James Sidney Rollins*, 1871 (A346), oil (33 x 30), collection Mr. David Westfall, Columbia, Missouri.

176. *Major James Sidney Rollins*, 1871 (A345), oil (30 x 25), State Historical Society of Missouri, Columbia.

177. *Thomas Hoyle Mastin*, ca. 1871 (A349), oil (34 x 27½), collection Mr. Hoyle M. Lovejoy, River Forest, Illinois.

178. *John Jerome Mastin, Jr.*, ca. 1871 (A350), oil (39 x 30), collection Mr. G. Edgar Lovejoy, Jr., Port Lavaca, Texas.

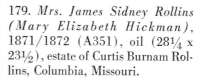

179. *Mrs. James Sidney Rollins (Mary Elizabeth Hickman)*, 1871/1872 (A351), oil (28¼ x 23½), estate of Curtis Burnam Rollins, Columbia, Missouri.

180. *Mrs. James Thomas Birch (Margaret Elizabeth Nelson)*, 1870 (A330), oil (26½ x 21½), collection Mrs. Benjamin E. Reed, St. Louis, Missouri.

181. *Washington Crossing the Delaware*, 1856/1871 (A261), oil (36¼ x 57¼), collection Mrs. Thomas E. Keck, Kansas City, Missouri.

182. William Ranney (1813-1857), *Marion Crossing the Pedee* (1850), engraving (7⅞ x 11⅞), Charles Kennedy Burt (1823-1892) after painting. Published by the American Art-Union, New York [1851]; entered 1852.

183. *Mrs. B. W. Clarke (Mary Jane Kin-
ney) and Brother*, 1874 (A366), oil (39^{13}⁄$_{16}$
x 30), William Rockhill Nelson Gallery of
Art, Kansas City, Missouri.

184. *The Puzzled Witness*, 1874 (A363), oil
(23 x 28), collection Mr. James E. Gibson,
Kansas City, Missouri.

185. *Studies of Figures*, ca. 1874 (S116, *verso*), pencil (9¼ x 7), State Historical Society of Missouri, Columbia.

186. *Studies of Heads of Men*, ca. 1874 (S120, *verso*), pencil (8⅝ x 6¾), State Historical Society of Missouri, Columbia.

187. *Miss Vinnie Ream*, 1876 (A372), oil (40 x 30), State Historical Society of Missouri, Columbia.

188. A photograph of Miss Vinnie Ream.

189. *Dr. Alexander M. Davison*, 1876
(A370), oil (29 x 24), collection Mr. J.
Porter Henry, Webster Groves, Missouri.

190. *Self-Portrait of the Artist*, ca. 1877 (A378), oil (26½ x 21½), Board of Education, Kansas City, Missouri.

191. Sir Edwin Henry Landseer (1802-1873), *Portrait of the Artist*, engraving after painting. Ill.: *Engravings from Landseer* (1876), frontis.

192. *Mrs. James Thomas Birch (Margaret Elizabeth Nelson)*, 1877 (A376), oil (40 x 32), collection Mr. James E. Birch, St. Louis, Missouri; Mrs. Fulton Stephens, Esparto, California.

193. Wenzel (*or* Wenceslaus) Hollar (1607-1677), *Spring*, etching, 1641 (Parthey 610).

194. *Palm Leaf Shade*, 1877/1878 (A380), oil (26¾ x 22½), collection Mrs. Kathleen T. Stier, Lexington, Missouri.

195. Thomas Sully (1783-1872), *Lady with Fan*, engraving (vignette: 2¼ x 1¾), John Cheney (1801-1885) after painting. Ill.: *The Gift . . . for 1839*, frontis.